# Permanent Neutrality

# Permanent Neutrality

*A Model for Peace, Security, and Justice*

Edited by
Herbert R. Reginbogin
and Pascal Lottaz

LEXINGTON BOOKS
Lanham • Boulder • New York • London

Published by Lexington Books
An imprint of The Rowman & Littlefield Publishing Group, Inc.
4501 Forbes Boulevard, Suite 200, Lanham, Maryland 20706
www.rowman.com

6 Tinworth Street, London SE11 5AL

Copyright © 2020 by The Rowman & Littlefield Publishing Group, Inc.

*All rights reserved.* No part of this book may be reproduced in any form or by any electronic or mechanical means, including information storage and retrieval systems, without written permission from the publisher, except by a reviewer who may quote passages in a review.

British Library Cataloguing in Publication Information Available

**Library of Congress Cataloging-in-Publication Data Available**

ISBN: 978-1-7936-1028-7 (cloth)
ISBN: 978-1-7936-1030-0 (pbk)
ISBN: 978-1-7936-1029-4 (electronic)

# Contents

Acknowledgments   vii

Preface   ix

Introduction   1
   *Pascal Lottaz and Herbert R. Reginbogin*

**Part I: Theory**

  1  A Tale of Two Strategies: Permanent Neutrality and Collective Security   15
     *Stephen C. Neff*

  2  Neutrality and Security: A Comparison with Alternative Models of National Security   39
     *P. Terrence Hopmann*

  3  The Logic of Neutrality   57
     *Pascal Lottaz*

**Part II: Practice**

  4  The Model of Neutrality: The Example of East-Central European States   89
     *Heinz Gärtner*

  5  Neutral and Nonaligned States in the European Union   111
     *Gunther Hauser*

  6  Neutral Power Russia   129
     *Glenn Diesen*

  7  America's Experience with Neutrality: An Epoch of Neutrality   145
     *Herbert R. Reginbogin*

**Part III: Application**

  **8** The Nomos of Neutrality in East Asia    167
     *Herbert R. Reginbogin and Pascal Lottaz*

  **9** Taiwanese Neutrality: Solving the Conundrum    191
     *Pascal Lottaz and Herbert R. Reginbogin*

  **10** Case Studies of Contemporary Neutrality Advocacy    209
     *Lu Hsiu-lien, Michael Tsai, and Michael O'Hanlon*

Conclusion    221
    *Pascal Lottaz and Herbert R. Reginbogin*

Index    227

About the Contributors    237

# Acknowledgments

We would like to thank, first and foremost, our colleagues and co-contributors. Without their engaged participation, this book could not explore as fully and in-depth the role of state neutrality in the contemporary international world order. Their research and viewpoints are invaluable in this collaborative effort to seek a new security architecture for peace, security, and justice in the twenty-first century. Secondly, our deepest gratitude goes to the Catholic University of America (CUA), Waseda University, and the Democratic Pacific Union for their generous logistical and financial support to bring together movers and shakers from around the world to ponder seriously about a durable peace across Asia-Pacific and Europe. We want to especially thank CUA Columbus Law School professor Marshall J. Breger, Professor Robert A. Destro, the director of the Institute for Policy Research, and Stephen E. Young, librarian at CUA Columbus Law School, for their continuous collaboration. In addition, we thank Shawn Turner, professor of National Security Communication at Michigan State University. Furthermore, it would not have been possible to organize the 2019 Conference on Permanent Neutrality without the administrative support of Susan Kelly and Womishet Negash at CUA. At Waseda University, we want to thank Kazuhisa Tenjin, Akiko Suda, and Noriko Kato for their logistic support in creating this volume. Our deepest appreciation and thanks also go to Professor Bruce Bagley, at the University of Miami, and Professor Vipasha Bansal at Temple University (Japan campus) for their helpful suggestions regarding sections of the manuscript. We would also like to express our gratitude for the teamwork and collaboration we have had together over the years. Lastly, we thank our families for their continuous devoted support and patience, enabling us to complete this book: Karin and Michael Reginbogin, and Susanne, Raphael, and Alexander Lottaz.

# Preface

This book is the product of a conference held in Washington, DC on March 25, 2019. The venue, "Permanent Neutrality, a Model for Peace, Security, and Justice," was convened to discuss the potential of permanent neutrality in the twenty-first century. Some might question if neutrality ever played a role in world politics or argue that it is on the verge of disappearing. The historical record shows, however, that such assumptions are not warranted. Neutrality as a principle and an institution has been going through different phases over the past millennia, and there is no reason to believe that it will disappear before universal and lasting peace is achieved. As long as there are conflicts and wars, there will be those who choose one side, those who choose another, and those who choose not to choose.

Discussing and understanding the role of neutral states in any security environment remains an important part of the research of international politics. Since the end of World War II, International Relations has often ignored neutrality as a principle and a concept. Despite its paramount importance in the nineteenth and early twentieth century, its centrality at the Hague Peace Conferences, and the volumes and volumes of scholarly work created before 1939, it has been replaced—not entirely but mostly—by new concepts like "balancing," "hedging," or "bandwagoning." Proponents of realism often fail to account for neutral states in their explanations, while constructivism has focused attention on the social origins and norms of neutrality, but it does not usually deal with the security function of neutral states. The lack of proposals to use neutrality—especially permanent neutrality—in contemporary world politics to pacify areas of contestation is symptomatic to this change in International Relations.

This book argues that serious thought should be given to the resurrection of permanent neutrality and the practice of "neutralization." Not every conflict can be solved through permanent neutrality, but there are good reasons to consider its useful functions. They can contribute to keeping global security architectures stable during times of global change in the distribution of power.

# Introduction

## Pascal Lottaz and Herbert R. Reginbogin

This book explores state neutrality in the contemporary international system. It begins from an underlying assumption that was most ruthlessly expressed by Stalin when he said; "I am sorry, gentlemen, we cannot do anything about geography."[1] The dictator supposedly confronted a delegation of Finish Diplomats with this fatalism shortly before he ordered the invasion of their country to increase Soviet military security at the western border. It is a crude principle that geography is the fundamental determinant of foreign policy,[2] but one that will remain valid for as long as the Westphalian state system exists. Or, as Henry Kissinger put it, "geography has been the predominant factor in determining the fate of nations, from pharaonic Egypt to the Arab Spring."[3] Geography decides which resources states have at their immediate disposition and what they have to obtain from the outside. It determines the vulnerabilities and strengths of their military positions. It is the source of strategy, demography, transportation, even culture. Geography drives states' decisions on how to cope with their shortcomings, on the one hand, and how to capitalize on their strengths, on the other. Finally, geography also determines and drives security, threat, and threat perception. In this context, neutral states play roles that are not "aloof" of world affairs but embedded in them since they take up physical space while not joining the wars and conflicts of others. This book explores their special position and the potential it harbors to create security for the past, present, and (conceivable) future.

Pascal Lottaz and Herbert R. Reginbogin

# INTERNATIONAL POLITICS OF THE TWENTY-FIRST CENTURY

The context of this book is geopolitics, which is constant. Concepts of geographical belonging, however, are not. The colonial empires that were built around the brutal and exploitative subjugation of remote territories for the value of their natural resources, indigenous labor, and strategic positions were the driving geopolitics of the eighteenth and nineteenth centuries. The beginning of the twentieth century was marked by more territorial conflicts between the old and new empires, ridden by ideological extremism. The Second World War was not a definite settlement of the question "who governs how" because two distinct socioeconomic models emerged. Soviet aggression against its neighboring states, together with the western "containment" strategy to incarcerate the communist ideology on the Eurasian mainland led to much suffering in the territories in which the Cold War turned hot. The focus on ideology overshadowed the national and geographical nature of the state system of the Cold War. That the globe was made of more than just a "red world" and a "free world" became apparent in the latter part of the twentieth century, when the fault lines began to shift; China emerged not as an acolyte of the Soviets but as a power in its own right, that had many conflicts with the "white" communists to the west. Communist Vietnam turned from an arch-nemesis of the United States into a quasi-ally in South East Asia. The friendly Taliban who fought communism with US support in Afghanistan started turning their weapons against its empire, once the former enemy had been defeated. The impact of their unprecedented form of asymmetric warfare culminated in the United States' most traumatic experience in half a century. 9/11 became the source of an entire redefinition of warfare that, in the end, transformed "combatants" to "noncombatants" and "terrorists," mostly disabling the applicability of the law of war and justifying many forms of cruelty against the enemy. Several wars in the Middle East followed with the world community sanctioning only one as expressed through the United Nations (UN). The Middle East today remains the most volatile and brutalized region on the planet. As the pendulum of history swings back, ideology is trumped again by geostrategic interests; the abusive, dictatorial regimes of Saudi Arabia and Egypt—one governed by an absolute monarchy, the other by a military junta—are some of the closest allies of US interests while the theocracy of Iran is being ostracized as the greatest threat to peace and security in the Middle East. All of them score equally low in freedom house rankings. That the former two are US allies while the latter is an "enemy" has nothing to do with political ideology but with Iran's geostrategic goals in the region—aiming at military expansion and threatening the state of Israel—while the others support the United States' tactical interventions.

As grim as these developments are, others are remarkable for their positive change. The violent aggrandizement of nation-states, be it through colonialism or political incorporations of territories, has largely (but not completely) ended. South and North America have not had significant border changes for over a century; neither did East Asia or Africa since the independence of the former colonies. Except for the occasional emergence of a newly independent territory, not many modifications occurred over the past seventy years in the fundamental distribution of national jurisdictions. The most volatile continent in this regard is still Europe.

On the one hand, the peaceful collapse of the Soviet Union gave birth to fifteen new states (in Europe and Asia) reunified two (the Germanies) and split one (Czechoslovakia), while the violent dissolution of Yugoslavia added another seven.[4] On the other hand, the continent has witnessed the first lasting attempt at pan-Europeanization. The "European Project" has pacified a continent whose states, for centuries, used to be at each other's throats. The European Union (EU) is today in an unprecedented situation, somewhere between a large customs union and a full nation-state. The carefully negotiated, voluntary pooling of sovereignty through supranational institutions has created a construct that blurs the lines of the Westphalian system but has, for the first time, achieved lasting peace in Europe.

Yet, geography remains, states remain, and politics remains. Despite the laudable achievements of humanity in the second half of the twentieth century—never before has the species been as prosperous as today[5]—the challenge of collective management of the planet has not changed. The Kantian world society under a unified and universally accepted government has not (yet) been achieved. International Relations is still a domain that is inherently anarchic, lacking a global leviathan to impose *enforceable* law for all. Although international organization for the collective management of goods, rules, and conflicts exist, the disagreement among states on how to use them, or which rulings to accept and which ones to ignore, are challenging assumptions about a law-based international order. This is not to argue that humanity is actually living in a state of absolute anarchy, but the underlying operating system of the order is built not on law but power. However, there are many constraints on states—norms are among the most important. No country today is entirely free to do as it pleases, unimpacted by the reactions of others. Even the largest powers, like the United States, Russia, and China, are constrained in their actions by what other states would tolerate without taking counter measures. But there are limits of enforceability to laws and norms. Absolute sovereignty (often in conjunction with nationalism) is a dangerous idea that adversely impacts totalitarian and democratic societies alike; in its name, China does not follow the United Nations Law of the Sea (UNCLOS)—while the United States has not even ratified it. A majority of the British voted to leave the EU, and the Swiss voted to infringe on agreements with the bloc. Poland is breaking its own constitution, while the Philippines kills drug victims, the United States ignores fundamental human rights of people fleeing to its shores, and China incarcerates minority populations. States can and do move the boundaries of the acceptable—internally and externally. But any action produces a reaction. When NATO promised membership to Russia's immediate neighbors, Moscow started fueling internal conflicts that disqualified them. Inversely, when Russia invaded Crimea, the EU and the US enacted economic sanctions. When the United States removed itself from a multilateral accord with Iran—against the wishes of the other treaty partners—the same partners tried to save the agreement by creating new institutions that would allow the circumvention of US sanctions. Should the approach succeed, the resulting mechanisms would permanently weaken the structural power of the United States to use its economy as political leverage. Large powers can impose their will much more readily on smaller ones, but nothing comes without political costs.

## NEUTRALIZATION, SECURITY ARCHITECTURE, AND SECURITY DILEMMA

World politics is the background against which this book proposes to view permanent neutrality as a building block for *regional security architectures*. It argues that neutrality is an underestimated and underutilized tool of International Relations that can be deployed to increase trust, mediate conflicts, and most importantly, defuse the security dilemma.[6] After the Second World War, a perception has developed that neutrality is a policy of "aloofness," synonymous to the pejorative "isolationism" of the United States in the interwar period, and that is only still practiced by small and feeble states who have no other choice but to hide behind the indecisiveness of a neutral posture.[7] This view is neither historically accurate nor an apt description of the contemporary world. Small and large states have been using the politics of neutrality for centuries, either for themselves or by imposing them on others to further their grand strategic interests. In the nineteenth century jurisprudential terms arose out of these practices, most importantly that of "neutralization," which in this context does not mean the colloquial "elimination" but simply "to make neutral."[8] A neutralized state or territory is one that has been declared and recognized as permanently neutral by other countries. The two expressions are synonymous.[9]

Another important concept that this book uses is the popular International Relations metaphor of security as a "house" with an underlying "architecture." There are several definitions for what a "security architecture" means,[10] but this book understands it as the way in which different states (and state-like actors) in a particular geography interlock in a complex system of military and civil matters to create a regional environment that does not rely on physical violence or coercion to deal with inter-state relations like commerce, politics, the exploitation of natural resources, or military developments. There is, in this sense, no working security architecture in place in the Middle East, since many actors try to influence each other by use of force. Europe, the Americas, Asia, and most of Africa, on the other hand, do have relatively stable security architectures, which, albeit, do not necessarily rely on the same building blocks. Europe's security architecture is crafted around the multilateralism ordained by the EU and NATO. It extends to North America but does not include Russia—a flaw that Glenn Diesen, in chapter 7, criticizes as castigating Moscow from the "common European home," which is a primary driver for its current foreign policies. He argues that Russia, today, is using and encouraging more neutrality in its neighborhood and uses neutralist policies itself to increase its security toward Europe and China.

Permanent neutrality has a hybrid character, combining realist assumptions about the role of power in the international system (the politics of neutrality) with constructivist approaches to International Relations—mainly due to its paramount importance to the development of norms of International Law (the law of neutrality). Its realist appeal for regional security architectures is that neutrals take up physical space that becomes "no man's land" for the geopolitical strategizing of rival parties while, at the same time, they remain autonomous actors who influence the action–reaction calculations of other states. That neutrals have "international value" as buffer zones and intermediaries is nothing revolutionary. In fact, the neutralization debate is about 200 years old, and strategies of neutrality on land and sea are even older.[11] It used to be well understood that permanent neutrality was a "significant means to manage power in the international system."[12] Especially in the nineteenth century, Great Powers used to declare their neutrality occasionally when they had nothing to gain from a third-party conflict or had an overarching interest to use the neutrality of other states to maintain their empire—foremost Britain.[13] Meanwhile, they also imposed permanent neutrality on other states to keep them away from the gravitational pull of rivals. Sometimes this happened through multilateral agreements to territories that would have been too valuable to go to either side of a conflict constellation; Switzerland in 1815 or Austria in 1955 are examples thereof—albeit in very different security environments. On the other hand, "neutralization" could also happen unilaterally and under the guise of policies that were not called such; the Monroe Doctrine, for example, effectively neutralized the South American states to keep them out of the sphere of influence of the European powers.[14] The Finno-Soviet "Agreement of Friendship, Cooperation, and Mutual Assistance" of 1948 served the same purpose but with the USSR as its primary beneficiary and with Finland as the neutralized state.[15] Also the

Antarctic Treaty, which prohibits its militarization of Antartica, was, in effect, another neutralization to manage geography by removing it from the realm of military strategy.[16] Neutralization also happened to waterways like rivers or channels[17]—even the high seas under the shipping laws of maritime neutrality.[18] Except for uninhabited territories, neutralization from the outside and the status of permanent neutrality from the inside need to go hand in hand to succeed. No state maintains a neutral posture if it does not recognize it as beneficial to itself. As a policy, neutrality is always a means to achieve the higher goals of the state—usually the security and welfare of its people. Even the staunchest neutralists today, the Swiss, proclaim that "time and again, neutrality must be harmonized with the changes in the security environment. The abandonment of [our] neutrality could only be considered if the gain from a new security was greater than the loss of the old one."[19] There is no value in neutrality for its own sake.

## THE CHAPTERS OF THIS BOOK

In recognition of the security function of neutrality the aim of this book is to explain the utility of permanent neutrality as a concept to manage international conflict. This stands in contrast to approaches that study the neutralities of different countries only in terms of what their foreign policies were in times of crisis—if the neutrals kept to the predicaments of international law, and if their legal status was observed by the belligerents or not. Infringements from both sides (by neutrals and by belligerents) are routinely portrayed as "failures" of neutrality that "proof" the futility of neutral policies in the face of threat or moral outrage.[20] The irony of this introduction, for example, is that Stalin, who was quoted in the beginning, invaded Finland in 1939 because Helsinki was not willing to trade some of its territories with Moscow. The Finnish Government argued that it could not do so because it had to maintain its neutrality.[21] This led to Stalin taking by force what he could not get through negotiation. In this case, the neutralist approach failed to save the Finns from the Winter War. Nevertheless, only a few years later, the same Soviets went on to neutralize Finland again—coming full circle. Stalin did so not because he suddenly developed respect for the Finnish desire to be neutral but because their neutrality became useful to him after a change in the regional security environment (the defeat of the Axis Powers).[22] It is hardly surprising that neutrality is not a silver bullet against war and aggression. It is only one of several strategies for countries to try to create security. That is the topic of the theoretical first section of this book.

In chapter 1, Stephen C. Neff gives a historical overview by contrasting permanent neutrality with the alternative of collective security. Comparing the intellectual origins of both, he shows that the collective security model is a "top-down" architecture—because it necessitates large, international institutions—while the idea of security through permanent neutrality is "bottom-up"—envisioning stability through a decentralized structure of states that abstain from conflict and thereby "quarantine" war. Naturally, the two approaches do not mix well, which many commentators have noticed; "neutrality and collective security are complementary concepts; the more there is of one, the less there is of the other."[23] This became painfully clear, for example, in the late 1930s, when the first global collective security attempt through the League of Nations failed and the collapse of the system immediately lead to the resurgence of neutral states right before the outbreak of the Second World War.[24] In chapter 2, P. Terrence Hopmann scrutinizes these alternative security approaches for the twentieth and twenty-first centuries. Differentiating between Alliances, Collective Security Institutions, neutrality, and nonalignment, he shows how each approach has its benefits but also harbors risks. In chapter 3, Pascal Lottaz takes the theoretical discussion one step further by exploring what he calls the origins of "the neutral idea," it's surprising success, and the resulting "logic of neutrality." He argues that neutrality has a simple appeal to states, founded in realism, and that the positions of neutral actors have particular impacts on conflict dynamics. He models those graphically to explain neutral-belligerent interactions and the workings of different kinds of neutrality.

The second section of this volume deals with the contemporary practice of neutrality. In chapter 4, Heinz Gaertner expands on the model of neutrality by discussing it in the context of Europe, how it served the continent already and how its broader application can help Eastern Europe, especially Ukraine, to thrive in partnership with NATO, OSCE, and Russia alike. Chapter 5, by Gunther Hauser, dives into the different policies of the EU's current neutrals, showcasing how diverse and multifaceted neutrality policies are. They are adapted to the needs and historical developments of their states. There is not "one" monolithic form of being neutral and even membership in the European Union or collaboration with NATO's Partnership for Peace program does not disqualifies countries from using the label of neutrality. In chapters 6 and 7, Glenn Diesen and Herbert R. Reginbogin show how also for Russian and American neutrality was and still is of importance.

The third and last section of the book discusses potential applications of permanent neutrality where it is not yet in use. Herbert R. Reginbogin and Pascal Lottaz argue in chapter 8 that besides the various security challenges in East Asia there exists already a "nomos" of neutral behavior there, which, if further expanded, would benefit the military stability of Asia Pacific by creating a neutral corridor between the United States and China. In conjunction to this, the same authors show in chapter 9 how the appeal of neutrality has already lead to an indigenous movement in Taiwan for the neutralization of the contested island and how a "Neutral Taiwan" might be a way to "square a circle" of this unfinished issue of World War II. Finally, the last chapter contains three primary sources of concrete policy thinking on contemporary neutrality; taken from public presentations given at the 2019 Permanent Neutrality Conference in Washington, DC, Lu Hsiu-lien (Annette Lu), former vice president of the Republic of China (ROC–Taiwan) outlines in her own words the political vision for the "Peace and Neutrality" of Taiwan and the reason why she has been advocating it for years. Her colleague, Michael Tsai, former Minister of Defense of the ROC, adds his own comments to the same idea. And, finally, Michael O'Hanlon, a senior fellow at the Brookings Institution and former member of the external advisory board at the Central Intelligence Agency, explains his thinking on a neutral solution for Ukraine. Together, these excerpts represent modern thought about permanent neutrality as a tool of statecraft by practitioners.

## WHY STILL THINK ABOUT NEUTRALITY?

There are signs that the ideal of "real" collective security, enforced through the United Nations, is as distant as it always was. Too many ongoing conflicts are blocking unanimous decision-making in the Security Council. There is no unanimity on Syria, no solution for Palestine, no agreement on Ukraine or Georgia, no collective action on Yemen, and no consensus on Northern Cyprus. There is not even a shared vision for the future of Taiwan or the rightful belonging of the waters of the South and East China Sea. Most strikingly, though, there is little agreement for the time that will be known as "Post-Pax-Americana."[25] What is next? Nothing has ever lasted forever. NATO is seventy years old already, so is the US–Japan alliance and the United States' extensive base system around the world. Everything ends sometime. If, as some argue, the "rise of China" and the "Resurgence of Russia" together with America's slow but steady withdrawal from international security really signify a return to a multipolar world order,[26] there will be a strong need for the redefinition of many of the current security architectures in the East and the West. What this volume proposes is not to forget about the potential of permanent neutrality. It is a serious and realistic security model that harbors the potential to support a balance of power through the provision of "hard" military security corridors (buffers), on the one hand, while it can also fill the need for human-centered ontological security by providing an understanding for the Do's and Don'ts of international behavior, on the other. After all, the challenges of the twenty-first century are not "just" reducible to military threat. If no collective effort is achievable to reverse climate change, our shared human security will be in the gravest of dangers. Cooperative security architectures are needed to achieve the unity necessary to face this universal and existential nonmilitary threat of our age.

The model of neutrality is in the following pages discussed to show its potential. Through the ten chapters of this book, the editors hope to illuminate the theoretical and practical benefits that permanent neutrality as a model for peace, security, and justice has to offer.

## NOTES

1. As quoted in Gunnar M. Hägglöf, "A Test of Neutrality: Sweden in the Second World War," *International Affairs* 36 (1960): 153.
2. Ibid.
3. This part of Kissinger's assessment of Robert Kaplan's book "The Revenge of Geography." For the full quote see http://robertdkaplan.com.
4. Or six, depending on whether or not to count Kosovo as an independent country.
5. Steven Pinker, *The Better Angels of our Nature: Why Violence has Declined* (New York: Viking, 2011).
6. See chapter 3 of this volume. Compare also with Charles L. Glaser, *Rational Theory of International Politics: The Logic of Competition and Cooperation* (Princeton: Princeton University Press, 2010).
7. See, for example, the conclusion in Nils Orvik, *The Decline of Neutrality 1914–1941. With Special Reference to the United States and the Northern Neutrals* (Oslo: Johan Grundt Tanum Forlag, 1953). See also the depiction of small neutrals in the Cold War by Joseph Kruzel, "The Future of European Neutrality," in *Between the Blocs: Problems and Prospects for Europe's Neutral and Nonaligned States*, ed. Joseph Kruzel and Michael H. Haltzel (Washington, DC: Woodrow Wilson International Center for Scholars, 1989).
8. Brian Havel made the case that the word "neutralization" should be replaced by a less pejorative term for which he proposed the word "neutralitization." It is an interesting idea but this book does not adopt his neologism. On the one hand because it lacks in elegance, on the other it would complicate historical discussions for which the common lingo was that of "neutralization" and "permanent neutrality." See Brian F. Havel, "An International Law Institution in Crisis: Rethinking Permanent Neutrality," *Ohio State Law Journal* 61 (2000).
9. Cyril E. Black et al., *Neutralization and World Politics* (Princeton: Princeton University Press, 1968), vi. For a short discussion, see also Christine Agius, "Transformed beyond Recognition? The Politics of Post-Neutrality," *Cooperation and Conflict* 46, no. 3 (2011): 268.
10. See Tow and Taylor, who defined it as "an overarching, coherent and comprehensive security structure for a geographically-defined area, which facilitates the resolution of that region's policy concerns and achieves its security objectives." William T. Tow and Brendan Taylor, "What Is Asian Security Architecture?," *Review of International Studies* 36 (2010): 96. See also, for example, Ramon Pacheco Pardo, "China and Northeast Asia's Regional Security Architecture: The Six-Party Talks as a Case of Chinese Regime-Building?," *East Asia: An International Quarterly* 29, no. 4 (2012); Paul D. Williams, "Reflections on the Evolving African Peace and Security Architecture," *African Security* 7, no. 3 (2014).
11. Leos Müller, *Neutrality in World History* (New York: Routledge, 2019); Stephen C. Neff, *The Rights and Duties of Neutrals: A General History* (Manchester: Manchester University Press, 2000); Philip C. Jessup and Francis Deak, *Neutrality: Its History, Economics and Law: The Origins*, 4 vols., vol. 1 (New York: Columbia University Press, 1935).
12. Black et al., *Neutralization and World Politics*, v.
13. Maartje M. Abbenhuis, *An Age of Neutrals: Great Power Politics, 1815–1914* (Cambridge: Cambridge University Press).
14. Erving Winslow, "Neutralization," *American Journal of International Law* 2 (1908): 379.
15. Quincy Wright, "The American Civil War, 1861–1865," in *The International Law of Civil War*, ed. Richard A. Falk (Baltimore: Johns Hopkins Press, 1971).
16. Black et al., *Neutralization and World Politics*, 90.

17. Harry S. Knapp, "The Real Status of the Panama Canal as Regards Neutralization," *The American Journal of International Law* 4, no. 2 (1910).

18. Leos Müller, "The Forgotten History of Maritime Neutrality, 1500–1800," in *Notions of Neutralities*, ed. Pascal Lottaz and Herbert Reginbogin (Lanham, MD: Lexington, 2019); *Neutrality in World History*.

19. Eidgenössisches Departement für Verteidigung, Bevölkerungsschutz und Sport (VBS), "Die Neutralität der Schweiz," (Berne: Schweizerische Eidgenossenschaft, 2014). Original in German. Translated by the author.

20. See, for instance, the criticism raised by Roger Cohen, "The (Not So) Neutrals of World War II," *The New York Times*, 1997; Christian Leitz, *Sympathy for the Devil: Neutral Europe and Nazi Germany in World War II* (New York: New York University Press, 2001).

21. Eloise Engle and Lauri Paananen, *The Winter War: The Soviet Attack on Finland, 1939–1940* (Mechanicsburg: Stackpole Books, 1992), 3–14.

22. On Finland and Stalin see Peter Ruggenthaler, *The Concept of Neutrality in Stalin's Foreign Policy, 1945–1953* (New York: Lexington, 2015); "Neutrality as an Instrument of Soviet Foreign Policy, 1945–1953," in *Notions of Neutralities*, ed. Pascal Lottaz and Herbert Reginbogin (Lanham, MD: Lexington, 2019).

23. This was a statement by Hersch Lauterpacht and quoted affirmatively by Hans Morgenthau in Hans J. Morgenthau, "The Resurrection of Neutrality in Europe," *American Political Science Review* 33 (1939): 478.

24. Ibid.

25. Christopher Layne, "This Time It's Real: The End of Unipolarity and the 'Pax Americana,'" *International Studies Quarterly* 56, no. 1 (2012); Charles A. Kupchan, "After Pax Americana: Benign Power, Regional Integration, and the Sources of a Stable Multipolarity," *International Security* 23, no. 2 (1998); Steven Simon and Jonathan Stevenson, "The End of Pax Americana: Why Washington's Middle East Pullback Makes Sense," *Foreign Affairs*, no. 6, Council on Foreign Relations, 2015.

26. Christopher Layne, "The US–Chinese power shift and the end of the Pax Americana," *International Affairs* 94, no. 1 (2018).

## SELECTED REFERENCES

Abbenhuis, Maartje M. *An Age of Neutrals: Great Power Politics, 1815–1914*. Cambridge: Cambridge University Press, 2014.

Agius, Christine. "Transformed beyond Recognition? The Politics of Post-Neutrality." *Cooperation and Conflict* 46, no. 3 (2011): 370–95.

Black, Cyril E., Richard A. Falk, Klaus Knorr, and Oran R. Young. *Neutralization and World Politics*. Princeton: Princeton University Press, 1968.

Cohen, Roger. "The (Not So) Neutrals of World War II." *The New York Times*, 1997.

Eidgenössisches Departement für Verteidigung, Bevölkerungsschutz und Sport (VBS). *Die Neutralität der Schweiz*. 4 ed. Berne: Schweizerische Eidgenossenschaft, 2014.

Engle, Eloise, and Lauri Paananen. *The Winter War: The Soviet Attack on Finland, 1939 – 1940*. Mechanicsburg: Stackpole Books, 1992.

Glaser, Charles L. *Rational Theory of International Politics: The Logic of Competition and Cooperation*. Princeton: Princeton University Press, 2010.

Hägglöf, Gunnar M. "A Test of Neutrality: Sweden in the Second World War." *International Affairs* 36 (1960): 153–67.

Havel, Brian F. "An International Law Institution in Crisis: Rethinking Permanent Neutrality." *Ohio State Law Journal* 61 (2000): 167.

Jessup, Philip C., and Francis Deak. *Neutrality: Its History, Economics and Law: The Origins*. 4 vols. vol. 1. New York: Columbia University Press, 1935.

Knapp, Harry S. "The Real Status of the Panama Canal as Regards Neutralization." *The American Journal of International Law* 4, no. 2 (1910): 314–58.

Kruzel, Joseph. "The Future of European Neutrality." In *Between the Blocs: Problems and Prospects for Europe's Neutral and Nonaligned States*, edited by Joseph Kruzel and Michael H. Haltzel. Washington, DC: Woodrow Wilson International Center for Scholars, 1989.

Kupchan, Charles A. "After Pax Americana: Benign Power, Regional Integration, and the Sources of a Stable Multipolarity." *International Security* 23, no. 2 (1998): 40–79.

Layne, Christopher. "This Time It's Real: The End of Unipolarity and the 'Pax Americana.'" *International Studies Quarterly* 56, no. 1 (2012): 203–13.

———. "The US–Chinese Power Shift and the End of the Pax Americana." *International Affairs* 94, no. 1 (2018): 89–111.

Leitz, Christian. *Sympathy for the Devil: Neutral Europe and Nazi Germany in World War II*. New York: New York University Press, 2001.

Lottaz, Pascal, and Herbert Reginbogin, eds. *Notions of Neutralities*. Lanham, MD: Lexington, 2019.

Morgenthau, Hans J. "The Resurrection of Neutrality in Europe." *American Political Science Review* 33 (1939): 473–86.

Müller, Leos. "The Forgotten History of Maritime Neutrality, 1500–1800." In *Notions of Neutralities*, edited by Pascal Lottaz and Herbert Reginbogin, 67–86. Lanham: Lexington, 2019.

———. *Neutrality in World History*. New York: Routledge, 2019.

Neff, Stephen C. *The Rights and Duties of Neutrals: A General History*. Manchester: Manchester University Press, 2000.

Orvik, Nils. *The Decline of Neutrality 1914–1941. With Special Reference to the United States and the Northern Neutrals*. Oslo: Johan Grundt Tanum Forlag, 1953.

Pacheco Pardo, Ramon. "China and Northeast Asia's Regional Security Architecture: The Six-Party Talks as a Case of Chinese Regime-Building? *East Asia: An International Quarterly* 29, no. 4 (2012): 337–54.

Pinker, Steven. *The Better Angels of our Nature: Why Violence Has Declined*. New York: Viking, 2011.

Ruggenthaler, Peter. *The Concept of Neutrality in Stalin's Foreign Policy, 1945–1953*. New York: Lexington, 2015.

———. "Neutrality as an Instrument of Soviet Foreign Policy, 1945–53." In *Notions of Neutralities*, edited by Pascal Lottaz and Herbert Reginbogin, 161–84. Lanham, MD: Lexington, 2019.

Simon, Steven, and Jonathan Stevenson. "The End of Pax Americana: Why Washington's Middle East Pullback Makes Sense." *Foreign Affairs*, no. 6, Council on Foreign Relations, 2015, 2–10.

Tow, William T., and Brendan Taylor. "What Is Asian Security Architecture?" *Review of International Studies* 36 (2010): 95–116.

Williams, Paul D. "Reflections on the Evolving African Peace and Security Architecture." *African Security* 7, no. 3 (2014): 147–62.

Winslow, Erving. "Neutralization." *American Journal of International Law* 2 (1908): 366–86.

Wright, Quincy. "The American Civil War, 1861–1865." In *The International Law of Civil War*, edited by Richard A. Falk, 30–110. Baltimore: Johns Hopkins Press, 1971.

*Part I*

# Theory

*Chapter One*

# A Tale of Two Strategies

*Permanent Neutrality and Collective Security*

Stephen C. Neff

There are many possible models for bringing peace, security, and justice to the world. One of them is empire or hegemony: putting one single power in command. Another is shared great-power management, along the lines of the nineteenth-century Concert of Europe. Another is the balance of power. International lawyers are particularly attracted to order brought about by adherence to a set of universal norms. Regional autarky is another possibility. So is technocratic management, along the lines advanced by the nineteenth-century St-Simonians. The list could be expanded more or less indefinitely. The present discussion will focus on the interplay and contrasts between two particular strategies: permanent neutrality and collective security. A couple of useful contrasts between these two may be pointed out from the outset.

Collective security, as the very name suggests, is a cooperative, community-oriented strategy. At its heart is the organization of the states of the world into a body with a shared mission of preserving peace and defeating—or, better yet, deterring—aggression. It is a social, solidaristic approach. It breathes an air of activity. As Theodore Roosevelt might have said, it is the strenuous life harnessed to the cause of peace. At its heart is the slogan associated with the Three Musketeers: "All for one, and one for all!" Permanent neutrality, in contrast, is the path of the loner. At its heart is the determination of individual states to safeguard themselves from the political and military squalls around them by resolutely refusing to take sides when quarrels break out. Its watchword is self-protection. Its goal is "business as usual" in the face of even the stormiest weather. Along these same lines, collective security may be thought of as a "direct approach" to peacekeeping, in which wrongdoers are explicitly identified, targeted, and sanctioned. It is a policing mechanism. Permanent neutrality, in contrast, is an "indirect approach," seeing peace arising as a beneficial side-effect of a general practice of dutiful law-observance, and self-restraint, on the part of each member of the community. Permanent neutrality is accordingly a decentralized path to peace, with power dispersed throughout the community. These two might be further thought of, by way of contrast, as "top-down" and "bottom-up" approaches to global security. Collective security is the top-down option. By its very nature, it only works if a sizeable portion of the world—and ideally the *entire* world—is pre-assembled for mutual supportive action. Collective security, therefore, can only work effectively if the international community itself is in reasonably good working order. That is, there must be a sensibly broad agreement on basic goals and values, combined with a degree of commitment to the broader community, that is, a willingness to expend resources and take risks for the benefit of the world at large. The great weakness of the collective security strategy, therefore, is the grave doubt as to whether the requisite degrees of consensus and commitment actually exist at any given time. Permanent neutrality, in contrast, is the bottom-up alternative, in that it can be implemented by stealth, so to speak, one state at a time, moving incrementally toward a world in which ever-larger numbers of states gear their national policies toward never going to war. No grand alliances need to be forged. No supra-national machinery or international organization is necessary. Grand summit conferences, with fluttering national flags, are not required. Photo opportunities are decidedly limited. The advantage, though, is that a security policy based on permanent neutrality can inch its way into existence incrementally. It can grow organically from tiny seeds. As more and more states adopt Swiss or Swedish or Irish policies of permanent neutrality, so the "contagion of peace" can gradually infect progressively greater portions of the world, without a need for central direction. In the (slightly altered) words of Bertrand Russell, the world will be at peace not because there is central authority enforcing it, but rather because everyone minds their own business.[1]

The question surrounding permanent neutrality is whether its egoistical and passive outlook can really successfully operate as a general strategy for peace and security. After all, it envisages global peace as, in effect, a beneficial side-effect of home-grown, nationally oriented policies, rather than as something that is directly and explicitly targeted, as is the case with collective security. One of the major questions about permanent neutrality as a peace mechanism is, as P. Terrence Hopmann is asking in his chapter,[2] whether this isolationist and egoistical aspect can somehow be transcended—whether it can somehow be made to serve in a concerted, systematic, consciously coordinated way to promote the larger collective goal of international peace and security. This discussion will be a contribution to answering that question. The focus will be on a comparison to and contrast with collective security as a rival strategy, with the primary emphasis on the experience of the interwar period.

The first section will point out the growing intellectual respectability of neutrality in the nineteenth century, culminating in optimistic assessments on the potential value of permanent neutrality for world peace. The second section will outline the rivalry between the collective security and neutrality visions in the early period of the League of Nations. The third will look to the little-known experience in the interwar period with coordinated efforts of neutral solidarity in the name of peace, and how they fared. The fourth section will briefly point out the continuing tension between the two in the post-1945 period. Finally, some thoughts will be offered about the implications for the contemporary world.

## Neutrality's Road to Respectability

Neutrality's early prospects as a strategy for world peace were inauspicious in the extreme. Writers in the medieval just-war tradition had no regard for neutrality. In fact, the medieval concept of just war carried within it, if only implicitly, a recognizable component of collective security thinking. This was evident in the principle that the overriding duty of states was to support the just side in a conflict and to refrain carefully from lending any support to the unjust party.[3] It is readily seen that there is a germ of the collective security mentality operating here. It is the duty of all states to aid victims of aggression and injustice—if not by actually joining in the hostilities, at least by providing all possible assistance from the sidelines.

Even then, however, there were some indications—if only grudging—that neutrality could play a legitimate part in international affairs. It was conceded that in doubtful cases—when the just side in a conflict could not be reliably identified—neutrality, in the sense of impartial treatment of the contending sides, would be justifiable.[4] This was a strong hint of things to come: that neutrality, even if it was reprehensible in principle, could still have a useful role to play in special circumstances. Initially, this marginal role for neutrality only envisaged that the various neutral countries would be tending to their own interests—staying out of war at a minimum or, as a possible bonus, profiting from the conflict by trading with both sides, including in weapons of war. Not until the nineteenth century did neutrality come to be thought of in broader, more communitarian terms as a policy which could work for the welfare of the world at large, and not merely for the egoistical interests of the neutral states themselves. For this change to take place, two important developments were necessary. One was the development of *permanent* neutrality—meaning, as the name clearly implies, a policy on a given state's part of *always* being neutral in all circumstances. The second was the acceptance of such policies by the major powers, together with their utilization, in the context of international politics, as a general war-prevention mechanism.

The earliest example of a consciously adopted policy of long-term neutrality was by the Netherlands in the eighteenth century.[5] After the War of the Spanish Succession (1701–1713), the Dutch made a more or less conscious decision to remain aloof from the various violent struggles for power in Europe and to remain at peace with all parties whenever war broke out. The reason for that was that their priorities had shifted from imperial conquest to trade. The neutrality policy was broadly successful in as far as it kept the country out of external European wars for nearly 200 years until World War II (not accounting for the many wars in the East Indies and the splitting away of Belgium), while driving home handsome profits from trade. It is worth noting, though, that it did not lead to the Dutch being particularly honored or liked by their fellow Europeans. Instead, it gave them the reputation as mercenaries, greedily exploiting the hardships and risks of other countries for the sordid goal of personal enrichment.

In the years after 1783, the Dutch were joined as stalwart neutrals by the newly independent United States. Neutrality, from early days, was an essential part of the American self-image, with the scrupulous avoidance of "entangling alliances," against which President Washington had so firmly warned. The Americans consequently became resolute champions of the rights of neutrals, as opposed to belligerents, when issues arose. Even more than the Dutch, the Americans were explicit about the larger role that they expected neutrality to play. It was a key part of the broader national policy of staying out of European conflicts, and thereby of promoting peace. The United States even had the distinction of going to war in 1812 against Great Britain over issues of neutrality.[6]

## Neutrality Meets World Peace

A key development for permanent neutrality as a strategy for peace was its recognition by the major powers as a useful tool for conflict management. This was a phenomenon of the nineteenth century.[7] It may be said to have begun in 1815, with the Congress of Vienna (1814–1815), which acknowledged the permanent neutrality of Switzerland as being in the greater interest of peace in Europe.[8] The neutrality of Switzerland was expressly stated to be in the general interest of Europe at large. A second important step in this direction came in the 1830s when Belgium was separated from the Netherlands as an independent state. Its permanent neutrality was provided for, once again, with guarantees from the major powers.[9] Then in 1867 came a comparable arrangement for the independence and neutrality of Luxembourg—an arrangement which survived the strains of the Franco-Prussian War of

1870–1871.[10] Portions of states could be covered as well. The Ionian Islands, for example, when they were transferred to Greece from the protection of Britain in 1863, were stipulated to "enjoy the advantages of a perpetual neutrality."[11] Such activity was not confined to Europe. In 1885, the Congress of Berlin made provision for the neutrality of the Congo Free State.[12] In Central America, a similar arrangement was made for the neutralization of Honduras in 1907.[13] Newly independent Albania was also granted neutral status in 1913 (with guarantees by the major powers).[14]

Other vital steps included neutralization regimes for the newly constructed Suez and Panama Canals.[15] The basic idea was to ensure that these crucial waterways remained open to all states without discrimination both in war and peace—and to ensure that no belligerent activity took place in or near them. In 1881, a bilateral treaty between Argentina and Chile provided that the Straits of Magellan were to be "neutralized forever," with free navigation for all states and a ban on fortification.[16] In short, these choke points were to be fenced off from international conflict and remain as zones of peace.

By the end of the nineteenth century, there was significant recognition that neutrality could, and even did, play a role in the larger cause of world peace and security. This was explicitly recognized by the Swedish lawyer Richard Kleen, who was the foremost authority on the rights and duties of neutral states and a prominent champion of the rights of neutrals against belligerents.[17] Neutrality, explained Kleen, actually had two functions, a narrow and a broad one. The narrow one was to ensure the right of each state to remain at peace if it so chose whenever a war between other countries broke out. This was clearly a right of individual state autonomy. The broader purpose was nothing less than the promotion—in the long run, at least—of "universal peace."[18] It is in the interest of this larger goal, as well as for their own parochial state interest, that neutral states should stand up for the full respect of their neutral rights by the belligerents.

The high regard in which neutrality was held was confirmed by no less a source than the famous eleventh edition (1911) of the Encyclopedia Britannica, which informed the reading world that neutrality was "bringing the state system of the modern world nearer to the realization of the dream of many great writers and thinkers of a community of nations." Neutrality—or, more strictly, recognition and observance of the legal rights of neutrals—was seen as the critical mechanism for counteracting the role of "brute force" in international life.[19] This growing belief that the general concerns of those at peace should prevail over those at war would operate—it was hoped—as a process of gradually hemming in and confining belligerents.[20] "The greater the number of neutralized states," posited an American anti-imperialism campaigner, "the more remote in a geometrical ratio, become the possibilities of war." He saw the tendency toward world peace "growing deeper and stronger as the spheres in which [neutrality] prevails become larger and more numerous."[21]

Admittedly, a certain leap of faith was being called for. World peace was going to arrive not so much as a consciously crafted and carefully guided policy, so much as an after-effect of the proliferation of ad hoc instances of permanent neutrality. There was, in this belief, a relatively high component of speculation.

Moreover, the old suspicion of neutrality was by no means a thing of the past. Even Kleen, resolute champion though he was of the rights of neutrals, insisted, in the spirit of old just-war thinking, that a neutral state should strive to be (or become) "an active factor in the maintenance of universal order."[22] Further in this vein, he conceded that neutrality found its chief justification in the uncertainty that typically prevailed in the determination of fault when war broke out. As international law advanced so as to make it possible to identify wrongdoers in the resort to war, neutrality would lose its *raison d'être* and would be replaced by a "duty of intervention" in favor of right against wrong. Kleen was therefore opposed to neutrality as a dogmatic and inflexible policy of states—that is, in effect, to a doctrinaire policy of permanent neutrality.[23] So powerful, even at the turn of the twentieth century, was the basic just-war mentality—and the low opinion which it harbored of neutrality.

## COLLECTIVE SECURITY VERSUS NEUTRALITY

Collective security, as an officially implemented policy, was an invention of the twentieth century. It was a child of desperation and disillusionment, in the aftermath of the First World War. It then had a second birth in the United Nations era in 1945. As a direct and high-profile approach to peacemaking, it has received far more attention than permanent neutrality. But it has not had the field entirely to itself.

### Collective Security's First Incarnation: The League of Nations

The essence of collective security is the idea that, when a country is a victim of aggression, the other members of the security arrangement should spring into action and assist the victim country. In numbers, there will be safety. That is to say, no aggressor could ever expect to be stronger than the collective security body as a whole. Therefore, if the collective rescue apparatus operated as planned (or hoped), then aggression would inevitably meet with defeat—and, by obvious extension, aggressors would be deterred from mounting attacks to begin with.[24]

In its purest form of this noble enterprise, the collective security corps would act immediately against aggressors. That is to say; the arrangement would basically be automatic, triggered by an act of aggression *per se*. That was the basic intention of the world's first global collective security arrangement, the League of Nations. It was articulated explicitly in the famous (or infamous) Article 10 of the League Covenant. Under this "guarantee provision," as it was commonly known, each League member undertook "to respect and preserve as against external aggression"[25] all of its fellow members. The League Council was to "advise" on the means of fulfilling this duty. But the duty *itself* arose automatically upon the occurrence of an act of aggression.

Broadly similar to the guarantee provision was the sanctions arrangement set out in Article 16 of the Covenant. This was more narrowly focused than the guarantee in that it was directed only against misconduct by the League's own member states, but the basic idea was the same. If one (or more) League member state was to resort to war against another in violation of the Covenant (i.e., without first going through relevant peaceful-settlement mechanisms), this would be regarded as an "act of war" against all other League members, which would then be obligated "immediately" and automatically to impose a range of economic sanctions against the wrongdoer.

These two collective security provisions were the polar opposite in spirit to the concept of permanent neutrality. At their very heart was a policy of instant involvement by all League member states in conflicts involving any one of them. It is hardly surprising, then, that the heartiest champions of collective security were also the most resolute critics of the very idea of neutrality. Woodrow Wilson, the principal proponent of the League of Nations, made it clear that, according to his ideal of the League, "it shall be understood that there is no neutrality where any nation is doing wrong."[26]

The American international lawyer (and collective security advocate) Charles Fenwick, speaking in similar terms, derided neutrality as "the policy of international *laissez-faire* in regard to war."[27] Another international legal observer concluded, with evident satisfaction, that, in the new collective security era, "neutralization . . . would appear to be distinctly on the wane, if not on the high road to extinction."[28] Another American lawyer (and collective security enthusiast), Quincy Wright, made an explicit comparison between the medieval just-war era and the League period—and concluded that neutrality was equally incompatible with both.[29] He disputed the thesis that neutrality made any contribution to world peace, contending instead that, if anything, it operated to encourage aggression, by giving would-be aggressors confidence that neutral states would treat them on a strict par with their victims.[30]

One of the most outspoken figures in this vein was Nicolas Politis, sometime foreign minister of Greece, international-law scholar and general knight-errant of the solidaristic vision of international law.[31] He held neutrality to be "a true anachronism" in the collective security age and gladly pronounced it to be "inevitably doomed" and "destined to disappear."[32] Like Wright, he contended that "the attitude of disinterestedness" operated "to favor war" rather than to restrict it.[33] More specifically, Politis maintained that, even if a League member state declined to participate in armed action against an aggressor, it would not have the option of remaining neutral in the traditional sense. For one thing, it would be entitled to discriminate against the aggressor, for example, in its economic policies. In addition, the "neutral"—or rather nonparticipating—state would have no ground for complaint if the collective security side were to infringe some of its traditional neutral rights, in the larger cause of defeating aggression.[34]

However, even if it were accepted that there was a broad inconsistency between collective security and neutrality, there were many who contended that the latter was not wholly a thing of the past. One of the most vigorous spokesmen for this view was the Danish lawyer and diplomat Georg Cohn.[35] It was pointed out that, for one thing, neutrality still remained an option for states that were not members of the League. Moreover, many contended that, even for League members, neutrality was still possible in cases where the aggressor or wrongdoing party was not clearly identified. Neutrality could also be justified in cases in which *both* sides were wrongdoers.

## The Fall of Collective Security

Events in the interwar period proved unkind to the vision of collective security.[36] The guarantee provision of Article 10 was never invoked. The economic-sanctions provision of Article 16 was resorted to on just one occasion, the Italian invasion of Ethiopia in 1935–1936, where it proved to be a humiliating failure. Italy completed its conquest of Ethiopia before the sanctions could have any serious effect.

This embarrassing failure of collective security led to a bout of intense soul-searching at the League and within the various member states. In July 1936, in the immediate wake of the Ethiopian fiasco, seven neutral countries issued a joint declaration which regretted that the Covenant had been applied "incompletely and inconsistently." In Britain, Prime Minister Neville Chamberlain of Great Britain candidly admitted in 1938 that the small states of the world should not harbor any illusions that the League's collective security system would be able to provide them with effective protection.[37] In debates at the League in 1938, the government of Sweden contended that "a practice has become established," outside the text of the Covenant, in which League members no longer regarded themselves as "bound to take coercive action against an aggressor State." The League's vision of "automatic and obligatory sanctions," it lamented, had become a "fiction."[38]

An immediate consequence of this failure of collective security was a renewed interest in, and respect for, traditional neutrality. In truth, there had always been a belief that, even with collective security in force, there was room for neutrality to operate interstitially—that is, that, whenever gaps or cracks appeared in the collective security system, neutrality would become permissible.[39] Even Politis had conceded that.[40] In the wake of the Ethiopian crisis, it was apparent that the cracks were distressingly large—and hence that the scope for neutrality policies was correspondingly much broader than had initially been hoped. This view received notable support from the International Law Association,[41] which concluded at its 1938 meeting that the sanctions provision of the League Covenant was now "inoperative" because of "general nonobservance." As a result, "[a]ccording to the practice of nations, neutrality is not abrogated, even as between members of the League."[42]

It is hardly surprising, then, that a number of traditionally neutral states reasserted their pre-League policies in the wake of the Ethiopian crisis. Belgium was one of these. In 1937, it was released by Britain and France from its defensive-alliance obligations under the Locarno Treaty of 1925 (which was designed to stabilize the western borders of Germany), shifting over to a policy which it characterized as "realistic neutrality."[43] The Netherlands too went back to its general policy of neutrality.[44] The Swiss government similarly announced that it was reverting, "by an instinct of self-preservation, to its full traditional neutrality."[45] It formally notified the League in April 1938 that it would no longer participate in economic sanctions. In taking note of this position the following month, the League Council effectively conceded that its collective security system was no longer viable.[46]

## NEUTRAL SOLIDARITY AND WORLD PEACE

Neutrality did not merely survive in the challenging vicissitudes of the interwar period. It also underwent a certain transformation, which has received very little attention from scholars of the period. This transformation consisted of an aligning of the policies of neutral countries into a common front for the promotion of international peace. Neutrality came to be envisaged as a kind of parallel, or underground, counterpart of the formal collective security apparatus of the League. In this regard, neutrality ceased to be a purely egoistic practice of individual states in isolation and became instead a coordinated and collective policy directed toward the welfare of the world at large—an attempt to fulfill Kleen's call for neutrality to become "an active factor" in the promotion of peace instead of a mere congeries of egoistic and isolationist state policies. The experience with this policy in the interwar period was every bit as interesting as the better known (and unedifying) experience with formal collective security.

The centerpiece of this policy of neutral solidarity was the embargoing of arms shipments to the belligerent parties. This was contrary to the law and practice of traditional neutrality, which barred *governments* from supplying arms to warring parties, but was permissive when it came to arms shipments by private parties. Under the traditional law of neutrality, private companies were permitted to supply weapons, subject only to the risk that the arms shipments might be captured and confiscated *en route* by the opposing side. However, there was nothing to prevent neutral governments from prohibiting arms shipments by their nationals as a matter of their own *national* laws.

Just such an idea formed a central plank in the campaign for a so-called "new neutrality" in the United States, which, in essence, proposed the foregoing of certain traditional rights of neutrals—such as the right to permit arms exports—in the interest of remaining at peace.[47] This arms-embargo policy was then embodied in a series of neutrality laws beginning in 1935.[48] The goal of this "new neutrality" policy was to keep the United States *itself* out of any future conflicts.

For this policy to function on a global scale, as a viable international peacekeeping mechanism, it needed to be universalized and coordinated. The idea was that, if all (or most) neutral governments were to impose arms embargoes, then warring parties would be "starved" of foreign arms supplies and thereby driven into peace by the sheer inability to continue the hostilities. Clearly, such a strategy would work best when the belligerents were highly dependent on foreign suppliers for their armaments *and* when the neutral parties acted promptly and in unison to choke off arms shipments to *all* of the belligerents.

## The Chaco War

The first trial of this approach to peace-making occurred even before the Ethiopian test of the sanctions regime—in the Chaco War between Bolivia and Paraguay, which broke out in 1933. The experience, however, was not altogether encouraging. It began when the United States (not a League member) imposed an arms embargo against both sides in 1934. Several other countries followed suit. A Neutral Commission was formed at the League of Nations, which recommended the imposition of arms embargoes by neutral states against both warring sides.[49] This recommendation was widely adopted,[50] but the Commission made clear that these were voluntary unilateral acts by the states themselves.[51] It was noted, however, that, since the embargo policies were coordinated through the League, this invested the actions with "a collective and international character."[52]

The two contending states reacted to the embargo in instructively different ways. Paraguay praised the embargo as "a laudable, humanitarian object, . . . animated by a lofty desire to render the continuance of the hostilities more and more difficult."[53] Bolivia, in contrast, protested against what it called "the flagrant injustice of a uniform embargo.[54] The reason for this differential response was not difficult to guess. Paraguay was geographically favored by its access to the Paraná and Paraguay Rivers, as compared to the more isolated Bolivia. That is to say, Paraguay was far better positioned to benefit from smuggling, in violation of any arms embargoes, which would hit Bolivia harder.[55] The French government advanced another objection: that many states were not as conscientious as it was in imposing and enforcing embargoes.[56]

Matters took an interesting turn in January 1935, when the Neutral Commission found Paraguay to have been at fault in the crisis. Bolivia then pressed for the activation of the collective security provisions (the Article 10 guarantee and the Article 16 economic sanctions). This did not happen. But the League did recommend that the arms embargoes be lifted vis-à-vis Bolivia but kept in place against Paraguay. Nineteen League states (out of a membership of sixty) acceded to this recommendation.[57] Paraguay responded by withdrawing from the League of Nations.

### The Spanish Civil War

A second, and even more challenging, trial of neutral solidarity in the cause of peace came with the outbreak of the Spanish Civil War of 1936–1939. On this occasion, the League played hardly any role. Instead, the European states, on the initiative of France, formed themselves into a Nonintervention Committee. The basic policy was to ensure that outside powers stayed out of the contest and that there would be scrupulously even-handed treatment of the two contending sides. By September 1936, twenty-six European countries had signed on to the nonintervention program. The plan expanded from arms embargoes to the patrolling of frontiers, to prevent influxes of foreign participants. Plans were devised for the stationing of observers in Spain to monitor the entry of goods and volunteers into Spain. These were stationed on the French and Portuguese frontiers and in Gibraltar.

An arrangement was also devised for policing maritime traffic, comprising ship observations, with monitoring by an international naval patrol. This patrol consisted of vessels of the four major European naval powers, which would fly a special pennant when engaging in this community service. Ships sailing to Spain from nonintervention states were expected to call first at designated observation posts and to take observation officers on board, to ensure that prohibited goods were not being carried. The naval patrol vessels were authorized to visit ships registered with any of the nonintervention states on the high seas, to check papers and ascertain the presence of observation officers on board.

The particular challenge of submarine attacks on neutral shipping was addressed by the Nyon Agreement of September 1937. Britain and France were charged with carrying out self-defense measures against this menace, by attacking submarines that attacked (or were thought to be attacking) neutral shipping in violation of prevailing international legal rules. A supplementary agreement extended this policy to cover aircraft and surface vessels of the contending parties.[58]

Provision was made for recognition of belligerency—an act which would have the effect, for all recognizing parties, of transforming the conflict into the full equivalent of an inter-state war, with the full panoply of the laws of war and neutrality then applying. Recognition of belligerency was, however, predicated on the occurrence of various conditions (chiefly on evacuations of foreign participants); and, in the event, these were not fulfilled. So it did not occur, and the struggle remained an internal conflict to its very end.[59]

The grand experiment of 1936–1939 in the Spanish Civil War cannot be said to have been a very encouraging precedent for a program of neutral solidarity and peace promotion. As in the case of the Chaco War, the problem of differential observance of the embargoes posed a problem. There were massive violations by Germany and Italy in favor of the Nationalist side. The Soviet Union aided the Republicans but to a much lesser extent. Since the observation schemes on land and sea only applied to nonintervention states and their nationals, there was ample scope for arms and volunteers to enter Spain. Moreover, the Nonintervention Committee did not possess any real enforcement powers over its members. The practical effect, then, was that the nonintervention program, as it worked, operated heavily in favor of the Nationalist side, since the Republicans' natural sympathizers, Britain and France, were more diligent in its observance than were the Nationalists' supporters.

## Visions of the Future

Alongside these ad hoc efforts to harness neutrality for the wider cause of peace, there were some more imaginative ruminations about what the future might look like—a future in which world peace efforts would be rooted in neutrality rather than in collective security. One such scheme came from Philip Jessup, a professor of international law at Columbia University, in 1936.[60] He frankly longed to find (or invent) some "alchemy to change the base nature of neutrality for selfish profit into partiality for the peace and happiness of mankind."[61] Neutrality, in his view, contained "the unfertilized seeds of collective action for bringing war to a close or for limiting its scope."[62] To make these seeds germinate, he proposed infusing neutrality with the spirit of collective security—and, more specifically, with the economic-sanctions provision of the League Covenant.

Inspired by the experience of the Chaco War, Jessup proposed that, when wars broke out, the neutral countries should stand together and prohibit arms shipments to both sides, to make the waging of the conflict "appreciably more difficult."[63] In addition to arms, Jessup proposed that the embargoing should apply to financial assistance as well. There would have to be diligent application of the embargo policies by the neutral states, including careful precautions against the re-exporting of materials by trading partners to the belligerents. As in the Chaco case, there should be room for adjusting the embargo policy in favor of the innocent party, once that was determined; but the main thrust of Jessup's plan was that there was to be equal treatment of the warring sides.

Jessup candidly acknowledged several problems with his plan. For one thing, there would be some economic hardship for the neutral states, in the form of trade opportunities foregone. But these hardships should be cheerfully borne in the larger interest of world peace. A major question concerned what materials other than arms should be embargoed. The greater the scope of the embargoes, the greater the hardship involved to the neutral states themselves (in the form of profits foregone), and also the greater the hardship for ordinary people in the belligerent states. The question of whether to embargo food shipments was particularly troubling. There was also the consideration of differential material effects of the policy. A self-sufficient belligerent would suffer less (if at all) from the embargoes, as compared to a highly trade-dependent state.

Another proposal, in a broadly similar vein, was advanced by Georg Cohn, the chief of the international law section of the Danish foreign office, in 1939. His plan was labeled "neo-neutrality."[64] Cohn was a prominent advocate of the idea that neutrality was not incompatible with the Covenant, and his neo-neutrality was an extended exposition of that thesis. He described it as "a policy of combination of both neutrality and solidarity,"[65] that is, a proposal "to isolate and restrict" war, without taking up arms against aggressors. War would not, on this plan, be eliminated or prevented altogether. Instead, it would be quarantined, and contained. It was a decidedly more modest plan than a straightforward collective security scheme, but it was arguably consistent with traditional neutrality policies and practices. It was also more realistic, in Cohn's view, to rely on the efforts of a large number of countries to contain war by means of neutrality policies, rather than counting on a small number of major powers to take up arms against aggressors.[66]

A notable feature of Cohn's plan was an explicit critique of what he called the moralistic or penal approach of collective security strategies, which were obsessed with identifying and punishing wrongdoers. The neo-neutrality approach, he argued, was more scientific and dispassionate, seeing war more as a disease or infirmity of the international system than as a crime.

On such a view, a policy of isolation and quarantine was more useful than one of punishment.

The neo-neutrality proposal was stated to be directed against war in general rather than against aggressors in particular.[67] Under this conception, the primordial duty of neutral states was to stay out of war. Cohn candidly held that a neutral state's ability "to keep a larger or smaller bit of the earth free from war" was actually a *more* valuable contribution to the cause of world peace than participation in military action against aggressors.[68] Once this main goal was achieved, the next duty of neutral states was stated (somewhat vaguely) to be the application of "any means to prevent or to stop the war to the limit of their ability without themselves participating in it."[69] To the extent that the traditional neutral duty of impartiality interfered with these goals, it was to be discarded.

Cohn's plan, like Jessup's, was designed to operate in situations in which aggressors or wrongdoers had not been clearly singled out. Some proposals, however, envisaged that aggressors could be identified and that, in such cases, the traditional neutral duty of impartiality must be abandoned as a matter of urgency. An example of this approach was a proposal by a research team based at Harvard Law School in 1939, in the form of a Draft Convention on the Rights and Duties of States in Case of Aggression.[70] The basic idea was that, in the case of a war of aggression, states that were not involved in the conflict would not be expected to join in—as they would under collective security—but instead they would become entitled to discriminate against the aggressor. Specifically, they would retain all of the traditional *rights* of neutrals vis-à-vis the aggressor country, while being relieved of all of the corresponding *duties* toward that loathsome state. That is, they would not be subject to the key duty of impartiality and would accordingly be entitled to act in favor of the victim state. Third states would, however, retain the option of acting impartially if they so chose.

Although the Harvard Draft Convention was never adopted, the ideas embodied in it were followed, with remarkable fidelity, by the United States during the period 1939–1941, before its entry into the Second World War. During that period, the country was "neutral" only in the sense that it was not an actual belligerent. Its policies were a very far cry from the twin duties of abstention and impartiality required by the traditional international law of neutrality. Washington was blatantly partial to the Allied side, most notably in the large-scale provision of war materials to the Allied powers through the Lend-Lease program instituted in early 1941. Even prior to its entry into the conflict, President Franklin Roosevelt was proudly proclaiming his country to be "the arsenal of democracy."[71]

There were loud objections to this American policy of "nonbelligerency," as it was sometimes called[72]—including from Jessup, who objected in principle to unequal treatment of the belligerents.[73] In technical legal terminology, the United States justified its policy in terms of countermeasures against Germany for its violation of the Pact of Paris of 1928, in which the states parties—including Germany—had grandly renounced resort to war as an instrument of national policy.[74] Whatever the strict legal merits of this American nonbelligerency policy, it stands as a striking illustration of how porous the line can become, in practice, between the very different policies of neutrality and collective security.

## THE UN CHARTER ERA

In the post-World War II period, the policies of collective security and neutrality have continued in their uneasy coexistence. Some of the differences from the interwar period may, however, be usefully noted. One is that the collective security design of the United Nations is, in key aspects, less ambitious than its League of Nations predecessor. This may come as a surprise to some, who believe the UN to be a more robust organization in its provision for the use of armed force as well as of economic sanctions in the cause of world peace. The crucial point, though, is that the automatic character of the League scheme was discarded, in favor of a discretionary approach—the discretion being that of the five major powers which wield the veto in the UN Security Council. The UN member states are obligated to act only when— and if—the Security Council so commands. There is no guarantee provision in the UN Charter comparable to Article 10 of the League Covenant, nor any provision for automatic economic sanctions as in Article 16.

As in the interwar period, there was considerable support for the view that neutrality was no longer tenable in a collective security system.[75] The nearest that the UN Charter came to an express endorsement of this view was in Article 2(5), which requires member states to give "every assistance" to the organization "in any action it takes" and, more specifically, to "refrain from giving assistance to any state against which the United Nations is taking preventive or enforcement action."[76] This certainly precludes neutrality in cases in which UN enforcement action is being taken, pursuant to guidance or instructions from the Security Council.

As before, though, there continued to be wide support for the idea that, if collective security failed to work as planned, neutrality would then be an option.[77] The effect, then, was that neutrality had a kind of vestigial or residual role to play, when the Security Council does not interfere or take sides. In its 1996 advisory opinion on the use of nuclear weapons, the World Court lent its imprimatur to the continuing existence of neutrality.[78]

In the practice of states, neutrality has continued to make at least sporadic appearances during the UN era.[79] The classic example was the Iran-Iraq war of 1980–1988, in which there was widespread adoption of explicit policies of neutrality—complete with insistence by the neutral states that the belligerents scrupulously respect the traditional legal rights of neutrals.[80] Even in the Kuwait conflict of 1991, an example of UN enforcement in action, Iran and Jordan issued declarations of neutrality.[81]

In addition, the list of permanently neutral states has expanded during the UN era, to take in Austria, Costa Rica, and Malta.[82] In 1962, in the course of Cold-War rivalries, an arrangement for the neutralization of Laos was agreed by the major powers.[83] In 1992, a similar agreement was made for the neutralization of Cambodia.[84] Moreover, permanently neutral states have not demonstrated any significant reluctance to become UN members, except Switzerland until its accession to the club in 2002.

## Collective Security and Neutrality in Action

In practice, and because of Cold-War constraints, the UN's collective security machinery has been activated only on select occasions. For present purposes, though, it is important to note the little-appreciated fact that UN action has tended to fall into two quite distinct categories. One involves action *against* some state for identifiable wrongdoing. This is punitive or corrective action. It took the form of comprehensive economic sanctions against Southern Rhodesia in 1966–1979. More visibly, there was armed action taken against North Korea in 1950–1953 and against Iraq for its occupation of Kuwait in 1990–1991. Force was also authorized (though not in the event actually applied) against Haiti in 1994 for the removal of a military government. These actions all fell clearly into the category of collective security.

The second type of action taken by the Security Council might be described as being more in the spirit of the neutral-solidarity efforts of the 1930s. These have been attempts to quarantine and contain conflicts, without actually taking sides. As in the interwar period, the policy of choice has been the arms embargo. Such policies are reminiscent of the Chaco War, and the Spanish Civil War noted above. They amount to coordinated neutrality efforts, in the interest of peace-promotion. What the post-1945 period has *not* seen, however, is any systematic thought given to this form of peace promotion, along the lines of Jessup and Cohn in the 1930s. The record has been one (for better or worse) of all practice and no theory.

As in the interwar period, the record of success for policies of neutral solidarity has been mixed at best. A comprehensive account is not possible in the present context. However, a brief look at the single most ambitious effort is instructive: the Bosnian Civil War of 1992–1995. That proved to be a sobering experience. The resemblances to the Chaco and Spanish Civil War experiences were striking and disturbing. As in the Spanish case, the underlying policy was to prevent outside involvement in the conflict. To that end, an arms embargo was instituted, which (as in the Spanish case) was neutral on its face.[85] In addition, a monitoring committee was established.[86] It demanded that all forms of outside interference in the conflict be ended.[87] Another policy, which had not been attempted in Spain, was the establishment of several designated "safe areas."[88]

Also as in the Chaco and Spanish cases, however, it soon became apparent that violations of the arms embargo were having the practical effect of operating actively in favor of one side (the insurgents) against the other (the Bosnian government). For that reason, the United States (most conspicuously) pressed for the lifting of the embargo. Worse yet was the tragic failure of the safe-areas policy, most conspicuously in the form of a genocidal massacre in Srebrenica of some eight thousand victims in July 1995. The conflict was soon brought to an end, but not by the arms-embargo policy. An attack by Croatian forces (armed and advised by American interests), coupled with an aerial bombing campaign—not officially authorized by the UN Security Council—finally brought the warring sides to the peace table, with a peace agreement reached in December of that year. Neither collective security nor neutral solidarity had proved equal to the challenge.

On one notable occasion (so far), there has been an authorization to neutral states to take more robust action than an arms embargo. This occurred in the Libyan civil conflict of 2011, in which the government of Muammar Qaddafi was overthrown by various insurgent forces. On that occasion, the Security Council gave general permission to UN member states to use armed force for two stated purposes: first, "to protect civilians and civilian populated areas under threat of attack"; and second, to enforce a ban on air flights over Libya.[89] That is to say, no mandate was given to intervening states to take one side against another in the actual struggle. There was to be, in effect, neutrality even as armed force was being employed. Here was neutrality in its most active guise.

This Libyan experience, like the Bosnian one, proved to be somewhat unhappy. There was a widespread (and probably well-founded) concern that Britain, France, and the United States went beyond these two designated purposes in their deployments of force and effectively aided the anti-government insurgents.[90] Based on this experience, it is hardly surprising that the UN Security Council did not approve similar intervention in the Syrian Civil War of 2011–2019.

## FINAL THOUGHTS

It cannot be said that either collective security or permanent neutrality has anything resembling an impressive historical track record for the promotion of world peace. Policies of direct confrontation of wrongdoings, along the lines of the action against Iraq in 1990–1991, have been rare in the extreme.

And the parallel, neutralist policy of isolating and containing conflict through such means as arms embargoes has no striking successes to its name. It is therefore hardly surprising that some find that alternatives, such as hegemonic or spheres-of-interest strategies, might hold out greater promise for the future. These are the solutions that have some attraction to thinkers of a realist persuasion—that is, of those who hold international affairs to be a constant jostling of competing national interests and clashes of rival state powers. Believers in both perpetual neutrality and collective security are of a more idealistic turn of mind, and in that sense are soulmates. To be more precise, they are believers in the idea of a genuinely international community, in which shared global interests are stronger than the parochial ambitions of individual states.

Although, as just noted, advocates of perpetual neutrality and collective security are fellow believers in a global vision, the forms of their beliefs are nevertheless quite distinct—rather like religious denominations which carve out distinctive paths to a common deity. We may go further along this line and liken the collective security and permanent-neutrality approaches to the Catholic and Protestant outlooks in Christianity. Collective security is the Catholic road to global peace, a sort of salvation through good works, carried out under the firm but benevolent auspices of a central organization (the United Nations). The good works involve a dutiful sacrifice of national interests in the common good, at the command of the UN Security Council.

Permanent neutrality, in contrast, may be seen as the Protestant road to global peace. It is more individual, imbued with a kind of international counterpart of the Protestant ethic, in which personal prosperity, far from being a bar to salvation, is regarded as being a sign of it. As in Protestantism, there is a strong current of salvation by faith rather than by works. Peace comes about not directly through the performance of mandatory community service—a sort of high-level conscription—but instead indirectly, as a by-product of constant attention to one's own affairs. Neutrality can be put forward as an inspiration to the world at large, as a concrete demonstration of the joys that await those who choose to stand aside from the storms of great-power rivalry. The more states that stand aside, the less will be at stake in that rivalry.

It is difficult to conclude on an optimistic note. Just as neither the Catholic nor the Protestant faiths have brought virtue and love to the world, so neither the collective security nor the permanent-neutrality strategies has led to even the more modest goal of global peace. In favor of the neutrality path, it may be said that, in general, it is more feasible to implement, precisely because it demands less of its practitioners. It calls for restraint and non-involvement rather than the riskier role of armed service. It may, therefore, be sensible to promote this as the more realistic—if also more modest—path to international security than the collective security one. As Jessup and Cohn emphasized, however, in the interwar period, neutrality as a peace strategy calls for more than merely doing nothing. It too calls for coordination and careful attention to detail. Neutrality as a peace strategy cries out for—but so far lacks—intellectual champions of the caliber of Jessup or Cohn to bring it forcefully to the attention of the statesmen and general public of the world. A careful study of past experience might be a useful first step in that direction.

## NOTES

1. Russell's reference was to the solar system rather than to the political world. See Bertrand Russell, *The Analysis of Matter* (New York: Harcourt Brace, 1927), 74.
2. See chapter 2 of this volume.
3. See, for example, Alberico Gentili, *The Three Books on the Law of War*, trans. John C. Rolfe (Oxford: Clarendon Press, 1933 [1598]), 67–73.
4. Hugo Grotius, *On the Law of War and Peace*, trans. Francis W. Kelsey (Oxford: Clarendon Press, 1925 [1625]), 786–87.
5. See generally Alice Clare Carter, *Neutrality or Commitment: The Evolution of Dutch Foreign Policy 1667–1795* (London: Arnold, 1975).
6. See generally Bradford Perkins, *Prologue to War: England and the United States 1805–1812* (Berkeley: University of California Press, 1961).
7. For a useful survey of neutralization practice in the nineteenth century see Maartje M. Abbenhuis, *An Age of Neutrals: Great Power Politics, 1815–1914* (Cambridge: Cambridge University Press, 2014), 45–62.
8. "Acte D'Accession, en Date de Zurich, le 27 Mai 1815, de la Confédération Suisse a la Déclaration des Puissances Réunies au Congrès de Vienne, en Date du 20 Mars 1815," in *Actes du Congrès de Vienne: Publiès d'apres un des Originaux Dépausé aux Archives du Département des Affaires Étrangères* (Paris: L'Imprimerie Royale, 1816). See also Act of Nov. 20, 1815, 65 C.T.S. 299. On Swiss neutrality, see Jacques Vergotti, *La neutralité de la Suisse: Son évolution historique et ses aspects dans les relations internationales de la première moitié du XXe siècle* (Lausanne: La Concorde, 1954).
9. Treaty of London, Apr. 19, 1839, 88 C.T.S. 411, art. 2, art. 7 of Annex. See generally Émile Banning, *Les origines et les phases de la neutralité belge* (Brussels: Albert Dewit, 1927); Édouard Eugène François Descamps, *La neutralité de la Belgique au point de vue historique, diplomatique, juridique et politique: Étude sur la constitution des États pacifiques à titre permanent* (Brussels: F. Larcier, 1902); and Daniel H. Thomas, *The Guarantee of Belgian Independence and Neutrality in European Diplomacy, 1830s—1930s* (Kingston: R. I.: D. H. Thomas, 1983).
10. Treaty Relative to the Grand Duchy of Luxembourg, May 11, 1867, 135 C.T.S. 1.
11. Treaty Relative to the Ionian Islands, Nov. 14, 1863, 128 C.T.S. 277, art. 2.
12. General Act of the Congress of Berlin, Feb. 26, 1885, 165 C.T.S. 485, arts. 10–12.
13. General Treaty of Peace and Amity, Dec. 20, 1907, 206 C.T.S. 63, art. 3. See also Rodriguez Salvador Gonzalez, "The Neutrality of Honduras and the Question of the Gulf of Fonseca," *American Journal of International Law* 10 (1916): 509–42.
14. Organic Statute of Albania, July 29, 1913, 213 C.T.S. 280, art. 3.
15. On the Suez Canal, see the Constantinople Convention, Oct. 29, 1888, 171 C.T.S. 241. See also Yves van der Mensbrugghe, *Les guaranties de la liberte de navigation dans le Canal de Suez* (Paris: Librairie de Droit et de Jurisprudence, 1964); and Benno Avram, *The Evolution of the Suez Canal Status from 1869 up to 1956: A Historico-juridical Study* (Geneva: E. Droz, 1958). On the Panama Canal, see Great Britain-USA, Hay-Pauncefort Treaty, Nov. 18, 1901, 190 C.T.S. 215, art. 3; and Panama-USA, Convention for the Construction of a Ship Canal, Nov. 18, 1903, 194 C.T.S. 263, art. 18. See also Norman J. Padelford, *The Panama Canal in Peace and War* (New York: MacMillan, 1943).
16. Argentina-Chile, Boundary Treaty, July 23, 1881, 159 C.T.S. 45, art. 4.

17. See Richard Kleen, *Lois et usages de la neutralité d'après le droit international conventionnel et coutûmier des États civilisés*, 2 vols. (Paris: A. Chevalier-Marescq, 1898–1900).

18. 1 Kleen, *Lois et usages*, 154–58. On permanent neutrality in the nineteenth century, see also Curt Ekdahl, *La neutralité perpetuelle avant le Pacte de la Société des Nations: Étude de droit des gens* (Paris: A. Pedone, 1923); Rudolf Laun, *Die Internationalisierung der Meeren und Kanale* (The Hague: M. Nijhoff, 1918); Emmanuel Descamps, *L'État neutre à titre permanent: Étude de droit international comparé* (Paris: Sirey, 1912); Dimitre Tswettcoff, *De la situation juridique des États neutralisés en temps de paix* (Geneva: Kündig, 1895); and Cyrus French, *Neutralization* (London: Oxford University Press, 1911).

19. Quoted in Earl Willis Crecraft, *Freedom of the Seas* (New York: D. Appleton-Century, 1935), 49. See also Abbenhuis, *An Age of Neutrals: Great Power Politics, 1815–1914*, 144–77.

20. See, for example, Sidney Schopfer, *Le principe juridique de la neutralité et son évolution dans l'histoire du droit de la guerre* (Lausanne: Corbaz, 1894).

21. Erving Winslow, "Neutralization," *American Journal of International Law* 2 (1908): 370–73.

22. Kleen, *Lois et usages de la neutralité d'après le droit international conventionnel et coutûmier des États civilisés*, 157.

23. Ibid., 156–58.

24. See also, on the mechanisms of collective security, Terrence Hopmann's explanations in this volume.

25. League of Nations, "The Covenant of the League of Nations," *The Avalon Project: Documents in Law, History and Diplomacy* (Yale: Yale Law School, 2008 [1919]), http://avalon.law.yale.edu/20th_century/leagcov.asp.

26. Harley Notter, *The Origins of the Foreign Policy of Woodrow Wilson* (Baltimore: Johns Hopkins University Press, 1937), 569.

27. Charles G. Fenwick, "Neutrality and International Organization," *American Journal of International Law* 28 (1934): 337.

28. Malbone W. Graham, "Neutralization as a Movement in International Law," *American Journal of International Law* 21 (1927): 94.

29. Quincy Wright, "The Present Status of Neutrality," *American Journal of International Law* 34 (1940): 396–99.

30. Ibid., 409.

31. See generally Nicolas Politis, *Neutrality and Peace*, trans. Francis Crane (Washington, DC: Carnegie Endowment for International Peace, 1935).

32. Ibid., xiii.

33. Ibid., 42.

34. Ibid., 47–50.

35. See Georg Cohn, "Neutralité et la Société des Nations," in *Les Origines et l'Oeuvre de la Société des Nations*, ed. P. Munch (Copenhagen: Rask-Ørstedfonden, 1924), 153–204. See also Malbone W. Graham, "The Effect of the League of Nations Covenant on the Theory and Practice of Neutrality," *California Law Review* 15 (1927): 357–77.

36. The best general history of the League remains F. P. Walters, *A History of the League of Nations* (London: Oxford University Press, 1952).

37. H.C., Feb. 22, 1938, 332 Hansard (5th ser.) 227.

38. L.N. Off. J., Special Supp. No. 180, 9–10.

39. See, to this effect, Philip C. Jessup, "The Birth, Death and Reincarnation of Neutrality," *American Journal of International Law* 26 (1932): 792.

40. Politis, *Neutrality and Peace*, 50.

41. A nongovernmental association of international lawyers.

42. International Law Association, *Report of the Fortieth Conference* (London 1938), 89.

43. Release of Belgium from Locarno Treaty Obligations, Apr. 24, 1937, 178 L.N.T.S. 185. On the political atmosphere in Belgium at the time, see E. H. Kossmann, *The Low Countries 1780–1940* (Oxford: Clarendon Press, 1978), 589–91.

44. Amry Vandenbosch, *Dutch Foreign Policy since 1815: A Study in Small Power Politics* (The Hague: Martinus Nijhoff, 1959), 186–90.

45. Ibid., 11.

46. On the Swiss position, see Nils Orvik, *The Decline of Neutrality 1914–1941. With Special Reference to the United States and the Northern Neutrals* (Oslo: Johan Grundt Tanum Forlag, 1953), 180–83; and Hans J. Morgenthau, "The End of Switzerland's Differential Neutrality," *American Journal of International Law* 32 (1938): 558–62.

47. On the "new neutrality" proposals, see Stephen C. Neff, "A Three-fold Struggle over Neutrality: The American Experience in the 1930s," in *Notions of Neutralities*, ed. Pascal Lottaz and Herbert R. Reginbogin (Lanham, MD: Lexington, 2019), 9–22.

48. *See generally* Robert A. Divine, *The Illusion of Neutrality: Franklin D. Roosevelt and the Struggle over the Arms Embargo* (Chicago: University of Chicago Press, 1962); and Elton Atwater, *American Regulation of Arms Exports* (Washington, DC: Carnegie Endowment of International Peace, 1941).

49. For the details, see "Report to the Council by the Chairman of the Committee of Three . . . on the Prohibition of the Export and Re-export of Arms and War Material to Bolivia and Paraguay" in League of Nations, *League of Nations Official Journal* 15 (1934): 837–39. For the texts of state responses to the Commission, see ibid., 827–37.

50. For a summary of the action taken, see ibid., 1594–609.

51. Committee of Three, Memorandum on the Question of the Embargo on Arms, ibid., 1585–86.

52. Note . . . by the Committee, Sep. 6, 1934, ibid., 1588–89.

53. Statement at mtg. of Sep. 19, 1934, ibid., 1535–36.

54. Ibid., 845.

55. *See*, to this effect, Letter Bolivia to S-G, July 11, 1934, ibid., 1582–85.; and Letter Bolivia to S-G, Sep. 11, ibid., 1589–93.

56. Statement at mtg. of Sep. 19, 1934, ibid., 1535–36.

57. F. Bottié, *Essai sur la genèse et l'évolution de la notion de neutralité: Thèse pour le doctorat en droit* (Paris: Les Éditions Internationales, 1937), 345–48.

58. On the Nyon Agreement, see Norman J. Padelford, *International Law and Diplomacy in the Spanish Civil Strife* (New York: Macmillan Company, 1939), 603–9.

59. On the Spanish Civil War and neutrality issues, see generally ibid.; and William E. Watters, *An International Affair: Non-intervention in the Spanish Civil War, 1936–1939* (New York: Exposition Press, 1971).

60. Philip C. Jessup, *Neutrality: Its History, Economics and Law: Today and Tomorrow*, 4 vols., vol. 4 (New York: Columbia University Press, 1936), 160–206.

61. Jessup, "The Birth, Death and Reincarnation of Neutrality," 793.

62. Jessup, *Neutrality: Its History, Economics and Law: Today and Tomorrow*, 179.

63. Ibid., 181.

64. Georg Cohn, *Neu-neutrality*, trans. Arthur S. Keller and Einar Jensen (New York: Columbia University Press, 1939).

65. Ibid., 173.

66. Ibid., 339–40.

67. Ibid., 254–81, 332–35, 339–44.

68. Ibid., 281.

69. Ibid., 254.

70. *American Journal of International Law* 33: *Supplement* (1939): 819–909.

71. Franklin D. Roosevelt, Radio Address, December 29, 1940, in Department of States, *Peace and War: United States Forein Policy, 1931–1941* (Washington, DC: United States Government Printing Office, 1943), 598–607.

72. See, for example, Edwin Borchard, "War, Neutrality and Nonbelligerency," *American Journal of International Law* 35 (1941): 618–25.

73. Charles Cheney Hyde and Philip C. Jessup, "Lifting Arms Ban Now Is Held Unlawful," *New York Times*, September 21, 1939, at 17, col. 6.

74. See Address of Robert H. Jackson, March 27, 1941, *American Journal of International Law* 35 (1941): 348–59.

75. See, for example, Hersch Lauterpacht, "The Limits of the Operation of the Law of War," *British Year Book of International Law* 30 (1955): 237–39.

76. United Nations, "Charter of the United Nations," no. 1 UNTS XVI (1945), www.un.org/en/charter-united-nations.

77. See, for example, Robert W. Tucker, *The Law of War and Neutrality at Sea* (Washington, DC: GPO, 1955), at 171–80; and T. Komarnicki, "The Problem of Neutrality under the United Nations Charter," *Transactions of the Grotius Society* 38 (1952): 85–86.

78. Legality of the Threat or Use of Nuclear Weapons, 1996 International Court of Justice, Rep. 226, paras. 88–89.

79. See Patrick M. Norton, "Between the Ideology and the Reality: The Shadow of the Law of Neutrality," *Harvard International Law Journal* 17 (1976): 257–78.

80. See Francis V. Russo, "Neutrality at Sea in Transition: State Practice in the Gulf War as Emerging International Customary Law," *Ocean Development and International Law* 19 (1988): 381–99.

81. Department of Defense Report to Congress on the Conduct of the Persian Gulf War—Appendix on the Role of the Law of War, Apr. 10, 1992, in *International Legal Materials* 31 (1992): 637–40.

82. On Austria, see Gerald Stourzh, *Geschichte des Staatsvertrages 1945–1955: Österreichs Weg zur Neutralität* (Graz: Styria, 1985). On Costa Rica, see Andreas Maislinger, ed., *Costa Rica: Politik, Gesellschaft und Kultur eines Staates mit Ständiger Aktiver und Unbewaffneter Neutralität* (Innsbruck: Inn, 1986). On Malta, see Jean-François Flauss, "La neutralité de Malte," *Annuaire Français du Droit International* 29 (1983): 175–93.

83. See John J. Czyzak, "The International Conference on the Settlement of the Laotian Question and the Geneva Agreements of 1962," *American Journal of International Law* 57 (1963): 300–17; and Arthur J. Dommen, *Conflict in Laos: The Politics of Neutralization* (New York: Praeger, 1964).

84. See Steven J. Ratner, "The Cambodia Settlement Agreements," *American Journal of International Law* 87 (1993): 32–35.

85. S.C. Res. 713, Sep. 25, 1991.

86. S.C. Res. 724, Dec. 12, 1991.

87. S.C. Res. 752, May 15, 1992.

88. S.C. Res. 824, May 6, 1993.

89. S.C. Res. 1973, Mar. 17, 2011.

90. See Teimouri Heidarali and Subedi Surya P., "Responsibility to Protect and the International Military Intervention in Libya in International Law: What Went Wrong and What Lessons Could Be Learnt from It?," *Journal of Conflict and Security Law* 23 (2018): 3–32. See also UK House of Commons Foreign Affairs Committee, "Libya: Examination of Intervention and Collapse and the UK's Future Policy Options," HC 119 (2016), 10–22.

## SELECTED REFERENCES

Abbenhuis, Maartje M. *An Age of Neutrals: Great Power Politics, 1815–1914*. Cambridge: Cambridge University Press, 2014.

"Acte D'Accession, en Date de Zurich, le 27 Mai 1815, de la Confédération Suisse a la Déclaration des Puissances Réunies au Congrès de Vienne, en Date du 20 Mars 1815." In *Actes du Congrès de Vienne: Publiès d'apres un des Originaux Dépausé aux Archives du Département des Affaires Étrangères*, 226–28. Paris: L'imprimerie Royale, 1816.

Atwater, Elton. *American Regulation of Arms Exports*. Washington, DC: Carnegie Endowment of International Peace, 1941.

Avram, Benno. *The Evolution of the Suez Canal Status from 1869 up to 1956: A Historico-juridical Study*. Geneva: E. Droz, 1958.

Banning, Émile. *Les origines et les phases de la neutralité belge*. Brussels: Albert Dewit, 1927.

Borchard, Edwin. "War, Neutrality and Non-belligerency." *American Journal of International Law* 35 (1941): 618–25.

Bottié, F. *Essai sur la genèse et l'évolution de la notion de neutralité: Thèse pour le doctorat en droit*. Paris: Les Éditions Internationales, 1937.

Carter, Alice Clare. *Neutrality or Commitment: The Evolution of Dutch Foreign Policy 1667–1795*. London: Arnold, 1975.
Cohn, Georg. *Neu-neutrality*. Translated by Arthur S. Keller and Einar Jensen. New York: Columbia University Press, 1939.
———. "Neutralité et la Société des Nations." In *Les Origines et l'Oeuvre de la Société des Nations*, edited by P. Munch. Copenhagen: Rask-Ørstedfonden, 1924.
Crecraft, Earl Willis. *Freedom of the Seas*. New York: D. Appleton-Century, 1935.
Czyzak, John J. "The International Conference on the Settlement of the Laotian Question and the Geneva Agreements of 1962." *American Journal of International Law* 57 (1963): 300–317.
Department of States. *Peace and War: United States Forein Policy, 1931–1941*. Washington, DC: United States Government Printing Office, 1943.
Descamps, Édouard Eugène François. *La neutralité de la Belgique au point de vue historique, diplomatique, juridique et politique: Étude sur la constitution des États pacifiques à titre permanent*. Brussels: F. Larcier, 1902.
Descamps, Emmanuel. *L'État neuter à titre permanent: Étude de droit international comparé*. Paris: Sirey, 1912.
Divine, Robert A. *The Illusion of Neutrality: Franklin D. Roosevelt and the Struggle over the Arms Embargo*. Chicago: University of Chicago Press, 1962.
Dommen, Arthur J. *Conflict in Laos: The Politics of Neutralization*. New York: Praeger, 1964.
Ekdahl, Curt. *La neutralité perpetuelle avant le Pacte de la Société des Nations: Étude de droit des gens*. Paris: A. Pedone, 1923.
Fenwick, Charles G. "Neutrality and International Organization." *American Journal of International Law* 28 (1934): 334–39.
Flauss, Jean-François. "La neutralité de Malte." *Annuaire Français du Droit International* 29 (1983): 175–93.
French, Cyrus. *Neutralization*. London: Oxford University Press, 1911.
Gentili, Alberico. *The Three Books on the Law of War*. Translated by John C. Rolfe. Oxford: Clarendon Press, 1933 [1598].
Gonzalez, Rodriguez Salvador. "The Neutrality of Honduras and the Question of the Gulf of Fonseca." *American Journal of International Law* 10 (1916): 509–42.
Graham, Malbone W. "The Effect of the League of Nations Covenant on the Theory and Practice of Neutrality." *California Law Review* 15 (1927): 357–77.
———. "Neutralization as a Movement in International Law." *American Journal of International Law* 21 (January 1927): 79–94.
Grotius, Hugo. *On the Law of War and Peace*. Translated by Francis W. Kelsey. Oxford: Clarendon Press, 1925 [1625].
Heidarali, Teimouri, and Subedi Surya P. "Responsibility to Protect and the International Military Intervention in Libya in International Law: What Went Wrong and What Lessons Could Be Learnt from It?" *Journal of Conflict and Security Law* 23 (2018): 3–32.
International Law Association. *Report of the Fortieth Conference*. London 1938.
Jessup, Philip C. "The Birth, Death and Reincarnation of Neutrality." *American Journal of International Law* 26 (1932): 789–93.
———. *Neutrality: Its History, Economics and Law: Today and Tomorrow*. 4 vols. Vol. 4. New York: Columbia University Press, 1936.
Kleen, Richard. *Lois et Usages de la Neutralité d'après le Droit International Conventionnel et Coutumier des Etats Civilises*. 2 vols. Paris: A. Chevalier-Marescq, 1898–1900.
Komarnicki, T. "The Problem of Neutrality under the United Nations Charter." *Transactions of the Grotius Society* 38 (1952): 77–91.
Kossmann, E. H. *The Low Countries 1780–1940*. Oxford: Clarendon Press, 1978.
Laun, Rudolf. *Die Internationalisierung der Meeren und Kanale*. The Hague: M. Nijhoff, 1918.
League of Nations. *League of Nations Official Journal* 15 (1934).
———. "The Covenant of the League of Nations." In *The Avalon Project: Documents in Law, History and Diplomacy* Yale: Yale Law School, 2008 [1919]. http://avalon.law.yale.edu/20th_century/leagcov.asp.

Maislinger, Andreas, ed. *Costa Rica: Politik, Gesellschaft und Kultur eines Staates mit Ständiger Aktiver und Unbewaffneter Neutralität.* Innsbruck: Inn, 1986.

Morgenthau, Hans J. "The End of Switzerland's Differential Neutrality." *American Journal of International Law* 32 (1938): 558–62.

Neff, Stephen C. "A Three-fold Struggle over Neutrality: The American Experience in the 1930s." In *Notions of Neutralities*, edited by Pascal Lottaz and Herbert Reginbogin. Lanham, MD: Lexington, 2019.

Norton, Patrick M. "Between the Ideology and the Reality: The Shadow of the Law of Neutrality." *Harvard International Law Journal* 17 (1976): 249–312.

Notter, Harley. *The Origins of the Foreign Policy of Woodrow Wilson.* Baltimore: Johns Hopkins University Press, 1937.

Orvik, Nils. *The Decline of Neutrality 1914–1941. With Special Reference to the United States and the Northern Neutrals.* Oslo: Johan Grundt Tanum Forlag, 1953.

Padelford, Norman J. *International Law and Diplomacy in the Spanish Civil Strife.* New York: Macmillan Company, 1939.

———. *The Panama Canal in Peace and War.* New York: MacMillan, 1943.

Perkins, Bradford. *Prologue to War: England and the United States 1805–1812.* Berkeley: University of California Press, 1961.

Politis, Nicolas. *Neutrality and Peace.* Translated by Francis Crane. Washington, DC: Carnegie Endowment for International Peace, 1935.

Ratner, Steven J. "The Cambodia Settlement Agreements." *American Journal of International Law* 87 (1993): 1–41.

Russell, Bertrand. *The Analysis of Matter.* New York: Harcourt Brace, 1927.

Russo, Francis V. "Neutrality at Sea in Transition: State Practice in the Gulf War as Emerging International Customary Law." *Ocean Development and International Law* 19 (1988): 381–99.

Schopfer, Sidney. *Le principe juridique de la neutralité et son évolution dans l'histoire du droit de la guerre.* Lausanne: Corbaz, 1894.

Stourzh, Gerald. *Geschichte des Staatsvertrages 1945–55: Österreichs Weg zur Neutralität.* Graz: Styria, 1985.

Thomas, Daniel H. *The Guarantee of Belgian Independence and Neutrality in European Diplomacy, 1830s–1930s.* Kingston, RI: D. H. Thomas, 1983.

Tswettcoff, Dimitre. *De la situation juridique des États neutralisés en temps de paix.* Geneva: Kündig, 1895.

United Nations. "Charter of the United Nations." no. 1 UNTS XVI (1945). www.un.org/en/charter-united-nations.

van der Mensbrugghe, Yves. *Les guaranties de la liberte de navigation dans le Canal de Suez.* Paris: Librairie de Droit et de Jurisprudence, 1964.

Vandenbosch, Amry. *Dutch Foreign Policy since 1815: A Study in Small Power Politics.* The Hague: Martinus Nijhoff, 1959.

Vergotti, Jacques. *La neutralité de la Suisse: Son évolution historique et ses aspects dans les relations internationales de la première moitié du XXe siècle.* Lausanne: La Concorde, 1954.

Walters, F. P. *A History of the League of Nations.* London: Oxford University Press, 1952.

Watters, William E. *An International Affair: Non-intervention in the Spanish Civil War, 1936–1939.* New York: Exposition Press, 1971.

Winslow, Erving. "Neutralization." *American Journal of International Law* 2 (1908): 366–86.

Wright, Quincy. "The Present Status of Neutrality." *American Journal of International Law* 34 (1940): 391–415.

*Chapter Two*

# Neutrality and Security

*A Comparison with Alternative Models of National Security*

## P. Terrence Hopmann

Even in a liberal international order in which humanitarianism is prioritized, states still need to be concerned about national security. Realist approaches to security tend to emphasize the role of alliances as a means through which states can pool their resources to provide security in response to external threats. Indeed, for many states in an international system in which security dilemmas arise, joining collective defense organizations is often a rational strategy. However, alliances are not the only option available for states to try to enhance their security in response to external threats; other choices are available.

In a classic realist work on international alliances, Stephen Walt argues that alliances may take the form either of "balancing" or "bandwagoning." Balancing consists of states, "allying with others against the prevailing threat." They ally to "protect themselves from states or coalitions whose superior resources could pose a threat."[1] This generally entails allying against the dominant global power to prevent it from achieving hegemony or from initiating aggression. By contrast, "bandwagoning" refers to joining with the source of the danger, either by trying to appease the superior power or perhaps to share in the spoils of victory.[2] In sum, "states tend to ally with or against the foreign power that poses the greatest threat."[3] Nowhere, however, does Walt, like most realists, consider other options, namely for states to join collective security organizations, to remain nonaligned, or to declare their neutrality in relation to major global powers. This chapter considers these alternative international postures, arguing that alignment is not the only choice available to states to enhance their security in a sometimes-threatening international environment.

The first option is participation in collective or cooperative security institutions, whether at the global level (i.e., the League of Nations and the United Nations) or at the regional levels [e.g., the Organization for Security and Cooperation in Europe (OSCE), the Organization of American States (OAS), or the Association of South East Asian Nations (ASEAN)]. Unlike alliances, these institutions do not rely primarily on military deterrence but on institutionalized norms of cooperation that depend more on confidence-building and diplomacy rather than on force to provide security. Under certain circumstances, these institutional arrangements may provide for collective defense when a member state or party within the system threatens the security or violates the sovereignty of other participating states and the entire community bands together to restore the *status quo ante* and to build peace within the region or the entire global community.

The second alternative to alliances takes the form of nonalignment, which is not necessarily the same as neutrality due to its more situational character. In another classic realist work on alliances, Liska notes that non-alignment is a legitimate alternative to alignment in which states under certain conditions, especially when opposing states or coalitions are approximately equal in power,[4] may refuse "to add their power to that of others." Instead, they may engage "in an active policy of playoff and unsolicited mediation between the great powers."[5] This was a stance taken by many states of the so-called "Third World" during the Cold War competition between the NATO and Warsaw Pact alliances. However, this stance is not necessarily permanent, nor does it require full neutrality on all issues between the opposing camps. Nonalignment may leave open the option of joining with others in the presence of an overwhelming threat without at the same time joining in "entangling alliances"[6] that entail binding commitments to come to the assistance of other states in future (mostly unforeseen) circumstances.

A third alternative to alliances is neutrality, in which states declare their "perpetual" or "permanent" neutrality regarding all global conflicts involving other states and therefore do not commit themselves to take military action in support of any state engaged in violent conflict, except possibly through the collective security mechanisms of the UN or regional institutions in the form of peacekeeping or peace enforcement operations. "Permanent neutrality" generally implies a commitment that one will never engage in violent conflict unless directly attacked. This may take the form of armed neutrality in which states try to discourage attacks by minimizing their threat to others while retaining a robust capability of self-defense if attacked (e.g., Switzerland, Sweden, Finland, and Austria). Alternatively, it may take the form of nonmilitarized neutrality, trying to minimize the likelihood of attack by presenting a nonthreatening posture toward others, and possibly relying on civilian resistance as an alternative to violence as a morally preferable form of self-protection (e.g., Costa Rica, which abolished its standing army in 1948).

This chapter does not assume that there is one system of security that is preferable for all states, and it further asserts that every state has the sovereign right to evaluate its security requirements in the light of its perceived security threats and vulnerabilities. In many cases, joining alliances may well be the optimal approach to deterring potential aggressors and providing for collective self-defense in the event of armed aggression. However, this is not the only or necessarily the best option for states in many cases. Reliance for security on one of the alternatives identified in this chapter should be considered as a viable option for many states in the current international system, especially if they are guided by humanitarian norms that seek to eschew resort to violence insofar as possible. In short, states may enhance their security, not by building up strong defenses in alignment with other powerful states, but rather by presenting a nonthreatening posture toward other states that makes them less likely to be targets for aggression in the first place.

## SECURITY THROUGH ALLIANCES

Alliances aggregate the power and resources of independent states to enhance their ability to deter, or, if deterrence fails, to defend against potential threats to their security; thus they are often referred to as "collective defense" organizations (as distinct from "collective security" institutions like the United Nations). Arguments about alliance formation—that is, both why states join specific alliances and what determines the overall composition of alliances—tend to break down into two: expediency versus shared ideology or a sense of common community.[7] Classical balance of power theories tend to argue that alliances form primarily based on relative power considerations. As noted above, states may either join forces with other states to balance the power of hegemonic states (or coalitions) that they perceive as threatening to their security, or they may "bandwagon" with a hegemonic power (or a coalition), hoping either to avoid complete conquest or perhaps to share even marginally in the spoils of victory. In the balance of power framework, however, if the power relationships shift too far in favor of the stronger coalition, a state belonging to that alliance must be prepared to switch alliances rather than fight regardless of their ideological or cultural affinity with their previous alliance partners. They do this in order to restore the approximate parity of power between the competing alliances, thereby maintaining balance in the international system as a whole. This was generally the practice of European states during the eighteenth and nineteenth centuries.[8] Alternatively, alliances may form around ideological blocs as occurred throughout much of the twentieth century, in which democracies often allied against authoritarian states and capitalist states allied against communist states.

At the same time, balance of power theories also recognize that alliances involve costs, mainly because member states may have to relinquish some portion of their sovereign control over decision-making, especially when they commit to defending allies, whether or not they hold any shared ideology or common sense of community. Thus in 1914 Britain and France supported their ally, Russia, in the Triple Entente, against the Dual Alliance of the Austro–Hungarian Empire and Germany as World War I escalated across the continent. They did this despite the absence of any ideological similarity between their liberal regimes and the absolutism of Tsarist Russia. In the long run, this cost them dearly in terms of blood and treasure. Therefore, in the traditional balance of power theories, states should limit the binding commitments they make to others, in large part by not enlarging their membership beyond a "minimum winning coalition," namely the minimum number of allies necessary to deter or defend against their rivals.[9] In this classical, realist approach, alliances should be cautious about adding new allies that contribute little to the collective defense effort while adding vulnerabilities that might drag their current members into a major war over issues of little importance to their overall security interests. This is especially significant if their new allies might either undertake provocative action against the opposing states or become easy targets of aggression by their opponents. In the practice dictated by the balance of power theory, alliance members' concerns about these costs of overextending alliance commitments often limit the overall size of alliances or make the commitments to mutual defense more ambiguous.

This has undoubtedly been an important issue for NATO since the end of the Cold War, as Article 5 of the NATO Treaty commits all alliance members to come to the aid of a member state that is attacked by an outside party, even if its own primary security interests are not at stake.[10] The Western alliance's eastward move has brought into membership all former Warsaw Pact States except for most of the successor states of the Soviet Union,[11] as well as three of the six states that once were part of nonaligned Yugoslavia.[12] These new members have brought NATO far more conventional military capabilities than those possessed by the Russian Federation, extending the alliance well beyond the requirements for a "minimum winning coalition," at least at the conventional arms level. However, by encroaching on the western borders of Russia, it has been perceived by Russians to threaten their security by bringing NATO into regions that Russia considers to be within its "sphere of influence," insofar as that concept is considered by some as a legitimate criterion for state policy in the twenty-first century; Russia has expressed concern about the entry of the three Baltic states into NATO, as well as the possibility of the former Soviet republics of Georgia and Ukraine joining the alliance in the future. This has created a classic circular security dilemma in which former Soviet allies fear Russian efforts to reassert control over them, but the response creates new fears in Russia for their own security.[13]

Given that the leadership in some of the former Soviet states proclaim intense anti-Russian attitudes in their rhetoric, this may raise concerns about possible provocations directed against Russia or perceptions of vulnerability among hardline Russian leaders. These mutual perceptions of threat increase the risk of violent conflict between NATO and Russia over issues that may not represent vital security interests for the majority of NATO member states. With the exception of the three Baltic republics, NATO has not so far taken in former Soviet Republics, in part out of concern that the liabilities of their membership might outweigh whatever contributions they might make to the security of NATO allies. Even the three Baltic states represent something of a risk for NATO, in part because NATO now surrounds the Russian enclave of Kaliningrad, posing a perceived threat to Russian interests that also could provoke a violent conflict in conditions where the vital interests of most NATO members are also not at stake.[14]

Although less important in most of the literature on international alliances, some authors have also argued that ideological, political, or cultural similarities may be a driving factor in the formation, enlargement, and even in the disintegration of alliances.[15] These integrative factors may include shared historical experiences, shared values and ideologies such as the differences between communist and capitalist regimes, shared political systems such as democratic versus authoritarian states, common cultural or even "civilizational" values that may include factors such as religion, cultural traditions, or other shared values. Even realists like Liska note that "ideology feeds on selective memory of the past and outlines a program for the future ... alliance ideology ... will be formulated so as to add incentive to joint action and to screen intra-alliance strains and splits."[16] These factors appeared to have some relevance during the Cold War between 1945 and 1989, where authoritarian states that adopted communist political and economic structures provided the ideological foundation for the Warsaw Pact alliance, whereas democratic states with fundamentally capitalist economic systems tended to provide the source of unity for the NATO alliance.

Given the role played by these ideological factors, it should hardly be surprising that the collapse of communism in Central and Eastern Europe led to the collapse of the Warsaw Pact, while the eastward spread of democratic politics and capitalist economic systems accompanied the eastward enlargement of the NATO alliance. Although fears of Russian "revanchism" were mostly absent in the first decade after the Cold War, the shared values of democratic governance and market economies provided the initial source of cohesion to an alliance that lacked a major threat from a rival state or bloc. However, as support for democratic governance has declined in some NATO states in the early decades of the twenty-first century, and as the economic and military rebound of Russia has introduced new security concerns for some of Russia's neighbors, these have combined to provide a new source of alliance cohesion for NATO even as shared ideology has waned.[17] In 2020, it remains to be seen whether Russia's renewed threats to its former Soviet states such as Ukraine, Georgia, Azerbaijan, and Armenia in its "near abroad" will lead NATO to be more eager to bring some or all of these states into the alliance despite their very imperfect democratic systems and frequently kleptocratic economies. In other words, it is an open question whether a shared perception of external threat to security will replace some of the ideological homogeneity as the glue that holds the NATO alliance together.

In short, states generally seek to join alliances when they perceive that their security is threatened so that alliance membership will add to their own defensive capabilities those of their allies, even despite the loss of some degree of independent decision-making over national security policy that alliance membership entails. As will be explained later, however, other states may perceive that this loss of independence is not worth the security benefits that alliance membership may provide, especially if there are alternative ways to mitigate threats from powerful states. At the same time, existing alliance members must consider, when deciding whether or not to add new member states, whether the new members' contributions to the collective security of the alliance outweigh the risk that, at a minimum, their participation may constrain the independence of their decision-making or, at a maximum, that their membership may add to the risks of confrontation with the states against whom the alliance is directed. In the latter case, the benefits of a new member's contribution to collective defense may be outweighed by the potential liabilities that the new members may present to the independence and security of the existing member states.

This analysis suggests that decisions about forming alliances or joining existing alliances are based on a rough cost-benefit analysis on the part of the involved states. Although such assessments are intrinsically subjective and may be composed of many factors, benefits are primarily calculated in terms of some combination of two factors: 1) the degree to which the formation or enlargement of the alliance enhances the capabilities of the alliance to provide security against external threats, and/or 2) the extent to which alliance membership increases the sense of community among a group of like-minded states. Conversely, costs are primarily determined by the degree to which membership in an alliance constrains a state's freedom of action in international relations or creates new liabilities, especially by posing new risks of unwanted engagement in conflict. This may be due to actions by individual alliance members that provoke adversaries by initiating violence that does not serve the interests of the majority of alliance members; alternatively, rivals may be tempted to take advantage of weaker, marginal alliance members by attacking them, thereby creating a dilemma for the alliance as a whole about whether and how to defend an alliance member when the vital interests of most allies are not at stake.

Furthermore, some states may value their independence so highly that they eschew alliance membership in favor of some other option. Similarly, they may perceive that alliance membership adds little to their security while increasing the risk of involving them in conflicts in which they have no direct interest. In either case, this may lead them to consider other alternatives to alliance membership to provide for their basic security needs. Alternatively, states seeking membership in alliances may find that the existing member states do not want to accept whatever liabilities might come along with adding new members to their alliance, leaving them without alliance membership as a viable option.[18] The remainder of this chapter will consider options available to states that do not seek to belong to collective defense alliances or find that they are not welcomed as partners to existing alliance frameworks.

## COLLECTIVE SECURITY INSTITUTIONS

Collective security institutions seek to create in some sense "alliances of the whole," whether at the global or regional level. Rather than being created in opposition to some external threat, they seek to bring into their membership all relevant states, including potential rivals. Within their structure, they define laws or normative rules governing all participating states intended to prevent threats or violent acts by any member state against another. If a participating state breaks these rules, then, in principle, all other participants will unify against that state to bring it back into compliance with the norms of collective behavior. In general, these institutions do not rely primarily, if at all, on the use of force to ensure compliance with those rules, but instead they try to use normative and political pressure to induce cooperation, and they place extensive reliance on preventive diplomacy and mediation to try to resolve disputes before they turn violent. In some cases, they may introduce sanctions or even military force to coerce parties to observe those rules, although gaining agreement to use force has often been difficult.[19]

The primary global collective security institution is the United Nations, the universal international institution in which virtually all of the world's states are members. Its collective security principles are mostly contained in chapters 6, "6 and a half," and 7 of the UN Charter. Chapter 6 focuses on the role of the UN in providing "good offices," conciliation, and mediation to resolve disputes before they turn violent or, if necessary, to bring an end to violent conflict. The primary mechanism in practice for accomplishing this mission has often entailed direct engagement by the Secretary-General (SG) himself or by appointed "Special Representatives of the SG" to deal with specific international and internal disputes.

Chapter "6 and a half," which does not exist in the charter but has become common practice since the early days of the UN, includes the use of UN-authorized military forces for peacekeeping, peace-making, or peace-enforcement.[20] UN missions have been deployed globally under these provisions to stand between belligerent forces, to enforce existing cease-fire and peace agreements, and to try to bring parties engaged in violent conflict to the negotiating table. However, many of these measures require the consent of the parties involved. Since state actors on the international level are often able to block collective Security Council resolutions that would run counter to their interests, the vast majority of UN peace operations have taken place in intrastate, civil conflicts rather than during interstate conflicts. As a result, as necessary as this activity has been in many ways, its value as an alternative to alliance membership has been diminished by the inability of the UN in most cases to respond to acts of aggression or other forms of violence by one-member state against another.

Chapter 7 empowers the Security Council to "take such action by air, sea, or land forces as may be necessary to maintain or restore international peace and security."[21] Such action can only be taken when none of the five permanent members of the Security Council (US, France, United Kingdom, USSR [later Russia], and China) exercises its right to veto. For this reason, Chapter Seven "collective security" decisions to authorize force have seldom been adopted. Two exceptions exist, however, which provide the only examples of effective UN action in defense of a state that has been subject to aggression, but both occurred under very unusual circumstances. The first collective security mission began in 1950 when North Korea invaded South Korea, and the UN adopted a resolution authorizing the use of force by a large coalition of UN member states led by the United States against North Korea and later against China when it entered the war in support of the North Koreans. A potential veto in the UN Security Council was averted by the fact that the Soviet Union had walked out of the Council in protest after the victory of the Chinese Communist Party in 1949, when the UN failed to turn over to the communist regime in Beijing the seat held by the Republic of China (ROC) that fled the mainland for Taiwan. The result was that the Soviets were unable to exercise their veto, while the ROC voted along with the US, UK, and France in support of the collective security resolution. Similarly, in 1990, when Iraq invaded and occupied Kuwait, a UN member state, in the immediate aftermath of the end of the Cold War, it was again possible to authorize a UN collective security action to force Iraq out of Kuwait's territory and to restore its sovereignty. A grand coalition of UN member states led by the US used military force to compel Iraq to withdraw from Kuwait. This outcome was the result of a global collective action undertaken under UN auspices to reverse a clear violation of one of the most fundamental principles of the UN Charter that was important at the time to all permanent members of the Security Council, including the Soviet Union under President Gorbachev (which voted for the resolution) and to a lesser extent China (which abstained), namely respect for the sovereignty of all member states and opposition to conquest by one member state or another.

These two cases illustrate how the UN collective security system was supposed to work under the terms of the UN Charter to provide an alternative to alliance membership to protect the sovereignty and freedom from aggression of UN member states; if this system had been entirely successful in practice, then alliances should have become essentially irrelevant as mechanisms to provide security for all states throughout the world. Of course, the political divisions of the Cold War, reinforced by the veto power granted by the UN Charter to the five permanent members of the Security Council, had prevented the UN from fulfilling this role except in these two cases that arose at unique moments in history when the Security Council veto was not invoked. It is, therefore, the failure of this system of collective security that has made alignment such a popular option in the post-1945 world, although these cases illustrate that, in principle, nonaligned states could find security guarantees in the UN collective security system if it were allowed to operate on the terms introduced in the UN Charter at the time of its founding.

In addition to the UN, cooperative institutions with (sometimes limited) security functions exist in different forms at the regional level. They include the African Union (AU), the European Union with its "common foreign and security policy," the Association of South East Asian Nations (ASEAN), the Organization of American States (OAS), and, most significantly, the Organization for Security and Cooperation in Europe (OSCE). Founded by the Helsinki Final Act of 1975, amid the Cold War and initially called the Conference on Security and Cooperation in Europe (CSCE), it included 35 states of Europe and North America "from Vancouver to Vladivostok the long way around."[22] All member states of the NATO and Warsaw Pact alliances signed the Final Act, and the neutral and nonaligned states of Europe, especially Finland, Sweden, Austria, Switzerland, and Yugoslavia, took a leading role in its creation.[23] In its early years, its primary security role came from the creation of a set of "confidence and security-building measures" (CSBMs) in which all participating states agreed to give advance notice of military maneuvers and to invite all other participating states to observe them *in situ*. The basic premise of these CSBMs was that no state would invite its potential victims to observe maneuvers that they intended to use as a disguise for preparing for aggressive military action; this practice of giving prior notice about military exercises would increase confidence in all other states that these were ordinary training activities and not preparations for aggression. Conversely, any unannounced maneuvers to which observers were not invited would give early warning to potential target states of possible aggression. This would both allow time to open negotiations to resolve the conflict, while also permitting potential targets of an attack to prepare their defenses, thereby possibly deterring an attack or at least aiding those states to deploy successful defense against any ensuing act of aggression. In short, these measures increased transparency and stability along the Cold War line of division through Central and Southeastern Europe in the last decades of the Cold War.[24]

The role of the CSCE changed dramatically after the end of the Cold War. In the years immediately after 1989, the organization became fully institutionalized, leading to its renaming as the "Organization for Security and Cooperation in Europe." The OSCE established a permanent secretariat in Vienna, headed by a Secretary-General. It is governed by a Permanent Council in which all states, amounting to 57 in 2019, are represented at the ambassadorial level. A Conflict Prevention Centre was established in Vienna, which has coordinated the work of some 25 Missions of Long Duration stationed in many participating states to promote conflict prevention, resolution, and post-conflict reconciliation. An Office of Democratic Institutions and Human Rights was created in Warsaw to, among other things, monitor democratic elections, promote human rights, and support other efforts to strengthen democratic institutions throughout the region. Through a series of so-called "Vienna Documents," the OSCE has enlarged the confidence and security-building measures beyond those negotiated during the Cold War. It has played the lead role in mediating conflicts in eastern Ukraine, the Transdniestria region of Moldova, and the conflict between Armenia and Azerbaijan over the status of the Nagorno-Karabakh region.[25] However, it does not to date have any role in peacekeeping or in the application of coercive measures to deter conflict, relying almost entirely on the normative foundations of the Helsinki principles and the active efforts of preventive diplomacy. Decisions in the Permanent Council are made on the basis of consensus, and thus in the decade since 2008 difficulties in finding common ground among Russia, the United States, and the European Union have limited its role in conflict management. Participants in the OSCE include all members of NATO, all former Warsaw Pact states, and all of the successor states of the Soviet Union, Yugoslavia, and Czechoslovakia. A key leadership role, however, has been played by the neutral and nonaligned states, which have held the rotating chair of the Permanent Council more often than former and current members of military alliances. While the effect of the consensus rule has at times significantly limited its engagement in conflicts where the interests of the most powerful states are at stake, it has generally been viewed as a useful institution for supporting the security of smaller states of Europe, including those that have refrained from joining military alliances—namely NATO on the one hand and the Central States Treaty Organization (CSTO) composed of Russia and several other former Soviet states on the other. Therefore, participation in the OSCE, as in the UN, is not inconsistent with membership in alliances, nonalignment, or permanent neutrality. To the major powers, it is clearly subordinated to their alliance commitments, but it is viewed by many smaller states, including neutral and nonaligned states, as a useful instrument to assure their security in an uncertain environment still dominated by competing military coalitions.

## SECURITY THROUGH NEUTRALITY AND NONALIGNMENT

Although neutral and nonaligned states both refrain from membership in alliances, the terms frequently take on very different meanings. Formally, neutrality defines the noninvolvement of states in armed hostilities between other parties and has a specific status under international law that mandates that neutral states have both rights and obligations in times of war.[26] They may not provide assistance to belligerents in armed conflicts nor allow their territory to be used by belligerents as a base for military operations. In exchange, they should not be attacked or occupied by belligerent states and they are accorded freedom of passage for nonmilitary goods and civilians on the high seas and in some cases across the territory of combatants. Beyond these legal requirements for all states that wish to remain officially neutral during conflicts, there are also more specific provisions for "permanently neutral countries": even in peacetime they may not join military alliances nor allow their territory to be used by others for military purposes. They may either adopt this status unilaterally (e.g., Sweden in the nineteenth and twentieth centuries) or as part of an international agreement (e.g., Switzerland in 1815 or Austria in 1955).[27] In the former case, respect for neutrality depends largely on the forbearance of belligerents to respect their neutrality, whereas in the latter case, they are bound by international agreements to respect that neutrality.[28] By refusing to take sides in armed conflict, they seek to remove incentives for belligerents to attack and occupy their territory; the very fact of their neutrality reduces the likelihood that mutual security dilemmas might prompt others to engage in military aggression against them.

At the same time, most permanent neutrals also seek to enhance their security by maintaining relatively large, well equipped, and trained armies. Switzerland is a case in point; it keeps a large citizen army which, along with its mountainous terrain, can make military attacks extremely costly for any potential aggressor, no matter how powerful in absolute terms. Others, such as Costa Rica, take a different approach; Costa Rica abolished its standing army in 1948, although it does maintain a substantial domestic police force in relation to its size. However, by demonstrating clearly to its neighbors that it does not offer any threat to their security, Costa Rica seeks to discourage others from engaging in military hostilities against it. Similarly, the Vatican, located in the center of Italy, a NATO member state, and Liechtenstein, located between two neutral states, Switzerland and Austria, do not see a need to maintain large armed forces to defend their neutrality. In short, as K. J. Holsti argues: "States that are neutral or neutralized limit their freedom of choice (avoid alliances and other military arrangements) in order to reduce vulnerabilities and threats."[29] Through their formal declaration of permanent neutrality, they seek international recognition of their desire not to be drawn into the armed conflicts of other global actors. In short, their security emanates from their not presenting a threat to others, in the expectation that other states will reciprocate by not threatening military action against them.

Nonalignment, by contrast, does not provide the same tight constraints on states. Most nonaligned states remain relatively self-reliant in their security policies, but they retain the option of receiving support from alliance members should conditions change in ways that threaten their security. Indeed, during the Cold War period, several members of the global "nonaligned bloc" actually had formal security agreements with major states, as for example both India and Cuba had security agreements with the Soviet Union. Nonetheless, the vast majority of states belonging to the global nonaligned movement refrained from joining military alliances with the major global powers, though some joined regional security institutions. For example, Indonesia served as a leader of both the neutral and nonaligned movement while participating in ASEAN. Others, such as nonaligned Yugoslavia, pursued policies of self-reliance to provide security. Nonaligned states may also play an active role in promoting the reduction of tensions on the global level by refusing to join in great power competition and, as Liska notes, by serving "as insulating buffer states, mediators, and international policemen."[30]

This aspect of neutrality has been further extended by Gärtner's concept of "engaged neutrality," which he defines as "active participation in international security policy in general and in international peace operations in particular."[31] He further notes that engaged neutrality does not imply neutrality about fundamental international norms such as democracy, human rights, prohibitions against torture, and other war crimes. Also, it does not permit a double standard that so often characterizes the policies of aligned countries that must sometimes turn a blind eye toward the violation of fundamental international norms and laws when committed by allies, while denouncing those same behaviors when committed by members of opposing coalitions. Neutrality thus both facilitates and demands involvement in international security policy and crisis management without, of course, allowing participation directly in hostilities on behalf of one party or another. Indeed, for countries like Switzerland, Austria, Finland, Sweden, and Costa Rica, engaged neutrality becomes a constituent part of their very identity. Insofar as this particular identity is accepted and recognized by other states in the international system, it provides them with a special status that includes strong normative prohibitions against engaging in hostile action toward them. In short, the status of engaged neutrality provides unique protection against threats from potentially predatory states that might otherwise endanger their security. This very identity itself becomes the primary guarantor of security for the internationally engaged neutral party.

## CONCLUSION

This essay has underscored that there are many paths for states to enhance their security in an anarchic and often threatening international environment.[32] As sovereign entities, states are free to choose how best to assure their own security against potential threats depending on their own specific circumstances. Even the classical realist, George Liska, recognized long ago the significance of this choice:

> Fear of an external threat often stimulates very pragmatic calculations. These may produce alignment or nonalignment. The option will be affected by such intangibles as historical experience and political culture as well as by the nature of specific, tangible threats.[33]

Without discounting these pragmatic considerations, contemporary international relations scholarship would also add to these factors normative principles and beliefs about the promotion of cooperative security in a global context in which all peoples and states face existential threats from a largely uncontrolled arms race and rampant climate change. In this context, security ought to take on a broader meaning than merely resisting threats from other hostile states; today's threats are also systemic and are thus beyond the control of any single state. In a world in which military force and competition for global resources and political power remain essential factors, traditional aspects of state security cannot be neglected, and states must decide how best to respond to those threats. That said, the broader systemic threats to humanity cannot be met by any single form of alignment or nonalignment. Instead, they require approaches that respond to the common threats to all humanity. Although we still live in a global system composed of sovereign nation-states, we also live in a world that presents numerous severe threats to all humanity collectively. No alliance or any group of neutral states can meet these challenges unilaterally. In the final analysis, the systemic threats to human survival can only be met by collective action that is directed at solving these common problems rather than focusing on narrow conceptions of state security that disregard the collective challenges to humanity as a whole. Resolving these collective threats to humanity requires new ideas and approaches to common security above and beyond a focus on national security. Without disregarding the requirements for state security, therefore, we must begin to explore new structures for international engagement that extend beyond the boundaries of international institutions and state policies as currently conceived. Alliances divide states into competing camps, and traditional neutrality can isolate states from engagement in the management of international peace and security.[34] In the face of existential threats such as climate change and a renewed arms race utilizing new and dangerous technologies heretofore unforeseen, new global structures are required to assure our survival. Since neutral states do not generally insist upon dividing the world into hostile, competitive blocs, they can play an essential role in leading the global system in the search for new institutional structures that respond to twenty-first century challenges to global security. In order to play this role, however, they must not seek "splendid isolation," but instead, they must take the lead in overcoming global rivalries that divide us and instead promote joint action in responding to the shared threats to human civilization as a whole.

## NOTES

1. Stephen M. Walt, *The Origins of Alliances* (Ithaca, NY: Cornell University Press, 1987), 17–18.
2. Ibid., 21.
3. Ibid., 21.
4. "Power" in this chapter, adopts a classic definition by J. David Singer. "Inter-Nation Influence: A Formal Model." *The American Political Science Review* 57, no. 2 (1963): 420–30: "the techniques and resources" one party utilizes to bring their *expectations* of what the other party would do in the absence of influence to "coincide as nearly as possible" with their own *preferences* regarding the other's behavior. Elements of those "techniques and resources" collectively constitute a definition of power and may include military might, economic resources, status and prestige, political commitment to the goal, quality of diplomacy, among other capabilities, to exert influence over another party.
5. George Liska, *Nations in Alliance: The Limits of Interdependence* (Baltimore: Johns Hopkins Press, 1962), 203–4.
6. The term "entangling alliances" originates with President George Washington's "farewell address" to the US Congress, in which he advised the young United States to "to steer clear of permanent alliance with any portion of the foreign world." See David Fromkin. "Entangling Alliances." *Foreign Affairs* 48, no. 4 (1970): 688–700.
7. Ole R. Holsti, P. Terrence Hopmann, and John D. Sullivan, *Unity and Disintegration in International Alliances: Comparative Studies* (New York: John Wiley & Sons, 1973), 4–6.
8. See Gulick, Edward Vose. *Europe's Classical Balance of Power: A Case History of the Theory and Practice of One of the Great Concepts of European Statecraft.* New York: Norton, 1967.
9. Ole Holsti, Hopmann, and Sullivan, *Unity and Disintegration in International Alliances: Comparative Studies,* 6–10.
10. NATO, "The North Atlantic Treaty" (Washington, DC, 1949).
11. Three former Soviet states in the Baltic region—Estonia, Latvia, and Lithuania—have become NATO members; the other twelve successor states have not joined NATO, although Georgia and Ukraine have at various times indicated an interest in joining.

12. Of the six former Yugoslav republics, Croatia, Montenegro, and Slovenia are NATO members in 2019; the Republic of North Macedonia was granted a membership protocol in February 2019, and full membership is contingent upon ratification by all current member states.

13. On Russian perceptions of threat from NATO see chapter 6 of this volume by Glenn Diesen.

14. See Wolfgang Zellner (coordinator) et al., *Reducing the Risks of Conventional Deterrence in Europe: Arms Control in the NATO-Russia Contact Zones* (Vienna: OSCE Network of Think Tanks and Academic Institutions, 2018), 11–13.

15. Ole Holsti, Hopmann, and Sullivan, *Unity and Disintegration in International Alliances: Comparative Studies*, 10–14.

16. Liska, *Nations in Alliance: The Limits of Interdependence*, 61.

17. See David Yost, *NATO's Balancing Act* (Washington, DC: US Institute of Peace Press, 2014), especially chapters 1 and 8.

18. This appears to be the case for Ukraine in 2019, caught between Russian aggression on one side and the reluctance of NATO to assume the potential liabilities that would likely accompany granting it NATO membership. See Heinz Gaertner, "Conclusion," in *Engaged Neutrality: An Evolved Approach to the Cold War*, edited by Heinz Gaertner (Lanham, MD: Lexington, 2017), 203–4.

19. Sanctions have often been employed when there is insufficient international consensus to use force, such as in response to the Russian annexation of Crimea in 2014; as noted below, force has been adopted only in rare historical moments such as Korea in 1950 and Iraq's takeover of Kuwait in 1990.

20. See Michael W. Doyle and Nicholas Sambanis, *Making War and Building Peace: United Nations Peace Operations*. Princeton: Princeton University Press, 2006.

21. United Nations Charter, chapter 7, Article 42.

22. P. Terrence Hopmann, "Intergovernmental Organisations and Non-State Actors, Russia and Eurasia: The OSCE," in *Key Players in Regional Dynamics in Eurasia: The Return of the 'Great Game,'* edited by Maria Raquel Freire and Roger E. Kanet (Houndmills: Palgrave MacMillan, 2010), 238.

23. P. Terrence Hopmann, "From Helsinki I to Helsinki II: The Role of the Neutral and Nonaligned States in the OSCE," in *Engaged Neutrality*, edited by Heinz Gaertner (Lanham, MD: Lexington, 2017), 143–60.

24. For a short overview of OSCE confidence building measures, see Organization for Security and Co-operation in Europe, "Early Confidence- and Security-Building Measures of the Conference on Security and Co-operation in Europe," *Security Community*, no. 1 (2016), www.osce.org/magazine/248511.

25. For further information about the OSCE role in these three cases, see the following articles by this author: for Moldova, "The OSCE Role in Ukraine and Moldova," *Studien und Berichte zur Sicherheitspolitik*, Vienna, Austria, 1/2000, pp. 25–61; for Ukraine, "The OSCE's Contrasting Roles in Managing the Ukraine/Crimea Crises in 1992–1996 and 2014–2015," in *OSCE Yearbook 2015*, edited by Institute for Peace Research and Security Policy at the University of Hamburg (Baden-Baden: Nomos Verlagsgesellschaft, 2016) and "Negotiating the Ukraine-Crimea Crisis," in *Tug of War: Negotiating Security in Eurasia*, edited by Fen Osler Hampson and Mikhail Troitsky (Waterloo, ON: Queens-McGill CIGI Press, 2017); for Nagorno-Karabakh, "Minsk Group Mediation of the Nagorno-Karabakh Conflict: Confronting an 'Intractable Conflict,'" in *OSCE Yearbook 2014*, edited by Institute for Peace Research and Security Policy at the University of Hamburg (Baden-Baden: Nomos Verlagsgesellschaft, 2015).

26. For an in-depth treatment of the subject, see Stephen C. Neff, *The Rights and Duties of Neutrals: A General History* (Manchester: Manchester University Press, 2000).

27. K. J. Holsti, *International Politics: A Framework for Analysis*, 7th ed. (Englewood Cliffs: Prentice-Hall, 1995), 88–89.

28. Switzerland was neutralized through the 1815 Treaty of Paris. See "Acte d'Accession, en date de Zurich, le 27 Mai 1815, de la Confédération Suisse à la Déclaration des Puissances Réunies au Congrès de Vienne, en Date du 20 Mars 1815," in *Actes du Congrès de Vienne:*

*Publiés d'après un des Originaux, Déposé aux Archives du Département des Affaires Étrangères* (Paris: L'imprimerie Royale, 1816). The same happened to Austria through the State Treaty. See United Kingdom of Great Britain and Northern Ireland, Union of Soviet Socialist Republics, United States of America, France, and Austria, "State Treaty (with annexes and maps) for the re-establishment of an independent and democratic Austria. Signed at Vienna on 15 May 1955," in *Treaty Series: Treaties and International Agreements Registered or Filed and Recorded with the Secretariat of the United Nations* (United Nations, 1955).

29. K. J. Holsti, *International Politics: A Framework for Analysis*, 89.
30. Liska, *Nations in Alliance: The Limits of Interdependence*, 225.
31. Heinz Gaertner, "Introduction: Engaged Neutrality," in *Engaged Neutrality: An Evolved Approach to the Cold War*, edited by Heinz Gaertner (Lanham, MD: Lexington, 2017), 9.
32. See Alexander Wendt, "Anarchy is What States Make of It: The Social Construction of Power Politics," *International Organization*, 46, no. 2 (1996), 391–425.
33. Liska, *Nations in Alliance: The Limits of Interdependence*, 213.
34. This posture is changing especially in Europe. See the discussion of new forms of security engagement by neutral EU states in chapter 5 by Gunther Hauser of this volume.

## SELECTED REFERENCES

"Acte d'Accession, en date de Zurich, le 27 Mai 1815, de la Confédération Suisse à la Déclaration des Puissances Réunies au Congrès de Vienne, en Date du 20 Mars 1815." In *Actes du Congrès de Vienne: Publiés d'après un des Originaux Dépausé aux Archives du Département des Affaires Étrangères*, 226–28. Paris: L'imprimerie Royale, 1816.

Doyle, Michael W. and Nicholas Sambanis, *Making War and Building Peace: United Nations Peace Operations*. Princeton: Princeton University Press, 2006.

Fromkin, David. "Entangling Alliances." *Foreign Affairs* 48, no. 4 (1970): 688–700.

Gaertner, Heinz. "Introduction: Engaged Neutrality" and "Conclusion." In *Engaged Neutrality: An Evolved Approach to the Cold War*, edited by Heinz Gaertner. Lanham, MD: Lexington, 2017.

Holsti, K. J. *International Politics: A Framework for Analysis*. 7th ed. Englewood Cliffs: Prentice-Hall, 1995.

Holsti, Ole R., P. Terrence Hopmann, and John D. Sullivan. *Unity and Disintegration in International Alliances: Comparative Studies*. New York: John Wiley & Sons, 1973.

Hopmann, P. Terrence. "From Helsinki I to Helsinki II: The Role of the Neutral and Non-aligned States in the OSCE." In *Engaged Neutrality*, edited by Heinz Gaertner. Lanham, MD: Lexington, 2017.

_____. "Negotiating the Ukraine-Crimea Crisis." In *Tug of War: Negotiating Security in Eurasia*, edited by Fen Osler Hampson and Mikhail Troitsky. Waterloo, ON: Queens-McGill CIGI Press, 2017.

_____. "The OSCE's Contrasting Roles in Managing the Ukraine/Crimea Crises in 1992–1996 and 2014–2015." In *OSCE Yearbook 2015*, edited by Institute for Peace Research and Security Policy at the University of Hamburg. Baden-Baden: Nomos Verlagsgesellschaft, 2016.

_____. "Minsk Group Mediation of the Nagorno-Karabakh Conflict: Confronting an 'Intractable Conflict.'" In *OSCE Yearbook 2014*, edited by Institute for Peace Research and Security Policy at the University of Hamburg. Baden-Baden: Nomos Verlagsgesellschaft, 2015.

———. "Intergovernmental Organizations and Non-State Actors, Russia and Eurasia: The OSCE." In *Key Players in Regional Dynamics in Eurasia: The Return of the 'Great Game,'* edited by Maria Raquel Freire and Roger E. Kanet. Houndmills: Palgrave MacMillan, 2010.

_____. "The OSCE Role in Ukraine and Moldova," *Studien und Berichte zur Sicherheitspolitik*, Vienna, Austria, 1/2000, 25–61.

Liska, George. *Nations in Alliance: The Limits of Interdependence*. Baltimore: Johns Hopkins Press, 1962.

NATO. "The North Atlantic Treaty." Washington, DC, 1949.

Neff, Stephen C. *The Rights and Duties of Neutrals: A General History*. Manchester: Manchester University Press, 2000.

Organization for Security and Co-operation in Europe. "Early Confidence- and Security-Building Measures of the Conference on Security and Co-operation in Europe." *Security Community*, no. 1 (2016). Published electronically June 24. https://www.osce.org/magazine/248511.

Singer, J. David. "Inter-Nation Influence: A Formal Model." *The American Political Science Review* 57, no. 2 (1963): 420–30.

Union of Soviet Socialist Republics, United Kingdom of Great Britain and Northern Ireland, United States of America, France and Austria. "State Treaty (with annexes and maps) for the re-establishment of an independent and democratic Austria." Signed at Vienna on 15 May 1955." In *Treaty Series: Treaties and International Agreements Registered or Filed and Recorded with the Secretariat of the United Nations*, 223–379: United Nations, 1955.

Walt, Stephen M. *The Origins of Alliances*. Ithaca, NY: Cornell University Press, 1987.

Yost, David S. *NATO's Balancing Act*. Washington, DC: US Institute of Peace Press, 2014.

Zellner, Wolfgang (coordinator) et al., *Reducing the Risks of Conventional Deterrence in Europe: Arms Control in the NATO-Russia Contact Zones*. Vienna: OSCE Network of Think Tanks and Academic Institutions, 2018.

*Chapter Three*

# The Logic of Neutrality

## Pascal Lottaz

Neutrality is a practical affair; it does not rely on Theoreticians to flourish. There are, however, several theoretical ways to understand neutrality.[1] The most prevalent one is to focus on it as a legal concept under international law.[2] Another way is to study neutrality as a norm.[3] Alternatively, one can also look at neutrality's connection to values; like its relationship to national identities[4] or humanitarianism.[5] Finally, it is possible to focus on the structures that systems with neutral actors create.[6] While all approaches are important, this chapter focuses on the last one only. It borrows aspects from classical and structural realism to explain the logic position of neutral actors in different conflict constellations. As of now, no theoretical work has been conducted in modern International Relations on the logic of security systems with neutral actors. Network analysis or game-theoretical approaches have yet to be attempted. Hence, the absence of a theory of neutrality.[7] This chapter will not be able to offer a theory either, it will, however, propose an approach for the theoretical modeling of neutral actors in security systems. It argues that neutral behavior of states is common because their self-interest naturally leads to what the chapter calls the "neutral idea." That, in turn, gives rise to the "politics of neutrality" which, in contrast to the "law of neutrality," is not founded on international law but multilateral negotiations. The resulting position of neutral actors is that of a "third space" outside of a primary conflict but inside of a conflict dynamic. From this follows that neutrality in a system is a meta-relational property that arises naturally from the triangular logic of "being friends with enemies."

## PRACTICE MAKES LAW—
## BUT WHAT MAKES PRACTICE?

Let there not be any misunderstanding; neutrality, especially permanent neutrality, is deeply rooted in International Law.[8] In fact, contemporary international law, as it developed after the Hague Conventions of 1899 and 1907, is a combination of the Law of Peace on the one hand, and the Law of War and Neutrality on the other.[9] On land, legal neutrality dates back to bilateral treaties of thirteenth century Europe. On the sea, the origins of its codification are enshrined in the Catalan "Consolato del Mare."[10] However, international law is not the source of the neutral behavior of states. On the contrary, the legal codification of neutrality always followed the practice thereof; or, in the words of Stephen Neff, the "law of neutrality ... was made not, as it were, from the top-down by scholars and commentators, but rather form the bottom-up by statesmen, generals, admirals and traders."[11] Practices of great and small power neutrals alike became international law only after time. Powerful states like Great Britain, Russia, or the United States practiced neutrality in the eighteenth and nineteenth centuries in wars that they were not interested in long before the law of neutrality codified the rules thereof.[12] The same was true for small powers who pursued neutral statuses for themselves or their territories. Examples thereof are ancient Melos in 416 BC,[13] sixteenth-century Liège,[14] Switzerland in 1815,[15] Luxemburg in 1867,[16] the Congo in 1885,[17] Austria in 1955,[18] even Laos, in 1962.[19] While large, seafaring nations tended to be most interested in occasional neutrality as a means to continue trade and refrain from unwanted entanglement, for small countries "neutralization"[20] was most often a means to gain a political status in the international system that would guarantee their military security. These territories, which were not always independent states,[21] were highly contested areas, caught in unique security environments for which legally precise models often did not exist. The instruments of neutralization—the treaty documents that enshrined their permanent neutrality—therefore frequently contained novel provisions which qualified their particular neutrality while also creating precedents for new neutrality law. Switzerland's neutralization at the Congress of Vienna, for example, created the term "permanent neutrality" under international law in the first place.[22] The notion that neutrality could be "perpetual" (meaning that it would be a breach of the law if the neutralized state unilaterally abandoned it) had never been used in any treaty document before.[23] Austria's neutralization 150 years later was innovative not so much for its content, which was modeled explicitly after Switzerland, but for its method of combining a political declaration (the Moscow Memorandum) with a peace accord and subsequent bilateral acts of recognition that made it part of International Law.[24] Even the Laotian accord contained novel aspects of neutralization like article seven that required Laos to "accept direct and unconditional aid from all countries."[25] This is curious because permanent neutrality had never been understood to require indiscriminate acceptance of aid. But for Laos, which was struggling for a national solution to avoid a civil war as much as it was seeking an international solution, aid was an essential factor to create domestic unity among rival factions.[26] Innovation, in other words, is a hallmark of neutralization. The lack of a clear legal framework has never been a hindrance for the inception of neutralities when those served a purpose to the powers involved.

This raises an interesting question. If the Law of Neutrality is the outcome and not the source of neutral behavior, then what causes actors to seek neutrality in the first place? Neutral solutions have been anything but obvious for many cases where they became a legal arrangement. The pool of examples widens even further if one includes cases for which neutrality was seriously considered but not adopted. In 1952, there was a realistic Soviet proposal for a unified, neutral Germany, which failed only because Chancellor Adenauer did not trust Soviet intentions.[27] For Japan, local left-wing politicians and General MacArthur, too, argued for a decade after the war that permanent neutrality would be the best international status for Japan.[28] In Cambodia, Prince Norodom Sihanouk advocated just as much for a neutral solution for his country as did his counterpart, Souvanna Phouma, in Laos.[29] Furthermore, an entirely separate category of "neutralism"[30] emerged around the early 1960s when the Nonaligned Movement (NAM) became an informal association of dozens of nations who sought to distance themselves from the block dynamics of the Cold War.[31] Although their "neutralism" differed much from the older concept of permanent neutrality, the underlying idea to remain outside of an external power struggle was the same.[32] The "neutral and nonaligned" states found themselves subsequently in the same boat during the CSCE process of the mid-1970s.[33]

Even today, movements that seek a neutral solution are far from over. The NAM still exists, holding summits every four to six years. Turkmenistan and, to a lesser degree, Moldova joined the ranks of permanently neutral states in the mid 1990s.[34] Serbia declared its "military neutrality" in 2007,[35] and there are good arguments for the neutralization of Ukraine.[36] In Asia, former vice president of the Republic of China (ROC–Taiwan), Lu Hsiu-lien (Annette Lu), is leading a political movement that, albeit small, has real chances of holding a referendum on Taiwanese "peace and neutrality."[37] Despite the many commentaries declaring the death or at least the decline of neutrality,[38] there is still *something* intuitive about it that keeps motivating politicians to use it as a means to solve international problems.

It is not surprising that neutral policies keep reappearing over the centuries if one thinks about these situations from the perspective of the neutrals. Stephen Neff put it best when he said that there just never was a great "disposition on the part of princes to throw themselves into the quarrels of others when they perceived no interest of their own to be at stake."[39] It is only natural that those who have nothing to win (or everything to lose) from another party's dispute would seek to evade the conflict in the first place and continue "business as usual" whenever possible. Neutrality was simply always a way to uphold bilateral peace when there was no good reason for war from the standpoint of the neutral.

## THE NEUTRAL IDEA

The neutral idea is, in fact, so intuitive and common that it already existed before the word "neutrality" in western languages was coined. Robert A. Bauslaugh showed that although ancient Greek lacked the diplomatic vocabulary of a "neutral" state, the practice of not taking sides in third party conflicts was widespread.

> There are many examples: the Milesians in the mid-sixth-century B.C.; the Argives in 480; the Melians, Therans, Achaeans, and others in 431; the Agrigentines, Camarinaeans, and the majority of South Italian cities in 415; the Boeotians and Corinthians in 399; the Megarians from the 390s onward; the united Greek alliance in 362; Athens in the 340s; and a substantial number of states in the final struggle against Philip II in 338. The simple fact is that among surviving accounts of virtually every major conflict of the classical period there are references to states that remain—or seek to remain—in a posture friendly yet uncommitted to the belligerents.[40]

In the absence of a concrete concept, Greek writers resorted to descriptions. They ranged from notions of disengagement like "those standing aloof from both sides," over nonjudgmental statements like "those who were allies of neither side," and extended to positive expressions like "those remaining at peace."[41] It is clearly not the case as some researchers have indicated that neutrality as a foreign policy only emerged after the Middle Ages with the concept of sovereign states.[42] There are enough examples not only from ancient Greece but also from nonwestern backgrounds to conclude that foreign policies of *third spaces* (as explained below) are universal to power politics rather than dependent on the notion of sovereignty. In Asia, the "dual vassalage"[43] of the Ryukyu Kingdom to Ming-China and Edo-Japan is one,[44] while Japan's national seclusion ("sakoku") policy to expel European influences from its politics is another—albeit in the sense of standing aloof rather than remaining friends.[45]

The best classic description of the neutral idea stems, in fact, from the "patron scholar"[46] of realism; Thucydides in his Melian Dialogue cites the citizens of the island of Melos who wanted to preserve their neutrality in the war between Athens and Sparta as telling the hostile Athenians "we invite you to allow us *to be friends to you and foes to neither party*, and to retire from our country after making such a treaty as shall seem fit to us both."[47] This is the most useful portrayal of the subjective wish of a neutral actor, emphasizing the positive relational property of remaining friends with one conflict party, while, at the same time, refraining from becoming an enemy of the other. This makes Thucydides' definition slightly more comprehensive than definitions that focus only on what neutral states abstain from.[48] Take, for instance, Quincy Wright's definition that "neutrality, in the broadest sense, means nonparticipation in war," from which he deducts that "[i]t is, therefore the fact that the nonparticipants consider themselves neutral, that they are, at least in action, ready to be impartial and indifferent to the results, and to abstain from assisting or hampering either, so far as that is possible without sacrificing their own vital interest." Although he is correct in describing the attitudes of neutral actors and their rational expectations (nonpreference) toward the future, his portrait neglects the relationship of the actors during the actual conflict, which is one of friendship to all sides. That is why the more comprehensive way of describing the neutral idea for the time of warfare is that of Thucydides, which, in slightly different words, means *remaining friends with enemies*. The positive aspect (being friends) is important when interpreting the relationships of neutrals, as will be shown later. Importantly, a neutral remains friends with enemies with the full knowledge of that fact by all parties—as indicated in the Melians proposal for a treaty that would formalize the status and probably include the Do's and Don'ts of their neutrality. Unfortunately, for them, the neutral tactic did not bode well. The Athenians ultimately rejected their proposal, reasoning that allowing Melos not to succumb to Athens' demands (to become an ally against Sparta) might incite other peripheral states to do the same and thereby weaken the Athenian position in the Peloponnesian War. They declared war on Melos, killed all males of military age and enslaved the rest of the population.

Some commentators have interpreted this as proof for the futility of clinging to moral principles in interstate affairs (in the sense that "only might makes right").[49] The episode, however, also illustrates a principle of the neutral position; a neutral status can only be maintained if it is based on a mutual agreement. Melos was able to maintain its friendship with Athens and Sparta as long as both wanted that. As soon as the security environment changed and the strategic gain from a subdued Melos compared to a neutral Melos became higher to one of the two conflict parties, its doom was spelled. This is hardly surprising; there are dozens of similar examples. In the First and Second World Wars alone, neutral states were invaded *en masse* by all belligerents for their strategic values.[50] On the other hand, there were also those neutrals that escaped this fate because their neutrality served the belligerents more than subjugation would have—which always comes at a certain political, economic, or military price. It is therefore rather due to a crude cost-benefit analysis and much less because of values why the relatively homogeneous group of successful World War II neutrals survived the tragedy unharmed. Fascist Spain and Portugal, just like democratic Ireland, Sweden, and Switzerland and the young Muslim nation of Turkey had to offer economic benefits to all sides while their strategic value was not high enough to justify the military pain of an invasion.[51] That was different for neutral Iceland and Iran, which the Allies occupied because of their strategic positions, or for Belgium, the Netherlands, Denmark, and Norway which Hitler occupied for the sake of his war against France and the USSR. The Soviet Union swallowed the neutral Baltic states for pure aggrandizement while invading Finland to militarize its borders. The question if neutrality could provide security in the case of third-party wars has always been one of political expediency rather than moral imperatives.

## THE POLITICS OF NEUTRALITY

The understanding of neutrality as a bilateral or multilateral arrangement has also been called the "politics of neutrality"[52] because of its negotiated character.[53] Some scholars use the same expression when talking about domestic neutrality law[54] or when neutral foreign policy is supposed to achieve a national political goal—as in the Laotian example. That is, however, not the meaning that "politics of neutrality" has in international politics, where it means that sovereign states negotiate among themselves if they want to allow one actor to occupy a third space during a conflict.

Politics of neutrality was a common feature of European power politics before the sixteenth century, for which examples of big and small powers are abundant. In 1309, the city of Zürich concluded a treaty with Habsburgian Dukes to make sure that their armies would not enter their territory in return for the right to receive food supplies from Zürich's markets.[55] On a larger scale, in 1370, England and Flanders concluded a treaty specifying that the latter would refrain from supporting France militarily or economically because it was at war with England.[56] International lawyers have often cited such medieval examples as the beginning of the codification of neutrality. Many were, however, rather dismissive of these contractually agreed neutralities arguing that they were "only political" and not based on a deeper jurisprudential principle that would create a lawful status.[57] Especially those thinkers who saw in international law a "progress of civilization," did not think highly of politics of neutrality which was, after all, based on the assumptions of an anarchical world and the necessity of securing agreement to one's own position rather than calling on the abstract principles of (unenforceable) moral rights.[58]

Naturally, those who argued most ardently against a rigid legalist understanding of neutrality were realist scholars.[59] Among them was Hans J. Morgenthau, who probably had the most intimate understandings of the politics of neutrality. As a German Jew, trained in jurisprudence during the 1920s and 1930s, Morgenthau observed the legal idealism of the interwar period and the political tragedies in Europe firsthand. In contrast to his colleagues, he understood policies of neutrality as a function of a states' security needs to be combined with the development of the international environment:

> The legal and political status which we call neutrality, is intimately connected with the legal and political structure of the international society at a given historical moment. Any basic change in this structure necessarily affects the normative content and the effectiveness of the rules of neutrality. The rules of international law referring to the rights and obligations of neutrals have no independent normative existence of their own; they are only the expression of certain legal, economic, political, and military conditions to which they owe their existence. Should these conditions change, these rules change also; should these conditions cease to exist, these rules cease to exist. Only this legal and sociological background can provide a scientific understanding of the legal value and practical importance of the rules of neutrality in a changing international order.[60]

Morgenthau did not think much of unenforceable principles, exclaiming in one essay even that "there are no such things as rights and duties of neutrality." What neutrals can and cannot do depends entirely "on the development of the technique of warfare as well as on the military measures which the belligerents are likely to put into effect in [a] concrete war."[61] Nevertheless, he did not mean to say, like other realists did,[62] that the politics of neutrality was impossible or impractical in itself—rather that it must be based on an assessment of the "politico-moral tendencies" (the thread of Fascism and Communism to dissolve the state from within) as well as the "politico-military power"[63] (state-directed technology of warfare) to be correctly understood. Neutrality, he held, is a function of the balance of power. The concrete way a balance of power works dictates the policies that neutral states can choose to maintain peaceful relationships with all sources of threat. They must not make themselves targets—or, conversely, they have to recognize when they become targets to take the necessary steps. What he opposed were legalistic approaches to marry principles of political necessity with abstract jurisprudential concepts. He criticized the venture of combining the collective security principles of the League of Nations with the policies of permanent neutrality of small European states, especially Switzerland, that adopted the status of "differential neutrality" when it joined the League in 1920. Differential neutrality was an experiment to divorce the military requirements for permanent neutrals (to not join alliances) from economic cooperation with the League. Under this approach, neutral members of the League were obliged to carry out sanctions against offending members in accordance with Article 16 of its Covenant but were exempt from any military action. To Morgenthau, this made no sense as it completely disregarded the practical, political pressures that permanent neutrals were under to keep an impartial attitude toward the centers of power. He was not surprised when all European neutrals went back to "integral neutrality" in 1938, when the collective security mechanisms of the League completely failed.[64] Of course the neutrals reverted back—it was the only other security paradigm left. In times of serious threat, neutral states can only rely on their political ability to convince all belligerents to remain friendly to them, if they want to avoid war, and that necessitates diplomatic freedom of action.[65]

In the end, realism views the politics of neutrality under the lens of rational choice. There are many circumstances when it simply makes sense for states not to ally themselves with any other power but to pursue their goals from an independent, *neutral* position. That has always been the case for big and small power alike. Big powers tended to be occasional neutrals like the United States, Britain, or Russia during the eighteenth and nineteenth centuries, or, to give another example, Japan, the USSR, and the United States remained neutral in the early days of World War II.[66] It also was the case for small powers who used permanent and occasional neutrality in Europe before and during the World Wars, and it was also true for the neutralism of the Cold War which—not to forget—emerged from both sides of the iron curtain.[67] Whether states seek to maintain their security by claiming to be uninvolved in a conflict, or if they seek protection under a security umbrella depends solemnly on the political calculations form the point of view of the states involved.[68] Morgenthau understood this well when he wrote in 1961 (about the US disdain for the new Cold War neutralism) that "in our disparagement of neutralism we have refrained from asking: Does it make sense from the point of view of the neutralists? This is the only politically relevant question because nations align themselves with other nations (or refuse to do so) in view of their interests rather than on the basis of some abstract moral standard. And in view of their interests, the answer is bound to be yes."[69] Therefore, any systematic analysis of the logic that neutral actors create has to start from their point of view in strategic constellations.

## THE LOGIC OF NEUTRALITY: TRIANGULAR AND BILATERAL

The argument thus far has been that (1) the law of neutrality emerged from the practice of neutral behavior, which (2) itself stems from the intuitive neutral idea and (3) gives rise to the politics of neutrality. Now, since the sole purpose of the security function of neutrality is to assure a peaceful relationship of the neutral with belligerent parties (being friends with enemies), the politics of neutrality must *necessarily* take place in the realm of a conflict dynamic—actual or anticipated.[70] Using the realist understanding that neutral actors are not "aloof" but, in fact, dependent on the international system, the assumption can be made that neutral actors are not different from conflict parties—they participate in the system—but with different goals and strategies. This understanding enables the graphic modeling of actors and their relations. The basis for this model is Thucydides' definition: [*we are*] *friends to you and foe to neither* [*of you two*].

This premise implies three actors: a neutral and two conflict parties. Let the neutral actor take the name "A" and the two conflict parties be represented as belligerents "B1" and "B2." Furthermore, it is assumed that war and peace—or conflict and harmony—are binary. They are the two fundamental states in which actors can exist in relation to each other.[71] Although there are undoubtedly many intermediary steps between perfect-harmony and perfect-conflict, war and peace are assumed to be binary because (a) even a minor disagreement is a conflict toward which a third party can take a neutral

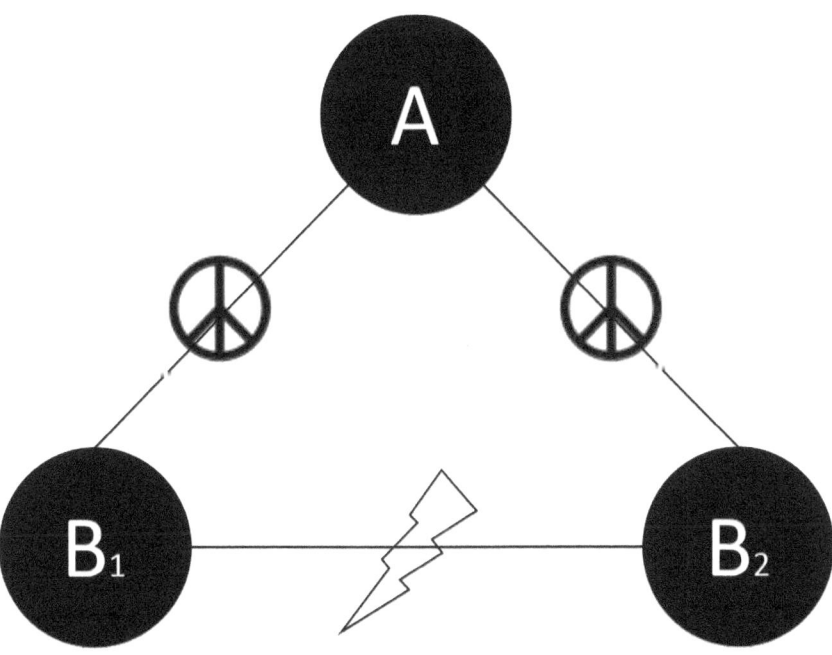

Figure 3.1. Base model of the neutral position, with two belligerents and a neutral.

stance, and (b) interndational law only distinguishes between the two "ideal types" of war and peace. They determine the two rulebooks that it knows; either the law of peace or the law of war. The law of neutrality is a byproduct of the law of war because it only has relevance when there actually is a war.[72] Hence, in the following model, the relationships of the actors are either "at peace" or "at war," which gives rise to a triangular constellation.

Figure 3.1 represents the base model of the neutral position, showing three important aspects of it. First, three actors render three relationships: two times "at peace," one time "at war." Second, the neutral position arises from the constellation of two types of properties, the actors themselves and their relationships. Modeled as such, it becomes clear that the intuitive notion that neutral actors are "in the middle" between two belligerents is misleading.[73] Neutral states might physically be located between belligerent territories, but since the relationships involved are always bilateral, the neutral position in diplomacy is outside of a primary conflict and is, therefore, a third space, external to the conflict.[74] Third, the neutral position does not create a neutral relationship with the other actors. There is no neutrality as such involved in the basic constellation because the neutral position arises naturally from the peaceful relationship with the actors who are at war with each other. This means that neutrality is, in fact, a separate property because it is *meta-relational*. Neutrality is the impartial disposition of an actor toward the conflict of belligerents. That is shown in figure 3.2.

Neutrality as a feature of a conflict system is directed toward the conflict (the "at war" relationship) of the belligerents, which is why neutrality necessitates a conflict in the first place. Without a conflict, there is nothing to be neutral toward. This is important: war and peace are states in which two actors exist. Neutrality, on the other hand, is an attitude directed toward a war (or a conflict), which can express itself in various forms. A militarily strong neutral—especially a great power neutral—might unilaterally enact foreign policies that are geared toward keeping it impartial while safeguarding its interests with both parties. That was the approach of the United States in the 1930s. The neutral might also call on the law of neutrality as a guide to its policies and hope the belligerents will recognize the validity of it. If that fails, the neutral might negotiate with both parties the terms of their wartime engagement—especially in the realm of economics—to come to a diplomatic understanding of how much interaction with its enemy each belligerent is willing to accept from the neutral. That was the approach that Melos took, or which the smaller European neutrals had to resort to during the World Wars. It is often the only option for pragmatic policymaking since neutral trade with belligerents frequently must pass through territory (on land or at sea) that is under the control of one belligerent to reach the shores of the other. Unsurprisingly, it is a hallmark of the law of neutrality that it explicitly guarantees the legality of neutral trade with belligerents. The only qualifica-

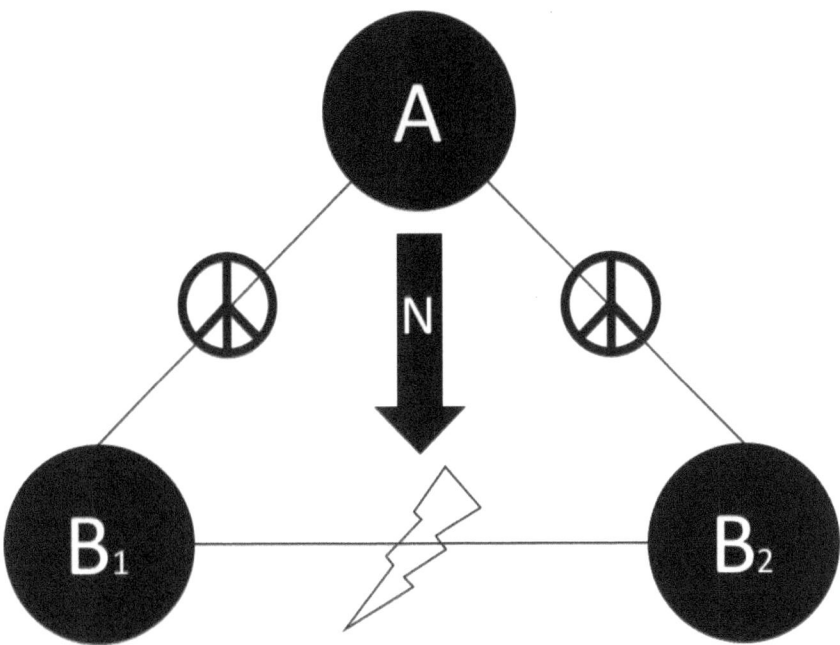

**Figure 3.2. Base model with meta-relational neutral attitude.**

tion is that belligerents might "blockade" their enemies in which case neutral cargo on belligerent ships (or neutral ships with belligerent cargo) can be seized legally by the blockading belligerent, thereby increasing the risk of commerce for neutral traders. But trade itself is explicitly allowed under neutrality law.[75]

The constellation of figure 3.2 is typical for so-called occasional neutrality, which is the position any country naturally assumes in case of a war between two other states. It does not require a declaration of neutrality nor any special national policy. Occasional neutrality arises "ipso facto"[76] from the constellation. Also in International Law, neutrality law immediately applies once a war breaks out unless A wishes to ally itself with one of the two parties. The neutral position is valid for any form of neutrality during a conflict and usually requires an equidistant position—especially for small states—to prevent the situation where one conflict party would receive more favors from a neutral than the other and thereby provoke the latter into eliminating the source of its enemy's benefit. The opposite, "benevolent neutrality" (the practice of favoring one belligerent over another) also exists, but it is only feasible in cases where a neutral actor can be sure that the disfavored party has no power to stop the practice. For example, if the benev-

68                           *Pascal Lottaz*

olent neutral is geographically much closer to the state it favors than the one it deprives of equal treatment (e.g., South American countries in World War II who often favored the Allies over the Axis) or when the neutral in question is a major power to be reckoned with (e.g., the United States in the first years of the First and Second World Wars). In other cases, where the balance of power is relatively equal among belligerents, smaller neutral states that are in the immediate vicinity of the belligerents can only succeed in the delicate neutral balancing act through credible *impartiality* (which was a common feature in Greek descriptions of neutral behavior and is an integral part of neutrality law).[77] "Benevolent neutrality" can be modeled by indicating defensive alliances or preferential treatment of one belligerent over the other by the weight of the relationship stroke (figure 3.3).

If more actors are introduced, the number of bilateral relationships naturally multiplies.[78] Applying the model, for example, to United States and Japanese neutralities[79] during the years 1939–1941 (until Pearl Harbor) the situation of figure 3.4 emerges. For the sake of simplicity, the diagram reduces the number of belligerents to the main actors. It shows how both Japan and the United States during the first period of warfare in Europe maintained

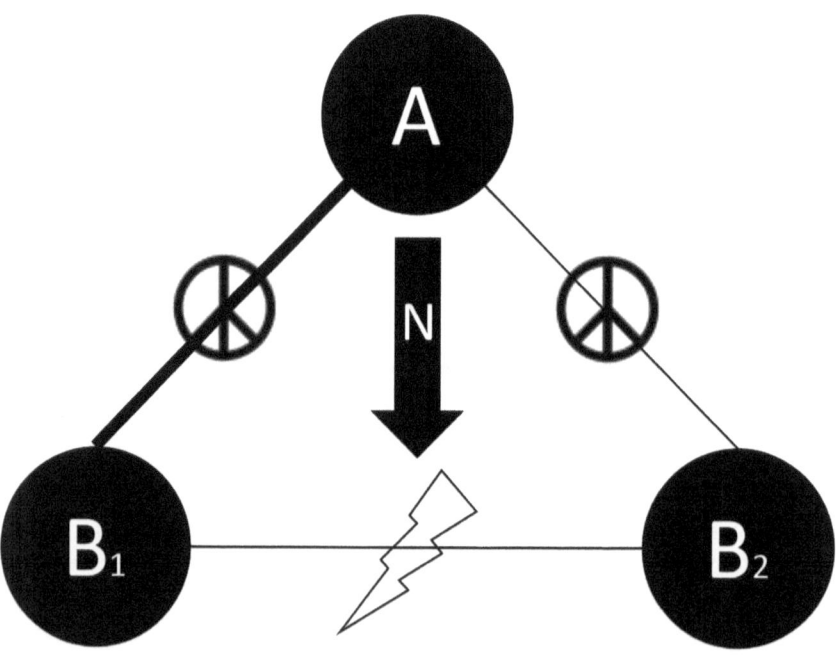

**Figure 3.3.   Benevolent neutrality, where one conflict party receives more favors than the other.**

peaceful relationships with both sides, albeit favoring and supporting the opposite parties.

The same can be done for Japanese–USSR relations during the period for which their (mutual) neutrality pact kept them at peace (1941–1945) while they were fighting each other's allies in the other theaters of the war.[80] It was a bizarre constellation and Switzerland's top diplomat in Tokyo, Minister Camille Gorgé, once called it "the strangest neutrality that one has ever seen."[81] But looking at the situation from the viewpoint of Japan and the Soviet Union, the pact made absolute sense as it reduced the war fronts for both of them. The situation was mutually beneficial until the Soviet Union had the capacity (after the end of the war with Germany) to break the treaty and enter the war in the last days before Japan's surrender.[82] Since the pact bound the two to observe strict neutrality toward each other, their neutralities were directed at the wars that their allies were fighting with the pact partner and not toward the primary conflict, in which they both were fighting the same enemies as their allies.

The neutralities of the USSR and Japan are cases of "belligerent neutrality" because the countries in question were simultaneously neutral toward one conflict while at war in another (figure 3.5). This constellation is not even unique; the seventeenth, eighteenth, and nineteenth centuries saw many such cases.[83] The World War II examples show why it is important to focus on bilateral relations in order to understand the rationale of neutral behavior. If neutrality is understood as a status in the sense of an enduring property that is universal and aimed at avoiding any war, a situation like the above makes

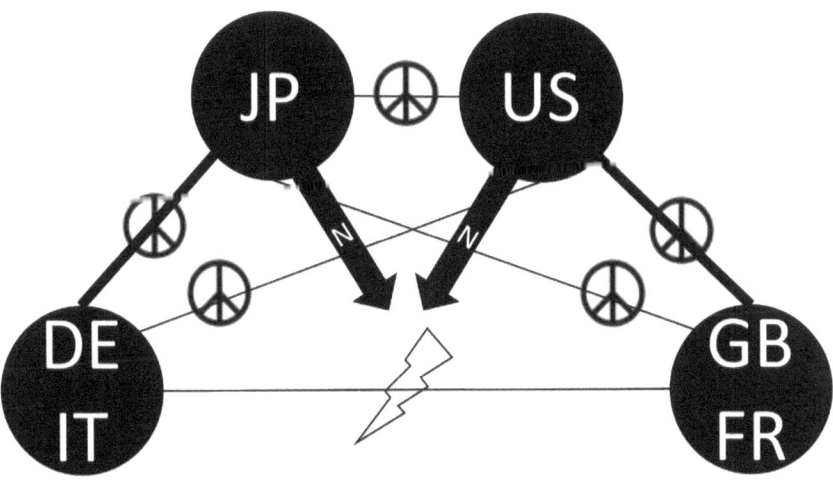

Figure 3.4. US and Japanese neutralities toward the European war 1939–1941.

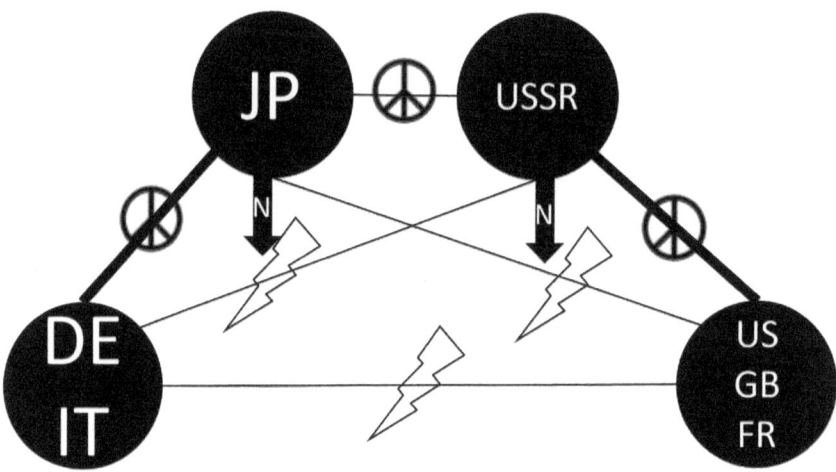

**Figure 3.5.** Japanese–USSR neutrality or "belligerent neutrality."

no sense. While a bilateral understanding of the politics of neutrality demonstrates the validity of the neutral proposal, even when a neutral is fighting a war somewhere else. Occasional neutralities are, in this sense, better described as tools to avoid *unwanted* wars, not all wars.

## PERMANENT NEUTRALITY AND THE SECURITY DILEMMA

In contrast, permanent neutrality is a different affair. Although the basic premise of bilateral relations remains the same, permanent neutrality replaces the precondition of an actual conflict with that of a *potential* conflict. Anticipating conflict in the future, permanent neutrals promise not to take anyone's side (under any circumstance) and to adjust their foreign and military policies accordingly, as not to create a situation in which they would be forced to join a war on one or the other side. Permanent neutrals are, in this sense, pessimistic about the future. They expect the possibility of conflict, which then becomes a guide to their peacetime policies. Adjusting the model to this situation, permanent neutrality can be expressed as shown in figure 3.6. The neutrality in the system, as well as the potential future conflict of B1 and B2, are expressed through dotted lines to indicate that they are not part of the actual constellation—since all actors are at peace with each other—but that the potential conflict and the potential neutrality toward it are components of the logic.

It makes much more sense to speak of neutrality as an enduring state in the case of permanent neutrality than for occasional neutrality because the

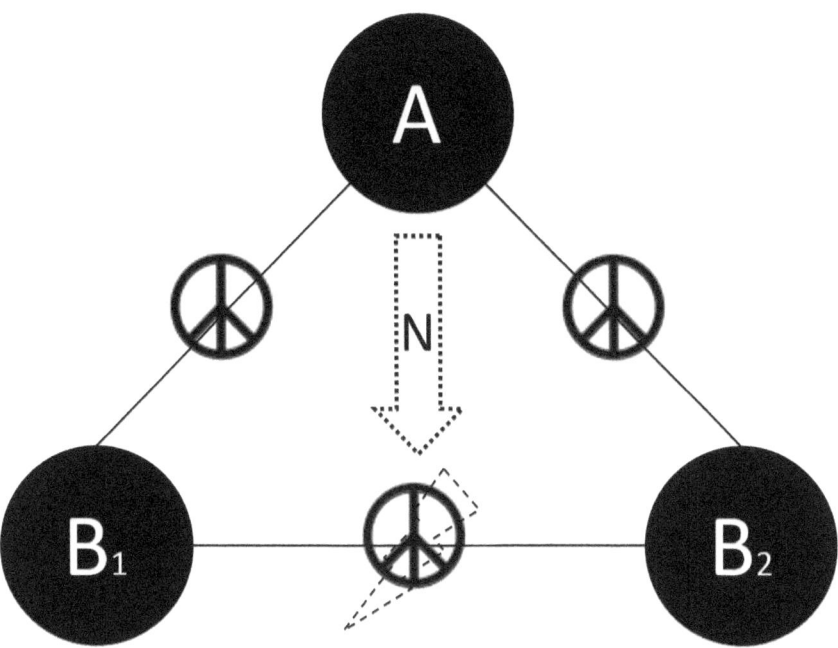

Figure 3.6. Triangular relationship with two potential adversaries and a permanent neutral.

promise that it implies is that regardless of the existence of an actual war the bilateral relationship between the neutral and its peers will remain the same now and in the future. The status of the relationship between third parties becomes irrelevant to the disposition of the permanent neutral, which by default, is that of neutrality. Unless an aggression by either belligerent occurs against the permanent neutral (which would result in a relationship of war among them) a permanently neutral country commits to not changing its relationship with either of them for the sake of the other. This amounts to the renunciation of war for the settlement of international disputes.[84] From this elucidated that for permanent neutrals, military alliances (offensive or defensive) are incompatible foreign policies and that they must be interested in relatively equal (impartial) relationships with all other actors in the system as this reduces the risk of any potential belligerent to change its relationship with the permanent neutral from peace to war. As such, the permanent neutral position can be understood as a slight modification of Thucydides dictum: [*We are*] *friends to all and foe to none*.

Since permanent neutrality does not require war of third parties as a precondition, and aims at maintaining peaceful relations at all times, it inti-

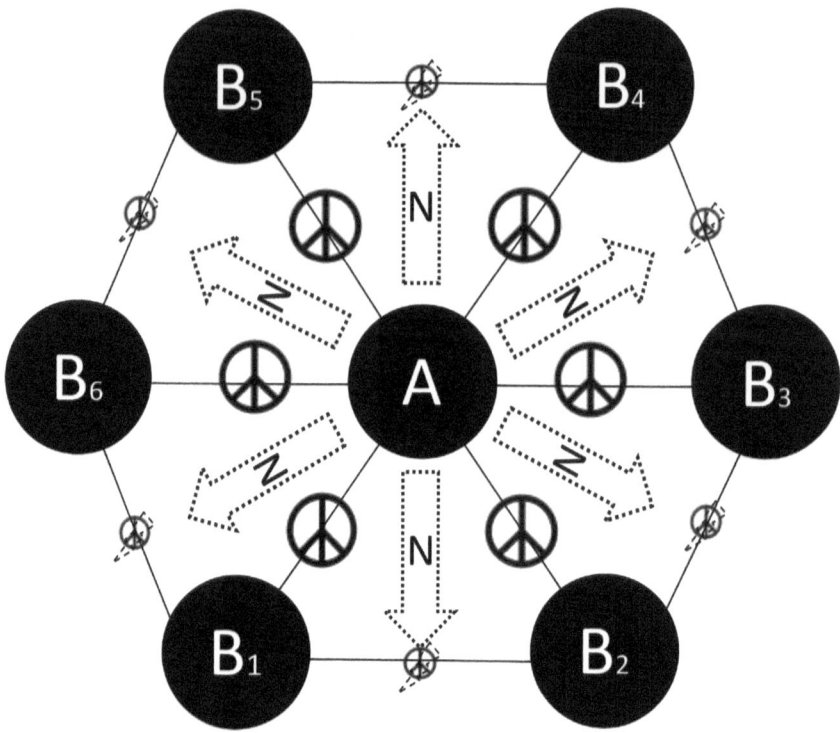

**Figure 3.7. The multilateral configuration of permanent neutrality.**

mately ties the neutral idea to an environment of peace. As a security approach, permanent neutrality prohibits states from seeking alliances, which naturally incentivizes them to act as mediators in international disputes (figure 3.7). Their position facilitates such functions as they remain friends to all sides. Some states take this logic to its extreme, renouncing even their militaries—like the Vatican and Costa Rica—while other permanent neutrals maintain armies for their national defense but simultaneously try to bridge the conflicts of their partners in the system. Austria, Sweden, Finland, and Switzerland all built an international reputation when they served as meeting ground for great power rivals before and during the Cold War. This neutral "mediation function" is not restricted to permanent neutrals but can be performed by any actor who succeeds in maintaining friendly ties with adversaries. In 2015, Singapore served as a neutral meeting ground for the leaders of the People's Republic of China (PRC) and the Republic of China (ROC-Taiwan).[85] Singapore did the same again in 2018 for the United States and North Korea. A year later, Japan's prime minister who enjoyed cordial relations with Iran and the United States, tried to broker an understanding between them during a serious military crisis in the Middle East.[86] Services of mediation are not conditioned on an actor being permanently neutral, merely on them being accepted as friends by both parties. Since that is the bread and butter of permanent neutrals, they are the most likely to play this role often.

Somewhat paradoxically, the ability to mediate rests largely on behavior that both conflicting parties might condemn. For example, neutrals during World War II were strongly pressured by both sides to cease trading with their respective enemies. Despite them functioning as diplomatic service providers to all belligerents (through their "Good Offices"),[87] their friendship to the enemy was a constant annoyance to both sides.[88] Even after the war, much historiography was produced that condemned neutral trading with the Axis powers.[89] This, however, misunderstands the situation of neutrals. Since a neutral status implies friendly relationships with all belligerents, trade and exchange are only the natural results thereof. If states are not at war, they are at peace, and if they are at peace then friendly relations on all levels of interstate exchange are the norm.

The most important implication of permanent neutrality as a model of structural realism is its impact on the security dilemma.[90] Kenneth Waltz described the security dilemma as "the condition in which states, unsure of one another's intentions, arm for the sake of security and in doing so set a vicious circle in motion. Having armed for the sake of security, states feel less secure and buy more arms because the means to anyone's security is a threat to someone else who in turn responds by arming."[91] The vicious cycle of mutual distrust, uncertainty, and militarization, in the end, leads to decreased security for everyone and, in the worst case, to war. The security dilemma gets amplified when taking into consideration the dynamics of alliances. On the one hand, they are a form of militarizing by other means; through the collectivization of the military potential of a group of states. Instead of increasing one's threat potential through conventional militarization, allied states try to achieve the same outcome by bonding together. But creating deterrence through combined force will naturally result in adverse effects from the other parties who might try to increase their conventional armaments or create counter alliances. The formation of rivaling security alliances happened, for example, during the Cold War. The Warsaw Pact was the Soviet Union's answer to the US-led North Atlantic Treaty Organization (NATO). Alliances also increase the risk of entrapment when states cannot escape security obligations that they made. Under such scenarios, a relatively minor incident can spark a chain reaction through which many become embroiled in a war that none of them had wished for.[92] The prime example of this is World War I for which Waltz said that "[t]he interdependence of allies, plus the keenness of competition between the two camps, meant that while any country could commit its associates, no one country on either side could exercise control. If Austria-Hungary marched, Germany had to follow; . . . If France marched, Russia had to follow; . . . And so it was all around the vicious circle."[93] Thus, Christopher Clark has argued that Europe "sleepwalked" into one of the greatest calamities of human history.[94]

The logical position of permanently neutral states has a benign impact on both of these aspects of the security dilemma. Permanent neutrals do not increase the threat level to any other state through their numbers—even a large number of permanent neutrals is not a threat to any other state—and they cannot cause chain reactions through alliances. Furthermore, permanent neutrality comes with the premise and promise of strict impartiality *in the future*, and that is verifiable through the foreign policy to abstain from alliances in peacetime. For example, Switzerland, Austria, Costa Rica, Turkmenistan, and Serbia are all verifiable permanent neutrals today (whether recognized in the legal sense or not) because they do not join alliance systems. Although this policy has no impact on the threat emanating from their domestic armament, their overall threat potential is reduced. Of course, the question of military cooperation is more nuanced in the real world,[95] but it remains true that all these states avoid formal security commitments as to credibly signal their harmlessness—while not completely giving up national defense (except for Costa Rica). At the same time, their abstention from alliances reduces the systemic risk of widespread entrapment, decreasing the risk of a belligerent chain reaction. Since the logic of permanent neutrality provides that they will maintain friendly relations to rivaling powers for as long as possible—until either power turns against them—their position decreases the uncertainty in the system which further lessens the security dilemma.

There is a geostrategic component to this, too. Depending on their location, permanently neutral countries are natural barriers between potential adversaries. Since they have to adhere to a set of clearly stated policies to remain credible (no alliances, impartial military policies) they provide a similar understanding for the rules of military rivalry as do security alliances—just with less emphasis on deterrence. It is this logic that stands behind proposals to create entire "neutralized regions" in Eastern Europe[96] and East Asia[97] to physically separate NATO from Russia, and the military might of the United States from China. These regions would be neutral "cordons sanitaires" that serve as buffer zones between major powers which, in turn, would reduce their need for extended deterrence and thereby again reduce the security dilemma. These proposals are not, however, akin to idealistic pacifism. They merely reconceptualize deterrence by factoring in the logic of permanent neutrality. Permanent neutrals are not defenseless since they can and do maintain their national forces. Even in an anarchic world, where "big fish eat small fish and small fish eat shrimp," they become, in the words of Singapore's Lee Kuan Yew, "poisonous shrimp."[98] Their force might not be enough to beat an aggressor, but their militaries still are a low-key deterrence, signaling that any attack or attempt at occupation would come at a high cost.

At the same time, permanent neutrals often also enjoy some form of unspoken security guarantees. A permanent neutral whose neutrality is recognized by the international community usually serves a specific purpose which creates security implications for all actors in the system. Switzerland in 1815 and Austria in 1955 were neutralized with the agreement of all great powers because their neutralities were beneficial to all powers. Had one of the great powers decided to change the status quo and occupied Switzerland or Austria, that might have well provoked other powers to intervene. Generally speaking, an attack on a permanent neutral whose neutrality is in the interest of all military powers in a region impacts everybody's security adversely. It might affect regional power dynamics so strongly that some powers might see the attack as a *casus belli* itself and enter into a war with the aggressor. For example, Great Britain and France did not declare war on Germany in 1939 because Hitler attacked them. They declared war on Germany because of Hitler's attack on Poland. The Damocles Sword of a chain reaction from its adversaries still looms over the head of an aggressor state, even if there is no alliance system in place. The mere fact that permanent neutrality rests on the premise that it is in the interest of all parties involved adds deterrence from each side toward the other. Even in the absence of formal arrangements, the security logic and self-interest of states still provide for deterrence structures. Permanent neutrals are not isolated and lone states. They are embedded in larger security complexes whose logic they impact.

## CONCLUSION

This chapter has argued that the logic of neutrality contrasts with the law of neutrality. While the latter is a normative set of rules, the former is a natural byproduct of a neutral's position outside of a primary conflict but inside a conflict complex. Neutrals occupy a "third space" that is defined by their friendly relationship with both (or all) parties of a conflict. Neutrality means to be friends with enemies. This position is a natural phenomenon which this chapter has called the "neutral idea." The position of neutrals automatically leads to "politics of neutrality," which is the bargaining between neutrals and (potential) belligerents about the Do's and Don'ts of their peaceful relationships. In cases where neutrality worked successfully, it did so because keeping neutrals neutral was in the best interest of all conflict parties. The logic of neutrality is different, however, between occasional neutrals and permanent neutrals. Only the latter comes with the premise and promise of avoiding military alliances and maintaining impartiality. Permanent neutrality affects the security dilemma positively by reducing uncertainty and decreasing the risk of belligerent chain reactions while, simultaneously, not eliminating a neutral's deterrence capacity.

In other words, as much as permanent neutrality has a domestic security function, its successful implementation has also an impact on entire security architectures. Further research on this impact is needed, especially regarding the dynamics of different systems, whether they are multipolar, bipolar, or unipolar. Permanent neutrals influence each security system differently and are, in turn, shaped differently by them. However, as this discussion has shown, the neutral idea is surprisingly resilient, and since there are no signs for its terminal decline, neutrality should be studied seriously as part of structural realist theory.

## NOTES

1. Theoretical approaches stand in contrast to practical research agendas of historians to uncover individual case studies of neutral policies. There is a lot of great historical research, for example: Neville Wylie, *European Neutrals and Non-belligerents during the Second World War* (New York: Cambridge University Press, 2002); Owen Chadwick, *Britain and the Vatican during the Second World War* (Cambridge: Cambridge University Press, 1988); Bent Bludnikow, "Denmark during the First World War," *Journal of Contemporary History* 24 (1989); Elie Podeh, "The Drift Toward Neutrality: Egyptian Foreign Policy During the Early Nasserist Era, 1952–1955," *Middle Eastern Studies* 32, no. 1 (1996); Detlev F. Vagts, "Switzerland, International Law and World War II," *The American Journal of International Law* 91 (1997); Georg Kreis, ed., *Switzerland and the Second World War* (London: Frank Cass, 2000).

2. Examples for the treatment of neutrality in international law are innumerable. Two of the most important classic works are; Lassa F. L. Oppenheim, *International Law: A Treatise—War and Neutrality*, vol. II (London: Longmans, Green, and Co., 1912). And Jessup's four volumes: Philip C. Jessup, *Neutrality: Its History, Economics and Law*, 4 vols. (New York: Columbia University Press, 1935–1936). Excellent recent scholarship on neutrality and law can be found in Stephen C. Neff, *The Rights and Duties of Neutrals: A General History* (Manchester: Manchester University Press, 2000); Alfred P. Rubin, "The Concept of Neutrality in International Law," *Denver Journal of International Law and Policy* 16 (1987–1988, 1987); Kentaro Wani, *Neutrality in International Law: From the Sixteenth Century to 1945* (New York: Routledge, 2017).

3. On neutrality as a norm, see Jessica L. Beyer and Stephanie C. Hofmann, "Varieties of Neutrality: Norm Revision and Decline," *Cooperation and Conflict* 46, no. 3 (2011); Daniel A Austin, "Realism, Institutions, and Neutrality: Constraining Conflict through the Force of Norms," *Commonwealth: A Journal of Political Science* 9 (1998); Laurent Goetschel, "Neutrality, A Really Dead Concept?," *Cooperation and Conflict* 34, no. 2 (1999); Christine Agius and Karen Devine, "Neutrality: A Really Dead Concept? A Reprise," *Cooperation and Conflict* 46 (2011); Harto Hakovirta, *East-West Conflict and European Neutrality* (Oxford: Oxford University Press, 1988). For older discussions, see also Philip C. Jessup, *Neutrality: Its History, Economics and Law: Today and Tomorrow*, 4 vols., vol. 4 (New York: Columbia University Press, 1936); Quincy Wright, "The Present Status of Neutrality," *The American Journal of International Law* 34 (1940); Peter Lyon, "Neutrality and the Emergence of the Concept of Neutralism," *The Review of Politics* 22, no. 2 (1960); Roderick Ogley, *The Theory and Practice of Neutrality in the Twentieth Century* (London: Routledge, 1970).

4. On neutrality as identity see, for example, Johanna Rainio-Niemi, *The Ideological Cold War: The Politics of Neutrality in Austria and Finland* (New York: Routledge, 2014); Karen Devine, "Stretching the IR Theoretical Spectrum on Irish Neutrality: A Critical Social Constructivist Framework," *International Political Science Review* 29, no. 4 (2008); "Values and

Identities in Ireland's Peace Policy: Four Centuries of Norm Continuity and Change," *Swiss Political Science Review* 19, no. 3 (2013); András Kovács and Ruth Wodak, *NATO, Neutrality and National Identity: The Case of Austria and Hungary* (Wien: Böhlau, 2003); Juhana Aunesluoma and Johanna Rainio-Niemi, "Neutrality as Identity? Finland's Quest for Security in the Cold War," *Journal of Cold War Studies* 18 (2016); Filip Ejdus, "Beyond National Interests: Identity Conflict and Serbia's Neutrality toward the Crisis in Ukraine," *Südosteuropa. Zeitschrift für Politik und Gesellschaft*, no. 3 (2014); Mikael af Malmborg, *Neutrality and Statebuilding in Sweden* (New York: Palgrave, 2001).

5. On neutrals and humanitarianism see Helena F. S. Lopes, "Inter-imperial Humanitarianism: The Macau Delegation of the Portuguese Red Cross during the Second World War," *The Journal of Imperial and Commonwealth History* (2018); Laurent Goetschel, "Neutrals as Brokers of Peacebuilding Ideas," *Cooperation and Conflict* 46, no. 3 (2011); "Bound to be Peaceful? The Changing Approach to Western European Small States to Peace," *Swiss Political Science Review* 19, no. 3 (2013); Antonion Donini, "Beyond Neutrality: On the Compatibility of Military Intervention and Humanitarian Assistance," *Fletcher Forum on World Affairs* 19 (1995); Christopher Greenwood, "The Applicability of International Humanitarian Law and the Law of Neutrality to the Kosovo Campaign," *Naval War College International Law Studies* 78 (2002).

6. Two wonderful book-length studies are: Maartje M. Abbenhuis, *An Age of Neutrals: Great Power Politics, 1815–1914* (Cambridge: Cambridge University Press, 2014); Wylie, *European Neutrals and Non-belligerents during the Second World War*. A noticeable work in International Relations is the quantitative study by Gregory A. Raymond, "Neutrality Norms and the Balance of Power," *Cooperation and Conflict* 32 (1997).

7. A theory of neutrality in international relations would not only have to be able to capture *all* instances of neutrality that the historical record provides us with, but also have "predictive power" concerning conflict constellations.

8. Neff, *The Rights and Duties of Neutrals: A General History*; Stefan Oeter, "Ursprünge der Neutralität: Die Herausbildung des Instituts der Neutralität im Völkerrecht der frühen Neuzeit," *Heidelberg Journal of International Law* 48 (1988); Abbenhuis, *An Age of Neutrals: Great Power Politics, 1815–1914*.

9. Oppenheim, *International Law: A Treatise—War and Neutrality*, II.

10. Elizabeth Chadwick, "The British View of Neutrality in 1872," in *Notions of Neutralities*, ed. Pascal Lottaz and Herbert Reginbogin (Lanham, MD: Lexington, 2019); Leos Müller, *Neutrality in World History* (New York: Routledge, 2019).

11. Neff, *The Rights and Duties of Neutrals: A General History*, 7. See also Wright, "The Present Status of Neutrality," 395–396.

12. Neff, *The Rights and Duties of Neutrals: A General History*, 1–26.

13. Thucydides, "The Melian Dialogue (Book VI)," in *The History of the Peloponnesian War* (London: Longmans, Green, and Co., 1874); Rubin, "The Concept of Neutrality in International Law," 255–56; Robert A. Bauslaugh, *The Concept of Neutrality in Classical Greece* (Berkeley: University of California Press, 1991), 113–17.

14. W. S. M. Knight, "Neutrality and Neutralisation in the Sixteenth Century-Liège," *Journal of Comparative Legislation and International Law* 2, no. 1 (1920).

15. Edgar Bonjour, *Geschichte der schweizerischen Neutralität : Kurzfassung* (Basel: Helbing & Lichtenhahn, 1978).

16. "Treaty Relative to the Neutralization of the Grand Duchy of Luxemburg," *The American Journal of International Law* 3, no. 2 (1909).

17. E. Delmar Morgan, "The Free State of the Congo," *Proceedings of the Royal Geographical Society and Monthly Record of Geography* 7, no. 4 (1885).

18. Alfred Verdross, "Austria's Permanent Neutrality and the United Nations Organization," *American Journal of International Law* 50, no. 1 (1956).

19. Jürg Martin Gabriel, "Neutrality and Neutralism in Southeast Asia, 1960–1970," in *The American Conception of Neutrality After 1941* (New York: Palgrave Macmillan, 2002); Arthur J. Dommen, "Neutralization Experiment in Laos," *Current History* 48, no. 282 (1965); William J Rust, *So much to Lose: John F. Kennedy and American Policy in Laos* (Lexington: University Press of Kentucky, 2014).

20. On the concept of "neutralization" see the introduction to this volume.

21. On "permanent territorial neutrality" see Lottaz and Reginbogin in chapter 9 of this volume.

22. "Perpetual Neutrality" became for the first time part of a multilateral treaty in 1815 through the "Acte d'accession, en Date de Zurich, le 27 Mai 1815, de la Confédération Suisse à la Déclaration des Puissances Réunies au Congrès de Vienne, en Date du 20 Mars 1815." The term was, however, invented before that. Already in the eighteenth-century, Grand Duke Leopold of Tuscany used the term to refer to the neutrality of Tuscany when he dissolved his army. See Neff, *The Rights and Duties of Neutrals: A General History*, 42.

23. The actual term was the French "neutralité perpétuelle." See Bonjour, *Geschichte der schweizerischen Neutralität: Kurzfassung*, 36–37.

24. Alfred Verdross, "Die Österreichische Neutralität," *Heidelberg Journal of International Law*, 19 (1958).

25. "Declaration on the Neutrality of Laos. Signed at Geneva, on 23 July 1962," ed. United Nations, vol. 456, *Treaty Series: Treaties and International Agreements registered or filed and recorded with the Secretariat of the United Nations* (New York: United Nations, 1964). Article 7.

26. See Edmund F. Wehrle, "A Good, Bad Deal": John F. Kennedy, W. Averell Harriman, and the Neutralization of Laos, 1961–1962," *Pacific Historical Review* 67, no. 3 (1998); Kenneth L. Hill, "President Kennedy and the Neutralization of Laos," *The Review of Politics* 31, no. 3 (1969).

27. It was disputed among historians for a long time whether Stalin was actually serious about his proposal to neutralize Germany and let it have free elections. After new Russian sources became available, Wilfried Loth concluded that Stalin "really wanted what he said; a united Germany outside of the western block." Wilfried Loth, "Die Entstehung der "Stalin Note," in *Dei Stalin-Note vom 10. März 1952: Neue Quellen und Analysen*, ed. Jürgen Zarusky (Oldenbourg: R. Oldenbourg Verlag, 2002), 62. (Original in German, translated by author). See also in English "The origins of Stalin's note of 10 March 1952," *Cold War History* 4, no. 2 (January 1, 2004). See also chapter 4 by Heinz Gaertner of this volume.

28. Jennifer M. Miller, "The Struggle to Rearm Japan: Negotiating the Cold War State in US-Japanese Relations," *Journal of Contemporary History* 46 (2011); Ivan. I. Morris, "Japanese Foreign Policy and Neutralism," *International Affairs (Royal Institute of International Affairs 1944–)* 36, no. 1 (1960).

29. Sihanouk Prince Norodom, "Cambodia Neutral: The Dictate of Necessity," *Foreign Affairs* 36 (1958).

30. On the term "neutralism" see Hans J. Morgenthau, "Critical Look at the New Neutralism," *New York Times* (August, 27, 1961); Lyon, "Neutrality and the Emergence of the Concept of Neutralism"; Efraim Karsh, *Neutrality and Small States* (New York: Routledge, 1988), 27–29. See also Gabriel, "Neutrality and Neutralism in Southeast Asia, 1960–1970"; Sandra Bott et al., *Neutrality and Neutralism in the Global Cold War between or Within the Blocs?* (New York: Routledge, 2016).

31. Lorenz M Lüthi, "The Non-Aligned Movement and the Cold War, 1961–1973," *Journal of Cold War Studies* 18 (2016).

32. On nonalignment and neutrality see Thomas Fischer, Juhana Aunesluoma, and Aryo Makko, "Neutrality and Nonalignment in World Politics during the Cold War," *Journal of Cold War Studies* 18, no. 4 (Fall, 2016).

33. Oliver Bange, "Changing Concepts and Understandings of Neutrality in the Cold War: The Neutral and Non-Aligned States (N+N)," in *Notions of Neutralities*, ed. Pascal Lottaz and Herbert Reginbogin (Lanham, MD: Lexington, 2019).

34. David Noack, "Politics of Neutrality in the Post-Soviet Space: A Comparison of Concepts, Practices, and Outcomes of Neutrality in Moldova, Turkmenistan and Ukraine 1990–2015," in *Notions of Neutralities*, ed. Pascal Lottaz and Herbert Reginbogin (Lanham, MD: Lexington, 2019).

35. Ejdus Filip, "Serbia's Military Neutrality: Origins, Effects and Challenges," *Croatian International Relations Review* 20, no. 71 (2014).

36. For an overview of the internal debate in Ukraine see Noack, "Politics of Neutrality in the Post-Soviet Space: A Comparison of Concepts, Practices, and Outcomes of Neutrality in Moldova, Turkmenistan and Ukraine 1990–2015." See also Michael O'Hanlon's commentary in chapter 10 of this volume. See also Micha el O'Hanlon, *Beyond NATO: A New Security Architecture for Eastern Europe* (Washington, DC: Brookings Institution Press, 2017); See also Heinz Gaertner's introductions and conclusion in the same book, and for newspaper articles see Heinz Gaertner, "Kiew sollte sich die Neutralität Österreichs ansehen: Bündisfreiheit zwischen EU und Russland als interessantes Modell für die Ukraine," *DerStandard*, March 3, 2014. John J. Mearsheimer, "Why the Ukraine Crisis is the West's fault: the liberal delusions that provoked Putin," *Foreign Affairs*, no. 5 (September/October, 2014); Henry Kissinger, "How the Ukraine Crisis Ends," *The Washington Post*, March 6, 2014.

37. "Taiwanese Neutrality" is discussed at length in chapters 8, 9, and 10 of this volume.

38. See, for example, the accounts in Nils Orvik, *The Decline of Neutrality 1914–1941. With Special Reference to the United States and the Northern Neutrals* (Oslo: Johan Grundt Tanum Forlag, 1953); Goetschel, "Neutrality, a really dead concept?"; Agius and Devine, "Neutrality: A Really Dead Concept? A Reprise"; Christine Agius, "Transformed beyond Recognition? The Politics of Post-Neutrality," *Cooperation and Conflict* 46, no. 3 (2011).

39. Neff, *The Rights and Duties of Neutrals: A General History*, 8.

40. Bauslaugh, *The Concept of Neutrality in Classical Greece*, xix.

41. Ibid., xx, 3–20.

42. Goetschel, "Neutrality, A Really Dead Concept?," 119.

43. Ronald P. Toby, *State and Diplomacy in Early Modern Japan: Asia in the Development of the Tokugawa Bakufu* (Princeton: University Press, 1984), 50.

44. Kazuyuki Tomiyama, "Ryukyu Kingdom Diplomacy with Japan and the Ming and Qing Dynasties," in *Self-determinable Development of Small Islands*, ed. Masahide Ishihara, Eiichi Hoshino, and Yoko Fujita (Singapore: Springer Singapore, 2016).

45. Toby, *State and Diplomacy in Early Modern Japan: Asia in the Development of the Tokugawa Bakufu*.

46. Jonathan Monten, "Thucydides and Modern Realism," *International Studies Quarterly* 50, no. 1 (2006): 3.

47. Thucydides, "The Melian Dialogue (Book VI)" 403 (emphasis added).

48. The negative definition of neutrality is popular. Morgenthau, for example, writes: "Neutrality as a status of international law results from the desire of a state not to be involved in a war waged by other states. Therefore, neutrality is essentially a negative status depending upon the existence of definite relations between two states, which the law calls war" Hans J. Morgenthau, "The Problem of Neutrality," *University of Kansas City Law Review* 7, no. 109 (1938): 112.

49. Archie W. Simpson, "Realism, Small States and Neutrality," in *Realism in Practice: An Appraisal*, ed. Davide Orsi, J.R. Augustin, and Max Nurnus (Bristol: E-International Relations Publishing, 2018), 122.

50. Malbone W. Graham, "Neutrality and the World War," *The American Journal of International Law* 17 (1923); Edgar Turlington, *Neutrality: Its History, Economics and Law: The World War Period*, 4 vols., vol. 3 (New York: Columbia Univ. Press, 1936); Wylie, *European Neutrals and Non-belligerents during the Second World War*; Johan den Hertog and Samuël Kruizinga, *Caught in the Middle Neutrals, Neutrality and the First World War* (Amsterdam: Aksant, 2011); Elizabeth Chadwick, "The 'Impossibility' of Maritime Neutrality During World War I," *Netherlands International Law Review* 54, no. 2 (2007).

51. Herbert R. Reginbogin, *Faces of Neutrality: A Comparative Analysis of the Neutrality of Switzerland and other Neutral Nations during WW II*, trans. Ulrike Seeberger and Jane Britten (Berlin: Lit Verlag, 2009).

52. Sometimes also referred to as "Diplomacy of Neutrality." See Lyon, "Neutrality and the Emergence of the Concept of Neutralism."

53. Oeter, "Ursprünge der Neutralität: Die Herausbildung des Instituts der Neutralität im Völkerrecht der frühen Neuzeit," 455; Goetschel, "Neutrality, A Really Dead Concept?," 119–22; Abbenhuis, *An Age of Neutrals: Great Power Politics, 1815–1914*, 126.

54. Thomas Fischer, Juhana Aunesluoma, and Aryo Makko, "Introduction: Neutrality and Nonalignment in World Politics during the Cold War," *Journal of Cold War Studies* 18 (2016): 7–8; Jürg Martin Gabriel, *The American Conception of Neutrality after 1941* (New York: Palgrave Macmillan, 2002), 12.

55. Oeter, "Ursprünge der Neutralität: Die Herausbildung des Instituts der Neutralität im Völkerrecht der frühen Neuzeit," 453.

56. Neff, *The Rights and Duties of Neutrals: A General History*, 9.

57. Oeter, "Ursprünge der Neutralität: Die Herausbildung des Instituts der Neutralität im Völkerrecht der frühen Neuzeit," 453; Oppenheim, *International Law: A Treatise—War and Neutrality*, II, §286. See also Wani, *Neutrality in International Law: From the Sixteenth Century to 1945*, 17–44.

58. This is not to argue that scholars of international law did not recognize the political necessities of legal principles. L. F. L. Oppenheim, for example, writes clearly that "Just as third States have no duty to remain neutral in a war, so they have no right to demand that they be allowed to remain neutral. History reports many cases in which States, although they intended to remain neutral, were obliged by one or both belligerents to make up their minds and choose the belligerent with whom they would throw in their lot. For neutrality to come into existence it is, therefore, not sufficient for a third State at the outbreak of war to take up an attitude of impartiality, but it is also necessary that the belligerents recognize this attitude by acquiescing in it and by not treating such third State as a party to the war." Oppenheim, *International Law: A Treatise—War and Neutrality*, II, §299.

59. Karsh, *Neutrality and Small States*, 5–6, 21.

60. Morgenthau, "The Problem of Neutrality," 109.

61. "The End of Switzerland's Differential Neutrality," *The American Journal of International Law* 32 (1938): 560.

62. Machiavelli, for example, held that "[t]hus it will always happen that he who is not your friend will demand your neutrality, whilst he who is your friend will entreat you to declare yourself with arms. And irresolute princes, to avoid present dangers, generally follow the neutral path, and are generally ruined." Niccolò Machiavelli, ed., *The Prince* (Boston: Constitution Society, 1515), 109. On other criticism of the impracticality of neutrality see also Simpson, "Realism, Small States and Neutrality"; Johan den Hertog, "Dutch Neutrality and the Value of Legal Argumentation," in *Caught in the Middle*, ed. Johan den Hertog and Samuël Kruizinga, Neutrals, Neutrality and the First World War (Amsterdam University Press, 2011), 5–7.

63. Hans J. Morgenthau, "The Resurrection of Neutrality in Europe," *American Political Science Review* 33 (1939): 483.

64. Ibid.

65. "The Problem of Neutrality," 120.

66. Pascal Lottaz, "Neutrality and Wartime Japan," in *Notions of Neutralities*, ed. Pascal Lottaz and Herbert R. Reginbogin (Lanham, MD: Lexington, 2019).

67. The Polish revolt of 1956 was a step toward a "neutral" Polish direction, albeit terminated later, and so was the Hungarian revolt during which Imre Nagy declared Hungary to be neutral. Meanwhile, Josip Tito steered Yugoslavia into the NAM, defying Soviet wishes repeatedly and China, too, joined the NAM, adding to the perception that the group was just a steppingstone toward communism. As it turned out, that was not the case.

68. Naturally, "political calculations" is a brought term that captures many different factors, like national political practices and conditions, identity, the perception of threat, morals, religion, and more notions that influence how the political process of a state determines its foreign policy.

69. Morgenthau, "Critical Look at the New Neutralism," 76.

70. An actual conflict dynamic is an ongoing one, whereas an anticipated conflict dynamic is one that could potentially happen in the future, which has implications especially for permanent neutral states.

71. Both states only come into existence because there is more than one actor. If the world was made of only one single country, interstate wars could not occur because there would be no "inter." But as soon as there is more than one actor, and if those actors are in some form of

contact to each other, then they must necessarily exist in a relationship which is either harmonious or in conflict.

72. See the distinctions made by Lassa F.L. Oppenheim, *International Law: A Treatise—Peace*, vol. I (London: Longmans, Green, and Co., 1912); *International Law: A Treatise—War and Neutrality*, II.

73. The notion of neutrals being "between" is prevalent. See Joseph Kruzel and Michael H. Haltzel, *Between the Blocs: Problems and Prospects for Europe's Neutral and Nonaligned States* (Cambridge: Cambridge University Press, 1989); Bott et al., *Neutrality and Neutralism in the Global Cold War between or Within the Blocs*; Hertog and Kruizinga, *Caught in the Middle Neutrals, Neutrality and the First World War*.

74. The Latin root of the word neutrality "neuter"—a compound word made of "ne" (not) and "uter" (either)—meaning "neither (of two)" is somewhat closer to this understanding than its translation in Chinese "zhōnglì" or Japanese "chūritsu," both written as 中立, literally meaning "middle stance."

75. The provisions for neutrality law and trade are highly complex and include the provisions of so-called "contraband of war." Good overviews can be found in Neff, *The Rights and Duties of Neutrals: A General History*; Leos Müller, "The Forgotten History of Maritime Neutrality, 1500–1800," in *Notions of Neutralities*, ed. Pascal Lottaz and Herbert Reginbogin (Lanham, MD: Lexington, 2019); *Neutrality in World History*; Abbenhuis, *An Age of Neutrals: Great Power Politics, 1815–1914*. See also Chadwick, "The 'Impossibility' of Maritime Neutrality During World War I"; "The British View of Neutrality in 1872."

76. Oppenheim, *International Law: A Treatise—War and Neutrality*, II, 299.

77. Bauslaugh, *The Concept of Neutrality in Classical Greece*, 10–11; Oppenheim, *International Law: A Treatise—War and Neutrality*, II, §285.

78. With every additional actor, the number of relationships increases by the triangular number sequence (0, 1, 3, 6, 10, 15, 21, 28, 36, 45, 55, 66, 78, 91, etc.)

79. On US and Japanese neutralities see Lottaz, "Neutrality and Wartime Japan."

80. Boris. Slavinsky, *The Japanese-Soviet Neutrality Pact: A Diplomatic History, 1941–1945*, trans. Geoffrey Jukes (London: RoutledgeCurzon, 2004).

81. Quote by Camille Gorgé, see Pascal Lottaz, "Neutral States and Wartime Japan: The Diplomacy of Sweden, Spain, and Switzerland toward the Empire" (National Graduate Institute for Policy Studies, 2018), 145.

82. Lottaz, "Neutrality and Wartime Japan," 116–19.

83. Neff, *The Rights and Duties of Neutrals: A General History*, 29.

84. In fact, under international law, even the case in which a neutral is attacked and has to use military force to defend itself is not considered an act of war. It is a sovereign right to do so and regarded as the upholding of its neutral status. See Oppenheim, *International Law: A Treatise—War and Neutrality*, II, §320.

85. "As a small state, Singapore must remain neutral and principled," *Channel New Asia*, May 14, 2018, channelnewsasia.com/news/singapore/small-state-singapore-remain-neutral-principled-chan-chun-sing-10231998 . "Singapore summit: what we learned from the Trump-Kim meeting," *The Guardian*, June 12, 2018, theguardian.com/world/2018/jun/12/singapore-meeting-what-we-know-so-far .

86. "Man on a mediation mission: Japan's Abe heads to Iran," *France 24*, June 10, 2019, france24.com/en/20190610-man-mediation-mission-japans-abe-heads-iran .

87. On neutral "Good Office Services" during World War II see Lottaz, "Neutral States and Wartime Japan: The Diplomacy of Sweden, Spain, and Switzerland toward the Empire."

88. Walther Hofer and Herbert Reginbogin, *Hitler, der Westen und die Schweiz 1936–1945* (Zürich: NZZ libro, 2001); Reginbogin, *Faces of Neutrality: A Comparative Analysis of the Neutrality of Switzerland and other Neutral Nations during World War II*; Wylie, *European Neutrals and Non-belligerents during the Second World War*.

89. Christian Leitz, *Nazi Germany and Neutral Europe during the Second World War* (Manchester: Manchester University Press, 2000); Roger Cohen, "The (Not So) Neutrals of World War II," *The New York Times*, 1997.

90. The "security dilemma" was coined by John Herz. See John H. Herz, "Idealist Internationalism and the Security Dilemma," *World Politics* 2 (1950).

91. Kenneth N. Waltz, *Theory of International Politics* (Reading: Addison-Wesley, 1979), 186.
92. This dynamic has also been called "chain ganging." See Thomas J. Christensen and Jack Snyder, "Chain Gangs and Passed Bucks: Predicting Alliance Patterns in Multipolarity," *International Organization* 44, no. 2 (1990).
93. Waltz, *Theory of International Politics*, 167.
94. Christopher Clark, "The Sleepwalkers: How Europe Went to War in 1914" (London: Penguin Books, 2012).
95. On the real-world cooperation of European neutrals, see chapters four and five in this volume.
96. O'Hanlon, *Beyond NATO: A New Security Architecture for Eastern Europe*.
97. See chapter 10 in this volume.
98. Lee-Kuan Yew, "Big and Small Fishes in Asian Waters" (Singapore: Singapore Government Press, 1966). See also "S'pore must be a 'poisonous shrimp' to survive in a world of 'big fish,' LKY said in 1966," Ong Anya and Lay Belmont, Mothership, December 10, 2018, mothership.sg/2018/12/singapore-poisonous-shrimp.

## SELECTED REFERENCES

Abbenhuis, Maartje M. *An Age of Neutrals: Great Power Politics, 1815–1914*. Cambridge: Cambridge University Press, 2014.
Agius, Christine. "Transformed beyond Recognition? The Politics of Post-Neutrality." *Cooperation and Conflict* 46, no. 3 (2011): 370–95.
Agius, Christine, and Karen Devine. "Neutrality: A Really Dead Concept? A Reprise." *Cooperation and Conflict* 46 (2011): 265–82.
Aunesluoma, Juhana, and Johanna Rainio-Niemi. "Neutrality as Identity? Finland's Quest for Security in the Cold War." *Journal of Cold War Studies* 18 (2016): 51–78.
Austin, Daniel A. "Realism, Institutions, and Neutrality: Constraining Conflict through the Force of Norms." *Commonwealth: A Journal of Political Science* 9 (1998): 37–56.
Bange, Oliver. "Changing Concepts and Understandings of Neutrality in the Cold War: The Neutral and Non-Aligned States (N+N)." In *Notions of Neutralities*, edited by Pascal Lottaz and Herbert Reginbogin, 19–40. Lanham: Lexington, 2019.
Bauslaugh, Robert A. *The Concept of Neutrality in Classical Greece*. Berkeley: University of California Press, 1991.
Beyer, Jessica L., and Stephanie C. Hofmann. "Varieties of Neutrality: Norm Revision and Decline." *Cooperation and Conflict* 46, no. 3 (2011): 285–311.
Bludnikow, Bent. "Denmark during the First World War." *Journal of Contemporary History* 24 (1989): 683–703.
Bonjour, Edgar. *Geschichte der schweizerischen Neutralität: Kurzfassung*. Basel: Helbing & Lichtenhahn, 1978.
Bott, Sandra, Jussi M Hanhimäki, Janick Marina Schaufelbuehl, and Marco Wyss. *Neutrality and Neutralism in the Global Cold War between or Within the Blocs?* New York: Routledge, 2016.
Chadwick, Elizabeth. "The British View of Neutrality in 1872." In *Notions of Neutralities*, edited by Pascal Lottaz and Herbert Reginbogin, 87–112. Lanham: Lexington, 2019.
———. "The 'Impossibility' of Maritime Neutrality during World War I." *Netherlands International Law Review* 54, no. 2 (2007): 337–60.
Chadwick, Owen. *Britain and the Vatican during the Second World War*. Cambridge: Cambridge University Press, 1988.
Christensen, Thomas J., and Jack Snyder. "Chain Gangs and Passed Bucks: Predicting Alliance Patterns in Multipolarity." *International Organization* 44, no. 2 (1990): 137–68.
Clark, Christopher. *The Sleepwalkers: How Europe Went to War in 1914*. New York: HarperCollins, 2012.
Cohen, Roger. "The (Not So) Neutrals of World War II." *The New York Times*, 1997.

"Declaration on the Neutrality of Laos. Signed at Geneva, on 23 July 1962." In *Treaty Series: Treaties and International Agreements Registered or Filed and Recorded with the Secretariat of the United Nations,* edited by United Nations. New York: United Nations, 1964.
den Hertog, Johan. "Dutch Neutrality and the Value of Legal Argumentation." In *Caught in the Middle,* edited by Johan den Hertog and Samuël Kruizinga. *Neutrals, Neutrality and the First World War,* 15–34. Amsterdam: Amsterdam University Press, 2011.
Devine, Karen. "Stretching the IR Theoretical Spectrum on Irish Neutrality: A Critical Social Constructivist Framework." *International Political Science Review* 29, no. 4 (2008): 461–88.
———. "Values and Identities in Ireland's Peace Policy: Four Centuries of Norm Continuity and Change." *Swiss Political Science Review* 19, no. 3 (2013): 376–409.
Dommen, Arthur J. "Neutralization Experiment in Laos." *Current History* 48, no. 282 (1965): 89–115.
Donini, Antonion. "Beyond Neutrality: On the Compatibility of Military Intervention and Humanitarian Assistance." *Fletcher Forum on World Affairs* 19 (1995): 31–45.
Ejdus, Filip. "Beyond National Interests: Identity Conflict and Serbia's Neutrality toward the Crisis in Ukraine." *Südosteuropa. Zeitschrift für Politik und Gesellschaft* no. 03 (2014): 348–62.
Filip, Ejdus. "Serbia's Military Neutrality: Origins, Effects and Challenges." *Croatian International Relations Review* 20, no. 71 (2014): 43–69.
Fischer, Thomas, Juhana Aunesluoma, and Aryo Makko. "Introduction: Neutrality and Nonalignment in World Politics during the Cold War." *Journal of Cold War Studies* 18 (2016): 4–11.
———. "Neutrality and Nonalignment in World Politics during the Cold War." *Journal of Cold War Studies* 18, no. 4 (Fall, 2016).
Gabriel, Jürg Martin. *The American Conception of Neutrality after 1941.* New York: Palgrave Macmillan, 2002.
———. "Neutrality and Neutralism in Southeast Asia, 1960–1970." In *The American Conception of Neutrality after 1941,* 119–218. New York: Palgrave Macmillan, 2002.
Goetschel, Laurent. "Bound to be Peaceful? The Changing Approach to Western European Small States to Peace." *Swiss Political Science Review* 19, no. 3 (2013): 259–78.
———. "Neutrality, a Really Dead Concept?" *Cooperation and Conflict* 34, no. 2 (1999): 115–39.
———. "Neutrals as Brokers of Peacebuilding Ideas." *Cooperation and Conflict* 46, no. 3 (2011): 312–33.
Graham, Malbone W. "Neutrality and the World War." *The American Journal of International Law* 17 (1923): 704–23.
Greenwood, Christopher. "The Applicability of International Humanitarian Law and the Law of Neutrality to the Kosovo Campaign." *Naval War College International Law Studies* 78 (2002): 35–68.
Hakovirta, Harto. *East-West Conflict and European Neutrality.* Oxford: Oxford University Press, 1988.
Hertog, Johan den, and Samuël Kruizinga. *Caught in the Middle Neutrals, Neutrality and the First World War.* Amsterdam: Aksant, 2011.
Herz, John H. "Idealist Internationalism and the Security Dilemma." *World Politics* 2 (1950): 157–80.
Hill, Kenneth L. "President Kennedy and the Neutralization of Laos." *The Review of Politics* 31, no. 3 (1969): 353–69.
Hofer, Walther, and Herbert Reginbogin. *Hitler, der Westen und die Schweiz 1936–1945* [in German]. Zürich: NZZ libro, 2001.
Jessup, Philip C. *Neutrality: Its History, Economics and Law.* 4 vols. New York: Columbia University Press, 1935–1936.
———. *Neutrality: Its History, Economics and Law: Today and Tomorrow.* 4 vols. Vol. 4. New York: Columbia University Press, 1936.
Karsh, Efraim. *Neutrality and Small States.* New York: Routledge, 1988.
Kissinger, Henry. "How the Ukraine Crisis Ends." *The Washington Post,* March 6, 2014.

Knight, W. S. M. "Neutrality and Neutralisation in the Sixteenth Century-Liège." *Journal of Comparative Legislation and International Law* 2, no. 1 (1920): 98–104.
Kovács, András, and Ruth Wodak. *NATO, Neutrality and National Identity: The Case of Austria and Hungary*. Wien: Böhlau, 2003.
Kreis, Georg, ed. *Switzerland and the Second World War*. London: Frank Cass, 2000.
Kruzel, Joseph, and Michael H. Haltzel. *Between the Blocs: Problems and Prospects for Europe's Neutral and Nonaligned States*. Cambridge: Cambridge University Press, 1989.
Leitz, Christian. *Nazi Germany and Neutral Europe during the Second World War*. Manchester: Manchester University Press, 2000.
Lopes, Helena F. S. "Inter-imperial Humanitarianism: The Macau Delegation of the Portuguese Red Cross during the Second World War." *The Journal of Imperial and Commonwealth History* (2018): 1–23.
Loth, Wilfried. "Die Entstehung der "Stalin Note." In *Dei Stalin-Note vom 10. März 1952: Neue Quellen und Analysen*, edited by Jürgen Zarusky. Oldenbourg: R. Oldenbourg Verlag, 2002.
———. "The Origins of Stalin's Note of 10 March 1952." *Cold War History* 4, no. 2 (2004): 66–88.
Lottaz, Pascal. "Neutral States and Wartime Japan: The Diplomacy of Sweden, Spain, and Switzerland toward the Empire." National Graduate Institute for Policy Studies, 2018.
———. "Neutrality and Wartime Japan." In *Notions of Neutralities*, edited by Pascal Lottaz and Herbert Reginbogin, 113–34. Lanham: Lexington, 2019.
Lüthi, Lorenz M. "The Non-Aligned Movement and the Cold War, 1961–1973." *Journal of Cold War Studies* 18 (2016): 98–147.
Lyon, Peter. "Neutrality and the Emergence of the Concept of Neutralism." *The Review of Politics* 22, no. 2 (1960): 255–68.
Machiavelli, Niccolò, ed. *The Prince*. Boston: Constitution Society, 1515.
Malmborg, Mikael af. *Neutrality and State-building in Sweden*. New York: Palgrave, 2001.
Mearsheimer, John J. "Why the Ukraine Crisis is the West's fault: the liberal delusions that provoked Putin." *Foreign Affairs* no. 5, 2014 September–October, 2014.
Miller, Jennifer M. "The Struggle to Rearm Japan: Negotiating the Cold War State in US-Japanese Relations." *Journal of Contemporary History* 46 (2011): 82–108.
Monten, Jonathan. "Thucydides and Modern Realism." *International Studies Quarterly* 50, no. 1 (2006): 3–25.
Morgan, E. Delmar. "The Free State of the Congo." *Proceedings of the Royal Geographical Society and Monthly Record of Geography* 7, no. 4 (1885): 223–30.
Morgenthau, Hans J. "Critical Look at the New Neutralism." *New York Times* (August, 27, 1961): 25, 76–77.
———. "The End of Switzerland's Differential Neutrality." *The American Journal of International Law* 32 (1938): 558–62.
———. "The Problem of Neutrality." *University of Kansas City Law Review* 7, no. 109 (1938): 109–28.
———. "The Resurrection of Neutrality in Europe." *American Political Science Review* 33 (1939): 473–86.
Morris, Ivan. I. "Japanese Foreign Policy and Neutralism." *International Affairs (Royal Institute of International Affairs 1944–)* 36, no. 1 (1960): 7–20.
Müller, Leos. "The Forgotten History of Maritime Neutrality, 1500–1800." In *Notions of Neutralities*, edited by Pascal Lottaz and Herbert Reginbogin, 67–86. Lanham: Lexington, 2019.
———. *Neutrality in World History*. New York: Routledge, 2019.
Neff, Stephen C. *The Rights and Duties of Neutrals: A General History*. Manchester: Manchester University Press, 2000.
Noack, David. "Politics of Neutrality in the Post-Soviet Space: A Comparison of Concepts, Practices, and Outcomes of Neutrality in Moldova, Turkmenistan and Ukraine 1990–2015." In *Notions of Neutralities*, edited by Pascal Lottaz and Herbert Reginbogin, 267–88. Lanham: Lexington, 2019.
O'Hanlon, Michael. *Beyond NATO: A New Security Architecture for Eastern Europe*. Washington DC: Brookings Institution Press, 2017.

Oeter, Stefan. "Ursprünge der Neutralität: Die Herausbildung des Instituts der Neutralität im Völkerrecht der frühen Neuzeit." *Heidelberg Journal of International Law* 48 (1988): 447–636.

Ogley, Roderick. *The Theory and Practice of Neutrality in the Twentieth Century.* London: Routledge, 1970.

Oppenheim, Lassa F.L. *International Law: A Treatise—Peace.* Vol. I. London: Longmans, Green, and Co., 1912.

———. *International Law: A Treatise—War and Neutrality.* Vol. II. London: Longmans, Green, and Co., 1912.

Orvik, Nils. *The Decline of Neutrality 1914–1941. With Special Reference to the United States and the Northern Neutrals.* Oslo: Johan Grundt Tanum Forlag, 1953.

Podeh, Elie. "The Drift towards Neutrality: Egyptian Foreign Policy during the Early Nasserist Era, 1952–55." [In English]. *Middle Eastern Studies* 32, no. 1 (1996): 159.

Prince Norodom, Sihanouk. "Cambodia Neutral: The Dictate of Necessity." *Foreign Affairs* 36 (1958): 582–86.

Rainio-Niemi, Johanna. *The Ideological Cold War: The Politics of Neutrality in Austria and Finland.* New York: Routledge, 2014.

Raymond, Gregory A. "Neutrality Norms and the Balance of Power." *Cooperation and Conflict* 32 (1997): 123–46.

Reginbogin, Herbert R. *Faces of Neutrality: A Comparative Analysis of the Neutrality of Switzerland and other Neutral Nations during WW II.* Translated by Ulrike Seeberger and Jane Britten. Berlin: Lit Verlag, 2009.

Rubin, Alfred P. "The Concept of Neutrality in International Law." [In English]. *Denver Journal of International Law and Policy* 16 (1987–1988, 1987): 353–76.

Rust, William J. *So Much to Lose: John F. Kennedy and American Policy in Laos.* Lexington: University Press of Kentucky, 2014.

Simpson, Archie W. "Realism, Small States and Neutrality." In *Realism in Practice: An Appraisal*, edited by Davide Orsi, J.R. Augustin and Max Nurnus, 119–30. Bristol: E-International Relations Publishing, 2018.

Slavinsky, Boris. *The Japanese-Soviet Neutrality Pact: A Diplomatic History, 1941–1945.* Translated by Geoffrey Jukes. London: RoutledgeCurzon, 2004.

Thucydides. "The Melian Dialogue (Book VI)." Translated by Richard Crawley. In *The History of the Peloponnesian War*, 396–404. London: Longmans, Green, and Co., 1874.

Toby, Ronald P. *State and Diplomacy in Early Modern Japan: Asia in the Development of the Tokugawa Bakufu.* Princeton: Princeton University Press, 1984.

Tomiyama, Kazuyuki. "Ryukyu Kingdom Diplomacy with Japan and the Ming and Qing Dynasties." In *Self-determinable Development of Small Islands*, edited by Masahide Ishihara, Eiichi Hoshino and Yoko Fujita, 55–65. Singapore: Springer Singapore, 2016.

"Treaty Relative to the Neutralization of the Grand Duchy of Luxemburg." *The American Journal of International Law* 3, no. 2 (1909): 118–20.

Turlington, Edgar. *Neutrality: Its History, Economics and Law: The World War Period.* 4 vols. Vol. 3. New York: Columbia University Press, 1936.

Vagts, Detlev F. "Switzerland, International Law and World War II." *The American Journal of International Law* 91 (1997): 466–75.

Verdross, Alfred. "Austria's Permanent Neutrality and the United Nations Organization." *American Journal of International Law* 50, no. 1 (1956): 61–68.

———. "Die Österreichische Neutralität." *Heidelberg Journal of International Law*, 19 (1958): 512–30.

Waltz, Kenneth N. *Theory of International Politics.* Reading: Addison-Wesley, 1979.

Wani, Kentaro. *Neutrality in International Law: From the Sixteenth Century to 1945.* New York: Routledge, 2017.

Wehrle, Edmund F. ""A Good, Bad Deal": John F. Kennedy, W. Averell Harriman, and the Neutralization of Laos, 1961–1962." *Pacific Historical Review* 67, no. 3 (1998): 349–77.

Wright, Quincy. "The Present Status of Neutrality." *The American Journal of International Law* 34 (1940): 391–415.

Wylie, Neville. *European Neutrals and Non-belligerents during the Second World War.* New York: Cambridge University Press, 2002.
Yew, Lee-Kuan. "Big and Small Fishes in Asian Waters." MC.JUN.22/66(PM), 1966, http://www.nas.gov.sg/archivesonline/data/pdfdoc/lky19660615.pdf.

*Part II*

# Practice

*Chapter Four*

# The Model of Neutrality

*The Example of East-Central European States*

## Heinz Gärtner

After[1] the collapse of the Warsaw Pact, some of its former members joined the North Atlantic Treaty Organization (NATO) and later the European Union (EU). They saw NATO as a protection against Russia and the EU as a return to Europe. After a brief internal debate, they did not opt for neutrality. Other East and Central European states remained outside the alliance. NATO, on its part, followed an "open-door policy," leaving the possibility of membership open without yet inviting them to join. This chapter argues that neutrality might be one alternative option to NATO membership for these Eastern and Central European states. It will use the case of Austria's permanent neutrality as a point of comparison to argue for the usefulness of the "Austrian Model" as a security paradigm for Europe.

In some former Soviet states like Ukraine, Georgia, and Moldova, neutrality is a controversial option since some domestic forces are pursuing NATO membership.[2] Also, Russia remains suspicious of a "neutrality option" because it does not trust that NATO would respect it. That has to do with historical precedence; after a conversation between the US Secretary of State, James Baker, and the Soviet President, Michael Gorbachev, in 1990, Russian officials, commentators and Gorbachev himself argued that it had been agreed at this meeting that NATO would not expand to the East; they maintained that NATO enlargement was a broken promise. In contrast US-officials claim that there is no written confirmation.

The Final Report and Recommendations of the Panel of Eminent Persons on European Security as a Common Project, November 2015, formulated some practical lessons for the OSCE from the crises in and around Ukraine. It sought to provide reassurance to Eastern European countries that found themselves "in-between" Russia and the West. The proposals included elements such as a treaty on European security, alliance membership, military co-operation outside the alliance framework, permanent or time-limited neutrality, neutrality but with military links to NATO, and an nderstanding of what neutrality means in the present context. Austria's Chairmanship of the OSCE in 2017 could have raised the issue of neutrality for Ukraine. As a diplomatic solution, the Austrian model could be an attractive alternative for Ukraine and other in-between states.[3] The Austrian EU Presidency in the second half of 2018 offered another opportunity to address the issue of neutrality for Eastern European States, including Moldova and Belarus.

This chapter focuses on neutrality as a model for the new Eastern Europe. It applies, to these countries, lessons learned from Austria's experience with neutrality. It examines options for the security architecture in the Eastern Partnership countries, including the role of NATO, the OSCE, and neutrality/ military nonalignment. Furthermore, it looks at options for neutrality and military nonalignment, drawing on the experience of Austrian neutrality and argues that most of the measures of the Minsk Agreement of 2015 can only be implemented in the context of a long-term solution.

The concept of neutrality has proven time and again that it can adapt to new situations.[4] The notion that neutrality is a phenomenon particularly of the Cold War[5] is false in many ways. First, the history of neutrality is much older; the Swiss idea of neutrality dates back to the fifteenth and sixteenth centuries and received its legal basis at the Congress of Vienna in 1815. Second, neutrality was not constitutive of the Cold War but was its anomaly. In Europe, the conflict was about building blocks; neutrality was about staying out of them. Whereas the bloc mentality was the norm, neutrality was the exception. Michael Gehler,[6] for example, argued that Austria's neutrality played an important role in the debate in the early 1950s as a potential model for Germany and other Central European states to stay out of the two military blocs. P. Terrence Hopmann,[7] on the other hand, recently concluded that the neutral and nonaligned states of Europe heavily influenced the content of the Helsinki Final Act of 1975 as well as the outcome of negotiations within the Conference on Security and Cooperation in Europe (CSCE). Many of these states saw in the CSCE an opportunity to break down barriers between the two dominant alliance systems in Europe—NATO and the Warsaw Treaty Organization (WTO)—and to try to override Cold War divisions with a new normative structure to enhance security in the divided Europe.

Thirty years after the end of the Cold War, these are all considerations of the past that hold only limited value for the new Europe. The new challenges after the end of the Cold War are the proliferation of weapons of mass destruction, terrorism (which potentially holds new dangerous dimensions in combination with nuclear proliferation), and fragile, dysfunctional states—which can be breeding grounds for terrorism as well as a source of uncontrolled immigration, and foster organized crime. Neutral states are well suited (in many ways better than other states) for making important contributions to the fight against these new dangers. European neutrals are often more readily accepted as brokers of peace and mediators than members of alliances. They can assist with reconstruction and humanitarian aid efforts in war-torn countries within the frameworks of the UN, EU, OSCE, or NATO Partnerships. For neutral states the possibility for participation in EU common foreign policy and crisis management is explicitly permitted. Europe's neutrals are also part of robust deployments such as these within the NATO Partnership for Peace (PfP).[8]

## NATO'S NEW ROLE

Non-membership in an alliance, anchored in neutrality law or political convention, is a clear characteristic of neutrality. The most important features of an alliance are mutual obligations of assistance, which are incompatible with neutrality. As long as NATO sees itself as a military alliance, there can be no membership for neutral states in it. But within the PfP framework of partnerships, crisis management, and cooperative security, they can provide capacities that are similar to those of the members while remaining outside of the alliance structure.

After the end of the Cold War, collective defense was no longer the only or even primary item on the NATO agenda. In addition to territorial defense (covered by Articles 5 and 6 of the Washington Treaty), the Alliance started to take into account the global context. Alliance security interests could be affected by risks of a wider nature, including acts of terrorism, sabotage, organized crime, and by the disruption of the flow of vital resources (arrangements and consultations as responses to risks of this kind can be made under Article 4). NATO, therefore, shifted its attention toward a second core task of crisis management and expeditionary missions, especially in regions outside defined alliance borders ("out of area"), like in the former Yugoslavia or Afghanistan ("out of continent"), and the inclusion of non-members within the framework of the PfP and the Euro-Atlantic Partnership Council (EAPC). In addition, NATO introduced "cooperative security" as a third core task in its 2010 Strategic Concept, which was adopted at its Lisbon Summit.[9] This task was intended to coordinate the network of partner relationships with non-NATO countries and other international organizations around the globe. Cooperative security should contribute to arms control, nonproliferation, and disarmament. It should provide a framework for political dialogue and regional cooperation, increase military interoperability, and prepare for operations and missions. Cooperative security is not limited to European countries but includes a wide range of partners globally. These initiatives need to be seen and assessed against the backdrop of two developments. First, NATO completed its main combat mission in Afghanistan, which moved the Alliance and partners to look for ways to sustain and reinforce relations in general, and interoperability in particular, for the upcoming period. Second, uncertainty and insecurity began to increase, especially in Eastern Europe in the face of developments in Ukraine, and turmoils in the Middle East. The Alliance was confronted with the need to find ways of projecting security and stability and to assist partners in enhancing their defense capabilities. For many Eastern European countries, partnership with NATO acted as a stepping stone on the way to full membership, helping prepare them for admission. For NATO, on the other hand, partnerships have acted as a sort of transmission belt to project security and stability corresponding to the notion of cooperative security. They helped foster compatibility between NATO forces and the militaries of partner countries, consequently leading to the expansion of the pool of potential contributors to crisis management operations. Of course, the concept of partnership has not been static as such and has transformed over time.[10]

After the Russian annexation of the Crimean Peninsula, an integral part of Ukraine, and intrusions by Russian forces across the Ukrainian mainland in the eastern region of the Donbas in 2014, it seemed that NATO reverted back to traditional territorial and collective defense rather than concentrating on crisis management or cooperative security. That was, however, rather a shift of public perception. In fact, NATO had never given up collective defense; it was rather a question of priorities. The crisis merely refocused NATO's attention to Europe's east. In the wake of the continuous Russian-supported insurgency in Ukraine, NATO's core task of territorial and collective defense received priority attention again. At the Wales Summit in 2014, NATO allies included the concept of a Very High Readiness Joint Task Force (VJTF) into the overall NATO Response Force (NRF) structure to enhance the capabilities of the NRF in order to respond to the emerging security challenges posed by Moscow. Although it should also counter the risks emanating from the Middle East and North Africa, it is mainly based on collective defense. However, since partners cannot be part of collective defense operations, their possibilities for participation are becoming more limited. It would be especially unfortunate for neutral states if crisis management were more and more replaced by collective defense. Meanwhile, the threats and challenges from the South did not disappear. Human security, dysfunctional states, regional conflicts, refugee flows, natural disasters, terrorism and nuclear proliferation remain a threat to Europe's security for the foreseeable future. The emergence of the "Islamic State" is a case in point. The unraveling of the Westphalian System in many states of the Middle East and the Mediterranean will produce more dysfunctional states and more radical nonstate actors. The monopoly of the use of force by the state is being dissolved, leading to the privatization of violence and a new medievalism. It will probably produce a much larger challenge than is currently known.

## NEUTRALS IN THE EU

Enshrined in the Treaty of Lisbon of the EU is a solidarity clause (Article 222), which requires member states to support other member states in case of natural and man-made disasters (e.g., terrorist attacks). Contributions from member states are voluntary and happen upon request from the state concerned and European cooperation in the realms of police and justice takes priority over military means. Behind the solidarity clause again stands the idea of collective security.[11] It aims at enhancing the security among its member states—while the concept of collective defense is aimed against an outside enemy. However, this clause is not part of the Common Security and Defense Policy (CSDP) and must not be confused with assistance obligations under Article 42.7 which holds that member states must provide each other with "aid and assistance by all means in their power" in case of armed aggression toward a member state. This includes the promise to use military force. The so-called Irish Formula in the Treaty of Lisbon makes an exception for neutral and nonaligned countries. It states that this Article "shall not prejudice the specific character of the security and defense policy of certain member states."[12] The formulation applies not only to the neutral and nonaligned states but also to NATO members. They have to "be consistent with commitments under the North Atlantic Treaty Organization, which . . . remains the foundation of their collective defense and the forum for its implementation."[13] The Treaty, therefore, allows neutral EU members and NATO allies alike to opt-out. In other words, the Treaty of Lisbon indicates exceptions for all EU member states in their mutual security commitments because of their prior commitments to (or their abstention from) the NATO Treaty. This puts the meaningfulness of the Lisbon Treaty into serious question.

On the other hand, the principles of the EU's neighborhood policy (the promotion of democracy, the rule of law, and market economy) are also essential to consider. The Eastern European countries (Ukraine, Moldova, Georgia, Armenia, Azerbaijan, and Belarus) are part of this so-called "European Neighborhood Policy" (ENP), which focuses on relations with the EU in such areas as trade and investment, finance, energy, and transport, among others. These states are caught in a "geopolitical dilemma"[14] in their foreign and security policy orientation toward Brussels and Moscow; closer political association and economic integration with the EU stands in sharp rivalry to an improved partnership with Russia and the Eurasian Economic Union (EEU; comprising Russia, Kazakhstan, Belarus, Armenia, and Kyrgyzstan). In contrast, a neutral status for these countries could facilitate closer economic cooperation between the EU and the EEU and end their in-between-status, which is unsustainable and undesirable.[15] Under one vision offered by the Scenario Group Ukraine 2027,[16] the continuous policy of détente between Russia and the West could result in new security agreements in which Ukraine is recognized as a permanently neutral country. This status might be acceptable to Brussels, Moscow, Washington, and Kyiv. It would guarantee that no side uses force to change its status while a neutral Ukraine would still be armed, resembling, in principle, the Austrian model.

## THE AUSTRIAN MODEL

In October 1955, the Austrian National Assembly adopted permanent neutrality, which was Vienna's guarantee to the Great Powers that the country would not join any Eastern or Western military alliances. Ever since neutrality has been at the center of Austria's foreign and security policy. In the early, formative years, Austrians understood neutrality to be synonymous with independence. It helped the country develop a strong identity for the first time since World War I, which is why Austrians still cling to neutrality by almost a three quarters majority.[17] The essence of Austria's permanent neutrality correlates to the nature of the country's military role and was enshrined in the neutrality law declaration:[18] Austria may neither join any military alliances, nor allow foreign troops on its territory. The legal principle that neutral states are not allowed to participate in a war, in the sense of international law, was not regulated directly by this declaration, but resulted from the prevailing understanding of permanent neutrality. In stark contrast, the Chancellor of the Federal Republic of Germany (West Germany), Konrad Adenauer, rejected permanent neutrality as a concept for a reunified German state altogether. He suspected a conspiratorial tactic,[19] seeing the concept of "armed neutrality" in Austria as a put-to-sleep-approach by the Kremlin. He could not be swayed even by US President Eisenhower who supported the idea when he said in May 1955: "It seems that the idea has developed that one could build a number of neutralized states from North to South through Europe. Now, remember: The Treaty regarding the neutralization of Austria does not mean that Austria would be disarmed. It is not a void, not a military void, it is along the lines of Switzerland. . . . This kind of neutrality is very different from a military vacuum."[20]

That Adenauer's perception was too pessimistic and that the NATO allies were committed to the neutral status of Central European countries became clear a year later. During the Hungarian uprising in 1956, the Soviet Union suspected that the rebels would use Austria's territory as their hinterland. The State Department of the newly re-elected Eisenhower administration warned Moscow to respect Austria's neutrality and even stated that its violation would be a case for a Third World War.[21] In the end, Austria's neutrality protected Vienna during the Cold War from outside intervention by both blocs. Member states of the two alliances, on the other hand, were less fortunate. Although NATO and the Warsaw Pact countries rivaled each other, they informally recognized their respective territories. Eisenhower did not come to the aid of the Hungarian insurgents, although the United States supported them rhetorically, and President Johnson was silent during the uprising of the Prague Spring in 1968. Also, President Reagan only verbally supported the Polish protests in 1981. Using this analogy, Ukraine eventually cannot rely on the United States to go to war with a nuclear-armed Russia.

## DISENGAGEMENT AND A NUCLEAR-FREE ZONE IN CENTRAL EUROPE

Despite Adenauer's adverse reaction toward Stalin's notes on a "coalition free" Germany in 1952, there were still other suggestions made for a neutral Central Europe, modeled after Austria's neutrality. George F. Kennan, the US ambassador to Moscow after 1947, and the father of the policy of "containment," suggested, in 1956 and 1957, creating a neutral Central Europe because he did not believe there would be another way to unify Germany.[22] He called Central Europe the "in-between-zone."[23] German Chancellor Adenauer, again, called this proposal "suicidal."

Nevertheless, there were other attempts. US Senators Hubert H. Humphrey and William F. Knowland started a bipartisan initiative. Their plan of 1956–1957 was to create a buffer zone and a simultaneous withdrawal of US and Soviet troops from Germany and from the members of the Warsaw Pact. Eventually, this buffer zone should have been linked to the existing neutral states, Austria, Finland, Sweden, and Switzerland. Similar ideas came from the chairman of the British Labour Party, Hugh Gaitskell.[24] However, by that time, the wind in Washington had changed. US Secretary of State John Foster Dulles, said at a classified meeting of the National Security Council on February 6, 1958, that the United States and the Soviet Union had agreed that a unified neutral Germany in the center of Europe could not be controlled and that unification should not be a goal of US policy. Meanwhile, the United States should do everything to "keep the [West] Germans happy."[25]

Some neutral countries, such as Sweden and Switzerland, experimented with the development of nuclear weapons, even as they sought to stay out of the military blocs of the Cold War. Western-bloc nations such as Canada and Germany did the same. But Austria had already provided, in the mid 1950s, a different model.[26] After declaring its neutrality, it became a model for the concept of a geographical zone without nuclear weapons in Central Europe, a concept known as the "Rapacki Plan."[27] The State Treaty itself (through which Austria regained its independence, and adopted in the same year as the Treaty on Neutrality in 1955) required its nuclear-free status, defining that "Austria shall not possess, construct or experiment with (a) any atomic weapon, [and] (b) any other major weapon adaptable now or in the future to mass destruction and defined as such by the appropriate organ of the United Nations."[28] According to the Rapacki Plan, Poland, Czechoslovakia, the German Democratic Republic (GDR) and the Federal Republic of Germany (FRG) should become neutral like Austria. Because of the emerging concept of Mutual Assured Destruction, however, the plan was not implemented, albeit it never ultimately died.[29] Non-nuclear weapon states renounced nuclear weapons entirely when they joined the Nuclear Non-Proliferation Treaty (NPT) in 1969. Most of them reasoned that this would be one way to avoid becoming a primary target in case of a nuclear war. By abandoning its Soviet-era nuclear weapons in 1994, Ukraine created the precondition for a nuclear-free status.[30] However, through a potential membership in NATO it would lose this status because the club considers itself an alliance based on nuclear deterrence—able to count on the nuclear arsenals of the US, the UK, and France.

In the case of Austria, the neutrality policy was increasingly supplemented with an active foreign policy. Contrary to the Swiss model of "sitting still,"[31] Austria joined the United Nations the very year it regained its independence (1955), the Council of Europe in 1956, and the European Free Trade Association in 1960. Austria presented itself as a meeting point by hosting, for example, meetings between the presidents of the United States and the Soviet Union, John F. Kennedy and Nikita Khrushchev in 1961, and Richard Nixon and Leonid Brezhnev in 1973, both in Vienna. Last but not least, thanks to this policy of neutrality, Vienna was chosen as the third UN capital and seat of the International Atomic Energy Agency (IAEA), UN specialized agencies (e.g., UNIDO) and the secretariats of OPEC and OSCE (formerly CSCE).

## NEUTRALITY AS A MODEL FOR THE SOVIET PERIPHERY IN EAST AND WEST: FINLAND AND AFGHANISTAN

Austria was not alone. Since the end of the Second World War, and until the demise of the Soviet Union, neutral solutions were sporadically proposed, or actively pursued, around the immediate vicinity of the Soviet sphere of influence. In Finland, for example, neutrality was a quasi-dictum imposed on Helsinki by Stalin. In contrast to Austria's legality-based neutrality that was adopted by the Austrian parliament and validated under international law through the multilateral State Treaty, Finland's neutrality was founded on a bilateral agreement with Moscow, a "Treaty of Friendship, Cooperation, and

Mutual Assistance" (FCMA Treaty of 1948). Whereas the Austrian version did not entail bilateral linkages to the Soviet Union,[32] the Finish model was a Soviet-imposed neutralization of its immediate neighbor. According to the treaty, the Soviet Union could publicly raise the question of the need for mutual consultations. These obligations made Finland's neutrality inherently vulnerable to Cold War pressures.

However, Austria's neutrality treaty reinforced Finland's interpretation of a rather independent neutrality vis-à-vis the FCMA. The examples of the Austrian, and also the Swiss and the Swedish models, quickly made the Soviet Union suspicious that Finland would not meet its commitments under the FCMA. As a result, the concept of neutrality was deleted from all bilateral Soviet-Finnish diplomatic documents in the latter half of the 1960s. After the Prague crisis in 1968, the Soviet disapproval of neutrality grew ever more explicit—not least because of the fear of a spillover effect of neutrality on the Eastern bloc countries (i.e., Hungary in 1956). The FCMA treaty was extended in 1973 and 1983, but Finland's neutrality was no longer mentioned in any official Soviet-Finnish documents or diplomatic connections until 1989.[33]

Also on the Asian continent neutrality became a concept that the USSR was confronted with. In Afghanistan, it had always played a role in the kingdom's foreign and security policies. Throughout the nineteenth century, Afghanistan was considered a buffer state separating the territories of the rival British and Russian empires. Since regaining full independence in 1919—in particular independence in making its own foreign policy—almost all rulers of Afghanistan have advocated some form of neutrality in their official policy statements.[34] Most significantly, in the immediate aftermath of the Soviet military invasion, British Foreign Secretary, Lord Carrington, proposed modeling Afghanistan's neutrality after Austria's. US President Jimmy Carter supported the idea and, in a letter to Yugoslav President Tito, offered "to help guarantee Afghanistan's true neutrality." Carter saw this policy as a means to end the Soviet military occupation because their forces would have to be withdrawn—which was also the reason why it was immediately rejected by the Soviet Union and the communist regime in Kabul, who considered it an attempt by the West to undermine Soviet influence.[35]

## NEUTRALITY AS A PROBLEM-SOLVING MODEL?

Under some circumstances, the concept of neutrality can serve as a model for Eastern and Central European states. The question is whether neutrality is a phased-out model of a former policy between military blocs or whether it is a sustainable conceptual option for the future. Indeed, there are indications for the latter. The idea of neutrality, embedded in the debates about the "Finland

Option" and the "Austrian model," made a comeback especially in connection with the escalation of the Ukrainian question in the spring of 2014. Johanna Rainio-Niemi stresses the importance of the Austrian model:

> According to the Austrian model of neutrality as proposed in Austria, a "self-chosen," sovereignly-determined decision on "nonalignment and even neutrality" would not prevent a country from adopting and developing (Western type of) the rule of law and strong democratic institutions. Further, it would not prevent a country from cultivating a free-market economy and cooperating on these terms with both West and East. Exactly this had been the case with Austria in 1955–1995, and the strategy brought economic prosperity, social equality, a stable political order and democracy. By adopting neutrality, Austria had grown into "a symbol of cooperation and not of conflict between the East and the West" and had been able to find a niche as an internationally acknowledged bridge-builder and mediator across the divides in world politics and between the East and the West in the Cold War era.[36]

Neutrality could be a sustainable conceptual option for the future also. Among others, both, the former security adviser to US President Carter, Zbigniew Brzezinski,[37] and former US secretary of state, Henry Kissinger, have suggested that the Finland option could offer a model for Ukraine.[38] This analogy draws upon Finland's long territorial border with Russia, its good relations with both East and West, and its military nonalignment.[39]

In a Brookings Marshall Paper, Michael O'Hanlon[40] argues that now is the time for Western nations to negotiate a new security architecture for neutral countries in Eastern Europe to stabilize the region and reduce the risks of war with Russia. He believes NATO expansion has gone far enough. The core concept of this new security architecture would be one of permanent neutrality.[41] He argues that, to reduce the conflict with Russia, NATO should not expand further and includes in his list Finland, Sweden, Ukraine, Moldova, Belarus, Georgia, Armenia, Azerbaijan, Cyprus, and Serbia, as well as (possibly) other Balkan states. Interestingly, he does not mention Austria and Switzerland, which are the only countries with a permanent neutral status based on international law. Moscow might accept the neutrality of these states only if it is based on international law.[42] Self-declared neutralities, like those of Turkmenistan, Serbia, or Moldova, however, are not recognized by international law and can easily be abandoned. O'Hanlon is right that, ideally, these nations would endorse and promote this concept themselves in the first place as a more practical way of ensuring their security than the current situation or any other plausible alternative. It would have to be substantiated with legal provisions, however.[43]

Also Stephen Walt[44] argues that the solution to this crisis is for Ukraine to be a permanent neutral buffer state that could sustain itself economically with the support of the EU and other international institutions.[45] Dimitri

Trenin observes that the Kremlin wants Ukraine to serve as a buffer between Russia and NATO, which suggests that Moscow might accept a neutral Ukraine, which, in turn, does not exclude future EU membership, but would exclude NATO membership.[46] He argues, furthermore, that arming Ukraine would only lead to escalation.[47] It would not enable Ukrainian forces to defeat the far stronger Russian military. On top of this, it must be recognized that Moscow will be willing to pay a higher price in this confrontation since Ukraine is strategically more important to Moscow than to Washington. Also, since the local balance of power favors Russia, Moscow would not capitulate but escalate the conflict. Ukraine should be armed with defensive weapons not before but only after it adopts the status of neutrality solemnly, to defend this status, its sovereignty, and its territorial integrity. This would be analogous to the case of Austria which, when it adopted "armed neutrality," its State Treaty also renounced the right to acquire offensive weapons for the very same reason, to prevent abuse of a purely defensive military policy for escalation in the case of conflict.

Graham Allison makes a more far-reaching suggestion of neutrality.[48] If all of the territory of Ukraine (minus Crimea) shall remain a sovereign, independent, nonbloc state, Ukraine would have to "agree with all the parties that it would remain neutral for the next quarter century" in its military and economic relations. Allison thus does not define neutrality in military terms only. In his conception, Ukraine would neither become a member of NATO nor of the EU, nor of equivalent Russian-led institutions. Allison includes domestic affairs in his proposal under which Ukraine would have to commit "to meet the highest EU standards for guaranteeing minority rights, including those of Russian speakers." For historical analogies, Allison refers to Belgium in the nineteenth century and to Austria and Finland after World War II. On the other hand, he also argues that a neutrality agreement should not be imposed on Ukraine; its government would have to be party to any resolution, but that neutrality is preferable to other feasible alternatives. He concludes that Ukraine's survival as an independent political entity cannot be achieved without Russian acceptance.

## NEUTRALITY FOR UKRAINE?

Since the 1990s, NATO and Ukraine developed several forms of military and political cooperation. Ukraine joined the PfP in 1994 and in 1997 a joint NATO-Ukraine Commission was established. Ukraine contributed to NATO peace operations as, for example, in the Balkans. Despite the ongoing conflict with Russia in the Donbas, and contrary to the above-mentioned proposals, the debate on NATO membership of Ukraine continues.[49] However, when it comes to Ukraine, there is no military solution in sight. As a first step toward the political and diplomatic solution of the Ukrainian conflict, the leaders of Germany, France, Ukraine, and Russia agreed in 2015, in the Belarusian capital of Minsk to a ceasefire. Further provisions in the package of measures for the implementation of the Minsk Agreements[50] are:

1. An immediate and comprehensive ceasefire in certain areas of the Donetsk and Luhansk regions of Ukraine.
2. Strict implementation as of February 15, 2015; withdrawal of all heavy weapons by both sides by equal distances in order to create a security zone, ensuring effective monitoring and verification of the ceasefire regime and the withdrawal of heavy weapons by the OSCE.
3. Implementation of constitutional reform in Ukraine with a new constitution entering into force by the end of 2015 providing for decentralization as a key element.

In the end, the deadlines of the agreement could not be met.

For Russia it might not be sufficient that NATO promises to not invite Ukraine into the alliance as a member. Those promises can be broken. Only under these conditions could the Minsk Agreement be fully implemented, namely the "withdrawal of all foreign armed formations, military equipment, as well as mercenaries from the territory of Ukraine under monitoring of the OSCE."[51] Engagement between the EU and the EEU could and should run in parallel to the political resolution of conflicts such as the Minsk process.[52]

On the one hand, in 2018, after years of conflict, Russia has consolidated its military and political control over its proxies in the Donetsk and Luhansk regions which stripped Ukraine of parts of its territory.[53] On the other hand, most Ukrainian combat-ready troops are concentrated in the Donbas.[54] Sanctions will do little to stop Russia's aggressive behavior. Therefore, the likelihood that the deployment of UN peacekeeping troops could stabilize the militarized conflict in Donbas (suggested by Russia in 2017) is not very high because Ukraine would not accept a ceasefire before a political solution is found.[55]

To use the Austrian analogy again, in addition to its neutrality law, the separate State Treaty guaranteed that Austria would not join a new union with Germany (Anschluss), as had happened in 1938. In the case of Ukraine, such a prohibition for the state (or parts of it) from joining Russia, together with a neutrality agreement, could guarantee its unity. At the same time Russia has to recognize that an independent Ukraine, including also independence from the Russian Federation, is the result of the political process of forming a Ukrainian state.[56] In addition, in the Austrian State Treaty, minority rights were regulated and certain capabilities of Austria's military were limited. In the case of Ukraine, a similar treaty could expressly detail the Russian minorities within the country's borders, as well as clarify the future status of Crimea with its different ethnic and language groups (Russians, Ukrainians, and Crimean Tartars), whereby the unity of Ukraine should be guaranteed. In fact, the basis for the respect for minority rights can already be found in the Minsk Agreement, which states that a new constitution should provide "for decentralization as a key element (including a reference to the specificities of certain areas in the Donetsk and Luhansk regions.)"[57] The Austrian analogy also offers the provision of 1969 for the German-speaking minority in South Tyrol in Northern Italy. Once successfully implemented, separatist tendencies vanished gradually since the autonomy solution improved the situation of the minority tremendously within the Italian territory.

In the immediate aftermath of World War II, Austria was divided into four zones and jointly occupied by the United States, Great Britain, and France in the West and South of the country, and in the East by the Soviet Union. Therefore, there was a danger of partition similar to the one in Germany. A similar fate might await Ukraine, since, under an alternative settlement of the current conflict, it too might end up partitioned, with the breakaway regions in the Donbas becoming legally recognized; which is a far-off scenario at the moment—since not even Russia as of 2019 recognizes the two "Republics"—but not an unthinkable outcome. The nongovernment-controlled areas in Ukraine cover about 20,000 km², the size of Slovenia, with 2.5 million inhabitants.

The principles of the EU's neighborhood policy, the promotion of democracy, the rule of law and market economy are essential for Ukraine. However, a solution without Russia will not be possible, as EU politicians and officials continue to indicate. Moreover, they also emphasize that becoming a NATO member is not on the Ukrainian agenda. Nevertheless, such statements will do little to stop Russia's aggressive behavior, which makes the Austrian model an even more interesting alternative for Ukraine.[58] Austria is a member of the EU but not of NATO and has developed splendidly in terms of its democratic institutions and its economy. Similarly, a democratic and economically developed Ukraine could, in the long run, be a valuable advantage for Kremlin. At the moment, European and American economic aid packages (similar to those received by other Euopean states through the post-World War II Marshall Plan) are now essential for Ukraine. As in Austria, these aid packages should also target the eastern part of the country. The combination of neutrality and the Marshall Plan was a definite success for Vienna precisely because the plan had political and economic dimensions. The primary aim was not to prevent a Soviet intervention in Western Europe, but the reconstruction of the target countries and their integration with the West. The plan was designed to portray the Western economic model as attractive and the communist model as unappealing. It announced the success of a market economy-based society with a parliamentary democracy. In his speech in June 1947, the US-Secretary of State George C. Marshall, explicitly included in his plan, besides Germany, Austria and other western European countries, the Soviet-occupied countries, and even the Soviet Union itself (although the Soviets rejected the plan and the money). Moreover, one could argue that Austria's neutrality law was the beginning of the détente policy between East and West.

There are other possible solutions to the Ukrainian crisis which, however, all come with major downsides. The "Cyprus model" would lead to a division of Donbas, especially if UN peacekeepers were to be deployed at the demarcation line as Moscow is proposing; this is unacceptable to Ukraine and also to the United States. Another scenario would be a model under which the Donbas is brought back gradually under Kyiv's full control with the assistance of international organizations; this would be a Kosovo-backwards model and this is unacceptable to Russia.[59] "However," as some security experts have argued "if the proposed UN peacekeeping mission will really be launched, it will de facto result in a close security cooperation between Russia and the West."[60]

## THE EXAMPLE OF GEORGIA

Georgia[61] joined the PfP in 1994 and sought closer relations with NATO. It participated in the NATO's International Security Assistance Force (ISAF) in Afghanistan. After the 2008 Russo-Georgian conflict, a NATO-Georgia Commission was established.[62] The conflict provoked a new debate, particularly within NATO, regarding the range and future of the military obligations of the alliance. Officially, NATO stands by its decision to continue its expansion into the east and south of Europe. If Georgia joined NATO and a further military conflict between Georgia and Russia should erupt (or be provoked), NATO could be dragged into a conflict with nuclear Russia, due to the commitment of assistance in Article 5 of its Treaty. If NATO did not act, its commitments would seem unreliable, both internally and externally, which could also have fatal consequences. Under these circumstances, what at first glance seems to be a strange solution becomes a viable political option: neutrality for Georgia and security guarantees from NATO and Russia.

Austria's status of neutrality was reached when all occupying forces agreed after World War II that they all would withdraw their troops from Austrian territory. The same model of neutrality could be an interesting solution for Georgia. Following the status of neutrality's logic, it would have to include the withdrawal of all Russian troops from Georgia, including from those rogue provinces which declared themselves independent (South Ossetia and Abkhazia). The price for the withdrawal—the waiving of Georgian membership in NATO—would not be so much a concession to Russia, but rather a requirement for a sovereign Georgia, free of foreign troops and with territorial integrity. This step would in no way exclude the possibility of close cooperation with NATO, such as the one practiced by Austria, Finland, and Sweden.

Just as in the argument above for minority rights in Ukraine, a treaty for Georgia, modeled after the Austrian State Treaty, could include wide-ranging guarantees for Georgia's ethnic minorities. The chances of a neutral solution being accepted are currently rather bleak as neither Georgia nor Abkhazia, South Ossetia, or Moscow seem enthusiastic about considering it. Certainly, though, it is an important political option for all involved parties to keep in mind.

## MOLDOVA AND BELARUS

Moldova, on the other hand, is neutral already. Its neutrality is self-declared through its constitution, which states in Article 11 that;"[t]he Republic of Moldova proclaims its permanent neutrality," and "[t]he Republic of Moldova shall not allow the dispersal of foreign military troops on its territory."[63] Hence, the country cannot join military alliances like NATO. However, self-declared neutrality has a weak status and its violation (from the Moldavian side) would not be an infringement of international law. In addition, it can be taken back by the country itself without the consent of external powers like members of the UN who would not have to be notified. This reduces the credibility of the status. As long as Russian troops are deployed in the separatist province of Transnistria, the condition that the dispersal of foreign troops is not allowed on Moldovan territory cannot be met. However, Moldova sees no contradiction with its status of neutrality and better relations with the EU and even NATO.[64] After all, it signed an Association Agreement with the EU and also the Deep and Comprehensive Free Trade Agreement and joined the PfP.[65]

For Belarus, neutrality remains an option. It will have to be based on international law as well, and also requires recognition by the member states of the UN with which it has diplomatic relations, including Russia. If Belarusian neutrality were accepted by Russia and by the West, it would have to be an armed neutrality that could serve as a buffer zone. It should not include offensive weapons that would weaken its neighbor's security. Again, it could be a similar provision as Article 13 of the Austrian State Treaty of 1955, holding that the neutral state should not possess, construct or experiment with any atomic weapons, or any other weaponizable technology, now or in the future, that could be used to construct weapons of mass destruction and defined as such by the appropriate organs of the UN. The prohibition also includes specially defined missiles.[66]

Meanwhile, neutrality may be the only viable long-term way for Belarus to improve relations with the East and West simultaneously. Other options, like tilting toward one military alliance or bloc, might provoke international and domestic opposition. Internal confrontation could be exploited by foreign powers—as the case of the conflict in Eastern Ukraine shows—and could even end in an open armed conflict.[67] Belarus' status in the Collective Security Treaty Organization (CSTO) would have to be negotiated and would probably be similar to Austria's PfP membership in relation to NATO, but without security obligations. On the other hand, membership in the Russian-lead Commonwealth of Independent States (CIS) should not be an obstacle, while also EU membership, in the long-term future, is not unthinkable. Membership in the Eurasian Economic Union and the CSTO are not necessarily incompatible with developing closer relations with the EU, as the example of Armenia shows.[68] To achieve such a "bridging function" realistically, Belarus' neutrality could be amended with a bilateral Russian-Belarus security treaty after the 1948 Soviet-Finnish bilateral security pact model which has already solved a security dilemma in that case; neutrality and the bilateral security pact were formally two separate issues—neutrality was desired primarily by Finland, and the security pact by the Soviet Union.[69] Combining the two gave security guarantees to both sides.

## THE FUTURE OF NEUTRALITY

How does a neutral state differ from a non-neutral one? In times of peace, it may not pre-emptively commit itself to support another state militarily in case of war. Such an obligation of mutual assistance was included in the North Atlantic Treaty in 1949 (Article 5) after heated discussions, because of the threat posed by the Soviet Union. That is why neutral states cannot join NATO without giving up their neutral foreign policy. This, however, is not necessarily to the detriment of neutral states. There are scenarios in which non-NATO states are by far better suited for peacekeeping operations than NATO members. A NATO mission in the Georgia conflict in 2008, for example, would probably have resulted in an escalation with unpredictable consequences. Similarly, non-NATO states are better suited for tasks in international, partisan conflicts where it is essential that peacekeepers are seen as truly impartial, like the crisis in Lebanon or a potential peacekeeping force in the Gaza strip. The EU humanitarian mission in Chad in 2007 is another case in point. The involved troops did not explicitly side with one of the conflict parties, a foreign power (i.e., France), the government, or the rebels, which would be the usual procedure in a war. Not a single neutral EU member state stood apart. Finland and Sweden provided troops; Ireland even supplied an operational commander, and Austria, the commander of special missions.[70]

In Ukraine, neither Russian nor Ukrainian or NATO troops should be part of a potential future peacekeeping mission. Instead, neutral European countries could be responsible for organizing UN-authorized operations. Besides, even India and China could be contributors, too.[71] It will have to be not just a military operation but a civil-military mission involving military, police, and civilian components.[72]

Neutrality is not a decision between right and wrong. Austria's neutrality is defined in negative terms as non-membership in a military alliance, non-participation in foreign wars, and the nondeployment of foreign troops on Austrian territory. However, neutral states can and should actively participate in crisis-management operations and conflict avoidance. This entails, among other things; preventive diplomacy, early detection and timely action, peaceful conflict settlement, but also the threat of sanctions, disarmament and military trust building. Membership in a military alliance, like NATO, is not necessary for the prevention of violent conflict. Crisis management and conflict prevention can also be conducted within the framework of the EU, NATO-Partnerships or the OSCE. Engaged neutrality[73] means active participation in international security policy in general and in international peace operations in particular.

## NOTES

1. Chapter 4 includes an excerpt of reprinted material from Heinz Gaertner, "Austrian Neutrality as a Model for the New Eastern Europe?" International Insititute for Peace (November 27, 2018), www.iipvienna.com/new-blog/2018/11/27/austrian-neutrality-as-a-model-for-the-new-eastern-europe.

2. Andrew Cottey, "Introduction: The European Neutral States," in *The European Neutrals and NATO: Nonalignment, Partnership, Membership?*, ed. Andrew Cottey (London: Palgrave Macmillan, 2018).

3. Instead, Austria's Chairmanship identified other priorities on how it would address the current threats and challenges in the OSCE area. First, since violent conflicts with numerous victims, displacements and destruction are becoming worse (or worsening), Austria intended to contribute to solve them. Second, radicalization and violent extremism was a major focus of the Chairmanship. Austria saw this as an imminent security risk in the entire OSCE area. A general goal was that Austria wanted to re-establish trust and confidence between states as well as citizens and facilitate confidence-building.

4. The most important features of any alliance are its mutual defense obligations. Neutrality and collective defense are negatively related. Neutrality means non-membership in an alliance based on political convention or on constitutional and international law. For a detailed discussion, see Heinz Gaertner, "Introduction: Engaged Neutrality," in *Engaged Neutrality: An Evolved Approach to the Cold War*, ed. Heinz Gaertner (Lanham, MD: Lexington, 2017).

5. See for example: Erich Reiter, "Neutralität als Österreichische Ideologie," in *Überlegungen zur Neutralität* (Wien: Internationales Institut Liberale Politik Wien, 2008); "Comments on the Objective of the Small States and Alliances Workshop," in *Small States and Alliances*, ed. Erich Reiter and Heinz Gaertner (Heidelberg: Physica Verlag, 2001).

6. Michael Gehler, "From an Offer for all Cases to a Model Case? Aspects of the Controversy about the Soviets' Germany, Austria, and Neutrality Policy, 1952–1955, in Current and Recent Research," in *Engaged Neutrality: An Evolved Approach to the Cold War*, ed. Heinz Gaertner (Lanham, MD: Lexington, 2017).

7. Terrence P. Hopmann, "From Helsinki I to Helsinki II: The Role of the Neutral and Nonaligned States in the OSCE," in *Engaged Neutrality: An Evolved Approach to the Cold War*, ed. Heinz Gaertner (Lanham, MD: Lexington Books, 2017).

8. On the various levels of engagement of current EU neutrals see chapter five, by Gunther Hauser, in this volume.

9. NATO, *Active Engagement, Modern Defence: Strategic Concept for the Defence and Security of the Members of the North Atlantic Treaty Organization* (Brussels: NATO Public Diplomacy Division, 2010).

10. Hakan Akbulut and Heinz Gaertner, eds., *NATO, Cooperative Security, and the Middle East—Status and Prospects: Experts Workshop, Vienna, 16 December 2016* (Vienna: Austrian Institute for International Affairs, 2016).

11. See also chapters 2 and 5 of this volume.

12. European Union, "Treaty on European Union," *Official Journal of the European Communities* 35, no. C191 (1992).

13. Ibid.

14. Velina Tchakarova, "Competing geopolitical approaches toward Eastern Europe," *Fokus*, no. 4 (2017).

15. Alexandra Vaileva, "Engage! Why the European Union Should Talk with the Eurasian Economic Union," *Perspective* (2017).

16. Scenario Group Ukraine 2027, "Foresight Ukraine, Four Scenarios for the Development of Ukraine," Friedrich Ebert Stiftung, 2017.

17. ATV, "Wie wichtig ist den Österreichern die Neutralität im 21. Jahrhundert?," Accessed August 29, 2019, www.ots.at/presseaussendung/OTS_20181025_OTS0144/atv-frage-der-woche-wie-wichtig-ist-den-oesterreichern-die-neutralitaet-im-21-jahrhundert.

18. StF: BGBl. Nr. 211/1955 (NR: GP VII RV 520 u. 598 AB 726 S. 80. BR: S. 109.) Availabel at www.ris.bka.gv.at/Dokumente/Erv/ERV_1955_211/ERV_1955_211.pdf

19. Konrad Adenauer, *Erinnerungen 1955–1959* (Stuttgart: Deutsche Verlags-Anstalt, 1966), 441–42.

20. Dwight D. Eisenhower, press conference 18 May 1955, quoted in ibid., 442.

21. Bild-Telegraf, November 7, 1956. National Security Council, Draft statement of US Policy toward Austria, 332. Paper Prepared by the NSC Planning Board, NSC 6020, Washington, December 9, 1960, approved by the President on January 18, 1961.

22. George F. Kennan, cited in Adenauer, *Erinnerungen 1955–1959*, 146–148.

23. George F. Kennan, *Im Schatten der Atombombe: Eine Analyse der Amerikanisch-sowjetischen Beziehungen von 1947 bis Heute* (Cologne: Kiepenheuer & Witsch, 1982), 21.

24. Andreas Hillgruber, *Europa in der Weltpolitik der Nachkriegszeit 1945–1963* (Vienna: Oldenbourg Verlag, 1979), 60–61.

25. National Security Council, "242. Memorandum of Discussion at the 354th Meeting of the National Security Council, February 6, 1958" (Washington: Office of the Historian, 1958).

26. See also: Heinz Gaertner, "A Neutral State's Perspective on the Ban—and a Compromise," *Bulletin of the Atomic Scientists*, August 15, 2017.

27. After the Polish foreign minister who expanded upon the idea and formally introduced it to the world. His plan was based on disengagement of the blocs and a nuclear-free status of the participating states.

28. United Kingdom of Great Britain and Northern Ireland, Union of Soviet Socialist Republics, United States of America, France and Austria, "State Treaty (with annexes and maps) for the re-establishment of an independent and democratic Austria. Signed at Vienna, on 15 May 1955," in *Treaty Series: Treaties and International Agreements Registered or Filed and Recorded with the Secretariat of the United Nations* (United Nations, 1955).

29. On the website of the Austrian Foreign Ministry one can find a modernized plan for a NWFZ in Europe. bmeia.gv.at/fileadmin/user_upload/Zentrale/Aussenpolitik/Abruestung/NWFZE_Finalversion.pdf; accessed August 13, 2019.

30. This was related to negative security guarantees provided to Ukraine by Russia, the US and the UK, and those guarantees have been violated by Russia and ignored by the US and UK.

31. Switzerland did not join any major international organizations for a long time. Only in 2002 it became a member of the United Nations.

32. Johanna Rainio-Niemi, "Cold War Neutrality in Europe. Lessons to be Learned?," in *Engaged Neutrality. An Evolved Approach to the Cold War*, ed. Heinz Gaertner (Lanham: Lexington, 2017).
33. Ibid. See also chapter 5, by Gunther Hauser, in this volume.
34. Nasir A. Andisha, "Neutrality in Afghanistan's Foreign Policy," *Special Report* No 360, United States Institute of Peace, March, 2015.
35. After the failure of Lord Carrington's initiative in the early 1980s, US expert Selig Harrison proposed the Finnish model. Ibid.
36. Rainio-Niemi, "Cold War Neutrality in Europe. Lessons to be Learned?"
37. Zbigniew Brzezinski, "Russia needs a 'Finland option' for Ukraine," *The Financial Times*, February 24, 2014.
38. Henry Kissinger, "How the Ukraine Crisis Ends," *The Washington Post*, March 6, 2014.
39. Rainio-Niemi, "Cold War Neutrality in Europe. Lessons to be Learned?"
40. Michael O'Hanlon, *Beyond NATO: A New Security Architecture for Eastern Europe* (Washington, DC: Brookings Institution Press, 2017).
41. Ibid.
42. Turkmenistan's neutrality was recognized by the UN-General Assembly in 1995. However, it is not binding according to international law.
43. Like in the case of Austria, all foreign troops would have to be withdrawn from the territory of these states while they would simultaneously receive guarantees for their territorial integrity. Austria's neutrality was not equidistant between blocs, but it adopted quickly Western values and became member of the EU as a neutral state.
44. Stephen M. Walt, "Why Arming Kiev Is a Really, Really Bad Idea," *Foreign Policy*, February 9, 2015. See also: Charles Kupchan, "Why giving Ukraine Lethal Weapons would be a Massive Mistake," *The Washington Post*, August 7, 2017.
45. Walt, "Why Arming Kiev Is a Really, Really Bad Idea." See also John J. Mearsheimer, "Getting Ukraine Wrong," *New York Times*, March 24, 2014.
46. Dmitri Trenin, "Avoiding US-Russia Military Escalation During the Hybrid War," *Carnegie Endowment for International Peace*, January, 2018.
47. Walt, "Why Arming Kiev Is a Really, Really Bad Idea"; Kupchan, "Why giving Ukraine Lethal Weapons would be a Massive Mistake."
48. Graham T. Allison, "Could the Ukraine Crisis Spark a World War?," *The National Interest* (2017).
49. Cottey, "NATO's Partnerships."
50. The Financial Times, "Full Text of the Minsk Agreement," February 12, 2015.
51. Ibid.
52. Scenario Group Ukraine 2027, "Foresight Ukraine, Four Scenarios for the Development of Ukraine."
53. Vladislav Inozemtsev, "Can Ukraine Change Russia?," in *The Russia File: Russia and the West in an Unordered World*, ed. Daniel S. Hamilton and Stefan Meister (Washington, DC: Center for Transatlantic Relations, The Johns Hopkins University, 2017).
54. Olexiy Haran and Petro Burkovskiy, "Ukraine's Foreign Policy and the Role of the West," in *The Russia File: Russia and the West in an Unordered World*, ed. Daniel S. Hamilton and Stefan Meister (Washington, DC: Center for Transatlantic Relations, Johns Hopkins University, 2017).
55. Trenin, "Avoiding US-Russia Military Escalation During the Hybrid War."
56. "To Understand Ukraine: A New Stage in the Russian State Project," *Russia in Global Affairs* (2017).
57. The Financial Times, "Full Text of the Minsk Agreement."
58. Heinz Gaertner, "Die Ukraine sollte sich die österreichische Neutralität ansehen," *Der Standard*, March 3, 2014.
59. Ibid.
60. András Rácz, "Wither or Return to the West? An Analysis of the New Russian Peacekeeping Proposal on Eastern Ukraine," *EU Frontier Policy Brief* No 23, Center for European Neighborhood Studies, 2018.

61. Heinz Gaertner, "Neutralität und Frieden," in *Handbuch Frieden*, ed. Bernhard Rinke and Hans J. Gießmann (Hamburg: Verlag für Sozialwissenschaften, 2011).
62. Cottey, "NATO's Partnerships."
63. The Republic of Moldova, "Constitution of 1994 with Amendments through 2006" (Constitute Project, 2006).
64. On Moldavian Neutrality see also David Noack, "Politics of Neutrality in the Post-Soviet Space: A Comparison of Concepts, Practices, and Outcomes of Neutrality in Moldova, Turkmenistan and Ukraine 1990–2015," in *Notions of Neutralities*, ed. Pascal Lottaz and Herbert Reginbogin (Lanham, MD: Lexington, 2018), 267–88.
65. Efforts in 2018 are concentrated on the implementation of the agreements on practical issues, signed between the sides and that has been endorsed in the Vienna Protocol of 2017. These are improving transport, communication, education and infrastructure.
66. The signatories of the treaty reserve the right to add to this Article prohibitions of any weapons which may be evolved as a result of scientific development.
67. Siarhei Bohdan and Gumer Isaev, "Elements of Neutrality in Belarusian Foreign Policy and National Security Policy," *Analytical Paper* No. 7, October 25, 2016.
68. Andrey Makarychev, "Incomplete Hegemonies, Hybrid Neighbours: Identity Games and Policy Tools in Eastern Partnership Countries," *CEPS Working Document*, February, 2018.
69. Rainio-Niemi, "Cold War Neutrality in Europe. Lessons to be Learned?"
70. See on these issues: Heinz Gaertner, ed., *Engaged Neutrality: An Evolved Approach to the Cold War* (Lanham, MD: Lexington, 2017), 129–50.
71. Rácz, "Wither or Return to the West? An Analysis of the New Russian Peacekeeping Proposal on Eastern Ukraine."
72. Richard Gowan, *Can the United Nations Unite Ukraine?* (Washington, DC: Hudson Institute, 2018).
73. Gaertner, "Introduction: Engaged Neutrality."

## SELECTED REFERENCES

Adenauer, Konrad. *Erinnerungen 1955–1959*. Stuttgart: Deutsche Verlags-Anstalt, 1966.
Akbulut, Hakan, and Heinz Gaertner, eds. *NATO, Cooperative Security, and the Middle East—Status and Prospects: Experts Workshop, Vienna, 16 December 2016*. Vienna: Austrian Institute for International Affairs, 2016.
Allison, Graham T. "Could the Ukraine Crisis Spark a World War?" *The National Interest* (May 2017).
Andisha, Nasir A. "Neutrality in Afghanistan's Foreign Policy." *Special Report* No 360, United States Institute of Peace, March, 2015.
ATV, "Wie wichtig ist den Österreichern die Neutralität im 21. Jahrhundert?" www.ots.at/presseaussendung/OTS_20181025_OTS0144/atv-frage-der-woche-wie-wichtig-ist-den-oesterreichern-die-neutralitaet-im-21-jahrhundert.
Bohdan, Siarhei, and Gumer Isaev. "Elements of Neutrality in Belarusian Foreign Policy and National Security Policy." *Analytical Paper* No 7, October 25, 2016.
Brzezinski, Zbigniew. "Russia needs a 'Finland option' for Ukraine." *The Financial Times*, February 24, 2014.
Cottey, Andrew. "Introduction: The European Neutral States." In *The European Neutrals and NATO: Nonalignment, Partnership, Membership?*, edited by Andrew Cottey, 1–20. London: Palgrave Macmillan, 2018.
———. "NATO's Partnerships." In *The European Neutrals and NATO: Nonalignment, Partnership, Membership?*, edited by Andrew Cottey, 45–72. London: Palgrave Macmillan, 2018.
European Union. "Treaty on European Union." *Official Journal of the European Communities* 35, no. C191 (1992).
Gaertner, Heinz. "Die Ukraine sollte sich die österreichische Neutralität ansehen." *Der Standard*, March 3, 2014.

———, ed. *Engaged Neutrality: An Evolved Approach to the Cold War*. Lanham, MD: Lexington, 2017.

———. "Introduction: Engaged Neutrality." In *Engaged Neutrality: An Evolved Approach to the Cold War*, edited by Heinz Gaertner, 1–14. Lanham, MD: Lexington, 2017.

———. "A Neutral State's Perspective on the Ban—and a Compromise." *Bulletin of the Atomic Scientists*, August 15, 2017.

———. "Neutralität und Frieden." In *Handbuch Frieden*, edited by Bernhard Rinke and Hans J. Gießmann. Hamburg: Verlag für Sozialwissenschaften, 2011.

Gehler, Michael. "From an Offer for all Cases to a Model Case? Aspects of the Controversy about the Soviets' Germany, Austria, and Neutrality Policy, 1952–1955, in Current and Recent Research." In *Engaged Neutrality: An Evolved Approach to the Cold War*, edited by Heinz Gaertner, 37–72. Lanham, MD: Lexington, 2017.

Gowan, Richard. *Can the United Nations Unite Ukraine?* Washington, DC: Hudson Institute, 2018.

Haran, Olexiy , and Petro Burkovskiy. "Ukraine's Foreign Policy and the Role of the West." In *The Russia File: Russia and the West in an Unordered World*, edited by Daniel S. Hamilton and Stefan Meister. Washington, DC: Center for Transatlantic Relations, The Johns Hopkins University, 2017.

Hillgruber, Andreas. *Europa in der Weltpolitik der Nachkriegszeit 1945–1963*. Vienna: Oldenbourg Verlag, 1979.

Hopmann, Terrence P. "From Helsinki I to Helsinki II: The Role of the Neutral and Nonaligned States in the OSCE." In *Engaged Neutrality: An Evolved Approach to the Cold War*, edited by Heinz Gaertner, 143–60. Lanham, MD: Lexington, 2017.

Inozemtsev, Vladislav. "Can Ukraine Change Russia?" In *The Russia File: Russia and the West in an Unordered World*, edited by Daniel S. Hamilton and Stefan Meister. Washington, DC: Center for Transatlantic Relations, The Johns Hopkins University, 2017.

Kennan, George F. *Im Schatten der Atombombe: Eine Analyse der Amerikanisch-sowjetischen Beziehungen von 1947 bis Heute*. Cologne: Kiepenheuer & Witsch, 1982.

Kissinger, Henry. "How the Ukraine Crisis Ends." *The Washington Post*, March 6, 2014.

Kupchan, Charles. "Why giving Ukraine Lethal Weapons would be a Massive Mistake." *The Washington Post*, August 7, 2017.

Makarychev, Andrey. "Incomplete Hegemonies, Hybrid Neighbours: Identity Games and Policy Tools in Eastern Partnership Countries." *CEPS Working Document*, February, 2018.

Mearsheimer, John J. "Getting Ukraine Wrong." *New York Times*, March 24, 2014.

National Security Council. "242. Memorandum of Discussion at the 354th Meeting of the National Security Council, February 6, 1958." Washington: Office of the Historian, 1958.

NATO. *Active Engagement, Modern Defence: Strategic Concept for the Defence and Security of the Members of the North Atlantic Treaty Organization*. Brussels: NATO Public Diplomacy Division, 2010.

Noack, David. "Politics of Neutrality in the Post-Soviet Space: A Comparison of Concepts, Practices, and Outcomes of Neutrality in Moldova, Turkmenistan and Ukraine 1990–2015." In *Notions of Neutralities*, edited by Pascal Lottaz and Herbert Reginbogin, 267–88. Lanham, MD: Lexington, 2018.

O'Hanlon, Michael. *Beyond NATO: A New Security Architecture for Eastern Europe*. Washington, DC: Brookings Institution Press, 2017.

Rácz, András. "Wither or Return to the West? An Analysis of the New Russian Peacekeeping Proposal on Eastern Ukraine." *EU Frontier Policy Brief* No. 23, Center for European Neighborhood Studies, 2018.

Rainio-Niemi, Johanna. "Cold War Neutrality in Europe. Lessons to be Learned?" In *Engaged Neutrality. An Evolved Approach to the Cold War*, edited by Heinz Gaertner, 15–36. Lanham, MD: Lexington, 2017.

Reiter, Erich. "Comments on the Objective of the Small States and Alliances Workshop." In *Small States and Alliances*, edited by Erich Reiter and Heinz Gaertner, 11–14. Heidelberg: Physica Verlag, 2001.

———. "Neutralität als Österreichische Ideologie." In *Überlegungen zur Neutralität*, 12–17. Wien: Internationales Institut Liberale Politik Wien, 2008.

Scenario Group Ukraine 2027. "Foresight Ukraine, Four Scenarios for the Development of Ukraine." Friedrich Ebert Stiftung, 2017.
Tchakarova, Velina. "Competing Geopolitical Approaches toward Eastern Europe." *Fokus*, no. 4 (2017).
*The Financial Times*. "Full Text of the Minsk Agreement." February 12, 2015.
The Republic of Moldova. "Constitution of 1994 with Amendments through 2006." Constitute Project, 2006.
Trenin, Dmitri. "Avoiding US-Russia Military Escalation During the Hybrid War." *Carnegie Endowment for International Peace*, January, 2018.
———. "To Understand Ukraine: A New Stage in the Russian State Project." *Russia in Global Affairs* (December 27 2017).
Union of Soviet Socialist Republics, United Kingdom of Great Britain and Northern Ireland, United States of America, France and Austria. "State Treaty (with annexes and maps) for the re-establishment of an independent and democratic Austria. Signed at Vienna, on 15 May 1955." In *Treaty Series: Treaties and International Agreements Registered or Filed and Recorded with the Secretariat of the United Nations*, 223–379: United Nations, 1955.
Vaileva, Alexandra. "Engage! Why the European Union Should Talk with the Eurasian Economic Union." *Perspective* (September 2017).
Walt, Stephen M. "Why Arming Kiev Is a Really, Really Bad Idea." *Foregin Policy*, February 9, 2015.

*Chapter Five*

# Neutral and Nonaligned States in the European Union

Gunther Hauser

Neutrality is a concept for avoiding involvement in wars of other states. This status was often proclaimed in history,[1] but its recognition was usually initiated not by the country in question but by a group of countries at war. Permanent Neutrality, as the introduction of this book explains, is a particular form of general neutrality. It was enshrined in international law through the Paris Agreement of November 20, 1815,[2] in which the major European powers recognized Switzerland's permanent[3] neutrality and guaranteed the inviolability of its territory.[4] Until the nineteenth century, two types of neutrality have been recognized: temporary (occasional) neutrality during wartime—from the beginning to the end of an armed conflict—and permanent neutrality. The permanently neutral state had to credibly arrange its peacetime trade and foreign policy to avoid potential entanglements in future conflicts. On October 18, 1907, the essential rights and duties of neutral states in wartime were codified for the first time in the Fifth and Thirteenth Hague Conventions. Alongside the rights of self-determination and nonparticipation in wars, another essential feature of the conventions for neutral states was that "[t]he territory of neutral powers is inviolable."[5] A neutral state is not allowed to start any war or to join a military coalition. Further obligations are impartiality toward belligerents, and agreements not to provide mercenaries for belligerents. The foreign policy of permanently neutral states must be arranged in such a way as to minimize the possibility of becoming entangled in any war.[6]

At the beginning of the Cold War, some European states decided to adopt permanent neutrality due to their geopolitical location between East and West. Not necessarily out of their free will, like Finland, that adopted neutrality policy as a way of "keeping distance to Soviet domination."[7] Sweden adopted a "policy of nonalignment in peacetime" aimed at "reducing tension in global politics and economics."[8] Furthermore, Sweden upheld and defended neutrality, "given a general state of belligerency."[9] The neutral status of Austria, also, was a condition for the withdrawal of post-war Soviet and allied occupation forces. Ireland had proclaimed its military neutrality while struggling for independence from Britain in 1921. Except Sweden, which joined the UN in 1946, all other neutrals became members of the UN in 1955. The opinion in these states was that UN membership would cause no damage to their neutrality. Neutral Sweden shared this point of view as it had joined already in 1946. Only the Swiss government thought their neutrality to contradict the collective security system of the UN. It joined only half a century later when, on September 10, 2002, Switzerland became the 190th member of the UN. For Austria, Finland, Ireland, Sweden, and Switzerland, neutrality also included an active, positive foreign policy in pursuit of international peace and justice to strengthen the rules of international law and contribute to European stability. The ingredients of such a policy have been the quest for disarmament, peacekeeping, championing the rights of developing nations, and the promotion of human rights within the framework of the United Nations and the CSCE/OSCE processes.[10] During the 1990s, European neutrals started to commit to the growing system of security and politico-military cooperation within the European Union (EU) and to support the tasks of NATO's Partnership for Peace (PfP), including humanitarian and rescue tasks, peacekeeping tasks, and tasks of combat forces in crisis management, including peace enforcement. Although the core principle of European Neutrals is still to avoid involvement in wars of other states, they are nowadays committed to the growing system of security and military cooperation within the NATO-PfP. The neutrality of EU member states (in the traditional sense as defined by the Hague Conventions) is becoming less and less relevant in strengthening integrated European security structures.[11] This chapter aims at analyzing and discussing the relevance of today's neutral and nonaligned policies of five EU member states (Austria, Ireland, Finland, Sweden, and Malta) in the context of the changing security environment.

## AUSTRIA

In Austria, neutrality has been ambiguous and ill-defined in the international context after the end of the Cold War. The best way to understand that is to compare it with military alliances that involve an obligation to collective defense.[12] Although being an EU member since 1995, Austria's national security policy continued along the lines of "pragmatic neutrality" by mainly participating in EU and NATO PfP tasks with a focus on interoperability.

Thus, pragmatic neutrality, which means that the Austrians today understand their neutrality as a Foreign Policy that mandates military noninvolvement in the case of third-party wars, but that allows "the armed forces of neutral states to work in cooperation with military alliances, mostly under the auspices of UN, EU, and NATO PfP for purposes such as peacekeeping and even peace enforcement."[13]

The history of this understanding reaches back to the post–World War II settlements of Europe. To regain its sovereignty after the war, Austria chose the option to become permanently neutral in 1955. Due to her geopolitical situation between East and West and because of the beginning of the Cold War, the Soviet Union had an interest in a friendly Austria that would not join the Western camp. In the so-called "Moscow Memorandum" of April 15, 1955, the Austrian delegation pledged that their country would adopt a neutral foreign policy similar to that of Switzerland. Austrian permanent neutrality was a product and a result of Soviet peaceful coexistence policy creating a neutral Alpine wedge (together with Switzerland) cutting the NATO Northern flank from the Southern flank.[14] Despite the foreign-induced character of the neutral posture, Austria portrayed its permanent neutrality as voluntary in order "to avoid the impression of a Soviet octroi."[15] Austria's subsequent balancing act in Europe was best characterized by Wolfgang Zecha, who said:

> Although Austria promised in the Moscow Memorandum to pursue a neutrality policy like Switzerland, the Austrian policy left this line by becoming a member of the UN in 1955. So the Austrian security policy started to walk a tightrope between neutrality and international solidarity because of her UN membership and membership in other organizations like EU or NATO Partnership for Peace (PfP) later on.[16]

When the Austrian National Assembly passed the Federal Constitutional Law on Austria's neutrality on October 26, 1955, it was taken for granted that its neutrality would be modeled after that of Switzerland. But very soon it deferred from that template on a central point: as early as December 1955, Austria joined the UN[17] together with fifteen other states (Albania, Bulgaria, Cambodia, Finland, Hungary, Ireland, Italy, Jordan, Lao PDR, Libya, Nepal, Portugal, Romania, Spain, and Sri Lanka). In 1995, Austria also joined the EU and became a participating state in the NATO-PfP. Ever since, Austrian security and its political situation have been directly linked with developments in the EU and NATO. This bond has been strengthened by a 1998 special provision that added to the Federal Constitution (Article 23f, Article 23j since 2010) that the 1955 Neutrality Act did not restrict Austrian participation in the intergovernmental Common and Foreign Security Policy (CFSP) of the EU. However, the relationship goes both ways as decisions to reach a common defense of the EU also require the resolution of the Austrian parliament; effectively granting neutral Vienna (like all other EU members) veto power over CFSP decisions.

The CFSP and CSDP are, in principle, purely EU affairs. However, Austria also collaborates with the much larger European security provider NATO. It signed the "PfP Framework Document" in February 1995 as the twenty-fifth participating state using the NATO Planning and Review Process (PARP) and the Political-Military Framework (PMF) for NATO-led PfP operations as a planning mechanism. This contributed to the Headline Goal of the European Security and Defense Policy within the framework of the *Tailored Cooperation Program*.[18] According to the Austrian PfP introductory document of May 1995, Austria's cooperation with NATO and the PfP participants aim, in particular, at cooperation regarding peacekeeping missions, humanitarian and disaster relief as well as search and rescue operations.[19]

For the past two decades, Austrian collaboration with NATO has occurred on several structural levels. Within the PfP, Austria runs the Centre for Operations Preparation, a Partnership Training and Education Centre. It also heads the Balkans Regional Working Group in the framework of the PfP Consortium of Defense Academies and Security Studies Institutes—a voluntary association funded by Austria, Germany, Switzerland, and the United States. Working in the spirit of the PfP, Austria "is actively participating in two of the three core tasks of NATO defined in its 2010 Strategic Concept: Crisis Management and Cooperative Security (the core task of Collective Defense being for members only)."[20] The initial intention of joining PfP and the Euro-Atlantic-Partnership Council (EAPC) was to enable Austria's participation in the transatlantic security dialogue. It provided access to the standards of education and training to back-up the Austrian Armed Forces' interoperability and contribution to NATO-led operations open to partners having a security policy interest. Austria has also contributed to Trust Fund projects in other PfP countries.[21] Along with individual allies and partners, it has made monetary contributions to support, for example, the destruction of mines and munitions in Albania, Kazakhstan, Montenegro, Serbia, and Ukraine.[22] Since 2012, Austria has participated in cyber exercises (such as Locked Shields) at the NATO Cooperative Cyber Defense Centre of Excellence in Estonia within the framework of the NATO-PfP.[23]

Despite the high-level collaboration with NATO, neutrality still enjoys much popularity among the Austrian people. According to various polls, more than two-thirds of Austrians still favor the policy. At the same time, a majority of the Austrian population also agrees to the deep integration of their Armed Forces into the Euro-Atlantic security process and comprehensive security coordination within Central Europe. Thus, in 2010, Austria launched the Central European Defense Cooperation (CEDC)—together with the Czech Republic, Hungary, Slovakia, Croatia, and Slovenia,[24] which the

Ministry of Defense describes as "a security policy coordination forum."[25] The CEDC fosters "regional military cooperation in selected areas through shared military projects."[26] The shared field of interest focuses on the sustained stabilization of the Western Balkans—cooperation by which security challenges are collectively met. In cross-border disaster relief, for example, the CEDC enables a regional military partnership in the sense of pooling and sharing, which promotes armed forces modernization through shared experience and synergies. In this area, Croatia is the framework nation for conducting training activities for Special Forces; exercises conducted in the past by the Croatian and Austrian Special Operation Forces. Hungary is the framework nation for conducting training activities for Forward-Air-Controllers, Air Traffic Controllers and in the field of Counter-Improvised Explosive Devices (IEDs).[27]

In 2012 Austria took the leading role in the EU Pooling and Sharing—Mountain Training Initiative, in order to standardize military mountain training and preparedness at the EU level enhanced by other European partners using this Austro-German initiative with nine permanent members (Austria, Belgium, Bulgaria, Croatia, Germany, the Netherlands, Poland, Slovenia, and Sweden). The program is closely coordinated with the NATO Centre of Excellence (COE) for Mountain Warfare in Slovenia to exchange experience within the lessons-learned process[28] to avoid duplication.[29] Furthermore, Austrian soldiers are part of EU Battlegroups since early 2011. The country also declared its readiness in 2017 to support EU Permanent Structured Cooperation (PESCO). It participates in five PESCO projects as follows: Deployable Military Disaster Relief Capability Package; European Union Training Mission Competence Centre (EUTMCC); Military Mobility; Cyber Threats; Incident Response Information Sharing Platform; and the CBRN[30] Surveillance as a Service (CBRN SaaS). Austria declared in 2018 her readiness to take the lead in this project to establish a persistent and distributed manned-unmanned sensor network consisting of Unmanned Aerial System (UAS) and Unmanned Ground Systems (UGS). It aims to be interoperable with legacy systems by providing a Recognized CBRN Picture to augment existing Common Operational Pictures used for EU missions and operations.[31]

At the same time, however, the position of the Austrian Government remains that this comprehensive coordination and collaboration within the EU security, crisis management, and military capability processes remain compatible with Austrian neutrality. Until today the argument remains that "the capability of the Austrian Armed Forces must be maintained and organized to make a solidarity-based contribution within a potentially developing common European defence."[32] The goal of this policy is not to ally Austria, but to strengthen its defensive capabilities inside the various European security institutions.

## IRELAND

While Austria promulgated neutrality as a constitutional act of Parliament, Irish neutrality is a matter of government policy rather than a rigid legal principle. Its origins lie in its struggle during the 1920s and 1930s for independence from Great Britain. Since its separation, neutrality is the officially accepted public policy by Ireland in military matters. The consensus has been in Ireland that neutrality is a policy of noninvolvement in military alliances, but allows for peacekeeping and peace enforcement where appropriate. Ireland became the first neutral member of the European Communities in 1973, which was the result of the ongoing CSCE (Conference on Security and Cooperation in Europe) process in the 1970s. It was an equally important part of the Soviet strategy for peaceful coexistence such as the German "Ostpolitik" aimed at peaceful relations with the Eastern bloc countries by recognizing the German–German border. The Soviets, therefore, approved that Ireland joins the European Communities (EC) even though they had opposed the initiative by Austrian politicians when they had proposed that their country should join the ongoing European integration process in the 1950s. The Soviet government argued that Austria would violate its neutrality by joining an economic alliance comprised of NATO member states even though the two most important economic partners of Austria were EC founding members—West Germany and Italy.[33]

For Ireland, the concept of neutrality has been fostered through the creation of a separate national identity and the assertion of statehood, primarily as a means of distinguishing itself from the great power next doors. A military alliance with the UK, it was argued, "is a threat to the sovereignty of the nation."[34] Thus, Irish society has embraced the concept of "military neutrality," which emphasizes the Irish insistence on avoiding alliance commitments. Since this stance depends on the unilateral Irish will to remain neutral and not international treaty agreements, Irish neutrality is much closer to the Finnish–Swedish models of neutrality than the Austro–Swiss models that make binding constitutional and treaty-based commitments to neutrality under international law.[35]

Militarily, Irish army personnel has successfully participated in UN missions, since 1959, in places such as Afghanistan, Angola, Cambodia, East Timor, El Salvador, Eritrea, Haiti, Iraq, Somalia, South Africa, West New Guinea, and Yugoslavia. Although in 1999 Ireland also joined NATO-PfP,[36] under its Defense Acts, the country will only participate in missions with a UN mandate.

Following the defeat of the first referendum proposal relating to the EU Treaty of Nice, the EU confirmed Ireland's neutrality in two declarations made in Seville in June 2002—signed by the Irish government and by the leaders of all fifteen member states at the time. The first declaration states that Ireland will uphold the principles of the UN Charter at every stage of its involvement in the EU CFSP while also reaffirming its commitment to the traditional status of military neutrality. The second declaration confirms that Ireland is under no obligation to participate in common defense policy. It also underscores that the development of the EU's capacity to conduct humanitarian and crisis management tasks do not involve the establishment of a European army. The purpose of the Seville Declarations

> Is to make clear, beyond any reasonable doubt, that the Treaty of Nice poses no threat to Ireland's traditional policy of military neutrality. The Declarations confirm that this understanding is shared by all 15 EU member states. This is in full conformity with the Government's position on ratification of the Treaty of Nice.[37]

This agreement was updated within the Lisbon Treaty negotiations during the late 2000s. Additionally, on June 19, 2009, EU leaders agreed on "guarantees" requested by the Irish government, which also consist of a declaration by Ireland relating to defense issues.[38] Thus, "Ireland is afforded guarantees under the Lisbon Treaty which maintain the country's traditional policy of military neutrality remains unchanged and unaffected by the ratification of the Treaty."[39] Neutrality, therefore, remains a powerful symbol highlighting Ireland's independence and sovereignty. It has remained flexible, stretching to accommodate the growing demands of Irish foreign policy. For Ireland, the concept of neutrality continues to be a potent symbol of its sovereignty and independence, which is based on geographical and historical circumstances.[40]

## FINLAND

In contrast to Ireland's relatively strong commitment to maintaining its neutrality policy—even seeking EU guarantees thereof—Finland changed its security policy status in 1995 to that of "nonalignment." Neutrality seized to be a Finnish goal that year when it started to participate "fully in the EU, security policy included."[41] The reasons for this change of heart are just as historical as they are for other cases.

Finland, independent only since 1917, did not have a long tradition of neutrality. During the interwar period (1918–1939), it declared itself neutral, but its foreign policy was not neutral enough to satisfy the security concerns of the Soviet Union. Finland was attacked by the Soviets in 1939, drawing the country directly into World War II. During the so-called "Winter War," Finland struggled to survive as an independent nation-state. After the fighting had ceased, the imposed treaties of Friendship, Cooperation, and Mutual Assistance of 1947 and 1948 mandated the existence of a Soviet military base on Finnish territory and created a defensive alliance between Helsinki and Moscow. It was, therefore, not easy for Finland to declare its neutrality during the Cold War, which officially, it still maintained. Its goal was to avoid involvement in any dispute with a major power for which the decision in early 1948 not to participate in the much-needed European Recovery Program (Marshall Plan) is an example. That was mainly due to Soviet contentions that the program was an effort on the part of the United States to divide Europe into two camps.[42] Under these circumstances, the Finish Government considered a policy of neutrality as the best alternative to prevent a new conflict with the Soviet Union. However, despite these "pro-soviet" steps, ideologically and economically, Finland deeply integrated into the Western capitalist camp.

Finland's Military Doctrine developed around a strategy of area defense—which denotes a manner of combat that utilizes a vast geographical area to protect especially essential locations. A particular element in this strategy and a pillar of Finland's "active neutrality policy" became the concept of a Nordic Nuclear-Weapons-Free Zone, consisting of Denmark, Finland, Iceland, Norway, and Sweden. President Urho K. Kekkonen first introduced the idea in May 1963 against the background of a Europe increasingly armed with nuclear weapons.[43] The zone could not be realized at the time when it was initially proposed because Denmark and Norway were members of NATO already and both considered the deployment of nuclear weapons on their territories in times of crisis.

Finland's efforts as a broker of disarmament and détente still came to fruition with the signing of the Final Act of the CSCE in Helsinki in 1975. This marked the climax of Finland's policy of "active neutrality," and, according to historian Martti Häikiö, it was also "proof that both superpowers recognized Finland's neutrality policy."[44]

In 1995, Finland joined the European Union together with Austria and Sweden. This was part of the international post-Cold War transformation.[45] EU membership, it is argued, gives Finland new opportunities for influencing change and stability in its security environment, while its military security remains its responsibility.[46] Finland has joined the EU as a militarily non-aligned country that wishes to play an active and constructive role in creating and implementing the CFSP. Its current military policy calls for increased cooperation with NATO and EU-led operations while, nevertheless, remaining outside formal alliances.

The term "neutrality" began to disappear from Finnish terminology in 1992–1993 when the country submitted its application to join the EU. After becoming a member, Finland felt that it could not be genuinely neutral anymore, because it would support the side of the EU, according to Finnish security policy expert Teija Tiilikainen.[47] Foreign policymakers replaced the concept of neutrality with that of "military nonalignment and an independent defense."⁴⁸ Although this marks a step away from classic neutrality, the Fins did not wholly abandon the concept (yet). Finland and Sweden both qualify for NATO membership, "but have chosen to remain outside of the Alliance for domestic political reasons—a position that has not resulted in free riding by member states."⁴⁹ Nordic leaders, however, not only "want to see a higher US and NATO presence in the Arctic High North and the Baltic Sea, but closer security-building and defense-strengthening interactions and collaboration with their militaries."⁵⁰ Especially the 2014 events around Russia's annexation of Crimea have fueled such feelings. All Nordic governments support US and EU trade sanctions and similar measures against Russia.

> Nordic governments favor a twin-track strategic approach to dealing with an expansionist Russia. On the one hand, this comprises defense-deepening. Secondly, Nordic leaders support maintaining a constructive, open dialogue with Moscow to enhance transparency and reduce the risk of a build-up of security and military tensions in the region.⁵¹

As a direct reaction to the annexation of Crimea, Finland started to increase interoperability with NATO which, in turn, provoked a frosty reaction by Russia's then-defense chief, General Nikolai Makarov. He held that it would be dangerous for Finland to join NATO and put the well-developed trade and political relations between the two countries at risk: "Were Finland to join NATO, then Finland, would constitute a threat to Russia, to which Russia would be forced to respond."⁵² In Finland, these remarks revived Cold War-era memories of Moscow meddling in Finland's sovereign affairs. Moscow's hostility toward the cooperation of EU member states that have been neutral but are now tilting toward joining NATO is not reserved to Finland only but extends to Sweden too. Its fear that both could join NATO is connected to the growing importance of the Baltic Sea for Russian oil and gas shipments and trade with Europe.

Moreover, Russia is nervous about the idea of having offensive missiles—or any part of NATO's ballistic missile defense system—located in neighboring Finland.⁵³ From a Swedish perspective, therefore,

> cooperation with Finland is a fundamental platform on our defense strategy. We have taken necessary steps, as two military nonaligned countries, to give our armed forces the tools to cooperate in case of crisis or war. The bilateral statement of intent with the United States is an important expression of common interest and mutual commitment. We have joined the British-led Joint Expeditionary Force and will continue to work closely with the UK.⁵⁴

In May 2018, Finland signed a trilateral statement of intent on defense cooperation with Sweden and the US aimed at strengthening transatlantic defense ties.⁵⁵

## SWEDEN

As for the case of Ireland, Swedish neutrality was not enshrined in any legal or formal context, but a policy established by unilateral declaration. It merely remains a principle of foreign policy that can be changed as necessary since it was neither guaranteed nor imposed by other states or constitutionally prescribed. In the wake of the ending Cold War, Conservative Prime Minister Carl Bildt, in 1992, gave a broader interpretation to the concept of neutrality that allowed Sweden to join NATO's PfP program. Furthermore, Sweden enacted a historical foreign policy change on February 11, 2002, with a proposal to drop the term *neutrality* altogether from its security policy doctrine. Sweden is to remain militarily nonaligned but would no longer adhere to strict neutrality.[56] The proposed new doctrine was drafted jointly by the governing Social Democrats, as well as the conservative Moderate Party, the Christian Democrats, and the People's Party. The Green Party and the Left Party were opposed to the change, which they saw as a step toward NATO membership.[57] The old doctrine dating back to 1992 stated that Sweden's militarily nonalignment was aimed at neutrality in wars that take place in nearby areas. However, in the view of the minister of foreign affairs, Anna Lindh, it would have been unrealistic to think that Sweden had remained neutral in a situation in which another EU member—or one of Sweden's neighbors—was attacked.[58]

In 2008, Sweden's coalition government, headed by the pro-NATO moderates and liberals, discussed the possibility of a "mutual jump" approach to NATO membership with Finland. Allan Widman, the Liberal's spokesman on defense, said: "There are few signs that Sweden is considering full membership in NATO" but that "as a very small and militarily weak country, we are in no condition to face serious challenges to our security independently. Excluding ourselves means both insecurity and little opportunity for influence."[59] In 2013, Sweden's military had "issued a wake-up call to government, warning that recent budget cuts and lack of investment have left the country unable to defend itself against a major attack for more than a week."[60] The "one-week" scenario represented the Armed Forces Command's (AFC) strategic assessment of Sweden's defense capability, Armed Forces commander General Sverker Göransson said:

> If Sweden is attacked on a broad military scale, we can possibly defend ourselves for one week. After that, we would need support from other countries. We do have the capacity to defend Sweden for a longer period if attacks have a limited objective, but for broader attacks from several different directions, we are talking about one week on our own.[61]

Defense Minister Karin Enström conceded that Sweden could not receive military assistance, including adequate airbase and naval station structures, but said measures "are being taken, independently by Sweden and together with its Nordic neighbors and cooperation partner NATO, to strengthen the country's capacity to provide and receive military support."[62] Sweden participated more actively than many NATO members during the campaign "Unified Protector in Libya," sending 122 personnel and 8 Gripen aircraft, at a monthly cost of 22 million US.[63]

Following Russia's 2014 invasion of Ukrainian territory, Sweden began to reassess its national security plans like many other nations in Europe. The Government of Sweden created a new web of bilateral military agreements with several countries—including a 2016 agreement with the US—while strengthening ties with its Nordic neighbors.[64] The impact of the agreement with the US has been that the two countries conduct more military exercises together, share information, and conduct strategic dialogues about the security situation in the northern part of Europe.[65]

However, despite all these steps toward military integration with NATO states, Sweden, as of 2019, is not seeking full NATO membership. It instead emphasizes the continuation of its cooperation based security approach outside the alliance, as the Defense Minister Peter Hultqvist said: "We have the strategy to upgrade the military capability at the national level and deepening our cooperation with other countries with bilateral agreements, multilateral agreements, and be very active in the NATO partnership and advance the procurement programme."[66] Sweden also builds units together with Finland—for example, Swedish–Finnish Naval Task Force. Both countries cooperate around amphibious capabilities, "and we have troops from Sweden in Finland exercising a scenario like defense of Finland, and we have Finish units in Sweden exercising defense of Sweden."[67] Furthermore, according to Hultqvist, "[o]n the military side, the Swedish government, has increased national defense spending about 25 percent to 2020, activated conscription and refocused efforts on national defense including civilian defense. . . . Furthermore, the transatlantic link is necessary for the stability in our part of Europe and must remain strong."[68] For this purpose, the Swedish government "has stationed permanent troops on the strategic island of Gotland located in the Baltic Sea, implemented NATO's Host Nation Support agreement, agreed to develop active cyber capabilities, intensified cooperation with our Baltic Sea partners and is acquiring next-generation submarines and fighter aircraft."[69] This Host Nation Support Agreement also prepares Sweden for receiving assistance from alliance troops in case of emergencies. A similar agreement is already in place for Finland. In the Swedish parliament, some 291 MPs backed the agreement against only 29 votes. Now it is easier to base NATO troops on Swedish territory, which Hultqvist commented by emphasizing that "cooperation with NATO is a priority, especially on information sharing and military exercises."[70] Sweden like Finland now defines its security status as nonaligned.

## MALTA

In contrast to Sweden, Malta's "neutrality is an understandably strategic position, coming from a country with a long history of colonial domination seeking to ensure the maintenance of independent sovereignty."[71] The islands of Malta are strategically located at the crossroads of the Mediterranean region, North Africa, and the Near East. John Paul Grech, Permanent Secretary to the Ministry of Foreign Affairs, stated in 2011 that "geographically we are Mediterranean, but everything about our political identity is European."[72] Especially during the 1970s and 1980s, Malta tried to make the most out of its geographic situation, leading its politicians to discuss and adopt the concept of neutrality for their foreign policy. The neutrality clause in the Constitution was drafted in 1987 and makes specific reference to nonalignment, which reads as follows: "Malta is a neutral state actively pursuing peace, security and social progress among all nations by adhering to a policy of nonalignment and refusing to participate in any military alliance."[73]

> Neutrality is our best security shield because if we are nobody's enemy, nobody will be against us. If NATO and Russia feel that their security is threatened, it transpires that a veritable security threat exists. If we join NATO and Russia, Malta will be subject to the same threat. Just because we are neutral we do not feel the fear that NATO and Russia feel.[74]

Maltese neutrality does not permit the country to be used as a military airbase, and it prevents Malta from falling into the vice of forming part of a military alliance. Malta joined the European Union on May 1, 2004, but decided not to participate in EU security operations. The island has been positioning itself "as a Mediterranean Bridge" since the 1970s when Malta blocked the CSCE Helsinki Act from passing until a chapter on Mediterranean security was incorporated. President Guido de Marco asserted in 2009, "how right was Malta to insist in the Helsinki summit of 1975 that no peace was possible in Europe unless there was peace in the Mediterranean."[75] In 2017, Foreign Minister Carmelo Abela emphasized again that "Malta wishes to be considered by all stakeholders in the Israel-Palestinian conflict as a bridgebuilder . . . this is our vocation."[76] Thus, Malta serves as Rapporteur of the UN Committee on the Exercise of the Inalienable Rights of the Palestinian People, but held that it was "constitutionally and structurally unable to contribute to international military combat operations."[77] Therefore, Malta collaborates in other spheres, "ranging from logistics to the sharing of intelligence, participation in counter-terrorism, and anti-human trafficking operations."[78]

Malta joined NATO's Partnership for Peace in 1995 under a Nationalist Party administration, then pulled out of the PfP after Labour won in the 1996 parliamentary election "amid concerns that it would violate the nation's constitutional neutrality."[79] In 2008, Nationalist Prime Minister Lawrence Gonzi reactivated the partnership with NATO, "and today there is consensus between the parties that cooperation can take place in line with Malta's neutral position."[80] During the 2011 Libya crisis, NATO's top military commander, US Admiral James Stavridis, "commended Malta for providing superb help to NATO with emergency landings and airspace."[81]

## CONCLUSION

Neutrality is defined by international law in the Hague conventions, but since 1945 its political meaning changed. In practice, neutrality "had a great deal to do with the size and consolidation of the state of the territory (territoriality), the geographical situation (geopolitics), the expansion of economic and trade relations (economy), but also with the changeability of politics (opportunism)."[82] Thus, the tendency toward neutrality "was closely connected not only with the safeguarding of territorial integrity and the striving for national independence but also with the will for national sovereignty."[83] Considering all the cases of contemporary neutral states discussed above, one can argue that nowadays, the essence of neutrality is primarily reduced to the status of nonalignment (nonparticipation in military alliances). In part, this is because all neutral states in the world have pledged to support the goals and resolutions of the United Nations, up to and including military actions. Most of the neutral states in the EU participate in EU, NATO, and UN missions and operations.

Furthermore, most of the neutral and nonaligned EU member states participate in wide-ranging military cooperation projects within PESCO —the Permanent Structured Cooperation process. Military cooperation in the sense of joint capability development in high technological, operational capabilities and international crisis management based on UN mandates does not pose a threat to the status of neutrality. However, joining a military alliance or a defense union would completely dissolve it. The EU does not plan to be a military alliance yet, although the Union introduced a limited mutual assistance clause in the Lisbon Treaty in case of armed aggression:

> If a Member State is the victim of armed aggression on its territory, the other Member States shall have toward it an obligation of aid and assistance by all the means in their power, in accordance with Article 51 of the United Nations

Charter. This shall not prejudice the specific character of the security and defence policy of certain Member States.[84]

According to that article (42:7), every EU member state defines contributions to mutual defense within the EU framework depending on their political will and interest. Additionally, twenty-two out of twenty-eight EU members (as of June 2019) determine their defense policies within NATO. This means that despite the above discussion about the various forms of military cooperation and integration, the EU neutrals are still solely responsible for their defense—while being under no formal obligation to aid other members militarily. Whether constitutionally and militarily neutral members like Austria, Ireland, and Malta or the nonaligned Finland and Sweden (who do not have any legal or political commitment to neutrality under international law)—they are not part of the mutual defense agreement like the other member states. On the international stage, the EU neutral and nonaligned states can strengthen international crisis management efforts and good offices policies. Their political influence in solving international disputes, on the other hand, remains limited.

## NOTES

1. Gunther Hauser, "Military Security and the Concept of Neutrality," in *Armed Forces and International Security: Global Trends and Issues*, ed. Jean Callaghan and Franz Kernic (Münster: LIT Publishing, 2003), 321.

2. Thomas Curson Hansard, ed., *The Parliamentary Debates from the Year 1803 to the Present Time*, vol. 37, The Parliamentary History of England from the Earliest Period to the Year 1803 (London: T. C. Hansard, 1816), 308.

3. The term used in the official documents is that of "perpetual neutrality" which today has become synonymous with the more prevalent expression of "permanent neutrality."

4. Stephen C. Neff, *The Rights and Duties of Neutrals: A General History* (Manchester: Manchester University Press, 2000), 101.

5. James Brown Scott, ed., *The Hague Conventions and Declarations of 1899 and 1907*, Carnegie Endowment for International Peace (New York: Oxford University Press, 1915). Article 1, Convention (V), Respecting the Rights and Duties of Neutral Powers and Persons in Case of War on Land.

6. For a detailed overview see: Neff, *The Rights and Duties of Neutrals: A General History*.

7. Martti Häikiö, "Finland's Neutrality 1944–1994," in *The Neutrals and the European Integration 1945–1995*, ed. Michael Gehler and Rolf Steininger (Vienna: Böhlau Publishing, 2000), 217.

8. Karl Molin, "The Central Issues of Swedish Neutrality Policy," in *The Neutrals and the European Integration 1945–1995*, ed. Michael Gehler and Rolf Steininger (Vienna: Böhlau Publishing, 2000), 261.

9. Ibid., 261.

10. Bundeskanzleramt, "Landesverteidigungsplan" (Vienna: Österreichische Staatsdruckerei), 23–26.

11. Gunther Hauser, "Visegrad and Austria–Comprehensive Relations," in *Visegrad countries in an enlarged trans-Atlantic community*, ed. Marek Stastný (Bratislava: Institute for Public Affairs, 2002), 113.

12. "Military Security and the Concept of Neutrality," 322.

13. "The Concept of Neutrality in Today's Security Environment," *Defensor Pacis* no. 18 (2006): 144.

14. "Austrian Security Policy–New Tasks and Challenges," *Obrana a strategy (Defense & Strategy)* 7, no. 1 (2007): 46.

15. Michael Gehler, "Different Roads to the European Union: Neutral States and Integration 1945–1995," in *The Convergence of Diversity: The European Model*, ed. Adrian-Ciprian Paun and Dragos Paun (Cluj: Cluj University Press, 2014), 56.

16. Wolfgang Zecha, "Austrian Security Policy Documents—A Walk on a Tightrope between Neutrality and International Solidarity," *AARMS (Academic and Applied Research in Military and Public Management Science)* 14, no. 4 (2015): 317.

17. Resolution by the Austrian Parliament, "Austrian Security and Defense Doctrine. General Considerations" (Vienna: Federal Chancellery [Republic of Austria], 2002).

18. Gunther Hauser, *Die NATO: Transformation, Aufgaben, Ziele* (Frankfurt am Main: Peter Lang Publishing, 2008), 45–47.

19. Ibid., 45–46.

20. Gerhard Jandl, "20 Years of Austrian Partnership with NATO—Record and Outlook," *Politorbis—Zeitschrift zur Aussenpolitik*, no. 61 (2016): 76.

21. Hauser, *Die NATO: Transformation, Aufgaben, Ziele*, 64.

22. North Atlantic Treaty Organization, "Relations with Austria" (2018).

23. Zecha, "Austrian Security Policy Documents—A Walk on a Tightrope between Neutrality and International Solidarity," 328.

24. Poland has observer status.

25. Federal Ministry of Defense and Sports (Austria), "Central European Defense Cooperation (CEDC)" (Vienna 2016).

26. Ibid.

27. Ibid.

28. The explanation in the Allied Joint Doctrine for the Conduct of Operations reads as follows: "The purpose of a Lessons Learned procedure is to learn efficiently from experience and to provide validated justifications for amending the existing way of doing things, in order to improve performance, both during the course of an operation and for subsequent operations. This requires lessons to be meaningful and for them to be brought to the attention of the appropriate authority able and responsible for dealing with them. It also requires the chain of command to have a clear understanding of how to prioritise lessons and how to staff them." NATO, *The NATO Lessons Learned Handbook*, 3rd ed. (NATO, Joint Analysis and Lessons Learned Centre, 2016).

29. Peter Grünwald, "Mountain Training Initiative," *Der Offizier. Zeitschrift der Österreichischen Offiziersgesellschaft*, no. 1 (2016): 24.

30. According to The Centre for Excellence in Emergency Preparedness (Ontario), "CBRN are weaponized or non-weaponized chemical, biological, radiological and nuclear materials that can cause great harm and pose significant threats in the hands of terrorists." The Centre for Excellence in Emergency Preparedness (Ontario), "Factsheet: What is CBRN?," Accessed June 15, 2019, www.ccep.ca/education/CBRNinfosheet.pdf.

31. Central European Defence Cooperation, "Rapid Deployment. Extended Reach. Enhanced Persistence. Superior Awareness," accessed June 15, 2019, http://cbrnsaas.eu.

32. Republic of Austria, "Austrian Security Strategy: Security in a new decade—Shaping Security," ed. Department IV—Coordination Federal Chancellery of the Republic of Austria, Division IV/6—Security Policy Affairs (Vienna 2013), 22.

33. The Soviet Union feared during that time that Austria as a buffer state between East and West silently could become a member state of NATO when joining the EC. For details see: Gunther Hauser and Mauro Mantovani, "Austria and Switzerland," in *The Handbook of European Defense Policies & Armed Forces*, ed. Hugo Meijer and Marco Wyss (Oxford: Oxford University Press, 2018), 108.

34. Brian William Lake, "Irish Neutrality and the Common Foreign and Security Policy: An Analysis" (Memorial University of Newfoundland, 2001), 12.

35. Ibid., 14.

36. Ibid.

37. Department of Foreign Affairs/An Roinn Gnóthaí, "Seville Declarations on the Nice Treaty," (Dublin, June 21, 2002).
38. Steve Peers, "Analysis: Lisbon Treaty guarantees for Ireland," *Statewatch* (2009).
39. Department of Foreign Affairs and Trade, "Neutrality: Ireland's Policy of Neutrality."
40. Lake, "Irish Neutrality and the Common Foreign and Security Policy: An Analysis," 12.
41. Häikiö, "Finland's Neutrality 1944–1994," 217.
42. Hauser and Mantovani, "Austria and Switzerland," 108.
43. Ibid.
44. Häikiö, "Finland's Neutrality 1944–1994," 213.
45. Finish Ministry for Foreign Affairs, "Security in a Changing World: Guidelines for Finland's Security Policy," ed. Council of State to the Parliament (1995).
46. Ibid.
47. Helsingin Sanomat International Edition, "Sweden to Adopt New Security Policy Doctrine—Drops Neutrality," February 12, 2002.
48. Ibid.
49. Erik Brattberg, "Smart Partnership for Smart Defense," *Project Syndicate* (2012): 2.
50. Defense News, "U.S. Supports Drive for Nordic Defense Cooperation," *O'Dwyer, Gerard*, May 23, 2016, 12.
51. Ibid.
52. Ibid., 23.
53. Ibid.
54. "The Need to up Security Cooperation in the EU," *Hultqvist, Peter*, December 11, 2017, 16.
55. "Cooperation based on Shared Interest," *Jussi, Niinistö*, December 10, 2018, 12.
56. Steve James, "Social Democrats Abandon 200 Years of Neutrality, World Socialist Web Site (WSWS)," International Committee of the Fourth International (ICFI), Accessed: June 15, 2019, www.wsws.org/en/articles/2002/04/swed-a12.html.
57. Gunther Hauser, *Das europäische Sicherheits-und Verteidigungssystem und seine Akteure*, 8th ed. (Vienna: Landesverteidigungsakademie, 2018), 109.
58. Gunnar Lassinantti, "Small States and Alliances—A Swedish Perspective," in *Small States and Alliances*, ed. Erich Reiter and Heinz Gärtner (Heidelberg: Springer, 2001), 108.
59. As cited in Defense News, "No NATO-Like Alliance For Nordic, Baltic Nations," *O'Dwyer, Gerard*, September 10, 2012, 23.
60. Ibid., 14.
61. Ibid.
62. Ibid.
63. Brattberg, "Smart Partnership for Smart Defense," 1.
64. Defense News, "Interview: Peter Hultqvist, Swedish Minister of Defense," *Mehta, Aaron*, June 12, 2017, 18.
65. Ibid.
66. Ibid.
67. Ibid., 19.
68. Defense News, "The Need to up Security Cooperation in the EU," 16.
69. Ibid.
70. Ibid.
71. Hillary Briffa, "Malta: Bridge of the Mediterranean: Neutrality as a Small State, Status Seeking Grand Strategy," *SSANSE: Small States and the New Security Environment*, no. 17 (2018): 3.
72. As cited in ibid., 4.
73. Chapter 1, Article 1, Paragraph 3. State of Malta, "Constitution of Malta," ed. Culture Ministry for Justice, and Local Government.
74. As cited in: Malta Today, "As Russia and US Join Hands, Karmenu Embraces Neutrality," *Sansone, Kurt*, June 2, 2002.
75. Briffa, "Malta: Bridge of the Mediterranean: Neutrality as a small state, status seeking grand strategy," 4.
76. Ibid.

77. Ibid.
78. Ibid.
79. Ibid., 5.
80. Ibid.
81. Ibid.
82. Gehler, "Different Roads to the European Union: Neutral States and Integration 1945–1995," 53.
83. Ibid., 59.
84. European Union, "Treaty on European Union," *Official Journal of the European Communities* 35, no. C191 (1992).

## SELECTED REFERENCES

Austria, Republic of. "Austrian Security Strategy: Security in a New Decade—Shaping Security," edited by Department IV—Coordination Federal Chancellery of the Republic of Austria, Division IV/6—Security Policy Affairs. Vienna, 2013.
Brattberg, Erik. "Smart Partnership for Smart Defense." *Project Syndicate* (2012).
Briffa, Hillary. "Malta: Bridge of the Mediterranean: Neutrality as a Small State, Status Seeking Grand Strategy." *SSANSE: Small States and the New Security Environment*, no. 17 (2018).
Bundeskanzleramt. "Landesverteidigungsplan." Vienna: Österreichische Staatsdruckerei, 1985.
Central European Defence Cooperation, "Rapid Deployment. Extended Reach. Enhanced Persistence. Superior Awareness." http://cbrnsaas.eu.
Defense News. "Cooperation Based on Shared Interest." *Jussi, Niinistö*, December 10, 2018, 12.
———. "The Need to Up Security Cooperation in the E.U." *Hultqvist, Peter*, December 11, 2017, 16.
———. "No NATO-Like Alliance For Nordic, Baltic Nations." *O'Dwyer, Gerard*, September 10, 2012, 23.
———. "U.S. Supports Drive for Nordic Defense Cooperation." *O'Dwyer, Gerard*, May 23, 2016, 12.
Department of Foreign Affairs and Trade. "Neutrality: Ireland's Policy of Neutrality."
Department of Foreign Affairs/An Roinn Gnóthaí. "Seville Declarations on the Nice Treaty." Dublin, June 21, 2002.
European Union. "Treaty on European Union." *Official Journal of the European Communities* 35, no. C191 (1992).
Federal Ministry of Defense and Sports (Austria). "Central European Defense Cooperation (CEDC)." Vienna, 2016.
Finish Ministry for Foreign Affairs. "Security in a Changing World: Guidelines for Finland's security policy," edited by Council of State to the Parliament, 1995.
Gehler, Michael. "Different Roads to the European Union: Neutral States and Integration 1945–1995." In *The Convergence of Diversity: The European Model*, edited by Adrian-Ciprian Paun and Dragos Paun. Cluj: Cluj University Press, 2014.
Grünwald, Peter. "Mountain Training Initiative." *Der Offizier. Zeitschrift der Österreichischen Offiziersgesellschaft*, no. 1 (2016): 24–27.
Häikiö, Martti. "Finland's Neutrality 1944–1994." In *The Neutrals and the European Integration 1945–1995*, edited by Michael Gehler and Rolf Steininger. Vienna: Böhlau Publishing, 2000.
Hansard, Thomas Curson, ed. *The Parliamentary Debates from the Year 1803 to the Present Time*, 37, The Parliamentary History of England from the Earliest Period to the Year 1803. London: T. C. Hansard, 1816.
Hauser, Gunther. "Austrian Security Policy–New Tasks and Challenges." *Obrana a strategy (Defense & Strategy)* 7, no. 1 (2007): 45–56.
———. "The Concept of Neutrality in Today's Security Environment." *Defensor Pacis*, no. 18 (2006): 140–64.

———. *Das europäische Sicherheits-und Verteidigungssystem und seine Akteure*. 8th ed. Vienna: Landesverteidigungsakademie, 2018.

———. *Die NATO: Transformation, Aufgaben, Ziele*. Frankfurt am Main: Peter Lang Publishing, 2008.

———. "Military Security and the Concept of Neutrality." In *Armed Forces and International Security: Global Trends and Issues*, edited by Jean Callaghan and Franz Kernic, 321–25. Münster: LIT Publishing, 2003.

———. "Visegrad and Austria–Comprehensive Relations." In *Visegrad countries in an Enlarged Trans-Atlantic Community*, edited by Marek Stastný, 113–38. Bratislava: Institute for Public Affairs, 2002.

Hauser, Gunther, and Mauro Mantovani. "Austria and Switzerland." Chapter 10. In *The Handbook of European Defense Policies & Armed Forces*, edited by Hugo Meijer and Marco Wyss, 197–213. Oxford: Oxford University Press, 2018.

Helsingin Sanomat International Edition. "Sweden to Adopt New Security Policy Doctrine—Drops Neutrality." February 12, 2002.

James, Steve, "Social Democrats Abandon 200 Years of Neutrality, World Socialist Web Site (WSWS)." International Committee of the Fourth International (ICFI), www.wsws.org/en/articles/2002/04/swed-a12.html.

Jandl, Gerhard. "20 Years of Austrian Partnership with NATO—Record and Outlook." *Politorbis—Zeitschrift zur Aussenpolitik*, no. 61 (2016): 75–80.

Lake, Brian William. "Irish Neutrality and the Common Foreign and Security Policy: An Analysis." Memorial University of Newfoundland, 2001.

Lassinantti, Gunnar. "Small States and Alliances—A Swedish Perspective." In *Small States and Alliances*, edited by Erich Reiter and Heinz Gärtner, 101–11. Heidelberg: Springer, 2001.

Malta Today. "As Russia and US Join Hands, Karmenu Embraces Neutrality." *Sansone, Kurt*, June 2, 2002.

Molin, Karl. "The Central Issues of Swedish Neutrality Policy." In *The Neutrals and the European Integration 1945–1995*, edited by Michael Gehler and Rolf Steininger. Vienna: Böhlau Publishing, 2000.

NATO. *The NATO Lessons Learned Handbook*. 3rd ed.: NATO, Joint Analysis and Lessons Learned Centre, 2016.

Neff, Stephen C. *The Rights and Duties of Neutrals: A General History*. Manchester: Manchester University Press, 2000.

News, Defense. "Interview: Peter Hultqvist, Swedish Minister of Defense." *Mehta, Aaron*, June 12, 2017.

North Atlantic Treaty Organization. "Relations with Austria." 2018.

Peers, Steve. "Analysis: Lisbon Treaty Guarantees for Ireland." *Statewatch* (2009).

Resolution by the Austrian Parliament. "Austrian Security and Defense Doctrine. General Considerations." Vienna: Federal Chancellery (Republic of Austria), 2002.

Scott, James Brown, ed. *The Hague Conventions and Declarations of 1899 and 1907*, Carnegie Endowment for International Peace. New York: Oxford University Press, 1915.

State of Malta. "Constitution of Malta." edited by Culture Ministry for Justice, and Local Government.

The Centre for Excellence in Emergency Preparedness (Ontario), "Factsheet: What is CBRN?" www.ceep.ca/education/CBRNintrosheet.pdf.

Zecha, Wolfgang. "Austrian Security Policy Documents—A Walk on a Tightrope between Neutrality and International Solidarity." *AARMS (Academic and Applied Research in Military and Public Management Science)* 14, no. 4 (2015): 317–30.

*Chapter Six*

# Neutral Power Russia

Glenn Diesen

Russia is not commonly associated with the concept of permanent neutrality due to its various levels of alliances during the Cold War and its role in the European alliance-systems before the Bolshevik Revolution. However, the geostrategic situation of the twenty-first century has increasingly produced incentives for Russia to promote neutrality as a foreign policy. The main threat and disappointment to Moscow have been the failure of the West to reach a post-Cold War settlement that would have established a new and mutually acceptable status quo. The prospect of a Common European Home[1] fell apart as Western governments opted for constructing a new Europe without Russia, expanding NATO and the EU toward Russian borders. In the absence of a Greater Europe that included Russia, Moscow was only left with two Grand Strategic options; either construct a new rival bloc of allies or create a beltway of permanently neutral states along its western border. The latter has emerged as its sole option since the people within many of its neighboring countries are divided among two camps—those who seek integration with both the West and Russia and those who seek integration only with the West to move away from Russia. In this environment, neutrality prevails as the most feasible option.

    The principal obstacle to legal agreements ensuring solutions of permanent neutrality on Russia's border has been the West's pursuit of a "Europe Whole and Free," aiming to unite the entire continent under shared institutions—but excluding Russia. The concept was first presented by President Bush in 1989 as a rival approach to Gorbachev's concept of a "Common European Home."[2] While they seem to be similar concepts, the former suggested integration under common values—implying US leadership, one-sided concessions, and even exclusion. The "open-door policy" of NATO and the EU has placed the concept of neutrality in direct conflict with the principle of sovereignty as the decision about foreign policy orientations falls upon third countries.[3] As a great power compromise, NATO and the EU could reach an agreement with Russia that neither side would expand their alliance structures toward the border of the other. By not opening the doors for new members, a neutral buffer zone would be maintained without infringing on the right to sovereign decision by neighboring states. In contrast, under the current status quo in which NATO is potentially open to any European state, Russia is incentivized to obstruct the expansionist impulses of NATO and the EU by preventing its Western neighbors from joining their alliance.

However, harmonizing neutrality and sovereignty requires agreements between the great powers. The EU-Russian Common Spaces Agreement is a key example of this problem as the EU agreed that integration initiatives in the common neighborhood must be mutually beneficial to avoid drawing dividing lines, while Russia agreed that participation in cooperation and integration initiatives is the sovereign decision of states. When the EU failed to live up to its commitments, Russia similarly abandoned its own. While Russia accuses the West of compelling states to choose sides and thereby divide Europe, the West accuses Russia of not allowing states to choose a side.

Russia responds to the challenge of Western expansionism by making conflict resolution in its neighboring countries conditional on the implementation of neutral settlements, as evident in Moldova, Georgia, and Ukraine. The rationale that a neutral geopolitical status is required to mitigate a polarized society is consistent with Russia's geostrategic interests in Europe. Meanwhile, NATO and the EU insist that Russia respects the sovereignty of its neighbors by allowing them to choose a "European path," which is consistent with the West's geostrategic ambitions. Due to the seemingly irreconcilable conflict with the West and the failure to construct a Greater Europe, Russia is pivoting to Asia in pursuit of alternative partners and toward integrating into Greater Eurasia. Politics of neutrality is also becoming a useful concept there as Moscow has been trying to avoid a formal alliance with China—since that would alienate other states such as India or Japan and thereby fragment Eurasia.[4]

## RUSSIAN REALISM AND THE END OF NEUTRALITY AFTER THE COLD WAR

For Russia, neutrality is a tool for "great power balancing," yet the exact meaning or application depends on the purpose it serves. Neutrality in Europe is a synonym for buffer states. A Greater Europe failed to materialize after the Cold War that would have replaced bloc-politics with an inclusive security architecture. As Europe remains divided, establishing a belt of neutral buffer states in the shared neighborhood would reduce conflict as a disruption to mutually beneficial economic cooperation. Neutrality in Asia, on the other hand, is about preventing the region from developing into a confrontational bloc-based system like Europe. A Greater Eurasia that includes various large powers on the supercontinent requires the absence of any formal alliance systems that polarize the region. For example, Russia would alienate India if it formed a formal alliance with China, and India would alienate Russia if it joined a formal alliance with the United States. The result would be that both Russia and India would be limited to an asymmetrical relationship with a more powerful state rather than diversifying their economic connectivity

Russia is renowned for its realist thinking in terms of the balance of power, creating systemic incentives and constraints on states.[5] The balance of power logic also informs Russia's views on the utility of permanent neutrality. That becomes a possibility when there is a balance of power. In realist theory, states have the option of either balancing or bandwagoning, while the third option of neutrality has received less attention. However, the realist theory makes a distinction between maximizing power and security. States accrue power to the extent that it advances their security, yet when balanced, a state has systemic incentives to reach a settlement to advance security for both sides. Neutrality for small states merely reflects the balance of power logic.[6] Larger powers support or impose neutrality on smaller states to mitigate the security dilemma, which is why neutral states are usually located in the border regions. The realist view on neutral countries is effectively that of a buffer state, which "declares non-involvement in a conflict or war, and indicates its intention to refrain from supporting or aiding either side."[7] This has a close bearing on the "Mitrany paradox," which denotes that security communities merely elevate inter-state conflicts to a higher level by constructing fewer, larger, and less compatible entities of power.[8] As alliances grow and become more diverse in terms of interests and values, they also have a greater need to distinguish themselves from outsiders through "othering." In this complex of geopolitical strategizing, neutrality functions effectively as a disarmament agreement if one thinks of alliances as institutions that replace a state's right to make war with a duty to make war.[9] Neutrality is a reflection of power, and the prospect of coercion is, therefore, necessary to preserve a neutrality regime. Both sides must have the possibility to respond and rebalance if the other encroaches upon the neutral as to ensure power maximization does not equate to security maximization. For this logic to function, it is important that neutrals prevent other states from using their territory or from strengthening the capabilities of any (potential) belligerent.

Following this logic, for several centuries, European powers used the concept of neutrality to mitigate the likelihood, scope, and destruction of war.[10] Neutrality ranged from occasional to permanent, with the former used to enable states to concentrate their forces temporarily on more pressing threats. For example, the neutrality pact between Moscow and Tokyo during the Second World War enabled the Soviet Union to concentrate its forces against Germany. After the Soviet Union defeated Germany, it attacked Japan in collaboration with the US.[11] The Cold War saw the emergence of more permanent neutral states that declared nonalignment in both peacetime and war. A belt of neutral states consisting of Sweden, Finland, Austria, Switzerland, and Yugoslavia reduced the front lines and mitigated the Cold War competition in Europe. Both the Soviet Union and the US argued in favor of neutrality when it served their foreign policy goals, yet usually opposed neutrality for states that would fall within their sphere of influence.[12]

The collapse of the Soviet Union severely skewed the balance of power and subsequently removed the incentive to support European neutrality. Because that was conditioned on the bipolar international distribution of power during the Cold War, it immediately began to erode after 1991. States still claimed to be neutral, yet the concept of neutrality became more ambiguous and flexible as the world shifted toward a unipolar international distribution of power. Morgenthau argued already in 1938:

> The legal and political status which we call neutrality is intimately connected with the legal and political structure of the international society at a given historical moment. Any basic change in this structure necessarily affects the normative content and the effectiveness of the rules of neutrality.[13]

After 1991, the cost-benefit consideration for remaining neutral had changed, and NATO proclaimed it had transformed into a democratic club rather than a military bloc intending to "keep the Russians out, the Americans in, and the Germans down."[14] Randall Schweller posited that states seek to bandwagon behind more powerful states that are considered to be the "wave of the future."[15] Case in point, Finland remained neutral throughout the Cold War before drifting toward NATO immediately after the demise of the Soviet Union. To some extent, Finland's neutrality came to an end five months after the Soviet Union collapsed by becoming an associate member of the North Atlantic Consultative Council (NACC) in June 1992.[16] The neutrality of Finland and Sweden has been gradually eroding as the EU continues to militarize and NATO attempts to absorb them into the alliance. In these states, NATO has become more controversial due to the predominantly military nature and anti-Russian posture of the alliance. The militarization of the EU is different as the union is predominantly about political and economic integration and less about military confrontation against Russia. As the EU militarizes and neutrality diminishes, it will also bring these states closer to NATO.[17]

The status for former communist states in Central and Eastern Europe who sought NATO and EU membership soon became an issue. NATO's Partnership for Peace program had initially been presented as an alternative to membership. Instead, it became a steppingstone by restructuring the armed forces of Central and Eastern European countries in line with NATO standards. While the West hoped to cultivate good relations with Russia, the new member states desired clear security guarantees and focused on Russia. The solution for NATO was to adopt a position of strategic ambiguity about Russia since a completely open debate could have undermined the justification for NATO's existence.[18] However, former US secretary of state James Baker cautioned that reinventing NATO as an insurance policy against a possible future Russian threat could make it become a self-fulfilling prophecy.[19] George Kennan was more direct in his criticism of NATO expansion:

> I think it is the beginning of a new cold war.... Of course, there is going to be a bad reaction from Russia, and then [the NATO expanders] will say that we always told you that is how the Russians are—but this is just wrong.[20]

From Moscow's perspective, the source of all conflicts between Russia and the West has been the failure to reach a political settlement after the Cold War that replaced the former system of bloc politics. Gorbachev had promoted the concept of a Common European Home from Vancouver to Vladivostok toward the end of the Cold War, yet the collapse of the Soviet Union derailed negotiations as the US was not required to make any compromises with a weakened and declining Russia. Former US ambassador to Russia, William Burns, argued that Putin "fundamentally misread American interests and politics"[21] by attempting to ally with the US after the September 11 attacks by facilitating military transit through Central Asia in return for halting NATO expansionism: "The Bush administration had no desire—and saw no reason—to trade anything for a Russian partnership against al-Qaeda. It had little inclination to concede much to a declining power."[22] Instead of recognizing Russia's role in Europe to make it a stakeholder in common security architecture, a new Europe was created without Russia–led by an expanding NATO and the EU. As President Putin posited:

> From the beginning, we failed to overcome Europe's division. Twenty-five years ago, the Berlin Wall fell, but invisible walls were moved to the East of Europe. This has led to mutual misunderstandings and assignment of guilt. They are the cause of all crises ever since.[23]

The new Europe did not merely present Russia with a new unfavorable status quo, but it created an antagonistic security structure, as the West committed itself to an "open Europe" that would gradually expand toward the Russian border. Subsequently, a zero-sum format to European integration emerged as the return to Europe meant that the shared neighborhood had to decouple from Russia, the largest European state, and instead look toward Washington and Brussels for leadership.

As the West has enjoyed asymmetrical power distribution in the unipolar era that followed the Cold War, the concept of neutrality has been fiercely rejected based on the argument that it undermined sovereignty.[24] The mantra that Russia should not get a veto over the right of other states to join political, economic, or military blocs is argued in defense of sovereignty. This logic presents the political, economic, and military blocs as merely passive agents with a duty to keep their alliances open, under the mantra of an open Europe. Arguing that the EU and NATO are really about democracy made it immoral to reject their expansion.

This expansionist bloc politics under the auspices of European integration becomes increasingly problematic the closer NATO and the EU get to Russian borders. First, Moscow perceived a US military presence in Ukraine and Georgia as an intolerable threat to its security. In its view, the prospect of war increases due to the threat of NATO's military adventurism, NATO's development of missile defense, and potentially the tail wagging the dog as the new members may pull NATO into a war. This is evident by Georgia's invasion of South Ossetia in 2008[25] on the assumption that the US and NATO would respond by providing support as a deterrent to any Russian response. Second, domestic stability in states such as Ukraine, Moldova, and Georgia unravels as these states are deeply polarized in terms of seeking a future with either the West or Russia.[26] In past presidential elections in Ukraine, before the 2014 coup, more than 90 percent in the western regions used to vote for a pro-Western/anti-Russian presidential candidate, while in the Eastern regions, more than 90 percent voted for a pro-Russian presidential candidate.

## RUSSIA PROMOTING AND IMPOSING NEUTRALITY IN EUROPE

Neutrality emerged as a Russian approach toward the rest of Europe over the past two decades, with some inconsistencies. Russia initiated a dual response to the failure in reaching a post-Cold War settlement; either the West would correct the mistake by creating a Greater Europe that included Russia or set up a buffer zone of permanent neutral states along its Western borders. With the West rejecting both options, Russia has responded to the continued division of Europe by unilaterally imposing neutrality on its neighborhood. At the 1999 OSCE Istanbul Summit, which called for elevating the role of the OSCE in European security, Russia had committed itself to withdraw its peacekeepers completely from Georgia and Moldova. As NATO commenced its march to the east, Russia began to walk back its previous commitments when it became evident that Russian peacekeepers would eventually be replaced by NATO peacekeepers—as opposed to OSCE peacekeepers representing a neutral solution. The Russian ambassador to Moldova explained that "a completely new reality has been created since" the OSCE Summit in Istanbul, as cooperative efforts had been replaced by Western unilateralism to marginalize Russia.[27] By proclaiming further NATO expansionism to be unacceptable, Moscow implicitly conditioned its withdrawal on settlements that would lay the foundation for the permanent neutralities of Moldova and Georgia.

In Moldova, Moscow negotiated the Kozak Memorandum in 2003, an agreement to reunite Moldova with the breakaway region of Transnistria under the condition that it would remain a neutral state in Europe. Moscow pressured its allies in Tiraspol to abandon demands for equal status with Chisinau in a united Moldova, albeit the agreement bestowed Tiraspol with enough power to obstruct decisions that affected Moldavian neutrality.[28] Neutrality primarily meant not joining NATO, and probably not even the EU in its current format due to the zero-sum organization of relations with Russia. The US and EU subsequently torpedoed the agreement on the day before the signing as it was seen to obstruct Moldova's "European" future. Article 11 of the Moldovan constitution proclaims permanent neutrality,[29] yet the durability of this is questionable due to stated ambitions to join the EU and the divisions in the population concerning NATO.[30]

In 2005, Russia appeared to have a breakthrough in obtaining EU support for neutrality in the shared neighborhood. The two signed the Common Spaces agreement that would, to some extent, construct a neutral belt between Russia and the West. The agreement recognized the need to prevent the development of new dividing lines with zero-sum integration incentives:

> The EU and Russia recognise that processes of regional cooperation and integration in which they participate and which are based on the sovereign decisions of States, play an important role in strengthening security and stability. They agree to actively promote them in a mutually beneficial manner, through close result-oriented EU-Russia collaboration and dialogue, thereby contributing effectively to creating a greater Europe without dividing lines and based on common values.[31]

Some ambiguity soon became evident as the EU implied that the first sentence rejected neutrality as sovereign states could choose to join the blocs of their choice. Meanwhile, Russia interpreted the second sentence as a commitment to neutrality by the regional blocs as they would not develop new dividing lines with zero-sum integration initiatives. The Common Spaces agreement was violated shortly after by the EU as it launched the Eastern Partnership initiative that pursues unilateral political integration with the shared neighborhood as support for energy and transportation infrastructure that bypasses and marginalizes Russia. In this context of greatest importance was the energy corridor, which through Georgia, Azerbaijan, and the Caspian Sea reaches Central Asia. The Eastern Partnership supports regional programs such as the Transport Corridor Europe-Caucasus-Asia (TRACECA), which is a transport corridor through Eurasia that bypasses Russia. The Eastern Partnership also supports INOGATE, an international energy cooperation program that includes all states of the former Soviet space—except Russia.[32] The Russian ambassador to the EU, Vladimir Chizhov, complained that "the road map for the external security space stipulated that integration processes in various parts of Europe were complementary, so to present the former Soviet Union nations with an 'us or them' choice is inappropriate and unequivocally unfair to them.[33]

By 2013, the EU was advancing its Association Agreements with the shared neighborhood that can be seen as imposing a civilizational ultimatum as "they must finally choose, so the narrative goes, between East and West."[34] But that fueled an Integration Dilemma because "it transform[ed] integration, a positive-sum process by definition, into a zero-sum game for the state that is excluded from the integration initiatives offered to its neighbors."[35]

The proposed Association Agreement divided Ukrainian society and sparked a powerful conflict with Russia. Already in the 1990s, the prospect of a future NATO membership had begun to deepen the polarization of Ukraine, since its population was split between pro- and anti-Russian camps.[36] Even NATO publications warned that "attempts to mobilize Ukraine against Russia would contribute to domestic division and make the task of nation-building more difficult."[37] Under President Kuchma (1994–2005), Ukraine had pursued closer relations with NATO in consultation and cooperation with Russia to avoid zero-sum integration initiatives.[38] The "common return" to Europe with Russia, consistent with Russia's ambitions for a Greater Europe, was derailed by the Western-backed Orange Revolution in 2004 that strongly favored NATO membership.[39] After Viktor Yanukovych came to power in 2010, he immediately stressed a "non-bloc status" and set Ukraine back on the path of neutrality. By 2013 Ukraine came under pressure as it rejected the Association Agreement to which the West responded by supporting a rebellion. Russia and Ukraine proposed a trilateral EU-Russia-Ukraine "trade commission" to harmonize tariff levels and make integration efforts compatible, but the EU immediately rejected Ukraine's efforts to remain neutral, arguing that "we do not need a trilateral agreement. The times of limited sovereignty are over in Europe."[40] Following the Western-backed coup in early 2014 against the Yanukovych Government, Ukrainian foreign policy returned to NATO ambitions and the new president, Petro

Poroshenko (2014–2019), oversaw a constitutional amendment that reflected EU and NATO accession ambitions.

Russia, in turn, reacted to the coup by repeatedly trying to impose neutrality on Ukraine. On March 15, 2014, the day before the referendum in Crimea, Russian Foreign Minister Sergei Lavrov proposed to his American counterparts to federalize Ukraine and declare it permanently neutral. Failing to reach an agreement, Moscow lent its military support to the pro-Russian rebels in Donbas, who contests the legitimacy of the new authorities in Kyiv. The rebellion subsequently prevented the central authorities in Kyiv from taking the entire country toward the West and away from Russia, since NATO accession rules exclude new members if they have ongoing conflicts on their territories. Meanwhile, the Minsk-2 agreement (the peace agreement to end hostilities in Eastern Ukraine) is a format to federalize Ukraine and decentralize government power that would enable the country's Eastern regions to maintain close ties with Russia. In other words, the Minsk-2 Agreement also imposes permanent neutrality in Ukraine. James Sherr posits that the Minsk Agreement was designed to make Ukraine "'federated,' 'neutral,' and without European prospects,"[41] while the US political commentator, Janusz Bugajski, criticized Russia's influence among its Western neighbors:

> Russia's revisionism targets specific neighbours for direct territorial acquisition or enforced federalization . . . Ukraine, Moldova, and Georgia are subject to violence, partition, economic warfare, and disinformation campaigns because they have decided to follow the European path of development. . . . In order to preclude broad regional opposition, Russia is also attempting to construct a belt of neutral or supportive states across Central Europe.[42]

This analysis inaccurately characterizes Russia's intention to impose a neutral belt along its borders. However, the revisionist label is peculiar as Russia is acting as a status quo power seeking to preserve the nonaligned status of its neighbors from the revisionism of NATO and EU expansionism.

As relations between the West and Russia continue to deteriorate, the ability of states to remain neutral has diminished. The West has reacted to the crisis by calling for further NATO expansion, increasing military deployments along Russia's borders and holding large military exercises with Russia as the target. Russia's reaction has been to demonstrate its preparedness to uphold its red lines and counter the West by holding large military exercises and take high risks by intercepting NATO military planes and ships.[43] The increased pressure from both sides makes it difficult to remain neutral yet risky to pick sides. For example, Serbia has aimed to maintain a neutral stance between the West and Russia by neither recognizing nor condemning Russia's unification/annexation of Crimea.[44] However, with the West's growing economic coercion against Russia, the EU is mounting increasing pressure on Belgrade to fall in line and scale back relations with Moscow to maintain a good relationship with Brussels.

## RUSSIA'S NEUTRALITY IN GREATER EURASIA

The Western-backed coup in Ukraine had a profound impact on Russia's geostrategic orientation by ending its centuries-old occidental era. Its former Greater Europe project was finally deemed to have failed and subsequently replaced with the Greater Eurasia initiative.[45] The "illusions about gradual integration with the West"[46] had been shattered, and the anti-Russian sanctions even convinced the remaining believers in Greater Europe that Russia had to pivot to Asia. The principal flaw in Russia's geoeconomic strategy for Greater Europe had been its excessive dependence on an unfavorable and asymmetrical economic partnership with the West—a relationship troubled with continued conflict due to zero-sum approach that "European integration" meant for Russia. The geoeconomics of Greater Eurasia, on the other hand, offers a better "balance of dependence" as Russia diversifies its economic connectivity to avoid becoming too dependent on any one state or region.[47] The concept envisions Russia to position itself as an essential pole of power within an economically integrated Greater Eurasia that encompasses Europe, China, South Korea, India, Iran, and everything in between.

The principal partner for this approach is China, due to its ability and intention to challenge the US-centric international economic system. Moscow has subsequently become the leading supporter of Beijing's efforts to restructure global value chains around China in terms of creating dependencies on rival technologies, strategic industries, transportation corridors, and financial instruments.[48] Russia is replacing supplies from Western strategic industries with Chinese suppliers and collaborating with Chinese corporations to develop Russia's tech-sector in areas such as 5G networks, artificial intelligence, and e-commerce. Russian energy projects previously earmarked for Western partners are now given to China. Russia is also supporting China's Belt and Road Initiative by promoting the use of Russia's vast territory, and even seeks to collectively develop the Northern Sea Route through the Arctic with China. Russia and China are also collectively developing alternative new financial instruments by developing common investment banks, harmonizing trade regimes, and "de-dollarizing."[49] Russia is apprehensive about becoming too reliant on Beijing due to the asymmetrical dependence, which would merely recreate a similarly unfavorable partnership which it already has with the West. Moscow seeks to mitigate this risk by establishing better economic connectivity with the rest of the vast continent.

Establishing a balance of dependence in Eurasia compels Russia to adopt a neutral stance in the region by not wedding itself permanently to any one partner in opposition to another. Its close ties with China will therefore not result in a formal alliance since that would alienate countries like India or Japan, fragment the Eurasian continent, and thereby leave Russia in an asymmetrical partnership with a more powerful state. That is why Russia became more comfortable in institutions like the Shanghai Cooperation Organization (SCO) after it included India and Pakistan because that meant that Chinese leadership in this forum could not transition into dominance. Similarly, Russia's growing cooperation with Iran cannot become an alliance in the future as it would undermine Russia's relations with the Arab world, and maintaining amicable relations with Iran's adversaries is imperative as a key mediator in the region.[50]

The Eurasian Economic Union (EAEU), an integration initiative in the post-Soviet space, appears at first glance to be an exception to Russia's neutral posture in Asia. The EAEU is primarily structured to use their collective bargaining power to integrate with larger economies such as China and the EU in a more favorable and symmetrical format. Case in point, Russia and China have agreed to harmonize their integration efforts in Central Asia and maintain the neutral status of the region by establishing cooperation between the EAEU and China's Belt and Road Initiative under the auspices of the SCO. The EAEU institutionalizes a privileged position for Russia in the region, yet it also offers China one tariff zone and a set of standards and legislation with the EU.[51]

## CONCLUSION

Russia's advocacy of neutrality for itself and neighboring states reflects its strategic interests as dictated by realist theory. The neutral posture is strategic for Russia as a status quo power that seeks to preserve its current influence—challenged by a revisionist West, that expands its alliance systems, and by a China on the rise. While the West rejects neutral solutions to mitigate tensions with Russia, China has demonstrated preparedness to preserve the neutral status of Central Asian states by harmonizing integrational efforts with Russia. The West's failure to recognize the foundation for Russia's advocacy for permanent neutrality in Europe results in flawed expectations and fears that Russia desired a sphere of influence in Europe, wanted to recreate the Soviet Union, or was in the process of constructing a formal alliance with China. As a new equilibrium after two decades into the twenty-first century, and with a new balance of power emerging, the possibility of permanent neutrality for smaller states should be reintroduced into the political discourse.

The failure to construct a neutral belt along Russia's western borders will continue to be the principal source of conflict between the West and Russia.

In the era of geoeconomics, the West will continue attempting to cripple the Russian economy with sanctions, cutting access to vital technologies and limiting Russia's access to finance and the payment systems SWIFT. Russia cannot accept further NATO and EU expansionism, and will, therefore, continue to look toward China in its efforts to reduce its reliance on Western technologies, industries, transportation corridors, and financial instruments. The West gradually recognizes that the Sino-Russian partnership has transitioned from a "marriage of convenience" to a strategic partnership. Western sanctions have enabled China to monopolize on the Russian market and develop geoeconomic capabilities that can rival the West. Permanent neutrality for the shared neighborhood in Eastern Europe appears to be the only solution to mitigate political tensions of a divided Europe, and thereby make economics a tool for engagement instead of coercion.

## NOTES

1. The Common European Home was part of Gorbachev's campaign for a New Political Thinking, which aimed to deconstruct the bloc-based security architecture in Europe and position the Soviet Union within a European political community. See Milan Svec, "The Prague Spring: 20 Years Later," *Foreign Affairs* 66, no. 5 (Summer, 1988).

2. George Bush, "A Europe Whole and Free: Remarks to the Citizens in Mainz" (1989), usa.usembassy.de/etexts/ga6-890531.htm.

3. NATO's open-door policy is based on Article 10 of the Washington Treaty, which states that membership is open to any "European state in a position to further the principles of this Treaty and to contribute to the security of the North Atlantic area." See NATO, "The North Atlantic Treaty" (Washington, DC, 1949).

4. Dmitri Trenin, *From Greater Europe to Greater Asia*, The Sino-Russian Entente (Moscow: Carnegie Moscow Center, 2015), 12.

5. Christian Thorun, *Explaining Change in Russian Foreign Policy: The Role of Ideas in Post-Soviet Russia's Conduct toward the West* (New York: Palgrave Macmillan, 2009).

6. Hans J. Morgenthau, *Politics among Nations: The Struggle for Power and Peace*, ed. Kenneth W. Thompson, vol. 6 (Beijing: Peking University Press, 1985).

7. Andrew Heywood, *Key Concepts in Politics and International Relations* (Macmillan International Higher Education, 2015), 144.

8. Ken Booth and Nicholas Wheeler, *The Security Dilemma: Fear, Cooperation, and Trust in World Politics* (Springer Nature, 2007), 188–89.

9. John H. Herz, "Power Politics and World Organization," *American Political Science Review* 36, no. 6 (1942): 1046–47.

10. Laurent Goetschel, "Neutrality, a Really Dead Concept?," *Cooperation and Conflict* 34, no. 2 (1999): 115.

11. Boris Slavinsky, *The Japanese-Soviet Neutrality Pact: A Diplomatic History, 1941–1945*, trans. Geoffrey Jukes (London: RoutledgeCurzon, 2004).

12. Jussi M. Hanhimäki, *Containing Coexistence. America, Russia, and the "Finnish Solution." 1945–1956* (Kent: Kent State University Press, 1997).

13. Hans J. Morgenthau, "The Problem of Neutrality," *University of Kansas City Law Review* 7, no. 109 (1938).

14. A sentence attributed to first NATO Secretary General Hastings Ismay. See Tony Judt, *Postwar: A History of Europe Since 1945* (New York: Penguin Press, 2005), 150.

15. Randall L. Schweller, "Bandwagoning for Profit: Bringing the Revisionist State Back In," *International Security* 19, no. 1 (1994).

16. David Arter, "Finland: From Neutrality to NATO?," *European Security* 5, no. 4 (1996). Consider inserting information about Finland's relation with the Soviet Union exposing the fear Finland has toward Russia.

17. Tuomas Forsberg and Tapani Vaahtoranta, "Inside the EU, Outside NATO: Paradoxes of Finland's and Sweden's Post-Neutrality," *European Security* 10, no. 1 (2001).

18. Oliver Thränert, "NATO, Missile Defence and Extended Deterrence," *Survival* 51, no. 6 (2009).

19. James A. Baker III, "Russia in NATO?," *Washington Quarterly* 25, no. 1 (2002).

20. *The New York Times*, "Foreign Affairs; Now a Word from X," *Friedman, Thomas L*, May 2, 1998, nytimes.com/1998/05/02/opinion/foreign-affairs-now-a-word-from-x.html.

21. William Burns, "How the US-Russian Relationship Went Bad," *Carnegie Endowment for International Peace* (2019), https://carnegieendowment.org/2019/03/08/how-u.s.-russian-relationship-went-bad-pub-78543.

22. Ibid.

23. Business Insider, "Putin: The Deterioration of Russia's Relationship with the West is the Result of many 'Mistakes,'" *Bertrand, Natasha*, January 11, 2016, finance.yahoo.com/news/putin-deterioration-russias-relationship-west-034104754.html.

24. See for example a recent article on the issue by the US American right wing think-tank Center for Strategy and International Studies: Heather A. Conley and Kathleen H. Hicks, "There is No Alternative to Sovereign Choice," *Commentary of the Center for Strategy and International Studies* (2017), www.csis.org/analysis/there-no-alternative-sovereign-choice.

25. For an overview, see Janusz Bugajski, *Georgian Lessons: Conflicting Russian and Western Interests in the Wider Europe* (Washington, DC: Center for Strategic and International Studies, 2010).

26. Glenn Diesen and Conor Keane, "The Two-Tiered Division of Ukraine: Historical Narratives in Nation-building and Region-Building," *Journal of Balkan and Near Eastern Studies* 19, no. 3 (2017).

27. Author interview, in Glenn Diesen, *EU and NATO Relations with Russia: After the Collapse of the Soviet Union* (London: Routledge, 2016).

28. Marius Vahl and Michael Emerson, "Moldova and the Transnistrian Conflict," *JEMIE—Journal on Ethnopolitics and Minority Issues in Europe*, no. 1 (2004).

29. The Republic of Moldova, "Constitution of 1994 with Amendments through 2006" (Constitute Project, 2006).

30. See also: David Noack, "Politics of Neutrality in the Post-Soviet Space: A Comparison of Concepts, Practices, and Outcomes of Neutrality in Moldova, Turkmenistan and Ukraine 1990–2015," in *Notions of Neutralities*, ed. Pascal Lottaz and Herbert Reginbogin (Lanham, MD: Lexington, 2019).

31. Kremlin, "Road Map on the Common Space of External Security" (Moscow: Presidential Executive Office, 2005).

32. Commission of the European Communities, "Commission Staff Working Document accompanying the Communication From the Commission to the European Parliament and the Council" (Brussels 2008).

33. Vladimir Chizhov, "Integration Is No Reason for Confrontation," *Russia Beyond the Headlines* 26 (2012), rbth.com/articles/2012/06/26/integration_is_no_reason_for_confrontation_15985.html.

34. Samuel Charap and Mikhail Troitskiy, "Russia, the West and the integration dilemma," *Survival* 55, no. 6 (2013): 49.

35. Ibid., 50.

36. Tor Bukkvoll, "Ukraine and NATO: The Politics of Soft Cooperation," *Security Dialogue* 28, no. 3 (1997): 368.

37. R Craig Nation, *NATO's Relations with Russia and Ukraine* (Brussels: NATO, Office of Information and Press, 2000), 19.

38. Taras Kuzio, *Ukraine under Kuchma: Political Reform, Economic Transformation and Security Policy in Independent Ukraine* (London: Macmillan, 1997).

39. Nicholas Ross Smith, "The EU and Russia's Conflicting Regime Preferences in Ukraine: Assessing Regime Promotion Strategies in the Scope of the Ukraine Crisis," *European Security* 24, no. 4 (2015).

40. Suzanne Lynch, "Russia Warned It Might Breach Helsinki Accord," *The Irish Times* (November 30, 2013).

41. James Sherr, *The New East-West Discord: Russian Objectives, Western Interests* (Clingendael: Clingendael Institute, 2015), 26.

42. Janusz Bugajski, "Moscow Dissects Central-Eastern Europe," *The American Interest*, (December 29, 2014).

43. Andrei P. Tsygankov, "The Sources of Russia's Fear of NATO," *Communist and Post-Communist Studies* 51, no. 2 (2018).

44. Filip Ejdus, "Beyond National Interests: Identity Conflict and Serbia's Neutrality toward the Crisis in Ukraine," *Südosteuropa. Zeitschrift für Politik und Gesellschaft*, no. 3 (2014).

45. Igor Ivanov, "The Sunset of Greater Europe," *Russian International Affairs Council* (2015), russiancouncil.ru/en/analytics-and-comments/analytics/zakat-bolshoy-evropy/.

46. Sergei Karaganov, "Eurasian way out of the european crisis," *Russia in Global Affairs* 8 (2015).

47. Glenn Diesen, *Russia's Geoeconomic Strategy for a Greater Eurasia* (Routledge, 2017).

48. Alexander Lukin, "Russia, China, and the Emerging Greater Eurasia," in *International Relations and Asia's Northern Tier: Sino-Russia Relations, North Korea, and Mongolia*, ed. Gilbert Rozman and Sergey Radchenko (Singapore: Palgrave Macmillan, 2018).

49. Gatev Ivaylo and Glenn Diesen, "Eurasian Encounters: The Eurasian Economic Union and the Shanghai Cooperation Organisation," *European Politics and Society* 17, no. 1 (2016).

50. Konstantin Truevstev, "Russia–Iran: In Syria and the Middle East," *Valdai Discussion Club* (2019), valdaiclub.com/a/highlights/russia-iran-in-syria-and-the-middle-east/.

51. Cordula Rastogi and Jean-François Arvis, *The Eurasian Connection: Supply-Chain Efficiency along the Modern Silk Route through Central Asia*, Directions in Development (Washington, DC: World Bank, 2014), 4.

## SELECTED REFERENCES

Arter, David. "Finland: From Neutrality to NATO?" *European Security* 5, no. 4 (1996): 614–32.

Baker III, James A. "Russia in NATO?" *Washington Quarterly* 25, no. 1 (2002): 93–103.

Booth, Ken, and Nicholas Wheeler. *The Security Dilemma: Fear, Cooperation, and Trust in World Politics*. Springer Nature, 2007.

Bugajski, Janusz. *Georgian Lessons: Conflicting Russian and Western Interests in the Wider Europe*. Washington, DC: Center for Strategic and International Studies, 2010.

———. "Moscow Dissects Central-Eastern Europe." *The American Interest* (December 29, 2014).

Bukkvoll, Tor. "Ukraine and NATO: The Politics of Soft Cooperation." *Security Dialogue* 28, no. 3 (1997): 363–74.

Burns, William. "How the US-Russian Relationship Went Bad." *Carnegie Endowment for International Peace* (March 8, 2019). https://carnegieendowment.org/2019/03/08/how-u.s.-russian-relationship-went-bad-pub-78543.

Bush, George. "A Europe Whole and Free: Remarks to the Citizens in Mainz" (1989), usa.usembassy.de/etexts/ga6-890531.htm.

Business Insider. "Putin: The Deterioration of Russia's Relationship with the West is the Result of Many 'Mistakes.'" *Bertrand, Natasha*, January 11, 2016, finance.yahoo.com/news/putin-deterioration-russias-relationship-west-034104754.html.

Charap, Samuel, and Mikhail Troitskiy. "Russia, the West and the Integration Dilemma." *Survival* 55, no. 6 (2013): 49–62.

Chizhov, Vladimir. "Integration is no reason for confrontation." *Russia Beyond The Headlines* 26 (2012). rbth.com/articles/2012/06/26/integration_is_no_reason_for_confrontation_15985.html.

Commission of the European Communities. "Commission Staff Working Document Accompanying the Communication From the Commission to the European Parliament and the Council." Journal.COM (2008), 823.
Conley, Heather A., and Kathleen H. Hicks. "There is No Alternative to Sovereign Choice." *Commentary of the Center for Strategy and International Studies* (April 27, 2017), www.csis.org/analysis/there-no-alternative-sovereign-choice.
Diesen, Glenn. *EU and NATO Relations with Russia: After the Collapse of the Soviet Union*. London: Routledge, 2016.
———. *Russia's Geoeconomic Strategy for a Greater Eurasia*. Routledge, 2017.
Diesen, Glenn, and Conor Keane. "The Two-Tiered Division of Ukraine: Historical Narratives in Nation-Building and Region-Building." *Journal of Balkan and Near Eastern Studies* 19, no. 3 (2017): 313–29.
Ejdus, Filip. "Beyond National Interests: Identity Conflict and Serbia's Neutrality toward the Crisis in Ukraine." *Südosteuropa. Zeitschrift für Politik und Gesellschaft*, no. 03 (2014): 348–62.
Forsberg, Tuomas, and Tapani Vaahtoranta. "Inside the EU, Outside NATO: Paradoxes of Finland's and Sweden's Post-Neutrality." *European Security* 10, no. 1 (2001): 68–93.
Goetschel, Laurent. "Neutrality, a Really Dead Concept?" *Cooperation and Conflict* 34, no. 2 (1999): 115–39.
Hanhimäki, Jussi M. *Containing Coexistence. America, Russia, and the "Finnish Solution." 1945–1956*. Kent: Kent State University Press, 1997.
Herz, John H. "Power Politics and World Organization." *American Political Science Review* 36, no. 6 (1942): 1039–52.
Heywood, Andrew. *Key Concepts in Politics and International Relations*. Macmillan International Higher Education, 2015.
Ivanov, Igor. "The Sunset of Greater Europe." *Russian International Affairs Council* (2015). russiancouncil.ru/en/analytics-and-comments/analytics/zakat-bolshoy-evropy/.
Ivaylo, Gatev, and Glenn Diesen. "Eurasian Encounters: The Eurasian Economic Union and the Shanghai Cooperation Organisation." *European Politics and Society* 17, no. 1 (2016).
Judt, Tony. *Postwar: A History of Europe Since 1945* [in English]. New York: Penguin Press, 2005.
Karaganov, Sergei. "Eurasian Way Out of the European Crisis." *Russia in Global Affairs* 8 (2015).
Kremlin. "Road Map on the Common Space of External Security" (Moscow: Presidential Executive Office, 2005).
Kuzio, Taras. *Ukraine under Kuchma: Political Reform, Economic Transformation, and Security Policy in Independent Ukraine*. London: Macmillan, 1997.
Lukin, Alexander. "Russia, China, and the Emerging Greater Eurasia." In *International Relations and Asia's Northern Tier: Sino-Russia Relations, North Korea, and Mongolia*, edited by Gilbert Rozman and Sergey Radchenko. Singapore: Palgrave Macmillan, 2018.
Lynch, Suzanne. "Russia Warned It Might Breach Helsinki Accord." *The Irish Times* (November 30, 2013).
Morgenthau, Hans J. *Politics among Nations: The Struggle for Power and Peace*. Edited by Kenneth W. Thompson, vol. 6. Beijing: Peking University Press, 1985.
———. "The Problem of Neutrality." *University of Kansas City Law Review* 7, no. 109 (1938): 109–28.
Nation, R. Craig. *NATO's Relations with Russia and Ukraine*. Brussels: NATO, Office of Information and Press, 2000.
NATO. "The North Atlantic Treaty" (Washington, DC, 1949).
Noack, David. "Politics of Neutrality in the Post-Soviet Space: A Comparison of Concepts, Practices, and Outcomes of Neutrality in Moldova, Turkmenistan and Ukraine 1990–2015." In *Notions of Neutralities*, edited by Pascal Lottaz and Herbert Reginbogin, 267–88. Lanham, MD: Lexington, 2019.
Rastogi, Cordula, and Jean-François Arvis. *The Eurasian Connection: Supply-Chain Efficiency along the Modern Silk Route through Central Asia*. Directions in Development. Washington, DC: World Bank, 2014.

Schweller, Randall L. "Bandwagoning for Profit: Bringing the Revisionist State Back In." *International Security* 19, no. 1 (1994): 72–107.

Sherr, James. *The New East-West Discord: Russian Objectives, Western Interests*. Clingendael: Clingendael Institute, 2015.

Slavinsky, Boris. *The Japanese-Soviet Neutrality Pact: A Diplomatic History, 1941–1945*. Translated by Geoffrey Jukes. London: RoutledgeCurzon, 2004.

Smith, Nicholas Ross. "The EU and Russia's Conflicting Regime Preferences in Ukraine: Assessing Regime Promotion Strategies in the Scope of the Ukraine Crisis." *European Security* 24, no. 4 (2015): 525–40.

Svec, Milan. "The Prague Spring: 20 Years Later." *Foreign Affairs* 66, no. 5 (Summer 1988): 981.

*The New York Times*. "Foreign Affairs; Now a Word from X." Friedman, Thomas L., May 2, 1998, nytimes.com/1998/05/02/opinion/foreign-affairs-now-a-word-from-x.html.

The Republic of Moldova. "Constitution of 1994 with Amendments through 2006" (Constitute Project, 2006).

Thorun, Christian. *Explaining Change in Russian Foreign Policy: The Role of Ideas in Post-Soviet Russia's Conduct toward the West*. New York: Palgrave Macmillan, 2009.

Thränert, Oliver. "NATO, Missile Defence and Extended Deterrence." *Survival* 51, no. 6 (2009): 63–76.

Trenin, Dmitri. *From Greater Europe to Greater Asia*. The Sino-Russian Entente. Moscow: Carnegie Moscow Center, 2015.

Truevstev, Konstantin. "Russia–Iran: In Syria and the Middle East." *Valdai Discussion Club* (July 3, 2019). valdaiclub.com/a/highlights/russia-iran-in-syria-and-the-middle-east/.

Tsygankov, Andrei P. "The Sources of Russia's Fear of NATO." *Communist and Post-Communist Studies* 51, no. 2 (2018): 101–11.

Vahl, Marius, and Michael Emerson. "Moldova and the Transnistrian Conflict." *JEMIE—Journal on Ethnopolitics and Minority Issues in Europe*, no. 1 (2004): 1–29.

*Chapter Seven*

# America's Experience with Neutrality

*An Epoch of Neutrality*

Herbert R. Reginbogin

What the nineteenth century brought to Great Britain, the twentieth century, did for the United States, resulting in each nation becoming the most powerful country of their era. The "American Century"[1] was shaped by a robust constitutional democracy promoting individual rights and influencing the concept of neutrality in many ways, from contributing to international humanitarian law to, ironically, even calling for its complete abandonment when fighting terrorism.[2] Contrary to America's early experience, when neutrality was a pillar of US foreign policy, after the Second World War, the US would never again adopt the status of neutrality, placing a "tombstone on an epoch." After the war, Washington embarked on the creation of a "new world order" based on the United Nations Charter, the Bretton Woods principles, and the Nuremberg Trials, in the spirit of "bellum iustum" (just war).[3] Meanwhile, other countries continued to practice neutrality based on the spirit of the Hague Conventions and of traditional sovereign rights until today. They delivered humanitarian services and contributed to the reduction of tensions among adversaries during the Cold War and beyond.[4]

To many Americans today, the meaning and experience of US neutrality are buried in history textbooks, as a memory of an unsuccessful past. When fascist nations in the 1930s and 1940s became outlaws of humanity, violating international law by committing crimes of aggressive war, the United States first tried not to become entangled in the Eurasian wars. US Congress passed four neutrality Acts, and the White House reminded hostile governments to respect US rights to trade and remain at peace with all parties. Nevertheless, the neutrality acts failed to keep the US out of another world war. In the end, America relinquished its 150 years of neutrality policy for a New World

Order. However, today that order based on the rule of law is once again changing

At a time of US-Russian proxy wars in Ukraine and Syria, on the brink of war between the United States and Iran, and an increasingly assertive China and North Korea, the risks of a future total war could occur due to a potentially fatal mistake.[5] New weapons such as unmanned drones and cyberweapons, heighten this danger, as there is no consensus around how states should respond to their use.[6] Although the unparalleled scope and scale of destruction of World War I and II resemble nothing like most violent conflicts today, great-power conflicts still exist. Understanding how they happened can help avoid future wars or at least limit their scale. But to determine that the potential for great-power war is to decline requires a clear conceptual understanding of what concept could alter the behavior of states.[7]

By exploring key moments of US neutrality history, this chapter argues that America's experience with neutrality can be a guideline for dealing with foreign and security challenges related to the threat of war. US precedence shows that a new security architecture built around beltways of countries employing the law and policy of neutrality would benefit not only orthodox state-centric security needs but also deliver improvements to nontraditional security aspects like economic, societal, environmental, and human security.

## THE EPOCH BEGINS

Neutrality is a dichotomy of war that evolved "not as a conceptually and judicially separate and independent idea," but as "a by-product of the concept of war,"[8] which states experience at times in a world of chaos and conflict. America was no different. In the state-centric and multipolar nineteenth and twentieth centuries, the United States was occasionally neutral during most European conflicts, inspiring optimistic platitudes of justice, free trade, and pro-actively contributing to the law of neutrality. For America in the nineteenth century, neutrality was a geopolitical statecraft to remain aloof of European entanglements. It was about a sovereign state that pursued its own interests, not embroiled in armed conflicts of other states. The policies it used to do so prohibited sovereign acts by belligerents within its jurisdiction, upheld its rights, and exercised the responsibilities as a neutral to treat belligerents impartially. The American Civil War became a catalyst for writings about the conduct of war, describing and dictating how soldiers should conduct themselves in wartime to mitigate the effects of armed conflicts, especially concerning civilians and captured forces. This "American humanitarianism" became an essential part of the Hague Peace Conference of 1899, which would evolve throughout the next century.

America's experience with neutrality also became a culturally constructed narrative, starting with President George Washington's proclamation of neutrality in 1793. That paved the road to promote the United States as a neutral country until 1941 when, on December 7, the Japanese attack on Pearl Harbor and Hitler's subsequent declaration of war upended America's neutrality once and for all. Until then, neutrality embodied for Americans a moralistic identity of upholding free trade and promoting overall general peace, internationalism, and prosperity. Freedom of commerce as part of international law was to benefit both belligerents and neutrals. It provided Americans with the opportunity to safeguard liberty and justice at home under domestic naturality laws, similar to what was the case for other nations in the seventeenth and eighteenth centuries.[9] So what happened to almost one hundred fifty years of America's praise for neutrality?

In 1794, as a newcomer to the society of nations, US Congress ratified its first Neutrality Act, adopting Washington's proclamation.[10] It regulated America's relations with belligerent countries, following a war that broke out between Revolutionary France and Great Britain (1793). The United States was itself fiercely divided between those who supported the French, including Secretary of State Thomas Jefferson, and those who supported the British, like Secretary of the Treasury, Alexander Hamilton. The neutrality act made US foreign policy transparent and clear internally and externally. It included provisions that outlawed private individual support for belligerent causes and militaries.[11] The legislation was innovative at the time and was later even called "the most significant impetus to the crystallization of the modern concept of neutrality."[12] It provided parts of the foundation for modern neutrality law.

Ironically, it was America's advocacy for neutral rights that eventually entangled it in the British-French conflict (1789–1815). Both sides paid lip service to the maritime rights of neutral vessels and their goods, which was central to America's economy.[13] The Revolutionary Government of France and French privateers caused significant losses to US shipowners, close to $20 million by 1800.[14] The American protests eventually led to an undeclared naval Quasi-War (1798–1800) waged primarily in the Caribbean during the beginning of John Adams's presidency in 1798.[15]

Adams sought peace with France on the conditions US neutrality was reaffirmed,[16] agreed to compensation payments for shipping losses, and its military obligations to France canceled that were still officially in force under the 1778 Treaty of Alliance. In the Convention of 1800 (Treaty of Mortefontaine), the Quasi-War was to end, and France agreed to return captured American ships. Compensating American citizens for damages inflicted by France on American shipping were discussed separately.[17] As for reaffirming US neutrality and reestablishing commercial relations after terminating the 1778 Treaty of Alliance, France accepted the provisions but on the condition of US "benevolent neutrality," which allowed French privateers access to US ports, while captured British ships would be auctioned in American prize courts.[18] Problematically, the commercial provisions directly contradicted the prior US commitments to Britain, outlined in the 1795 Jay Treaty, which was based on impartiality and not on the support of a belligerent, even when that was purely defensive in nature.[19] Despite these obstacles, at first US trade with Great Britain flourished. Britain recognized America's neutrality, which opened markets across the West Indies and the Pacific, including China, for more than a decade. This stands in contrast to European neutrals whose commercial activities were sharply hampered between 1793 and 1815 due to Anglo-French warfare, which entailed various economic blockades (especially after 1806) and sanctions that both states enforced violently on neutrals.[20] The United States was eventually drawn into the conflict in 1812 against Britain due to its defense of neutral commercial rights and the imprisonment of American seamen. The war ended 1814 through the Treaty of Ghent, which restored national boundaries as before the war and resolved fishery disputes and limited naval armaments on the Great Lakes. With the end of hostilities with Britain, commerce would flourish again, and for more than two centuries, peaceful relations between the US and Britain were only occasionally interrupted by disputes over the rights and duties of US neutrality.[21]

## A NATION RISES AND EXPANDS WITH NEUTRALITY AT ITS SIDE

The American policy of neutrality entered a new phase in the early 1820s, when several European powers attempted to expand their colonial influence, such as Russia, claiming territory from Oregon to Alaska. In Latin America, the US government feared Spain's supposedly critical interests to restore its Empire following a set of revolutions, like the Mexican War of Independence in 1821. Great Britain, too, had an eye on playing an active role in the political and economic future of the Americas. John Quincy Adams feared a subservient role for the United States in an Anglo-American alliance, which worried many Americans.[22] In response, President James Monroe, in 1823, invoked the so-called "Monroe Doctrine."[23] In his message to Congress, he referred to the United States again as a neutral who wanted to avert foreign entanglements. The US had, in Monroe's words, not interfered "in the wars of the European powers in matters relating to themselves . . . nor does it comport with our policy to do so" [and] "with the existing colonies or dependencies of any European power we have not interfered and shall not interfere."[24] The core message of the Monroe Doctrine was, however, that the US expected from European powers the same treatment of its interests in the

Americas. Monroe stated that the US would not tolerate European colonial interference in South or North America. The territories to the south of the US were to be free of their power politics, which could only harm US trade and security interests. This was the first time that the United States effectively asserted its power over foreign lands, and it did so by declaring these territories off-limits to Great Power politics. In effect, the Monroe Doctrine was the extension of US domestic neutrality policy by neutralizing the entire American continent. Although the policy itself does not mention neutralization per-se, the outcome was just that. This became clearer the further neutrality legislation in International Law progressed. Supreme Court Justice Winslow, for example, noted in 1907 that, "we have in the United States some continuing faith in what is popularly called the Monroe Doctrine, which, from what-ever motive, it was established, secures to the states of the South American continent conditions which may in a sense be called those of neutralization."[25] In other words, the US imposed a neutral status on Latin America, forbidding Europe from further colonizing the continent. The Monroe Doctrine, through unilateral neutralization, established US hegemony in the Western Hemisphere for decades to follow.

Neutrality remained an essential factor of US policymaking also for domestic affairs. From 1823 until the American Civil War, the United States pushed westward with both the identity of a neutral country and some Americans explaining the emergence of the US as a global power to be a divinely inspired plan. Explanations for America's exceptionalism was founded in the belief of "Manifest Destiny" that the US was predestined to expand across the North American Continent. It was the belief in the "hand of providence," that it was America's mission to defend and promote democracy, to embrace it throughout the world and the following centuries as expounded by US President Woodrow Wilson—often forgetting the brutal killings and treatment of indigenous men, women, and children on the path toward modernity.[26]

Over the next decades, America maintained a neutral position during the Texas War for Independence (1835–1836) and the Canadian Uprising of 1837 until the US was drawn into the Mexican-American War (1846–1848) that looked to some like simple land grabbing.[27] Not so for the newly elected President, James K. Polk (1845), who laid claim to the lands that would later become California, Utah, Nevada, Arizona, New Mexico, Colorado, and Wyoming following the victorious outcome of the Mexican War. The dispute erupted over the 1845 US annexation of Texas. The Mexican Government did not recognize the US claim at first, arguing that this infringed on the Treaties of Velasco, signed by Mexican caudillo President and General Antonio López de Santa Anna after the Texas Revolution a decade earlier. President Polk ordered troops to the disputed area where Mexican forces attacked US forces, after which the United States Congress declared war. It was not an extralegal military adventure, but the Old-World Order, according to Hugo Grotius, "On the Laws of War and Peace,"[28] granting states to have whatever territory they could win by force. Wars of aggression were legal at the time, as in Grotius's world, might makes right. This was true for neutral states, too.[29]

## THE AMERICAN CIVIL WAR: CONTRIBUTION TO INTERNATIONAL HUMANITARIAN LAW & NEUTRALITY

Eventually, during the American Civil War, the US government expected other countries to remain neutral while Washington focused on defeating the confederate states. That, however, proved to be a tricky affair. The British, for example, had a different understanding of what it meant to be neutral toward the United States. Most infamously, Great Britain allowed for the construction of merchant's vessels in England that were sold to the Confederate states who, unsurprisingly, used them also for belligerent purposes. These infringements of neutrality were to be ruled as a breach of neutrality in the so-called "Alabama Claims" arbitration case after the War.[30] More impactful than such occasional experiences that the United States had with the neutralities of other states was the impact the Civil War had on the development of America's own impartiality and humanitarianism when it came to the conduct of war to mitigate human suffering. In the so-called 'Lieber Code' (authored by the German-American legal scholar and political philosopher Franz Lieber), a set of humanitarian rules were dictated instructing the Generals of the US Army (General Order № 100),[31] how soldiers should conduct themselves in wartime. It ruled out torture to extract confessions, described the rights and duties of prisoners of war and their capturing forces, and detailed the handling of the state of war. The Union Army's Lieber Code represented the reemergence of the law of armed conflict synonymous with "the laws of war" or international humanitarian law in describing the contemporary jus in bello. The Lieber Code came into force with President Abraham Lincoln's signature on April 24, 1863. Similar milestones like the formation of the International Committee of the Red Cross and the subsequent drafting of the first-ever Geneva Convention in 1864 became relevant source material for scholars and politicians at The Hague Convention of 1899, along where many of its provisions were formulated into the "laws of war and neutrality" that finally became the backbone of International Humanitarian Law at the end of the century.

## THE NEUTRAL US CHALLENGED BY IMPERIALIST POWERS, INTERNATIONAL LAW, AND TOTAL WAR

In 1898 the US declared war on Spain for its interference in Cuba and the American hemisphere. In the process, the US became itself an imperial power that did not stop in its backyard, but took over even the Philippines, continuing the colonization of the archipelago from the Spanish. Thereby, America entrenched itself deeply in Asian affairs, which led to an increase in visibility through a stronger naval presence to strengthen its security and access to China and other Asian markets. In the same year, the US annexed Hawaii and solidified its interest with the building of the Panama Canal under President William Howard Taft. He sought to use American economic and military power to sustain political regimes friendly to American commercial interests. Taft defended America's expansionist economic interests through marine backed dollar diplomacy, which meant loans granted to foreign countries by US banks would be secured through having US armed forces sent to guarantee loans in case those were at risk due to political upheaval. In short, the United States had built an Empire across the Americas and the Pacific during a period of imperial expansion. Upon taking office in 1914, US President Woodrow Wilson immediately denounced the Taft administration's foreign policy. He backed Latin American nations' pursuit of self-governance devoid of American intervention and withdrew American support for investments in China.

Despite Wilson loathing military action in Latin America by his predecessor, the president deployed American troops to Mexico during the civil war and sanctioned military intervention in Haiti (1915) and the Dominican Republic (1916) to preserve its dominance in the region. He also kept in place the troops that Taft had stationed in Nicaragua, unwilling to diminish America's presence near the Panama Canal.[32] Looking toward Europe, there was a bush-fire that had turned into an uncontrollable inferno overnight with the outbreak of World War I. Wilson responded declaring US neutrality, especially defending the right of the US to trade with either side of the war until it, too, became a belligerent in 1917. With World War I and II, the advent of "total war" changed the nature of warfare itself. Tactics of attrition involved the complete mobilization of resources and people, affecting the lives of all citizens in the warring countries. Even the remotest parts of the world became a battleground. Under the logic of total war, impartiality toward belligerents became much trickier as war-faring states would consider almost any neutral trade with their enemy as illegitimate. Something that was not the case in earlier wars.[33] Almost a decade later, another discussion emerged about the validity of neutrality. For some, the signing of the Kellogg-Briand Pact in 1928 had made neutrality ideologically indefensible, because it condemned war as a legal principle itself and established new norms that allowed the prosecution of government leaders for crimes against peace without reservations.[34]

Still, Americans in the 1920s had no trouble practicing neutrality themselves during the Greco-Turkish War (1919–1922), Mussolini's temporary occupation of Corfu (1923), and the Spanish-French expeditions to reconquer Northern Morocco known as the Rif War (1920–1926).[35] Following the 1928 Kellogg Pact, wars of the 1930s were mostly waged without declaring war to avoid international condemnation such as Japan which invaded Manchuria in 1931, Mussolini's campaign to annex Abyssinia (Ethiopia) in 1935, the Spanish Civil War in 1936, or in 1937, Japan's invasion of China (Second Sino-Japanese War). The events sparked neither a great debate nor a crisis of conscience about American involvement. However, when it came to the German and Soviet invasions of Poland and the Soviet invasion of Finland in 1939, America's admiration for the principles of neutrality was tested as the United States uneven-handedly had not served peace, but granted assistance to financially stable, even aggressive, states.[36] US neutrality legislation of the 1930s was supportive of free trade, which was a right of neutrals under international law. It was probably the most important natural right, from the standpoint of neutrals, since it followed naturally from their position of being at peace with belligerents.[37] Still, the neutrality acts forbade Americans to trade in munitions with belligerents or sail on their ships and conduct other business that was perfectly legal under international law but brought Americans into the fray of battle. The neutrality acts aimed to do away with the scenarios that had led the nation into conflict in 1812, 1898, and 1917. In the interwar period, however, neutral American trade often ended up benefitting the more powerful aggressor states for having invaded another country instead of helping the victim, which left Americans with a bitter taste and a moral dilemma.[38] Only when America entered the Second World War, it ended the practice, even seeking to ban all other neutral nations from enjoying that same right. US Congress was divided over neutrality legislation with advocates of selective embargoes to send a strong message to the world's dictators (not to mention to keep trade lines open for the Ethiopians, Spanish Republicans, and then other democracies). The idea of initiating an embargo was by itself a self-righteous moralistic decision to decide that right and wrong now had a place in statecraft. In other words, the neutrality acts could be inaugurating a new era when Americans would make liberal use of sanctions and other short-of-war forms of coercion to impact the policies and conflicts of others.[39] The subsequent US opposition to neutrality was ironic considering that, during the interwar years, President Roosevelt's government enacted no less than four Neutrality Acts, ratified by Congress, which precisely defined the terms of American neutrality in the pre-war years of 1935, 1936, 1937, and 1939. They reflected a dispute over who specifically Americans should embargo—only those judged "aggressors" or all belligerents? The 1935 act banned munitions exports to belligerents and restricted American travel on belligerent ships. The 1936 act banned loans to belligerents. In 1937 that was extended to civil wars and gave the president discretionary authority to restrict munitions sales on a "cash-and-carry" basis, meaning that any US products and raw materials (no arms) had to be paid in full in US Dollars (no loans were granted) and that they had to be transported on the ships of the purchaser. Thanks to this inventive clause, lucrative US sales of much-needed war materials such as crude oil, cotton, copper, steel, trucks, etc. could flow to Ethiopia and the Spanish Republicans during much of the initial hostilities.[40]

As, in 1937, another conflict appeared on the horizon, this time between Japan and China, the newly introduced Cash-and-Carry provision in the Neutrality Act showed significant flaws. The regulation was not even-handed and did not serve peace, but granted assistance to financially stable, even aggressive, states like Japan. Powerful countries benefitted from the legislation because they were the only ones able to fulfill both requirements of paying in cash and maintaining naval forces strong enough to transport US goods back home. Financially weak nations became not only victims of military aggression but were left on the sidelines, unable to purchase much-needed war materials. Another weakness was the ineffectiveness of embargoes as the example of US policy toward the Second Sino-Japanese War showed. As long as an undeclared war existed between both countries, implementing an embargo under the neutrality legislation would have included both countries and not Japan alone. Roosevelt wanted to keep the option open to supply China with arms and to station American warships in its harbors. An official declaration of war by Japan against China would have quickly put a stop to shipments of American arms, and much needed other goods to China because it would have automatically triggered the Cash-and-Carry clause. In such a case, China being no naval power and lacking much-needed cash would have been unable to buy and transport much of anything from the USA. The snag was, though, that after officially declaring war on China, Japan would also have lost the opportunity of buying finished arms, which were not tradable under the Cash-and-Cary provisions. That led to Japan refraining from officially declaring war on China, allowing Japan to continue purchasing considerable amounts of war materials from America.[41]

This apparent contradiction in American neutrality policy was never revised, but for the "American people" writes the historian Akira Iriye, "confronted with a neutrality crisis they were compelled to recognize that in a world so sharply divided between forces of democracy and totalitarianism, the policy of neutrality was not something to be innocently indulged in but would have serious implications for the struggle between these forces."[42] In August of 1936 (an election year), Roosevelt still held that: "We shun political commitments which might entangle us in foreign wars. . . . We are not isolationists except in so far as we seek to isolate ourselves completely from war."[43] At the same time, the restrictions of American neutrality policies limited him from giving adequate support to the armaments of Western powers. A new Cash-and-Carry bill, designed to replace the Neutrality Act of 1937 (which had lapsed in May 1939) was set to allow for the purchase of military arms to belligerents on the same cash-and-carry basis. It was impossible for Roosevelt to find a Congressional majority and so he tried at least for prolonging the 1937 Cash-and-Carry clause. On more than one occasion, the House and Senate by a combination of neutralists rejected the legislation fearing that renewing the Neutrality Act would draw the US into the conflict in Europe.

After the German invasion of Poland, the US explicitly declared its neutrality on September 5, 1939. At that time, many Americans were only moved by one thought, the desire to keep out of the war at any cost. Three weeks after the invasion, Congress met in a special session to (1) extend the Cash-and-Carry clause, (2) repeal the president's authorization for imposing armament embargos, and (3) decide on a return to "neutrality under international law."[44] Although the United States insisted on being recognized as a neutral power, the country did slowly but consistently move away from the principles of neutrality with those conflicted with economic or political self-interest. Some of its activities differed considerably from the duty of impartiality, as in the case of supporting Great Britain's fight against the Axis Powers. It began with the release of surplus military supplies in the summer of 1940 and the destroyer-for-bases deal that September, which violated the Neutrality Acts' ban on the public sale of war supplies (leasing them was not allowed) to belligerents by neutral states, following the Lend-Lease Agreement of 1941. In short, the United States succumbed to new interpretations of neutrality (or nonbelligerency) like Franco Spain's "pro-Axis neutrality," Vichy's France "suspicious quasi-neutrality," Ireland's "against everybody neutrality" as well as Salazar's Portugal's "beneficial-to-everyone 'strict' neutrality" and the pope's "spiritual neutrality" as it took sides in the pending conflicts in the interwar years.[45] In a world of such diverse neutrals, the old fail-safe refuge of neutrality faded away as war became ever more likely. Later, grand narratives would arise about US good-neighborly relations in helping Britain continue its fight against Hitler, but forgetting its role in prolonging the Second World War by giving exemptions to American companies under the Trading with the Enemy Act.[46] By the time the United States turned into a belligerent, neutrality was deemed evil, and so were European neutrals who were still pursuing trade with Nazi Germany, although their behavior only mirrored that of the United States until it became a belligerent itself.

When Roosevelt adopted the Lend-Lease Policy in 1941 to help Great Britain continue its fight against Germany by providing arms, raw materials, and food to powers at war with the Axis, he made it all too clear that the United States had relinquished traditional neutrality. It meant taking the US far away from its status as a neutral country by violating the principle laws of neutrality it participated in creating and helped lay down in the two Hague Conferences.[47] Finally, following Japan's attack on Pearl Harbor and Hitler's subsequent declaration of war against the United States, America formally abandoned the banner of neutrality forever. Now the US, as a belligerent, adopted a moralistic assault on neutrality attempting to force neutral countries to become allies or be deemed an enemy while the US did not take any legal steps to stop its business conglomerates from trading with Nazi Germany while a neutral. American companies and banks collaborated with Nazi-German corporations on a full scale of business transactions raising the question of how much their efforts prolonged World War II.[48] It was not until 1974 that the American public learned about the impact the concentrated economic power of the Big Three (Ford Motor Company, General Motors, and Chrysler Automobiles) motor vehicle production had in both Allied and Axis territories. In Germany, as the US was a neutral country, "General Motor and Ford became an integral part of the Nazi war efforts. GM's plants in Germany built thousands of aircraft propulsion systems for the Luftwaffe at the same time that its American plants produced aircraft engines for the US Army Air Corps. . . . Due to their multinational dominance of motor vehicle production, GM and Ford became the principal suppliers for the forces of fascism as well as for the forces of democracy."[49] Documents in Russian archives confirmed that Ford decided to keep its majority stake in the German Cologne Ford plant and to support the continued involvement of US companies in German enterprises.[50] On January 6, 1944, the first in a series of lawsuits to follow were filed by the Department of Justice against a series of British and American chemical companies. They had violated the Sherman Anti-Trust Act alleging that they were part of cartels aiding Hitler Germany. The lawsuits put an abrupt end to the practiced 'business as usual' and charged American, British, including German companies for alleged cartel arrangements to control quotas and prices of certain market-segments around the world. During the year, several more lawsuits followed against the chemical giants American Dupont, British Imperial Chemical Industries, and German I. G. Farben as well as against British-American alkali producers like Borax Consolidated Limited, Pacific Coast Borax, Goldfields American Development Co. Ltd. besides the German-owned American Potash & Chemical Company. Also, other industrial segments having cartel arrangements were charged, such as members of the match cartel.[51]

## US NEUTRALITY-AMNESIA AFTER 1945

After 1945, the United States' role in the interwar years was rebranded, and the term neutrality disappeared. Americans came to believe that "unlike self-serving European imperialists who grasped for power, Americans had undertaken their benevolent reign only after being prodded out of their shell and only because it was a dirty job that somebody had to do."[52] The US eventually embraced collective security instead of neutrality to achieve peace and security. New narratives about a "good-neighborly nation that had finally overcome isolationism"[53] emerged. Forgotten were the inconvenient facts that the US was a neutral trading partner of Hitler Germany and forgotten was that "all Americans hard-fought battles over neutral rights since the Napoleonic Wars, [and] all the agonizing over their fate during the 1920s and 1930s."[54] Such is the price for referring to the interwar years as isolationism instead of what it really was: neutrality.

In the post-Cold War Restitution Era of the 1990s, neutrals were branded criminals and demons for their roles in World War II, as US courts were employed to seek justice for the stolen assets of Jewish victims of World War II. The US brand-marked European neutrals during World War II for their "business as usual" approaches and significant collaboration with the Nazis. The US judiciary accepted jurisdiction in the filing of class-action suits against European banks accused of holding dormant accounts of Holocaust victims, industry profiting from slave labor, and other stolen assets like paintings having not been returned to their legal Jewish owners. The political agitation was so vocal that economic and political boycotts were widely called for in the US against Switzerland, German industry and financial services, and other European countries.

After 9/11, the role of neutrality in international conflicts was critically accentuated by President George W Bush's phrase in September 2001, "Every nation . . . now has a decision to make: Either you are with us or, you are with the terrorists."[55] and that there could be no neutrality in the War against Terror. The climate of opinion called forth the concept of "bellum iustum" of the Middle Ages, with many Americans feeling righteous about their cause of war unwilling to accept a neutral attitude. Not taking sides was often perceived as a sign of cowardice, indifference, egotistic isolationism, profit mongering, or all taken together unless it was perceived as being useful to the international community.

The disastrous situation following the "coalition of the willing" invasion of Iraq in 2003, continuous US presence in Afghanistan, the fight against ISIS, and overall conditions of failed states Syria, Libya, Yemen, including the millions of refugees and displaced persons in the Middle East has prompted growing public disillusionment toward foreign intervention. Opportunity and a growing need to rethink American foreign policy have given rise to tactical concepts like "retrenchment," "offshore balancing," and "balance of threat" set out to bring an end to America's age of endless wars and to reduce America's military footprint around the world. Still, there is no grand American policy to balance the challenges between isolationist and internationalist foreign policy, a strategy needed to look beyond pro-active diplomacy and military restraint.

Central to American Foreign and Security Policy in the twenty-first century is to overcome the state-centric approach that deals only with military threats. A modern approach must also consider nontraditional security issues like threats that challenge economic, societal, political, and environmental security. This can point the way to a better understanding of human security. A new security architecture in this context would deal with global existential issues of the new millennium by calling for a reset by major adversaries to use the geopolitical tools and humanitarian norms of neutrality for the sake of the international community to increase trust among themselves while reducing geopolitical regional tensions and risks of a nuclear Armageddon.

As a political idea, the US experience of neutrality coupled with isolationist motives is comparatively different from countries like Austria, Finland, and Sweden actively engaged in international foreign affairs while still considering themselves neutral. In this context it is essential to differentiate between the policy and the law of neutrality. While the legal obligations only apply concerning ongoing war between states for occasional neutrals and future wars for permanent neutrals, the policy of neutrals describe measures expected of them during peacetime strengthening their credibility as a neutral. The laws of neutrality prohibit military assistance or interference but are entirely free to recognize and establish diplomatic relations with other countries or not, and address human rights or international humanitarian law violations.

Beltways of permanently neutral countries (voluntary neutralization) should become a bedrock of regional buffer zones useful to the international community. Their commitment to neutrality is a commitment not to resort to armed violence unless to protect its territorial integrity and to take non-violent measures against a state which gravely violates international law such as genocide, crimes against humanity, or war crimes[56]—thus contributing to international peace and security. Secondly, the new security architecture of neutrals constitutes a useful role in mediating and as honest brokers[57] work together with a vast array of Nongovernmental Organizations (NGOs), like the Red Cross or Doctors Without Borders. At the same time, the US Intelligence community, academicians, political decision-makers, and government bureaucrats would need to work together to enhance the polity of this new security architecture. The model could use America's experience of neutrality to reduce tensions between the US and its rival powers China and Russia. As recently as in early 2014, two of America's senior policy advisors of the

United States, such as Henry Kissinger and Zbigniew Brzezinski, proposed to deescalate the crisis in Ukraine through a neutral Ukraine.[58] It could serve as a model to achieve peace, security, and justice as a geopolitically buffer zone. America's experience with neutrality needs to be revived to better understand the far-reaching framework it holds for a New American Foreign and Security Policy.

## NOTES

1. Jürg Martin Gabriel, *Swiss Neutrality and the "American Century": Two Conflicting Worldviews*, vol. 14 (Zürich: Forschungsstelle für Internationale Beziehungen, Eidgenössische Technische Hochschule Zürich, 1998).
2. CNN, "You Are Either with Us or Against Us," November 6, 2001, edition.cnn.com/2001/US/11/06/gen.attack.on.terror/.
3. Stuart E. Eizenstat, "Eizenstat Report: US and Allied Efforts to Recover and Restore Gold and Other Assets Stolen or Hidden by Germany during World War II, Preliminary Report" (Washington, DC: US Department of State, 1997).
4. Heinz Gaertner, ed., *Engaged Neutrality: An Evolved Approach to the Cold War* (Lanham, MD: Lexington, 2017).
5. Alan F. Philips, "20 Mishaps That Might Have Started Accidental Nuclear War," Project of the Nuclear Age Peace Foundation, http://nuclearfiles.org/menu/key-issues/nuclear-weapons/issues/accidents/20-mishaps-maybe-caused-nuclear-war.htm.
6. Protocol Additional (PA) to the Geneva Conventions of 12 August 1949, and relating to the Protection of Victims of International Armed Conflicts (Protocol 1) Adopted on 8 June 1977 by the Diplomatic Conference on the Reaffirmation and Development of International Humanitarian Law applicable in Armed Conflicts, https://www.ohchr.org/EN/ProfessionalInterest/Pages/ProtocolI.aspx.
   State parties under Article 36 of PA I require that new weapons should be checked for legality, not merely at the point of deployment or use but also in their "study, development, acquisition or adoption of a new weapon, means or method of warfare." Law should constrain weapon development rather than new weapon technology drive the shaping of new law.
7. Tanisha M. Fazal and Paul Poast, "War Is Not Over. What the Optimists Get Wrong About Conflict," *Foreign Affairs* November/December 2019, https://www.foreignaffairs.com/articles/2019-10-15/war-not-over.
8. Efraim Karsh, *Neutrality and Small States* (New York: Routledge, 1988), 13.
9. See Stephen C. Neff, *Friends but No Allies: Economic Liberalism and the Law of Nations* (New York: Columbia University Press, 1990), 20–37.
10. George Washington—Proclamation of Neutrality—April 22, 1793, www.revolutionary-war-and-beyond.com/proclamation-of-neutrality-by-george-washington-april-22-1793.html
11. Hans Haug, "Neutralität und Völkergemeinschaftpar," *Revue Internationale de la Croix-Rouge* 44, no. 525 (1962): 5.
12. Efraim Karsh, *Neutrality and Small States*, 17. Also see Matthias Maas, *Small States in World Politics: The Story of Small State Survival 1648–2016* (Manchester: Manchester University Press), 53.
13. Donald R. Adams Jr., "American Neutrality and Prosperity, 1793–1808: A Reconsideration," *The Journal of Economic History* 40, no. 4 (December 1980), 732.
14. Curtis P. Nettels, *The Emergence of a National Economy, 1775–1815* (New York, 1962), 239. It is estimated, for example, that between June 1796 and the same month in 1797, the French navy and privateers combined took some 316 American ships. By 1800, US losses from similar seizures amounted to $20 million.
15. The Treaty of Alliance was about French support for the US Revolutionary War in exchange for the US defending French possessions in the Caribbean against foreign aggression.

That meant the US was obliged to support France against their opponents in the 1792–1797 War of the First Coalition while it proclaimed to be a neutral in 1794.

16. The Treaty of Amity and Commerce signed at the same time as the Treaty of Alliance on February 6, 1778 promoted trade and commercial ties between the two countries. It allowed the presence of consuls and recognized the US as an independent nation.

17. Discussions' on compensation were suspended until the issue of cancelling the Treaties of 1778 were resolved which finally led to US to compensate its own citizens for the claimed damages of $20 million, although it was not until 1915 that the heirs received $3.9 million in settlement.

18. Charles S. Hyneman, "Neutrality during the European Wars of 1792–1815: America's Understanding of Her Obligations," *The American Journal of International Law* 24, no. 2 (1930).

19. Emmerich de Vattel, more than a century after Grotius, published "Le droit de gens" (Leiden 1758), promoted the doctrines of international law in diplomacy and politics. Vattel prescribed that a state that declared itself neutral could choose between strict and benevolent neutrality. Strict neutrality consisted in observing an attitude of impartiality between the belligerents. The neutral state could for instance authorize or prohibit the passage of troops over its territory, but all belligerents must enjoy the same treatment. Benevolent neutrality, on the other hand, allowed an unequal economic treatment of the belligerents. It even permitted the neutral to maintain an alliance with one of the belligerents, on the condition that it was purely defensive in nature, that it was concluded before the outbreak of war, and that the conditions were fixed in advance. Hersch Lauterpacht, ed., *Oppenheim's International Law*, 7th ed., vol. II (London: Longmans, 1952), 627; "The Limits of the Operation of the Law of War," *British Yearbook of International Law* 30 (1955).

20. On Napoleon's Continental Blockade see Katherine B. Aaslestad and Johan Joor, eds., *Revisiting Napoleon's Continental System: Local, Regional and European Experiences* (London: Palgrave Macmillan, 2015). On neutral trade during the period see Maartje M. Abbenhuis, *An Age of Neutrals: Great Power Politics, 1815–1914* (Cambridge: Cambridge University Press, 2014), 29–38.

21. Office of the Historian, "The Trent Affair, 1861," history.state.gov/milestones/1861-1865/trent-affair; Elizabeth Chadwick, "The British View of Neutrality in 1872," in *Notions of Neutralities*, ed. Pascal Lottaz and Herbert Reginbogin (Lanham, MD: Lexington, 2019).

22. History.com (ed.) 1823, December 2 Monroe Doctrine, www.history.com/this-day-in-history/monroe-doctrine-declared

23. The "Monroe Doctrine" was mainly written by the Secretary of State John Quincy Adams.

24. US History.org, "Monroe Doctrine," at www.ushistory.org/documents/monroe.htm

25. Erving Winslow, "Neutralization," *American Journal of International Law* 2 (1908): 379.

26. Michael Adas, "From Settler Colony to Global Hegemon: Integrating the Exceptionalist Narrative of the American Experience into World History," *The American Historical Review* 106, no. 5 (2001); Michael Adas, "From Settler Colony to Global Hegemon: Integrating the Exceptionalist Narrative of the American Experience into World History," *The American Historical Review* 106, no. 5 (2001).

27. Oona A. Hathaway and Scott J. Shapiro, *The Internationalists: How a Radical Plan to Outlaw War Remade the World* (New York: Simon & Schuster, 2017).

28. Hugo Grotius, *On the Law of War and Peace*, edited and translated by Campbell A. C. (Kitchener: Batoche Books, 1625).

29. Hathaway and Shapiro, *The Internationalists: How a Radical Plan to Outlaw War Remade the World*.

30. Chadwick, "The British View of Neutrality in 1872."

The controversy began when Confederate agents contracted for warships from British boatyards. The most successful of these cruisers was the Alabama, which was launched on July 29, 1862. The Alabama Claims were a series of demands for damages sought by the government of the United States from the United Kingdom in 1869, for the attacks upon Union merchant ships by Confederate Navy commerce raiders built in British shipyards during the

American Civil War. The claims focused chiefly on the most famous of these raiders, the CSS Alabama, which captured 58 Northern merchant ships before it was sunk in June 1864 by a US warship off the coast of France.

31. Instructions for the Government of the Armies of the United States in the Field, Prepared by Francis Lieber, LL.D. and Revised by a Board of Officers (New York: D. Van Nostrand, 1863) at https://archive.org/details/governarmies00unitrich.

32. David Emory Shi and George Brown Tindall, "America and The Great War, 1914–1920," in: *America: A Narrative History*, chapter 22.

See, W.W. Norton & Co. https://www.wwnorton.com/college/history/america10_cp/ch/22/documents.aspx.

33. Quincy Wright and Clyde Eagleton, "Neutrality and Neutral Rights Following the Pact of Paris for the Renunciation of War," *Proceedings of the American Society of International Law at Its Annual Meeting* 24 (1930).

34. See, Kelly Dawn Askin, *War Crimes Against Women: Prosecution in International War Crimes Tribunals* (The Hague: Martinus Nijhoff, 1997), 46. It served to charge the top Axis leaders responsible for starting World War II with war crimes tried at the Nuremberg and Tokyo Tribunals with some being executed.

35. William Appleman Williams, *The Tragedy of American Diplomacy* (New York: Norton, 1988), 111–26.

36. Nils Orvik, *The Decline of Neutrality 1914–1941*. With Special Reference to the United States and the Northern Neutrals (Oslo: Johan Grundt Tanum Forlag), 121–34; Herbert R. Reginbogin, *Faces of Neutrality: A Comparative Analysis of the Neutrality of Switzerland and other Neutral Nations during WW II*, trans. Ulrike Seeberger and Jane Britten (Berlin: Lit Verlag, 2009), 25; Louis Clerc, "The Hottest Places in Hell? Finnish and Nordic Neutrality from the Perspective of French Foreign Policy, 1900–1940," in *Caught in the Middle*, ed. Johan den Hertog and Samuël Kruizinga, *Neutrals, Neutrality, and the First World War* (Amsterdam University Press, 2011); Karen Gram-Skjoldager, "The Other End of Neutrality: The First World War, the League of Nations, and Danish neutrality," in *Caught in the Middle*, ed. Johan den Hertog and Samuël Kruizinga, *Neutrals, Neutrality, and the First World War* (Amsterdam University Press, 2011), 139–72; Lloyd E. Ambrosius, *Woodrow Wilson and American Internationalism* (New York: Cambridge University Press, 2017), 161. The United Nations Charter, by contrast, would be far more hostile to neutral powers: Jürg Martin Gabriel, *The American Conception of Neutrality after 1941* (New York: Palgrave Macmillan), 211.

37. On the logic of neutrality see chapter 3 of this volume.

38. Carroll Quigley, *Tragedy and Hope: A History of the World in Our Time* (New York: MacMillan, 1966), 294–95.

39. Brooke L. Blower, "From Isolation to Neutrality: A New Framework for Understanding American Political Culture, 1919–1941," *Diplomatic History* 38 (2014): 345.

40. Reginbogin, *Faces of Neutrality: A Comparative Analysis of the Neutrality of Switzerland and other Neutral Nations during WWII*, 59.

41. Max Silberschmidt, *Der Aufstieg der Vereinigten Staaten von Amerika zur Weltmacht* (Aarau, 1941), 433.

42. Akira Iriye, *The Cambridge History of American Foreign Relations—The Globalizing of America, 1913–1945*, vol. 3 (New York, 1993), 155–56.

43. Roosevelt's Address at Chautauqua, New York, August 14, 1936, https://web.viu.ca/davies/H324War/FDR.Chautauqua.Speech.Aug14.1936.htm; William L. Langer and S. Everett Gleason, *The Challenge to Isolation, 1937–1940* (New York: Harper and Brothers, 1952), 16.

44. Samuel Eliot Morison, Henry Steele Commager, and William E. Leuchtenburg, *The Growth of the American Republic* (Oxford: Oxford University Press, 1962), 538. Blower, "From Isolation to Neutrality: A New Framework for Understanding American Political Culture, 1919–1941," 371.

45. See, for example, Christian Leitz, *Nazi Germany and Neutral Europe during the Second World War* (Manchester: Manchester University Press, 2000).

46. Walther Hofer and Herbert Reginbogin, *Hitler, der Westen und die Schweiz, 1936–1945* (Zürich: NZZ libro, 2001); Reginbogin, *Faces of Neutrality: A Comparative Analysis of the Neutrality of Switzerland and other Neutral Nations during WWII*.

47. Arthur L. Funk, "American Wartime Relations with Neutral European States: The Case of the United States and Switzerland," in *Les Etats Neutres Européens et la Seconde Guerre Mondiale* (Neuchâtel: La Baconniere, 1985), 283. Betsy Baker, "Hague Peace Conferences (1899 and 1907)," in *Oxford Public International Law* (2009), https://opil.ouplaw.com/view/10.1093/law:epil/9780199231690/law-9780199231690-e305.

48. Reginbogin, *Faces of Neutrality: A Comparative Analysis of the Neutrality of Switzerland and other Neutral Nations during WWII*.

49. Bradford C. Snell, "American Ground Transport: A Proposal for Restructuring the Automobile, Truck, Bus and Rail Industries. Committee of the Judiciary Subcommittee on Antitrust and Monopoly, United States Senate 16–24 (1974)," in *Hearings before a Subcommittee of the Senate Committee on the Industrial Reorganization Act*, 93rd Congress 2nd Session (February 26, 1974), Part 4A, p. A–22, http://libraryarchives.metro.net/DPGTL/testimony/1974_statement_bradford_c_snell_s1167.pdf.

50. Russian Military State Archives (RGVA), Stock 700-1-85, Effektenhandel zwischen Fa. Otto Wolff und der Schweiz und mit weiterem Ausland., 444–45; See Walther Hofer and Herbert R. Reginbogin, *Hitler, der Westen und die Schweiz* (Zurich, 2001).

51. Walther Hofer and Herbert R. Reginbogin, *Hitler, der Westen und die Schweiz* (Zurich, 2001); Herbert R. Reginbogin, *Faces of Neutrality*.

52. Blower, "From Isolation to Neutrality: A New Framework for Understanding American Political Culture, 1919–1941," 347.

53. Ibid., 375.

54. Ibid.

55. CNN—Transcript of US President Bush's address before the joint Congress of the United States on September 20, 2001, http://edition.cnn.com/2001/US/09/20/gen.bush.transcript/.

56. Dietrich Schindler, "Neutrality and Morality," *14 American University International Law Review* (1998), 169.

57. Peter Hostettler and Olivia Danai, "Neutrality in Land Warfare," in *The Msx Plank Encyclopaedia of Public International Law (MEPEPIL)*.

58. Zbigniew Brzezinski, "Russia needs a 'Finland option' for Ukraine," *The Financial Times*, February 24, 2014; Henry Kissinger, "How the Ukraine Crisis Ends," *The Washington Post*, March 6, 2014.

## SELECTED REFERENCES

Aaslestad, Katherine B, and Johan Joor, eds. *Revisiting Napoleon's Continental System: Local, Regional, and European Experiences*. London: Palgrave Macmillan, 2015.

Abbenhuis, Maartje M. *An Age of Neutrals: Great Power Politics, 1815–1914*. Cambridge: Cambridge University Press, 2014.

Adas, Michael. "From Settler Colony to Global Hegemon: Integrating the Exceptionalist Narrative of the American Experience Into World History." *The American Historical Review* 106, no. 5 (2001): 1692–720.

———. "Michael Adas, "From Settler Colony to Global Hegemon: Integrating the Exceptionalist Narrative of the American Experience into World History." *The American Historical Review* 106, no. 5 (2001): 1692–720.

Ambrosius, Lloyd E. *Woodrow Wilson, and American Internationalism*. New York: Cambridge University Press, 2017.

Baker, Betsy. "Hague Peace Conferences (1899 and 1907)." In *Oxford Public International Law*, 2009.

Blower, Brooke L. "From Isolation to Neutrality: A New Framework for Understanding American Political Culture, 1919–1941." *Diplomatic History* 38 (2014): 345–76.

Brzezinski, Zbigniew. "Russia Needs a 'Finland Option' for Ukraine." *The Financial Times*, February 24, 2014.

Chadwick, Elizabeth. "The British View of Neutrality in 1872." In *Notions of Neutralities*, edited by Pascal Lottaz and Herbert Reginbogin, 87–112. Lanham, MD: Lexington, 2019.

Clerc, Louis. "The Hottest Places in Hell? Finnish and Nordic Neutrality from the Perspective of French Foreign Policy, 1900–1940." In *Caught in the Middle*, edited by Johan den Hertog and Samuël Kruizinga. Neutrals, Neutrality and the First World War, 139–54: Amsterdam University Press, 2011.

Dawn Askin, Kelly. *War Crimes Against Women: Prosecution in International War Crimes Tribunals*. The Hague: Martinus Nijhoff, 1997.

Eizenstat, Stuart E. "Eizenstat Report: US and Allied Efforts to Recover and Restore Gold and Other Assets Stolen or Hidden by Germany during World War 2, Preliminary Report." Washington, DC, 1997.

Funk, Arthur L. "American Wartime Relations with Neutral European States: The Case of the United States and Switzerland." In *Les Etats Neutres Européens et la Seconde Guerre Mondiale*. Neuchâtel: La Baconniere, 1985.

Gabriel, Jürg Martin. *The American Conception of Neutrality after 1941*. New York: Palgrave Macmillan, 2002.

———. *Swiss Neutrality and the "American Century": Two Conflicting Worldviews*. Vol. 14. Zürich: Forschungsstelle für Internationale Beziehungen, Eidgenössische Technische Hochschule Zürich, 1998.

Gaertner, Heinz, ed. *Engaged Neutrality: An Evolved Approach to the Cold War*. Lanham, MD: Lexington, 2017.

Gram-Skjoldager, Karen. "The Other End of Neutrality: The First World War, the League of Nations, and Danish neutrality." In *Caught in the Middle*, edited by Johan den Hertog and Samuël Kruizinga. Neutrals, Neutrality and the First World War, 155–72: Amsterdam University Press, 2011.

Grotius, Hugo. *On the Law of War and Peace*. Edited and translated by Campbell A. C. Kitchener: Batoche Books, 1625.

Hathaway, Oona A., and Scott J. Shapiro. *The Internationalists: How a Radical Plan to Outlaw War Remade the World*. New York: Simon & Schuster, 2017.

Haug, Hans. "Neutralität und Völkergemeinschaftpar." *Revue Internationale de la Croix-Rouge* 44, no. 525 (1962): 474–75.

Hofer, Walther, and Herbert Reginbogin. *Hitler, der Westen und die Schweiz 1936–1945* [in German]. Zürich: NZZ libro, 2001.

Hyneman, Charles S. "Neutrality during the European Wars of 1792–1815: America's Understanding of Her Obligations." *The American Journal of International Law* 24, no. 2 (1930): 279–309.

Karsh, Efraim. *Neutrality and Small States*. New York: Routledge, 1988.

Kissinger, Henry. "How the Ukraine Crisis Ends." *The Washington Post*, March 6, 2014.

Langer, William L, and S. Everett Gleason. *The Challenge to Isolation 1937–1940*. New York: Harper and Brothers, 1952.

Lauterpacht, Hersch. "The Limits of the Operation of the Law of War." *British Yearbook of International Law* 30 (1955): 206–43.

———, ed. *Oppenheim's International Law*. 7th ed, Vol. II. London: Longmans, 1952.

Maas, Matthias. *Small States in World Politics: The Story of Small State Survival 1648–2016*. Manchester: Manchester University Press, 2017.

Morison, Samuel Eliot, Henry Steele Commager, and William E. Leuchtenburg. *The Growth of the American Republic*. Oxford: Oxford University Press, 1962.

Neff, Stephen C. *Friends but No Allies: Economic Liberalism and the Law of Nations*. New York: Columbia University Press, 1990.

Orvik, Nils. *The Decline of Neutrality 1914–1941. With Special Reference to the United States and the Northern Neutrals*. Oslo: Johan Grundt Tanum Forlag, 1953.

Quigley, Carroll. *Tragedy and Hope. A History of the World in Our Time*. New York: MacMillan, 1966.

Reginbogin, Herbert R. *Faces of Neutrality: A Comparative Analysis of the Neutrality of Switzerland and other Neutral Nations during WWII*. Translated by Ulrike Seeberger and Jane Britten. Berlin: Lit Verlag, 2009.

Williams, William Appleman. *The Tragedy of American Diplomacy*. New York: Norton, 1988.

Winslow, Erving. "Neutralization." *American Journal of International Law* 2 (1908): 366–86.

Wright, Quincy, and Clyde Eagleton. "Neutrality and Neutral Rights Following the Pact of Paris for the Renunciation of War." *Proceedings of the American Society of International Law at Its Annual Meeting* 24 (1930): 79–114.

*Chapter Eight*

# The Nomos of Neutrality in East Asia

Herbert R. Reginbogin and Pascal Lottaz

This chapter highlights the changes, challenges, and tensions arising in the Indo-Pacific region due to China's rise as a great power and explores the potential for neutral approaches of East Asian countries toward them. While China's rise offers new trade opportunities, it also poses security risks. The East Asian seas used to be marginal to western security thinking, but their long histories of contestation and their roles as global trade routes are central to the global economy. Their geography is also a critical part of the bilateral relationship between China and the United States. However, the vastly different value systems of a liberal democracy and a Communist-Leninist one-party state is inadvertently problematic and has already produced many conflicts.[1] Not only maritime disputes, but nuclear deterrence strategies impact the security of East Asian States profoundly, which are vital to understanding China's firm stand to establish a comprehensive maritime domain in the South China Sea. While containment, deterrence, and public diplomacy appear to have their limitations and are unable to deliver a reconciliation between the Great Powers, this chapter proposes a reset of the security architecture in East Asia. At the core of this new security architecture is the reconceptualization of permanent neutrality which could serve as an incentive for China to return to the liberal world order and resolve issues in the East and South China Seas in a peaceful and equitable madnner.

## US–SINO RELATIONS AND EAST ASIA

China's rise as a global power is ever more apparent in its determination to amend, challenge, and, at times, undermine the "operating system" of alliances, freedom of navigation, and sanctity of contracts established by the

United States since the end of the Second World War.[2] Due to China's economic development and military modernization, the strategic balance of power has changed in the Indo-Pacific region and particularly in the heartland of East Asia. This raises questions on the role of China, either as a benign and responsible power[3] or one that might attempt to assert coercive influence on its neighbors and elsewhere in the world militarily or socio-economically (through its "One Belt, One Road" initiative) to create "a world without American global supremacy, and revise the US-dominated economic and geopolitical world order."[4] Washington is especially concerned about China's growing military capabilities, while Beijing has been critical of the United States' alliance system and its "pivot to Asia" strategy since the Obama administration. Japan, the Republic of Korea (South Korea), and the Republic of China (ROC, Taiwan) are parts of the evolving North-East Asian regional order as essential allies of the United States. They are taking steps to uphold and promote a competitive, free, and open international order, which is at the center of Sino-US tensions. They are models of advanced democracies in East Asia, counterbalancing China's authoritarian model of economic development. On the continent, the economically weak post-communist Mongolia, sandwiched between Russia and the People's Republic of China (PRC), currently leverages its permanently neutral status to influence regional diplomacy, mediating trilaterally between North Korea, South Korea, and the US to advance peace in East Asia.[5] The US, at the same time, has been trying to mediate between its allies, Japan and South Korea, to overcome the "unfinished business" of World War II regarding reparations from Japan and Japanese companies for Korean forced labor and sexual slavery (the so-called "comfort women" issue). Naturally, this is a detriment to their alliance as well as the alliance with the US. Broader and united Japan–South Korea security coordination is needed not only to cope with North Korea's nuclear threat but also to balance the PRC's incredible economic rise and its repressive attitude toward democratization.

Further south, in the Taiwan Strait, more conflict is boiling. As international waters and part of the regional security interests, the US and its Allies continue to conduct freedom of navigation operations, just as they do in the South China Sea.[6] Beijing criticizes such maneuvers as provocations. However, Taiwan's contested political status and its geostrategic position have enormous implications for US-Sino relations. The "One China Principle," which Washington has accepted as the base for Sino-American relations since Nixon's rapprochement to Beijing in 1971, has led to a complicated situation. The principle holds that there is only one Chinese state and that the island of Taiwan is part of it. To Beijing, this is a sacrosanct principle, and it lashes out at anyone who claims otherwise or seeks independence for Taiwan.[7] To assert its standpoint, the PRC has steadily increased its military spending over the past decades. The build-up of its navy will enhance the power of its land forces and enable the PRC to challenge America's dominance along the South and the East China Seas,[8] which it perceives as a natural part for the security of its southern provinces, the most populated and developed parts of the country. It is a core national interest, and Beijing has made it clear that it wants to control this sea, and Taiwan with it.[9]

However, the territorial claims over an extensive range of islands and features in the South China Sea constitute the principal security concern also to Japan, South Korea, and several members of the Association of Southeast Asian Nations (ASEAN). Their region is increasingly becoming the primary node of global power politics.[10] The PRC has repeatedly signaled that it will not adhere to the established rules and mechanisms of conflict settlement. For example, it refuses to accept a ruling by the Permanent Court of Arbitration (PCA) at The Hague that what it calls "historical rights" over land features in the South China Sea are void and that their occupation is illegal under international law. The PRC even refuses to acknowledge the jurisdiction of the ICA and continues to expand its large land reclamation projects on the Spratly and Paracel Islands. Subsequent militarization of these features has drawn international criticism and raised the alarm among other claimants, most prominently the Philippines.[11]

The reasons for the PRC's assertive behavior are multifaceted and include Beijing's perception of the historical, symbolic, and economic meaning of the South China Sea, as well as the overall national security interest and its military strategy for space and the deep sea.[12] Not all reasons can be elaborated here, but it is essential to consider that recent Chinese history includes traumatic experiences of victimization and humiliation as, for example, through the western "open-door policy" and the horrific Opium Wars of 1839–1842 and 1856–1860, which resulted in ten to twelve million Chinese addicts and devastated many of the large coastal cities. In the twentieth century, China continuously suffered from colonial enterprises, including that of Japan, who split off Manchuria from the Chinese mainland and waged a brutal war for fifteen years (1931–1945) against the National Government. That conflict included terrible war crimes such as the notorious "Rape of Nanking," during which the capital city was destroyed, and tens of thousands of Chinese civilians were slaughtered by Japanese soldiers.[13] These experiences of suffering and victimhood cut as profoundly as the Civil War does in the US or the First and Second World Wars do in Europe. They are tragedies that shape perceptions for centuries. Proposals for security architectures in the Indo-Pacific have to deliver not only national and human security from current threats but must be commensurable with historical narratives to deliver ontological security as well.[14] Otherwise, proposals will run aground from local rejection. But first, the primary conflict dynamic between the two contesting super-powers needs to be studied. The following section explains common US perceptions of China's role in Asian Security affairs.

## THE US VIEW OF "THE CHINA CHALLENGE"

For over four decades, the United States assumed that "engagement" with the PRC would induce Beijing to cooperate with the West on a wide range of policy issues. The seasoned Chinese politician Deng-Xiaoping, in the 1980s, embraced the time-tested strategy; "hide your strength, bide your time, and never take the lead."[15] In 2015, the era of relative calm ended when, under President Xi Jinping, the Ministry of Defense issued a white paper titled "Chinese Military Strategy," which vowed to strengthen its naval power in support of Beijing's geopolitical objectives of safeguarding the PRC's maritime rights and interests. The document indicated the United States and other neighbors for taking "provocative actions" around the PRC's reefs and islands. It also held that the PRC would reinforce its "military presence on China's reefs and islands that they have illegally occupied"[16] and highlighted the importance of Taiwan's status of "Reunification," which it said, "is an inevitable trend in the course of national rejuvenation."[17] Over the years, Beijing's rhetoric has become even more blatantly bellicose, threatening the twenty-four million people of Taiwan with military intervention. "We make no promise to renounce the use of force and reserve the option of taking all necessary means,"[18] Xi said in his 2019 New Year speech, adding that the Taiwan issue was an internal matter and that China would permit "no external interference."[19] At the same time, however, Xi also indicated that China was aiming at taking center stage in the globalized world.[20] The bellicose language on security and the reconciliatory role of leadership internationally are at odds with each other but are part of Beijing's strategy of national development.

On the one hand, the PRC lifted hundreds of millions of people out of poverty and into the middle class over the past forty years. On the other hand, this coincided with a rising number of electoral democracies (tripling from 39 in 1974 to 125 today), of which many also achieved remarkable growth rates.[21] Xi wishes to reassert the PRC's greatness as the USA retrenches globally from international treaties and organizations. The election of US President Donald Trump in 2015 created doubt whether the country would remain interested in the global leadership role it took in the Cold War and after 1989. At the same time, Xi declared the arrival of a revolutionary "new era," underscoring his country's authoritarian model of development.[22] His portrayal of Chinese cultural and historical heritage provides a fundamental difference in leadership style compared to that exercised by Western powers. In the Auditorium of the Great Hall of the People in Beijing, on October 2017, he said, "it means the path, the theory, the system, and the culture of socialism with Chinese characteristics have kept developing, blazing a new trail for other developing countries to achieve modernization."[23] He continued to say, "it offers a new option for other countries and nations who want to speed up their development while preserving their independence, and it offers Chinese wisdom and a Chinese approach to solving the problems facing mankind."[24] Thus, the PRC committed itself to respect the choices of each State, that is, it promised not to intervene in the internal affairs of other countries as an alternative to western values of humanitarian intervention. However, what does this mean for the long-term development of the region? Will States that are economically dependent on China become "vassals" in the future, tactically intimidated by China's authoritarian model and prepared to care more for economic prosperity, stability, and security at the cost of giving up "a little liberty?"[25]

In addition to the PRC, the US views Russia as the other revanchist country on the Eurasian continent. It is an essential player in the region, posing challenges comparable to those of the PRC to the liberal international order—not the least because of its portrayal of encirclement by the West. The flight by two PRC H-6 and two Russian Tu-95 long-range, nuclear-capable bombers in the skies between Japan and South Korea backed up by a Russian A-50 early warning plane and its Chinese counterpart, a KJ-2000, on July 23, 2019, were intended to send a signal to the United States and its allies that the two powers were ramping-up military cooperation.[26] Albeit no direct nuclear military cooperation is intended, but nonetheless, Beijing and Moscow's political convergence is moving toward specific nuclear issues about America's more assertive nuclear weapons policy and the slow unraveling of arms limitations agreements.[27] The incident not only raised tensions in South Korea and Japan but overshadowed the growing hostility surrounding Taiwan and North Korea.[28]

The PRC and Russia have become partners in other areas too. For example, the PRC now receives oil supplies from Russia through an overland pipeline, decreasing Beijing's vulnerability to possible US oil sanctions. Beijing also profits from Moscow's military technology. It purchased aircraft engines, advanced weaponry, the S-400 air-defense system, and 24 SU-35 fighter jets from it. Notably, the S-400 system of antiaircraft missiles can strike unmanned aerial vehicles as well as cruise missiles. This system can contest the airspace near Taiwan and the Paracel and Senkaku Islands.[29] However, the cooperation between America's rivals goes beyond combined military maneuvers. As relations between them and the US have turned sour, the leaders of the PRC and the Soviet Union have declared their relationship to be at an "unprecedentedly high level." They have signed up to a joint statement on "Strategic Interaction Entering a New Era," and plan to undertake significant projects in the sectors of aerospace, energy, investments, and aviation. While Chinese direct investment in the US dropped by 90 percent from $46 billion in 2016 to $4.8 billion in 2018,[30] Russo-Chinese bilateral trade dramatically increased from $69.6 billion in 2016 to $107.1 billion in 2018, with Huawei, a PRC company, developing Russia's 5G network and

Russia becoming the PRC's largest supplier of crude oil. With Russia's economy still restrained by sanctions imposed after its annexation of Crimea, President Vladimir Putin promised to combine the Eurasian Economic Union with Xi Jinping's Belt and Road Initiative to form a "greater Eurasian partnership."[31] This marks a new level of cooperation and is indicative of Russia's turn to the east.[32] Although economic cooperation between the two powers is not of primary security concern to the US, the Russian armament of the PRC significantly complicates the security of America's allies and friends in the region, for which it seeks to take countermeasures. In April 2019, for example, the US Department of State approved an export license for 66 F-16 aircraft to Taiwan, worth $8 billion.[33]

While Russia is willing to divert the United States' strategic focus from Europe toward Asia by fortifying the PRC's military capabilities, there are still many shades of grey in this relationship. Russia remains impartial about maritime disputes in the South and East China Seas. Also, Russian and Chinese interests in the Indo-Pacific do not coincide. Beijing's ambition is to gain primacy in the region, whereas Moscow still has strategic priorities in Europe and the Middle East, and also needs to worry about economic difficulties at home. Russia is not willing to be dependent on the PRC and does not attempt to form a united front on maritime issues because that would undermine its relations with Vietnam, which has an ongoing maritime dispute with the PRC. While it may not be in Russia's interests to side with the regular US denunciations of PRC maritime expansionism, it is also not in the interest of the Kremlin that Beijing controls the multitrillion-dollar shipping lanes linking the Indian and Pacific oceans. Besides, Russian energy companies have a vested interest in the region. Rosneft, whose primary shareholder is the Russian government, but also Gazprom and Zarubezhneft,[34] can expect Russia to play the old-fashioned great-power politics to defend cash flows from them to the state.[35]

Warnings from Beijing continue that it is ready for war if there is a move toward Taiwan's independence as revealed again through the PRC's Defense white paper of July 24, 2019, outlining its military plans amid competing claims over the territory, including the South China Sea and Taiwan.[36] The US views these developments as unmistakable signs of the PRC's ambitions to project power over the Pacific and Indian Oceans, comparable to what it did in the nineteenth and twentieth centuries, along the coastlines in the Caribbean Sea and the Pacific Ocean. The Monroe Doctrine essentially neutralized the United States' backyard, assuring Washington's primacy in its immediate neighborhood.[37] At the same time, the United States used occasional neutrality as a foreign policy to remain outside the wars of Europe from which it had nothing to gain. The PRC's assertive actions in the South and East China seas have already been identified by US commentators as its version of the Monroe Doctrine,[38] while its 2019 white paper (quoted below) assures that Beijing will remain neutral in the sense of not joining military alliances. Its core interests are best served through the control over immediately adjacent waterways. Just as US control over its strategic waters allowed Washington to project power globally (even propelling its interventions into both world wars), a similar dominance of the immediate waterways and projection of power controlling the military and economic routes in the Indio-Pacific would allow Beijing to achieve a comparable primacy in Asia-Pacific. Officially, Beijing denies any such aspirations:

> committed to developing friendly cooperation with all countries on the basis of the Five Principles of Peaceful Coexistence. It respects the rights of all peoples to independently choose their own development path and stands for the settlement of international disputes through equal dialogue, negotiation and consultation. China is opposed to interference in the internal affairs of others, abuse of the weak by the strong, and any attempt to impose one's will on others. China advocates partnerships rather than alliances and does not join any military bloc. It stands against aggression and expansion and opposes arbitrary use or threat of arms. The development of China's national defense aims to meet its rightful security needs and contribute to the growth of the world's peaceful forces. History proves and will continue to prove that China will never follow the beaten track of big powers in seeking hegemony. No matter how it might develop, China will never threaten any other country or seek any sphere of influence.[39]

In stark contrast to this relatively benign self-image, the Defense Minister Wei Fenghe threatened just a few weeks earlier to "fight to the end, 'at all costs' over trade and Taiwan."[40] This was precipitated the day before on June 1, 2019, by the US Department of Defense, presenting an Indo-Pacific Strategy Report of an international coalition partnering against the PRC's growing might in the Indo-Pacific.[41] There are undaunting obstacles standing in the way of a peaceful resolution of the differences between the US and the PRC that could have a dire impact on the contested waterways—worth trillions of dollars in trade and responsible for more than half the world's oil shipping—from East Asia to the Middle East. Besides, there lie potentially large amounts of hydrocarbons under the sea beds that form part of Beijing's territorial claims in the South China Sea. They include hundreds of rocks and reefs that are also claimed by Brunei, Malaysia, the Philippines, Taiwan, and Vietnam, which creates intense clashes of interest. The United States regularly weighs in on behalf of the South East Asian nations causing the PRC to respond with bellicose rhetoric.

To Washington, US-Sino relations are set for an adversarial conflict, not because of the PRC's mass internment of Uighurs in Xinjiang, or the mistreatment of millions of Chinese activists,[42] the ongoing trade war, or a few rocks and islands in the corners of the Indo-Pacific region. Above all, the central conflict to the US is about the expanding economic and tactical coercion to control the autonomy of other countries and the build-up of China's military fleet and large air bases on those artificial islands reaching almost to the shores of Malaysia and Indonesia.[43] Both types of coercion are just under the threshold of using force to jeopardize the security, or the social and economic systems, of different countries.[44] As Admiral Philip S. Davidson, Commander, US Indo-Pacific Command, put the situation in his posture testimony before the Senate Armed Services Committee on February 12, 2019:

> China is leveraging military modernization, influence operations, and its economic instrument of power in ways that can undermine the autonomy of countries across the region . . . easy money in the short term, but these funds come with strings attached: unsustainable debt, decreased transparency, restrictions on market economies, and the potential loss of control of natural resources.[45]

The US interprets these actions as predatory check-book diplomacy. President Xi invested one trillion US dollars in ports and overland routes in more than sixty countries from all across Asia and Europe. In order to complete the One Belt, One Road Initiative, significant investments were also needed in Latin America and for opening markets in Africa. Countries like Greece demonstrated how dependent they had become on the PRC's direct investments in exchange for political goodwill by them limiting any criticism of its policies. Greece helped stop the European Union from issuing a consolidated statement against PRC aggression in the South China Sea, prevented the bloc from condemning its human rights record, and opposed the stricter screening of Chinese investments in Europe.[46] In 2018, Bangladesh banned one of the PRC's major state firms for attempted bribery,[47] and in the Maldives, Finance Minister Ibrahim Ameer blamed the PRC for inflating prices of infrastructure projects compared to those was previously agreed.[48] Pakistan, too, has recently started to feel the pressure of Chinese investments that it has been barely able to pay back.[49]

The United States interprets the above as examples of tactical coercion just below the bar of violating international law along with economic coercion, demonstrating the PRC's successful competitive strategy directed against the US and its partners in East Asia. However, in 2016, the PRC's claim to sovereignty over most of the South China Sea was invalidated by the Permanent Court of Arbitration (PCA) in The Hague.[50] Beijing's reaction was to simply not recognize the Court's jurisdiction to resolve its dispute with the Philippines or its interpretation against the legality of the so-called "nine-dash line."[51] The US and its allies failed to commit their support for the decision of the PCA, one of the institutions of the liberal world order, leaving the Philippines to fend for themselves to contain the PRC's bellicose actions. The Foreign Ministry of the Philippines called on all states to abide by the 2017 ASEAN-China Declaration on the Conduct of Parties in the South China Sea to reduce tension, mistrust, and uncertainty that could threaten regional peace and stability.[52] When in 2019 the Philippines government decided to upgrade its military facilities on the island Thitu of the Spratly Islands, Beijing again used the force of tactical coercion just below the threshold of armed conflict, in what is sometimes termed the grey zone between war and peace by deploying over one hundred PRC fishing ships with coast guard vessels instead of sending the Chinese Navy to hamper construction work. This time President Duterte's response was quick and to the point that unless the ships disappeared, he would send-in soldiers. The matter was resolved with the PRC respecting the sovereignty of the Philippines by withdrawing the vessels.[53] Still, Beijing is adamant about not resolving the South China Sea disputes in international institutions. Beijing's distrust and contempt of these mechanisms are seen in Washington as another sign of the PRC rejecting the 'operating system' and the rules of the existing liberal world order.

In other words, there are a plethora of commercial and military areas in which the US and the PRC have fundamentally different views. Meanwhile, to East Asian countries, the PRC's actions are aggravating, but they are also worried about the conflict potential that a US-PRC military conflict has for their region—even if they were not primarily involved. A war between these two advanced nuclear states would be disastrous for them. Thus, the question arises as to what can be done in the Asia-Pacific region to reduce the Great Power tensions?

## COLD WAR AND THE MILLENNIUM NEW SECURITY ARCHITECTURE

This passage explores how a geographical corridor of permanently neutral countries in a multipolar East Asia could become a new buffer zone, to allow the US and the PRC to transition their projection of power benignly and reduce the danger of a Sino-American war in the future. It uses precedence in the region as illustrations for existing neutralist policies that have already been serving local interests for many years. A formal "neutralization," however, would go further. As the introduction of this book explains, the practice of neutralization refers to multilateral treaty agreements to declare and uphold the permanent neutrality of a country, a territory, or a water way. The practice lay dormant for the past decades, but it is well defined under international law. At the same time, it is intuitive and malleable enough to adapt to the needs of this century, which revolve around new issues like human security, ecological economics, and global integration of production chains.

The world saw its first (and last) global, multipolar security system in the nineteenth century. The "Concert of Europe" was built around the idea that no single state should be powerful enough to exercise hegemony over Europe and that small, limited conflicts were an unavoidable means to retain the balance that would avoid a large-scale slaughter like the Napoleonic Wars that killed millions. Neutrality a fundamental premise of this arrangement because it kept the different centers of power economically prosperous and militarily secure, even when some of them were embroiled in local conflicts.[54] Neutral trading partners linked, for example, colonies to their motherlands when local shipping became impossible due to blockades or seawarfare between belligerents. They also function as buffer zones like Switzerland, Belgium, and Sweden. Even the UK and the US served this purpose in one way or the other until World War I.[55] In the case of a twenty-first century East Asian Security Architecture, a chain of states, extending from North-East Asia to ASEAN, would form a defensive Neutral-Bloc. It could include Mongolia, the Korean Peninsula, (or South Korea alone), Japan, Taiwan, and many ASEAN states. However, experiences of neutrality are not new to the region. There have been several local attempts and experiences with neutralist policies in the past decades.

## ASEAN

The history of European and Japanese occupation caused not only China to be wary of the Great Powers, but also Southeast Asia to prefer keeping the region neutral and free of external interference during the Cold War. It stems from the entanglement in the political and ideological challenges associated with the global distribution of power during this era and the disastrous impact of the Vietnam War.[56] At about the same time as European Détente began, the PRC and other Southeast Asian countries initiated steps to reduce tensions between East and West. An essential but underappreciated proposal at the time was one that came in the form of a neutral region surrounding the hot conflict zones around Vietnam, Cambodia, and Laos. The five founding members of ASEAN, Indonesia, Malaysia, the Philippines, Singapore, and Thailand signed a declaration that stated their ambition to become a "Zone of Peace, Freedom, and Neutrality" (ZOPFAN).[57] This caused regional Southeast Asian leaders to recognize the importance of greater self-reliance by pursuing the idea of neutrality, free of external interference by the Great Powers in Southeast Asia.[58] It underscored the policy of autonomy of a bloc of nations, which, by the beginning of the millennium, had become a convening power to discuss critical regional issues, emphasizing its impartiality. Its members had grown to ten by the 1990s, limiting the influence of the Great Power rivals even further. Since the end of the Cold War had led to a power balance between a continental power (PRC) and a maritime power (the US), each with its sphere of influence,[59] the divide in South East Asia between "communist" and "capitalist" countries also gave way to a rapprochement, especially after Vietnam's 1989 withdrawal of forces from Cambodia with the final resolution of the Cambodian Conflict in 1991.

The realignment of the Cold War conflict pattern during Détente in the 1970s offers a key element in explaining the onset of the East Asian Peace and East-West European Peace initiatives. The PRC and the US formed a kind of condominium, organizing East Asia into "two distinct spheres of influence," within which each held sway and ordered relations without the interference of the other.[60] This development brought about the expansion of ASEAN, and the notion of ASEAN neutrality evolved into a neutral form of response to conflict through impartiality. It has become an essential pillar of the security and strategic balance of the Asia-Pacific region, one of the world's most successful initiatives in regional conflict regulation and cooperation.[61]

> ASEAN's success in reducing tensions between the rival powers in East Asia is attributed to its engaging all the key players in bilateral or multilateral forums and making them come to the "table" with the underlying policy of guaranteeing each other's sovereign rights of territorial integrity, preventing efforts to exclude them, and an explicit principle of non-interference in each other's internal affairs. This also represents a form of "ideological neutrality" for the sake of finding the least-common denominators in their approaches to regional stability. The concept of neutrality has been repeatedly mentioned together with unity and solidarity, by ASEAN and its members as an ambition and as one of the main pillars supporting ASEAN's foreign policy over the last fifty years.[62] For ASEAN, the neutral aspect of *impartiality* and *non-interference* has always played a vital role in finding resolutions to regional conflicts.

## JAPAN

Japan, too, has some experience with principles that resemble those of neutral powers. It was cast (involuntarily) into a similar role of having to refrain from the use of force internationally because of the outcome of the War in the Pacific. Together with the Allies, the United States essentially dictated that the Japanese eliminate all nondefensive armed forces through the imposition of Article 9 of the new Japanese Constitution, which General Douglas MacArthur's headquarters wrote.[63] Its two paragraphs enshrine Japan's postwar pacifism:

> Aspiring sincerely to an international peace based on justice and order, the Japanese people forever renounce war as a sovereign right of the nation and the threat or use of force as means of settling international disputes.

> In order to accomplish the aim of the preceding paragraph, land, sea, and air forces, as well as another war potential, will never be maintained. The right of belligerency of the state will not be recognized.[64]

Paragraph one frames Japan's security unequivocally in pacifist and purely defensive terms. Total pacifism (meaning the complete absence of any armed forces) would have been the narrative and norm of Japanese foreign policy[65] had it not been for the Japanese government and the judiciary which interpreted Article 9 (1) to have no restrictions imposed upon the right of self-defense, just as Article 2 (4) of the UN Charter[66] is balanced with Article 51.[67] Japan, therefore, retains a national force but recognizes its pacifist meaning by naming them Air, Land, and Maritime Self-Defense Forces (SDF).[68] The problem is whether and to what extent Article 9 restricts the military capability that Japan can maintain. Under today's interpretation, Article 9 allows for overseas support of friendly nations—which raises the issue of collective self-defense and is an ongoing topic of debate.

The rejection of the use of force as a means for settling international disputes remains at the heart of Japan's military strategy. While the SDF is considered among one of the world's most potent conventionally equipped militaries, the international perception of its capabilities has been shaped by the narrowly defined use of force. In recent years Japan's security focus on the PRC has intensified because of Beijing's more assertive claims over the Senkaku Islands (known as Diaoyu islands to the PRC). At the same time, Tokyo increased cooperation with its allies, the United States, the United Kingdom, India, South Korea, and Australia. The scope of its engagements has surpassed its original mandate geographically, and the SDF today engages in international peacekeeping operations.[69] When it comes to the actual use of force, three principles that govern the SDF are:

1. There is an imminent threat to Japan.
2. No other means are available to defend Japan.
3. The use of force is limited to the minimum extent necessary.[70]

In 2014 Prime Minister Shinzo Abe's Government reinterpreted Article 9 to allow for the use of force not only in case of an attack against Japan proper (or its personnel and assets) but to also include the safety of its immediate military allies as part of the allowed reasons for the use of force.

Furthermore, the Abe Government passed an ambitious "peace and security legislation" that formally took effect in March 2016.[71] It set out to transform Japan's security policy and the roles and missions of its defense forces[72] coming on the heels of a significant revision of the Guidelines for Japan-US Defense Cooperation in 2015.[73] The main aims of the legislation were "to bolster deterrence to avoid armed conflict, especially through strengthening the US-Japan alliance; to protect Japanese nationals, and to better contribute to international peace and stability under "proactive pacifism" (*sekkyokuteki heiwashugi*)[74] in the form of peacekeeping.

Due to the 2014 reinterpretation of Article 9, the SDF has now enhanced both deterrence and readiness, especially regarding the US-Japan alliance.[75] Still, the restrictive and self-defensive nature of the Japan's military role lends way to how this could complement a neutral block of countries. First, it serves as a precedent for the nonoffensive nature of Japan's military role in North-East Asia, abnegating the sovereign right to declare war—just as permanently neutral countries do. Second, it allows for collective peacekeeping missions (in the sense of Hans Morgenthau's "collective defense of neutrality")[76] which would be an essential part of a mutual assistance agreement of a block of neutral states, in the sense of joint policing of the rule-based order in the overlapping maritime jurisdictions of the block, in accordance to the law of neutrality.[77] It would be part of the reset in which Japan would still uphold its role to defend its territory, limited to the minimum level of force necessary.

Consequently, there is space for Japan to be part of a buffer zone to reduce tensions between Beijing and Washington. Whether the revision of the Japanese Constitution will be the next step (to abolish or amend Article 9) remains tied to the country's interpretation of its security environment and the moral principles it has upheld over the decades. What is certain is that the undercurrent of Japanese foreign policy as a self-defensive mechanism is in alignment with the laws of neutrality as long as it does not have alliances with other countries that would go beyond the scope of Japan's constitutional obligation of defending only its territorial integrity.

## SOUTH AND NORTH KOREA

For the case of the Korean peninsula, it was, in fact, the North Korean President Kim Il-sung, who proposed neutralizing the entirety of Korea as a key to reunification and enhancing peace and security in East Asia. Kim deployed the help of former Soviet president, Mikhail Gorbachev, to deliver a confidential letter to US President Ronald Regan at their summit meeting on December 9, 1987, to engage in ways to reduce tensions between both countries. According to the Ministry of Foreign Affairs of South Korea (in a document declassified on March 29, 2018), this confidential letter from Kim to Reagan expressed the former's interest in terminating the Korean War and forming a neutral state based on a Korean Federation, thus, making the Korean Peninsula a buffer zone between the US and the Soviet Union.[78] Titled as the Democratic Peoples' Republic of Korea's proposal for establishing a neutral country and buffer zone, the document also included "the scaling down of the two Koreas' armed forces, removal of nuclear weapons on the Korean Peninsula and withdrawal of US troops stationed in South Korea. The two Koreas should dramatically cut the number of troops and reduce it to the point of self-defense," the document quoted North Korea as saying. "The two Koreas should keep the number of troops less than 100,000 for each. . . . All nuclear weapons and foreign troops must be withdrawn."[79]

South Korea's and the United States' response is best described by South Korea's Foreign Minister Choi Kwang-soo, who held that it was "grandiose and unrealistic." This opinion was officially shared by Washington.[80] But besides the skepticism, the following year President Reagan's "modest initiative" in 1988 opened-up an opportunity to allow "unofficial nongovernmental visits by North Koreans to the United States, easing of stringent financial regulations which impeded travel to North Korea by American citizens, permission for limited commercial export of US humanitarian goods to Pyongyang, and permission for US diplomats to engage in substantive discussions with North Koreans in neutral settings."[81] Thirty years later, the situation remains unchanged. The critical question for the United States still is whether moves by the North to improve relations with Seoul and Washington are tactical or represent a real strategic change in Pyongyang's policy to reduce tensions on the peninsula and improve the country's economic development.

In achieving a corridor of permanent neutral countries along with the Korean Peninsula, both South and North Korea would need to agree on several issues involving potential unification achievable through economic and political integration. Also, North Korea would need to destroy its nuclear weapons arsenal and disarm its intercontinental ballistic missiles, to be verified through the International Atomic Energy Agency's monitoring. In return, Pyongyang would gain the gradual relaxation of international sanctions. Arms control of conventional weapons would need to be implemented on the Korean Peninsula to ease security tensions and be made verifiable by an international supervisory body of military officials. On the other hand, Beijing and Washington would separately have to prepare for extended talks with diplomatic help from China to accelerate Pyongyang's denuclearization in exchange for the removal of the Terminal High Altitude Area Defense system from South Korea. Withdrawal of American troops needs to follow as well as the formal termination of the US-South Korean alliance. However, this isolated historical case does not, of course, mean that also the current North Korean President, Kim Jong-un, the grandson of the initiator of the proposal, still wants to see a neutral Korean Peninsula. Much remains to be explored diplomatically.

## TAIWAN

Even for the Island of Taiwan, there are strong arguments that it could and should join a new security architecture built on permanent neutrality in East Asia. In fact, it might be the primary beneficiary of such a fundamental change because, apart from the Korean peninsula, it is the only densely populated territory in the area that is seriously disputed and for which no post–World War II settlement exists. Politically, Taiwan is caught in a quagmire[82] as its official government narrative still is that Taipei is the capital of the ROC, which encompasses the entire Chinese territory as before the founding of the PRC in 1949. Unofficially, any aspirations to ever "recapture" the territories lost to Mao's communist forces have long been abandoned, and the political debate inside the self-governed island today gravitates around the question if Taiwan should declare its independence, uphold the status quo, or strive for reunification with the PRC. The first choice, as outlined above, is an absolute red line for the PRC and would, very likely, trigger its military intervention.

On the other hand, a reunification under the "One Country, Two Systems" principle offered by Beijing is to many citizens of Taiwan not an option either, as that would most likely set their political system toward a steady erosion of their liberal society (which by now even includes gay marriage and direct democracy) and lead to total central control by Beijing, as the case of Hong Kong exemplifies. The third option, to uphold the ambiguous status quo, is also under threat from both sides. Xi Jinping made it clear that it is a central interest of the PRC to integrate (and dissolve) the ROC into the motherland and, at the other end, there is a growing independence movement in Taiwan that is willing to take the risk of military confrontation to establish a "Republic of Taiwan." In short, there seems to be little room for maneuvering to create a situation that would satisfy all parties involved. Permanent neutrality, however, might well be the face-saving way out of this stalemate. Chapter 9 of this volume explains the rationale of "Taiwanese Neutrality" in-depth, but the central argument is that there is not only a homegrown neutrality movement currently in motion in Taipei,[83] but there are several essential precedents that make permanent territorial neutrality of the island a viable option.

First, the "neutralization" of Taiwan would, under international law, not require that it is recognized as a sovereign state. There are many examples of territories that were neutralized through international agreements but were not recognized nation-states. The Panama and Suez channels, the Greek islands of Corfu and Paxos, the Congo, Macau, and Portuguese Timor during World War II and even the Duchy of Luxemburg, were not recognized states while still settled—in different ways—as neutral territories.[84] It is entirely conceivable to discuss a "Neutral Taiwan" (with the liberty to forge its domestic legislation following the principles of self-determination) with Beijing, as a complementary concept to the "One Country, Two Systems" framework. A permanently neutral Taiwanese status would not conflict either with the PRC's stance of the "One China Principle," nor would it be incompatible with the PRC's own foreign policy, which, as outlined above, is also one of military nonalignment.[85]

Second, the status quo today is already, for all practical means, a form of neutralization of the island. Due to its disputed status and the lack of recognition of the ROC by international organizations, Taipei is not able to forge any form of military alliances. Its only security guarantee by the US, the "Taiwan Relations Act" of 1979, is a unilateral promise that "the United States will make available to Taiwan such defense articles and defense services in such quantity as may be necessary to enable Taiwan to maintain a sufficient self-defense capability."[86] Furthermore, it holds that the US would take "appropriate action" in case of "any threat to the security or the social or economic system of the people on Taiwan and any danger to the interests of the United States arising therefrom."[87] This law does not require Taiwan to act reciprocally and to take measures to support the United States in case of an attack by a third party on its assets or territory. Just like the "Treaty of Mutual Cooperation and Security between the United States and Japan," which established a one-way defensive obligation from the US toward Japan, the Taiwan Relations Act also binds the US only one-directionally to Taiwan—albeit without any enforceable promises of actual military assistance. Furthermore, it does not require Taiwan to host US military personnel or give the US the right to station its military on the island. In effect, the one-directional and "ambiguous"[88] nature of the Taiwan Relations Act, in conjunction with Taipei's incapacity of creating treaty relations with most countries or forging military alliances in its neighborhood, has already neutralized Taiwan to a large extent. In other words, the current situation is already one of *de-facto neutrality*. What is lacking is the explicit consent of the Super Powers together with a precise set of agreements on what this entails.

## STRATEGIC OPTIONS

Three strategic options appear feasible from a US perspective to halt the expansionism of the PRC and to influence its decision-making process. One is containment, another one deterrence, and diplomacy, and the third way is resetting the security architecture in East Asia through a belt of neutral countries. The strategy of containment is a product of the Cold War era, as a diplomatic doctrine set forth by the American diplomat George Kennan.[89] It played a critical role in the Cold War, prescribing US involvement in all theaters in Europe and Asia where the spread of the communist ideology needed to be stopped. Following this logic, the PRC should not be seen as a strategic partner, but as a rival and a challenger. Trade between the US and the PRC should be reduced to nonstrategic items, and an alliance of Asian states to contain China should be considered. This would include making Japan a pillar of a renewed US containment policy in the region. There is no doubt that the national interest of the United States is to resist the domination of any power in Asia. However, whether Tokyo, Seoul, Taipei, or Manila would want to participate in outright containment strategies is doubtful at best. Moreover, today's PRC does not aim at spreading communism or any other form of ideology. It explicitly refrains from any such initiatives under its policy of not interfering in the internal affairs of other states. The Cold War containment analogy, therefore, suffers severely because it was never designed to contain the military might of a state but only its political influence.

The second option, deterrence and diplomacy are about US public diplomacy backed by military power. Deterrence is a passive approach that is designed to discourage an opponent from action by threatening them with credible punishment. It is a strategy that necessitates military capabilities to dissuade an opponent from taking an undesirable action. This approach holds that international systems are stable when diplomacy is used effectively to deal with conflicts. Under this strategy, diplomacy and deterrence are complementary concepts—the more of the one, the less of the other—and the balance thereof depends on the willingness of all sides to engage constructively. When diplomacy as a tool is not used, relationships become focused on military strategy. This would be the beginning of an arms race in order to secure a strategic advantage and might lead to a confrontation which, in the end, could be the reason for war. America considers itself a liberal hegemon providing economic openness as a form of public diplomacy and using deterrence for global security. Deterrence is less provocative and requires less effort than containment. It is easier to achieve and less likely to fail. It is also worth noting that deterrence becomes successful when it is considered a legitimate exercise of power in the international community, and it is the modus-operandi of the US current approach when it conducts Freedom of Navigation Operations or deploys military assets to its bases in the Pacific. However, the hope that these tools will alter the PRC's behavior and contribute to a stable regional order appears to be misplaced as the current developments in the South- and East China Sea showcase.[90] Beijing remains critical of the US alliance system and its "pivot to Asia" strategy since the Obama administration. Another approach is needed to end to maritime disputes and deescalate tensions between the US and the PRC. Especially regarding the control of nuclear proliferation to limit the growth of nuclear arsenals in the Pacific that would best be achieved through a renewed, multilateral Intermediate-Range Nuclear Forces (INF) Treaty[91]—this time including all nuclear weapons states, chiefly the US, the PRC, and Russia.

The third option is to reset the security architecture in East Asia with a chain of neutral countries from the Pacific Northeast to the Philippines. Much remains to be explored in this regard, but a neutral buffer zone of the "first island chain" would allow Beijing to consider practical, time-tested precautions and not create a confrontation with the US through any miscalculation. A neutral Taiwan, together with an impartial Japan, neutralist ASEAN, and potentially a neutralized non-nuclear Korean peninsula could, in this sense, be the beginning of many benefits for the states involved and for their region. In short, a Pacific security architecture based on a neutral bloc of countries in East Asia operating under the norms of permanent neutrality could transform the Great Power Rivalry in the area back into a rule-based order. The security architecture could become the long-awaited grand design of American foreign policy to answer the security dilemma of the twenty-first century.

## NOTES

1. "The Meaning of China's Rise to Great Power Status," Institute for Security Policy at Kiel University accessed September 3, 2019 at https://www.ispk.uni-kiel.de/en/center-for-asia-pacific-strategy-and-security/the-meaning-of-china2019s-rise-to-great-power-status.

2. Center for Strategic and International Studies, *The Asia Chess Board—Grading the Game: An Interview with Dr. Kurt Campbell* (Pt. 1) July 29, 2019, www.csis.org/podcasts/asia-chessboard.

3. Taylor M. Fravel et al., "China is not an Enemy," *The Washington Post* (July 3, 2019), washingtonpost.com/opinions/making-china-a-us-enemy-is-counterproductive/2019/07/02/647d49d0-9bfa-11e9-b27f-ed2942f73d70_story.html.

4. Michael Pillsbury, *The Hundread-Year Marathon: China's Secret Strategy to Replace America as the Global Superpower* (New York: Henry Holt, 2015), 12.

5. Anthony V. Rinna, "How Mongolia Leverages its Neutrality to Influence Diplomacy with North Korea: Ulaanbaatar Is Increasingly Positioning Itself as a Mediating Force," *NK News*, June 25, 2019, http://nknews.org/2019/06/how-mongolia-leverages-its-neutrality-to-influence-diplomacy-with-north-korea.

6. Yoshihide Soeya, "The Case for an Alternative Strategy for Japan," in *Postwar Japan: Growth, Security, and Uncertainty since 1945*, ed. Micahel J. Green and Zack Cooper (Lanham, MD: Rowman & Littlefield, 2017), 29.

7. See chapter 9 of this volume.

8. James Stavridis, "Collision Course in the South China Sea: US and China Must Act Fast to Reduce Risks of Accidental Military Clashes," *Nikkei Asian Review*, May 22, 2019, asia.nikkei.com/Opinion/Collision-course-in-the-South-China-Sea.

9. People's Republic of China, "China's National Defense in the New Era," ed. State Council Information Office (Beijing: Foreign Languages Press, 2019), english.www.gov.cn/archive/whitepaper/201907/24/content_WS5d3941ddc6d08408f502283d.html.

10. Robert D. Kaplan, Asia's Cauldron: The South China Sea and the End of a Stable Pacific. 2014.

11. Marites Dañguilan Vitug, *Rock Solid: How the Philippines won its Maritime Case against China* (Quezon City: Bughaw, 2018).

12. For example, the PRC is creating several critical installations on the Hainan Island to gain advantages in submarine strategy. Sarah Kirchberger and Patrick O'Keeff, argue that "Die

weiter nördlich gelegenen Seegebiete nahe der chinesischen Küste sind wegen der geringen Wassertiefe ungeeignet für Operationen strategischer U-Boote. Aus Sicht der maritimen Geografie und Bathymetrie und in Ermangelung von Kontrolle über die Insel Taiwan, die sich geografisch gesehen noch besser für einen solchen Zweck eignen würde, ist Hainan daher der einzige geeignete Ort für eine strategische U-Boot-Basis in China (vgl. Abbildung 2). Wie Hans M. Kristensen und Robert S. Norris anmerken, sind alle chinesischen Atom-U-Boote des Typs 094 inzwischen auch in der neuen U-Boot-Basis Longposan in der Nähe von Yulin an der Südspitze Hainans stationiert, und nicht mehr in der alten SSBN-Basis der Nordflotte in der Nähe von Qingdao." Sarah Kirchberger and Patrick O'Keeffe, "Chinas schleichende Annexion im Südchinesischen Meer—die strategischen Hintergründe," *SIRIUS—Zeitschrift für Strategische Analysen* 3, no. 1 (2019).

13. Iris Chang, *The Rape Of Nanking: The Forgotten Holocaust Of World War II* (New York: Basic Books, 2012).

14. Jennifer Mitzen, "Ontological Security in World Politics: State Identity and the Security Dilemma," *European Journal of International Relations* 12, no. 3 (September 1, 2006).

15. Kevin Rudd, "What the West Doesn't Get About Xi Jinping," Harvard Kennedy School Blefer Center, March 20, 2018, belfercenter.org/publication/what-west-doesnt-get-about-xi-jinping.

16. State Council Information Office of the People's Republic of China, *China's Military Strategy* (Beijing: Ministry of National Defense of the People's Republic of China, 2015).

17. Ibid.

18. *The Guardian*, "'All Necessary Means': Xi Jinping Reserves Right to Use Force Against Taiwan," January 1, 2019, theguardian.com/world/2019/jan/02/all-necessary-means-xi-jinping-reserves-right-to-use-force-against-taiwan.

19. Ibid.

20. At the Nineteenth National Congress of the Chinese Communist Party in October 2017.

21. Ted Piccone, *Five Rising Democracies and the Fate of the International Liberal Order* (Washington, DC: Brookings Institution Press, 2016), 38–39.

22. Evandro Menezes de Carvalho, "The Twenty-First Century Finally Has Begun: The 'New Era' for China and the World," *People's Daily Online*, October 26, 2017, en.people.cn/n3/2017/1026/c90000-9285427.html.

23. Daniel W. Drezner, "China Elevates Xi Jinping to Mao Zedong's Level. Here's Why That's Unsettling," *The Washington Post*, October 25, 2017, washingtonpost.com/news/posteverything/wp/2017/10/25/china-elevates-xi-jinping-thought-heres-why-thats-unsettling/?utm_term=.840b5b90a0ff.

24. Daniel W. Drezner, "More Over, America. China Now Presents Itself As the Model 'Blazing a New Trail' For the World," *The Washington Post*, October 19, 2017, washingtonpost.com/news/worldviews/wp/2017/10/19/move-over-america-china-now-presents-itself-as-the-model-blazing-a-new-trail-for-the-world.

25. The ideal that "those who sacrifice a little liberty to gain temporary security deserve neither and will lose both" was a deeply ingrained principle of Benjamin Franklin, signatory of all four of the vital documents of the founding of the United States: the Declaration of Independence, the Treaty of Alliance with France, the Treaty of Paris and the United States Constitution.

26. Katie Stallard-Blanchette, "Putin and Xi's Buddy Act Could Blow Up East Asia: A Tense Aerial Standoff is the Latest Sign of Growing Chinese-Russian Military Ties," *Foreign Policy*, July 31, 2019, foreignpolicy.com/2019/07/31/putin-and-xis-buddy-act-could-blow-up-east-asia.

27. Franz-Stefan Gady, "The Significance of the First Ever China-Russia Strategic Bomber Patrol," *The Diplomat*, July 25, 2019, thediplomat.com/2019/07/the-significance-of-the-first-ever-china-russia-strategic-bomber-patrol.

28. "China Warns US, Allies on Regional Security, Taiwan," *Reuters*, July 24, 2019, aljazeera.com/news/2019/07/china-warns-allies-regional-security-taiwan-190724035256691.html.

29. Ibid.

30. Rebecca Fannin, "China-to-US Direct Investment Drops 84 Percent to Lowest Level In 7 Years Due to New Restrictions," *Forbes*, January 14, 2019, https://www.forbes.com/sites/

rebeccafannin/2019/01/14/china-to-us-direct-investment-drops-84-to-lowest-level-in-7-years-due-to-new-restrictions/#5e3255ad4dcd.

31. Katie Stallard-Blanchette, "Putin and Xi's Buddy Act Could Blow Up East Asia. A Tense Aerial Standoff is the Latest Sign of Growing Chinese-Russian Military Ties," *Foreign Policy*, July 31, 2019, foreignpolicy.com/2019/07/31/putin-and-xis-buddy-act-could-blow-up-east-asia.

32. See chapter 6 of this volume.

33. "US Risks China's Anger After Sealing $8bn Deal to Sell Taiwan 66 Fighter Jets," *The Guardian*, April 20, 2019, theguardian.com/world/2019/aug/21/us-taiwan-8bn-deal-66-f16-fighter-jets-china.

34. Gazprom operates already nearby in the South China Sea, as does Zarubezhneft, which is also wholly Russian-owned firm founded in 1967.

35. Bennett Murray, "Vietnam's Strange Ally in Its Fight with China. The Russian Oil Giant Rosneft is Quietly Backing Hanoi in its Clash with Beijing," *Foreign Policy*, August 1, 2019, http://foreignpolicy.com/2019/08/01/vietnams-strange-ally-in-its-fight-with-china.

36. "China Warns US, Allies on Regional Security, Taiwan," *Akjazeera*, July 24, 2019, aljazeera.com/news/2019/07/china-warns-allies-regional-security-taiwan-190724035256691.html.

37. See chapter 7 of this volume.

38. "China's Monroe Doctrine" *New York Times*, May 8, 2014, nytimes.com/2014/05/09/opinion/cohen-chinas-monroe-doctrine.html.

39. People's Republic of China, "China's National Defense in the New Era," 8.

40. "Chinese Defense Minister Vows to 'Fight to the End, At All Costs' Over Trade and Taiwan," *RT*, June 2, 2019, rt.com/news/460857-china-fight-trade-taiwan.

41. US Department of Defense, *Indo-Pacific Strategy Report: Preparedness, Partnerships, and Promoting a Networked Region* (Washington, DC: DoD, 2019).

42. Like those in Hong Kong, who, as of Summer 2019, are striving for more democracy.

43. Ana Swanson, "A New Red Scare Is Reshaping Washington," *New York Times*, July 20, 2019, nytimes.com/2019/07/20/us/politics/china-red-scare-washington.html.

44. Ketian Vivian Zhang, "Chinese Non-Military Coercion—Tactics and Rationale," *Brookings*, January 22, 2019, brookings.edu/articles/chinese-non-military-coercion-tactics-and-rational.

45. US Department of Defense, *Indo-Pacific Strategy Report: Preparedness, Partnerships, and Promoting a Networked Region*.

46. Jason Horowitz and Liz Alderman, "Chastized by EU, A Resentful Greece Embraces China's Cash and Interests," *New York Times*, August 26, 2017, nytimes.com/2017/08/26/world/europe/greece-china-piraeus-alexis-tsipras.html.

47. "Bangladesh Blacklists Chinese Construction Firm, Cancels Highway Deal After Bribe Claim," *South China Morning Post*, January 18, 2018, scmp.com/news/asia/south-asia/article/2129493/bangladesh-blacklists-chinese-construction-firm-cancels-highway.

48. "Maldives' New Finance Minister Names China for Inflating Prices of Infrastructure Projects," *South China Morning Post*, November 26, 2019, http://scmp.com/news/asia/south-asia/article/2175110/maldives-new-finance-minister-blames-china-inflatinChina's g-price.

49. Anthony B. Kim, "Is Pakistan About to Be Caught in China's 'Debt-Trap Diplomacy'?" *The Daily Signal*, August 8, 2018, dailysignal.com/2018/08/08/is-pakistan-about-to-be-caught-in-chinas-debt-trap-diplomacy.

50. Karen Lema "Philippines' Duterte Tells China to 'lay off' Island in Disputed Waters," *Reuters*, April 4, 2019, http://uk.reuters.com/article/uk-southchinasea-philippines/philippines-duterte-tells-china-to-lay-off-island-in-disputed-waters-idUKKCN1RG0LE.

51. Dañguilan Vitug, *Rock Solid: How the Philippines Won its Maritime Case against China*.

52. Declaration on the Conduct of Parties in the South China Sea, October 17, 2012, asean.org/?static_post=declaration-on-the-conduct-of-parties-in-the-south-china-sea-2; see Ankit Panda, "China, ASEAN Come to Agreement on a Framework South China Sea Code of Conduct," *The Diplomat*, May 19, 2017, thediplomat.com/2017/05/china-asean-come-to-agreement-on-a-framework-south-china-sea-code-of-conduct.

53. "Philippine President Rodrigo Duterte tells China to 'lay off' island in disputed South China Sea," *Reuters*, April 5, 2019, scmp.com/news/china/diplomacy/article/3004758/philippine-president-rodrigo-duterte-tells-china-lay-island.

54. See Maartje M. Abbenhuis, *An Age of Neutrals: Great Power Politics, 1815–1914* (Cambridge: Cambridge University Press, 2014).

55. See also Stephen C. Neff, *The Rights and Duties of Neutrals: A General History* (Manchester: Manchester University Press, 2000).

56. Nicholas Tarling, *Neutrality in Southeast Asia: Concepts and Contexts* (London: Routledge), 27.

57. Indonesia, Malaysia, the Philippines, Singapore and Thailand are the founding members of the Asian regional body established 1967 in Bangkok. Brunei Darussalam then joined on January 7, 1984, Vietnam on July 28, 1995, Lao People Democratic Republic (PDR) and Myanmar (Brunei) on July 23, 1997, and Cambodia on April 30, 1999. East Timor is still striving to become a member-state of ASEAN. See Truston Jianheng Yu, "2019: The year of Timor Leste in ASEAN?" *Jakarta Post*, December 13, 2018, thejakartapost.com/academia/2018/12/13/2019-the-year-of-timor-leste-in-asean.html.

58. Donald E. Weatherbee, *International Relations in Southeast Asia: The Struggle for Autonomy* (Lanham, MD: Rowman & Littlefield, 2005).

59. Robert S. Ross, "The US-China Peace: Great Power Politics, Spheres of Influence, and the Peace of East Asia," *Journal of East Asian Studies* 3 (2003).

60. Ibid., 370; Liselotte Odgaard, *The Balance of Power in Asia-Pacific Security: US-China Policies on Regional Order* (London: Routledge, 2007).

61. Amitav Acharya, Constructing a Security Community in Southeast Asia: ASEAN and the Problem of Regional Order-Politics in Asia (1996).

62. Ralf Emmers, "Unpacking ASEAN Neutrality: The Quest for Autonomy and Impartiality in Southeast Asia," *Contemporary Southeast Asia* 40, no. 3 (2018), 349–70.

63. US Department of State Office of the Historian, "Occupation and Reconstruction of Japan, 1945–1952," https://history.state.gov/milestones/1945-1952/japan-reconstruction.

64. Japanese Constitution, japan.kantei.go.jp/constitution_and_government_of_japan/constitution_e.html.

65. S. Hotaro Hamura and Eric Shiu, "Renunciation of War as a Universal Principle of Mankind–A Look at the Gulf War and the Japanese Constitution," *International and Comparative Law Quarterly* 44, no. 2 (1995): 430–31.

66. Article 2(4): All members shall refrain in their international relations from the threat or use of force against the territorial integrity or political independence of any state, or in any other manner inconsistent with the Purposes of the United Nations.

67. Article 51: Nothing in the present Charter shall impair the inherent right of individual or collective self-defense if an armed attack occurs against a Member of the United Nations, until the Security Council has taken measures necessary to maintain international peace and security. Measures taken by Members in the exercise of this right of self-defense shall be immediately reported to the Security Council and shall not in any way affect the authority and responsibility of the Security Council under the present Charter to take at any time such action as it deems necessary in order to maintain or restore international peace and security."

68. The SDF was renamed in 2012 to "The National Defense Force" but is often referred to as "Japan Self Defense Force" (JSDF); see Hitoshi Nasu, "Article 9 of the Japanese Constitution: Revisited in the Light of International Law," *ANU College of Law Research Papers* 26, no. 9 (2009).

69. Martin Fackler, "Japan Announces Defense Policy to Counter China," *New York Times*, December 10, 2016, nytimes.com/2010/12/17/world/asia/17japan.html.

70. Sheila A. Smith, *Japan Rearmed: The Politics of Military Power* (Cambridge: Harvard University Press, 2019), 141.

71. Adam P. Liff, "Japan's Security Policy in the 'Abe Era': Radical Transformation or Evolutionary Shift?," *Texas National Security Review* 1, no. 3 (2018).

72. Japanese Department of Justice, "Outline of the Legislation for Peace and Security," *Tokyo*, 2017, mod.go.jp/e/publ/w_paper/pdf/2016/DOJ2016_2-3-2_web.pdf.

73. *The Guidelines* provide a general outline of the scope of and respective responsibilities for operational coordination between the allies. They have been revised in 2015, 1997, and 1978, www.mod.go.jp/e/d_act/anpo/.

74. Atsuhiko Fujishige, "New Japan Self-Defense Force Missions under the 'Proactive Contribution to Peace' Policy: Significance of the 2015 Legislation for Peace and Security," Japan Chair Platform, Center for International and Strategic Studies, July 21, 2016, csis.org/analysis/new-japan-self-defense-force-missions-under-%E2%80%9Cproactive-contribution-peace%E2%80%9D-policy.

75. Ibid.

76. Hans J. Morgenthau, "The Problem of Neutrality," *University of Kansas City Law Review* 7, no. 109 (1938): 127.

77. Collective peacekeeping on the part of neutral countries in the case of illegitimate infringements on treaty agreements is explicitly allowed under the Law of Neutrality. L. F. L. Oppenheim holds that "there can be no doubt that neutral States, whether a complaint has been lodged with them or not, may either singly, or jointly and collectively, exercise intervention in cases of illegitimate acts or omissions of warfare being committed by belligerent Governments, or committed by members of belligerent forces if the Governments concerned do not punish the offenders." Lassa F. L. Oppenheim, *International Law: A Treatise—War and Neutrality*, vol. II (London: Longmans, Green, and Co., 1912), §246. It is also the basic principle upon which the so called "League of Armed Neutrality" was build by Catherina the Great. See Neff, *The Rights and Duties of Neutrals: A General History*, 38.

78. Joong Ang Ilbo, "North Korea proposed 'federal neutrality' to the US through the Soviet Union in 1987," March 3, 2018, mnews.joins.com/article/22490978#home. For the original documents see archival number of the document in Korean: 24754 722.12 UR/US 미국·소련 정상회담. Washington, DC, 1987.12.8-10 1987–1987 북미과/동구과 2017–0007 14 0001–0222 [Diplomatic documents in 87 years] Ministry of Foreign Affairs, Gorbachev, Reagan Conferring North Korea Proposal "Neutral Nation and Buffer Zone Declaration."

79. Yeo Jun-suk, "Cold War Document Reveals NK's Proposal of Neutral State on Peninsula," *The Korean Herald*, March 30, 2018, koreaherald.com/view.php?ud=20180330000803.

80. Ibid.

81. Joel Wit, "The United States and North Korea," *Brookings*, March 15, 2001, brookings.edu/research/the-united-states-and-north-korea.

82. On this point, see also, chapter 9 of this volume.

83. See the speech of Lu-Hsiu lien in chapter 10 of this volume.

84. See chapter 9 of this volume.

85. People's Republic of China, "China's National Defense in the New Era," 4, 8.

86. Article 3(a) of the Taiwan Relations Act. (Public Law 96-8, 22 U.S.C. 3301 et seq.)

87. Article 3(c) of the Taiwan Relations Act. (Public Law 96-8, 22 U.S.C. 3301 et seq.)

88. The vagueness of the wording of the Taiwan Relations Act is often referred to as "strategic ambiguity" on the part of the United States. See Mark Magnier, "Unloved but Essential: 40 Years On, the Taiwan Relations Act Remains Flexible, Durable, and Effective," *South China Morning Post*, April 10, 2019, scmp.com/news/china/article/3005465/unloved-essential-40-years-taiwan-relations-act-remains-flexible-durable.

89. David Mayers, *George Kennan and the Dilemmas of US Foreign Policy* (Oxford: Oxford University Press, 1990).

90. David C. Kang, China Rising: Peace, Power, and Order in East Asia (New York, 2007).

91. The bilateral Cold War INF treaty between the US and the Soviet Union (later Russia) was terminated in 2019. Matt Kord, "In Memoriam: The Intermediate-Range Nuclear Forces Treaty Dies at 32: The INF Treaty Is Survived By New START, But It Too Is In Danger," *The Nation*, August 2, 2019, thenation.com/article/intermediate-range-nuclear-forces-treaty-inf-obituary.

## SELECTED REFERENCES

Abbenhuis, Maartje M. *An Age of Neutrals: Great Power Politics, 1815–1914*. Cambridge: Cambridge University Press, 2014.
Chang, Iris. *The Rape Of Nanking: The Forgotten Holocaust Of World War II*. New York: Basic Books, 2012.
Dañguilan Vitug, Marites. *Rock Solid: How the Philippines Won its Maritime Case against China*. Quezon City: Bughaw, 2018.
Fravel, Taylor M., Roy J. Stapleton, Michael D. Swaine, Susan A. Thornton, and Ezra Vogel. "China is not an Enemy." *The Washington Post* (July 3, 2019).
Hamura, S. Hotaro, and Eric Shiu. "Renunciation of War As a Universal Principle of Mankind–A Look at the Gulf War and the Japanese Constitution." *International and Comparative Law Quarterly* 44, no. 2 (1995): 426–43.
Haythornthwaite, Philip J. *The Colonial Wars Source Book*. London: Caxton Editions, 2000.
Kirchberger, Sarah, and Patrick O'Keeffe. "Chinas schleichende Annexion im Südchinesischen Meer—die strategischen Hintergründe." *SIRIUS—Zeitschrift für Strategische Analysen* 3, no. 1 (2019): 3–20.
Liff, Adam P. "Japan's Security Policy in the 'Abe Era': Radical Transformation or Evolutionary Shift?" *Texas National Security Review* 1, no. 3 (2018).
Mayers, David. *George Kennan and the Dilemmas of US Foreign Policy*. Oxford: Oxford University Press, 1990.
Mitzen, Jennifer. "Ontological Security in World Politics: State Identity and the Security Dilemma." *European Journal of International Relations* 12, no. 3 (January 9, 2006): 341–70.
Morgenthau, Hans J. "The Problem of Neutrality." *University of Kansas City Law Review* 7, no. 109 (1938): 109–28.
Nasu, Hitoshi. "Article 9 of the Japanese Constitution: Revisited in the Light of International Law." *ANU College of Law Research Papers* 26, no. 9 (2009).
Neff, Stephen C. *The Rights and Duties of Neutrals: A General History*. Manchester: Manchester University Press, 2000.
Odgaard, Liselotte. *The Balance of Power in Asia-Pacific Security: US-China Policies on Regional Order*. London: Routledge, 2007.
Oppenheim, Lassa F.L. *International Law: A Treatise—War and Neutrality*. Vol. II. London: Longmans, Green, and Co., 1912.
Piccone, Ted. *Five Rising Democracies and the Fate of the International Liberal Order*. Washington, DC: Brookings Institution Press, 2016.
Pillsbury, Michael. *The Hundred-Year Marathon: China's Secret Strategy to Replace America as the Global Superpower*. New York: Henry Holt, 2015.
Ross, Robert S. "The US-China Peace: Great Power Politics, Spheres of Influence, and the Peace of East Asia." *Journal of East Asian Studies* 3 (2003): 351–75.
Smith, Sheila A. *Japan Rearmed: The Politics of Military Power*. Cambridge: Harvard University Press, 2019.
Soeya, Yoshihide. "The Case for an Alternative Strategy for Japan." In *Postwar Japan: Growth, Security, and Uncertainty since 1945*, edited by Micahel J. Green and Zack Cooper. Lanham, MD: Rowman & Littlefield, 2017.
State Council Information Office of the People's Republic of China. *China's Military Strategy*. Beijing: Ministry of National Defense of the People's Republic of China, 2015.
Tarling, Nicholas. *Neutrality in Southeast Asia: Concepts and Contexts*. London: Routledge, 2017.
US Department of Defense. *Indo-Pacific Strategy Report: Preparedness, Partnerships, and Promoting a Networked Region*. Washington, DC, 2019.
The People's Republic of China. State Council Information Office. "China's National Defense in the New Era." Beijing, Foreign Languages Press, 2019.
Weatherbee, Donald E. *International Relations in Southeast Asia: The Struggle for Autonomy*. Lanham, MD: Rowman & Littlefield, 2005.

*Chapter Nine*

# Taiwanese Neutrality

*Solving the Conundrum*

Pascal Lottaz and Herbert R. Reginbogin

For more than 70 years, the Republic of China (ROC)—Taiwan—and the People's Republic of China (PRC) have coexisted. Like the Korean peninsula, where the South is still technically at war with the North, Taipei and Beijing, have not achieved a peace settlement to end their conflict. After 20 years of relative calm in the Taiwan Strait, tensions in the Pacific are rising again with the PRC modernizing its military and increasing its naval strength. Beijing, Taipei, and Washington are caught in a multilayered, trilateral conflict constellation which is historically grown but increasingly fueled by the rivalry of the two superpowers. The unsettled business of World War II together with the United States' policy of "strategic ambiguity" toward Taiwan has led to an unstable status quo in East Asia that threatens to erupt into a hot conflict if the three parties do not find a mutual understanding of the status of Taiwan and a political solution that can deliver mutual military guarantees to avoid an escalating security dilemma. This chapter will first describe the current situation of Taiwan, the dangers that the status quo entails, and then propose to solve the Taiwanese conundrum, peacefully, through the armed permanent territorial neutrality of Taiwan.

## WORLD WAR II UNSETTLED

As with many unsettled issues of World War II, also the struggle over peace for Taiwan starts with an Empire. In this case, the Empire of Japan. After the forces of General Chiang Kai-shek, the nationalist leader of the ROC, defeated Japanese troops on the Chinese mainland, he sent his army on behalf of the Allied Forces to take over Taiwan that had belonged to Japan for fifty years. Since the Cairo Declaration of 1943, it had been clear that Japan would be forced to give up all claims on Taiwan. The communiqué unambiguously stated that "all the territories Japan has stolen from the Chinese, such as Manchuria, Formosa, and The Pescadores, shall be restored to the Republic of China."[1] The Potsdam Declaration in 1945 reaffirmed those terms. Formosa (Taiwan) would be returned to China. Even in the late forties, the US Department of State did not doubt that Taiwan belonged to China.[2] The unforeseen issue that soon arose, however, was the question *of which China*?

In 1949, Chiang's ROC forces had lost the bloody civil war to Mao Zedong's communists in all but name. The latter founded his People's Republic while Chiang was forced to flee to Taiwan for safety and regroup his army for later counter attacks. Chiang made Taipei his new capital city, establishing his rule without elections, due process, or the respect for the wishes of the local population. His forces killed an estimated twenty to thirty thousand who protested the invasive rule and mismanagement that the chaotic government brought with it.[3]

Despite the clear human rights abuses, the ROC under Chiang Kai-shek became for decades the official representative of China to the United Nations and most western countries. Meanwhile, Mao's Government in Beijing was initially only recognized by a handful of communist states. Chiang had planned for a full counter invasion,[4] but the nationalist Reconquista never came to fruition. When, in the 1950s, Kinmen and Matsu, small islands under ROC control, became targets of extensive shelling by Mao's forces, the United States neutralized the waterways between the two contenders by intervening with its Navi in the Taiwan Straits, putting pressure on both sides to stand down. Ever since, direct military engagement against each other has stopped mostly.[5] This effectively cemented the existence of the ROC and the PRC, living side-by-side—a course was set for a de facto existence of two Chinese states that neither of them had wanted.[6]

In 1971, the UN changed its recognition of "China" from the ROC to the PRC.[7] Taipei thereby lost its seat in the Security Council and was expelled from the UN system—a diplomatic disaster for Chiang. The fallout in realpolitikal terms, however, was limited, because a mutual-defense treaty with the United States (struck during the first Straight crisis in 1954) was still in effect. During the Cold War, the Island remained tightly integrated into the United States' Pacific security architecture of the "First Island Chain" (Japan–Taiwan–Philippines). On the other hand, also Washington changed its recognition of the Chinese Government to Beijing in 1979. At the same time it replaced the defense treaty with the Taiwan Relations Act, which was "to preserve and promote extensive, close, and friendly commercial, cultural, and other relations between the people of the United States and the people on Taiwan, as well as the people on the China mainland and all other peoples of the Western Pacific area."[8] The act established a people-to-people relationship rather than a state-to-state interaction. Its vague language assured quasi-diplomatic relations but ruled out to define Taiwan as a state. And despite containing security considerations, it did not *guarantee* the defense of the island, only that the US could, if it chose to do so, give military support to "provide Taiwan with arms of a defensive character."[9] This policy, known as "strategic ambiguity," has effectively frozen the conflict between the two Chinas. It allowed Taiwan to rule itself, to have its own military forces, customs, and border controls, and to develop a wealth of democratic freedoms unheard of in mainland China and much of the world.

## DANGER IN THE PACIFIC

Continuous US military support helped the ROC to prosper economically as one of the four "Asian Tigers,"[10] while, in world politics Taiwan became increasingly marginalized. After the PRC had taken a relatively reconciliatory approach toward Taiwan in the 2000s, the wind changed again under the leadership of President Xi Jinping. Beijing has decided to step up its campaign against Taipei by pressuring Taiwan's remaining allies to forsake their diplomatic ties with the ROC. The economic weight of the PRC has incentivized many to fall in line. As of 2019, only fifteen countries still recognize the ROC Government, and their number is shrinking.[11] On the political front, too, the pressure on Taipei is mounting. In 2015, three years after Xi came to power, the PRC's Ministry of Defense issued a highly assertive white paper titled, "Chinese Military Strategy" that vowed to strengthen the country's naval power,[12] safeguarding maritime interests in the East and South China Seas, and established that the reunification of Taiwan with the PRC was "an inevitable trend in the course of national rejuvenation."[13] Meanwhile, Xi has also signaled willingness to negotiate should the situation develop in favor of the PRC, most obviously when he agreed to a direct meeting with sitting ROC president, Ma Ying-jeou, in November 2015, in Singapore.[14] The thaw in cross-strait relations was short-lived, however, as the democratic change of Government in Taipei the following year exchanged the Kuomintang Party (KMT) with the Democratic Pacific Party (DPP), who takes a much firmer stance on Taiwan's independent political future than Ma's Kuomintang that has effectively started to campaign for reunification. Beijing's rhetoric has become even more blatantly bellicose since the change in Taiwan, threatening its nearly 24 million people with military intervention. "We make no promise to renounce the use of force and reserve the option of taking all necessary means,"[15] Xi said in his 2019 New Year speech, and the most recent whiter paper of June 2019 identifies that "The Taiwan authorities, led by the Democratic Progressive Party (DPP), stubbornly stick to 'Taiwan independence' and refuse to recognize the *1992 Consensus*, which embodies the one-China principle. . . . The "Taiwan independence" separatist forces and their actions remain the gravest immediate threat to peace and stability."[16] The paper leaves no doubt that the PRC would use even arms to resolve the issue, stating that; "[t]he PLA [People's Liberation Army] will resolutely defeat anyone attempting to separate Taiwan from China and safeguard national unity at all costs."[17]

This is bad news not only for the ROC but also for the United States, as the saber-rattling is another step in the derailment of US–Sino relations. Any escalation in the Taiwan Strait is closely monitored in Washington. Cultural and business ties between the ROC and the US are historically rooted and tightly knit through billion-dollar agriculture, commercial, and arms trade deals. Citizens of both countries enjoy visa-free travel, and the 2019 approval of the Department of State for 66 F-16 Fighter Jets to be sold to the ROC Government further underscores the US willingness to uphold the *de facto* independent status of the Taiwanese island.[18] Even under the administration of US President Donald Trump, Washington's commitments to Taiwan have not languished—unlike in the Middle East and Europe. On the contrary, ties were deepened last year through two new legislations; the "Taiwan Travel Act,"[19] that became law in 2018, and the "Taiwan Assurance Act"[20] that passed the House of Representatives and is set to pass the legislative process by 2020. Unsurprisingly, several US lawmakers voiced their support for Taipei after Xi's speech. Senator John Kennedy, for example, called his remarks "provocative" and "just bad diplomacy." Further measures have since been introduced in the US congress, including a "Taiwan Allies International Protection and Enhancement Initiative (TAIPEI) Act"[21] and a "resolution supporting measures taken by the Government of Taiwan to deter, or if so compelled, defeat, aggression by the Government of the People's Republic of China."[22] Xi's words backfired also locally. ROC President, Tsai Ing-wen, who used to be ambiguous and shaky on the question of independence, strengthened her rhetoric on the issue. The 62-year-old legal scholar (and Taiwan's first female president) affirmed that it was impossible for "any responsible politician in Taiwan to accept President Xi Jinping's recent remarks without betraying the trust and the will of the people of Taiwan."[23] She and the DPP, firmly rejected Xi's demand that Taipei consents to the "One Country, Two Systems" framework for the integration of the Taiwanese island into the PRC. Under the same formula, Hong Kong and Macau already saw their democratic liberties erode, which had become one of the driving factors for strong and prolonged civil protests in 2014 and 2019.[24]

The rhetoric blows between Xi and Tsai, and the escalation of bellicose language in Beijing and Washington lay bare this unresolved dilemma in East Asia—the *de facto* existence of two Chinese states. Officially, none of the two admits to this. Especially the PRC has been insisting vehemently on its standpoint that there is only one China and Taiwan is part of it. It forcefully defends the position that the "One-China Principle" is the only route for a political solution of the conflict.[25] The paradox is that also the ROC government (officially) does not claim otherwise. The so-called (but disputed) "1992 consensus," holds that Taipei and Beijing both accept that there is only one China but that they disagree on who its legitimate government is.[26] In recent years, the "consensus" has become the basis upon which Beijing wants to build its side of cross-strait relations, while the DPP rejects this approach.[27]

The vague idea of a "consensus" on the Taiwan Strait is shaky at best and on the verge of collapse at worst. The question of whether the current ambiguous situation of Taiwan can be transformed into an internationally recognized status that all stakeholders (internally and externally) can agree to, is at the heart of the question of a peaceful and stable future for the people of Taiwan. A Great Power stand-off between the US and the PRC is a nightmare scenario for Taiwanese politicians, who have warned with the African proverb that "when two elephants fight, it is the grass that is trampled."[28] In a hot conflict between the two, Taiwan would most likely not only be a casus belli but the battleground of a Sino-American war. Luckily, there are local efforts in Taipei to use a novel approach to the dilemma.

## A LOCAL PUSH FOR A NEUTRAL TAIWAN

In the early spring of 2018, Lu Hsiu-lien (Annette Lu),[29] a former democracy activist, feminists, and ROC Vice President (2000–2008), organized the first East Asia Peace Forum in Taipei which sported an oddly unfamiliar subtitle; "Peace in East Asia and the Neutrality of Taiwan." When she opened the forum, the veteran politician came quickly to the point: "People in Taiwan want to be the master of their destiny and do not wish to be annexed by Communist [*sic*]. . . . Beyond the Taiwan Strait, the People's Republic of China claims to own Taiwan, but it has never ruled Taiwan. . . . In recent years, concerned Taiwanese opinion leaders have launched a crusade to promote Taiwan's peace and neutrality via referendum. They hope to emulate Switzerland and Sweden which maintain remarkable self-defense capability [*sic*]."[30] Lu's remarks refer to herself and exponents of Tsai's DPP who are seeking to force the government to adopt a foreign policy of "peace and neutrality" by way of a plebiscite.[31] She started the political process for that when she presented the formal referendum proposal to the Central Election Commission in March 2019.[32] Although Lu suffered a setback when only a month later the Legislative Yuan changed the National Referendum Act, allowing plebiscites to take place only every other year—effectively banning any referendum until 2021[33]—her chances of success at the ballot box are not bad. Previous revisions to the law (effective since January 2018) considerably increased the likelihood of a positive vote.[34] The first successful referendums under the new rules in November 2018 demonstrated the direct democratic potential of the new instrument. Whereas no referendum had ever overcome the high statutory requirements for a valid plebiscite before, all ten referendums of that day were valid, and seven of them passed. On the other hand, the same referendums have also shown that the Taiwanese public is currently not in favor of taking risks regarding proclamations of sovereignty. Voters rejected a proposal that would have changed the name under which Taiwan competes in the Olympic Games from "Chinese Taipei" to "Taiwan."[35] The move would have certainly angered the PRC and infringed upon an agreement with the International Olympic Committee, which might have led to Taipei's expulsion from the Olympic Games—an argument of the no-committee that resonated strongly with voters. Together with the losses that the pro-independence leaning DPP had to register in local mayoral elections, the argument has gained ground that a majority of Taiwanese is not favoring a change in the status quo with the PRC. However, of all referendums that day, this one was the closest race, with 45 percent yes-votes to 55 percent rejections—a difference of only 1 million votes out of 20 million registered voters. This suggests that if a neutrality referendum was not framed as a move toward sovereignty, the proposal might succeed at the ballot box. However, if that was the outcome, what would a "Taiwanese neutrality" be?

## PERMANENT TERRITORIAL NEUTRALITY

In fact, neutrality is a promising, peaceful solution of the Taiwanese quagmire by squaring a circle: satisfying the basic needs of Beijing, Taipei, and the US under a new consensus that avoids the issue of sovereignty, while also providing a new shared narrative to continue cross-strait relations under the status-quo. Concretely, Taiwanese neutrality could become part of a local security architecture that would decrease the security dilemma between the PRC and the US, while also delivering security guarantees to the Taiwanese population but without military alliances. A neutrality proclamation in the absence of a war toward which it is directed is called *permanent neutrality*[36]—akin to the foreign policies of Switzerland, Sweden, or Austria. It is a perpetual state coming with the duty of impartiality toward armed conflicts and the promise to abstain from military alliances. A permanent neutral is not allowed to take sides during wars, nor can it allow third parties to use its territory or infrastructure for military purposes. At the same time, however, permanent neutrals are able to engage constructively in diplomacy, offer humanitarian services, mediate in conflict, and pursue their national interests like any member of the international community.

Since most historical instances of permanent neutrality involve sovereign governments, a unilateral Taiwanese declaration of neutrality might seem more of a provocation than a de-escalation in the standoff with the PRC, but that is not necessarily the case. Customary International Law distinguishes clearly between the concept of neutrality and sovereignty. They can go hand in hand—but they do not have to.[37] "The idea of neutralization does not of itself connote a territorial guarantee,"[38] Malbone W. Graham noted already in 1927. "Neutralization," in this context, refers to the act of several states agreeing in a treaty on the neutrality of a particular territory. What he and others[39] knew was that "neutrality" and "territorial integrity" were usually guaranteed separately under International Law. Switzerland and Belgium were neutralized with explicit (but separate) guarantees for the sovereignty over their territories. Meanwhile, the Greek islands of Corfu and Paxos, and the Belgian colony of the Congo (while occupied and exploited by its European rulers) were neutralized without such guarantees. Even the Grand Duchy of Luxemburg was neutralized in 1867 by the Great Powers of Europe without any promises for its territorial integrity.[40] It was neutralized but put under the sovereign control of King William III of the Netherlands.[41] Other examples of the late nineteenth and early twentieth centuries include the Aaland Islands, the Samoan Islands, the Rhineland, the Saar territory, even the city of Danzig.[42] Besides, also important waterways that flow through jurisdictions of sovereign governments have been permanently neutralized at various points in time, like the Panama Canal, the Suez Canal, the Straits of Magellan and, de facto, the Taiwan Straits (although the last one lacks any formal agreement thereof). Although these places were not declared sovereign, they still enjoyed the full protection of the law of neutrality. More importantly, they took a unique position in geopolitics. They were instances of what L. F. L. Oppenheim called "partial neutrality,"[43] or what can also be called "permanent territorial neutrality."[44]

Most cases of permanent territorial neutrality in International Law are European, but there are at least two precendences for territorial neutrality in Asia; Macau and Portuguese (East) Timor, during World War II. Both territories were colonies of neutral Portugal when the war in the Pacific broke out. Since they were regarded as extensions of the state under who's possession they were, Macau and East Timor became, by implication, neutral territories. Although East Timor was soon invaded—first by the Allied forces and then through a counter-offensive by Japan's Imperial Forces—the Japanese occupiers recognized the neutral status of the island. The official position of Tokyo was that Japan had to "liberate" the neutral territory and only stationed its troops on the island because the Portuguese colony was not able to guarantee that it would not be used by Japan's enemies—which is one of the principal duties of a neutral. The Japanese also granted the Portuguese administrators in East Timor the control over private civilian matters, refraining from provocative actions against the local population.[45] Even more interesting is Macau which remained outside the warfare and unoccupied for the entire time of the Second World War, despite the tiny peninsula being an easy target for the Imperial Forces that had no problem invading British Hong Kong. Tokyo exercised strategic constraint toward Macau not because it had an ingrained respect for neutral territory but for political and practical reasons. On the one hand, it had no intention to draw Portugal into the war on the Allied side. It was difficult enough to justify and appease Lisbon after the counter-invasion of Timor, but, more importantly, the neutral status of Macau made the territory a valuable hub for intelligence gathering (espionage and counter-espionage) and allowed for a frenzy of diplomacy toward all sides. Macau was more precious as a neutral territory than as a prize of war.[46]

As these examples show, there is no principle contradiction between a new consensus for a "One China Policy" and a declaration of permanent territorial neutrality. Taiwan could proclaim its permanent neutrality without announcing independence. Moreover, this new status would also be in line with the PRC's foreign policy of military nonalignment according to its most recent white paper, which holds that "China advocates partnerships rather than alliances and does not join any military bloc." In fact, a permanently neutral Taiwan would only strengthen that policy, not weaken it. There are other benefits that the PRC might get through a neutral Taiwanese island which will be explored below. But before that, the obvious elephant in the room to address is the security question. Some of the above examples are infamous because they ended with annexation or invasion; Portuguese Timor, the Saarland, Luxemburg, Danzig; they all were overrun by hostile forces who did not (or only partially) respected their neutral rights. Is this approach, therefore, invalidated? Permanent neutrality itself is not a magic potion that miraculously safeguards a state or a territory. Local security is just as dependent upon other factors like military preparedness, geostrategic position, and economic strength. The invaded neutral territories were all nearly defenseless. Luxemburg was not only neutralized but demilitarized. The other territories, too, had nearly no indigenous defenses, and, as described, the Japanese would most likely have refrained from invading Portuguese Timor had Portugal been able to repel the initial invasion by the Allied Forces under Australian command.[47] Macau, on the other hand, just like Switzerland or Spain in World War II, had more to offer to the belligerents than what they would have gained through attacking and occupying these places which would have inflicted military damage for no good gain. The peace dividend that neutrals have to offer is just as crucial (or even more important) than an abstract status under international law. These aspects are necessary to explain why some neutrals in history managed to stay unharmed, while others were invaded or drawn into wars. Strategically permanently neutral states or territories do not differ from others. There have been countless examples only in the past century during which collective security approaches failed to provide the security they were supposed to bring.[48] The Tripartite Pact did not save the Axis Powers of World War II from their demise (of their own making), South Vietnam's Alliance with the US did not rescue it from the North,[49] and the Warsaw Pact failed to protect the Soviet Empire. Besides, the proposition for Taiwan's permanent neutrality is not one to disarm the island. On the contrary, it is a proposal for an *armed neutrality*.

## TAIWANESE NEUTRALITY: PERMANENT, TERRITORIAL, AND ARMED

Permanent neutrality is often confused with pacifism because of its refusal to join alliances. In reality, many successful permanent neutrals depended heavily on the deterrent power of their Armed Forces. Switzerland and Sweden are prominent examples. During the World Wars, when the danger of invasion was real, they mobilized their (relatively) large Military Forces to guarantee that their territories would not be utilized by any of the belligerents for purposes of warfare, signaling that an invasion would come at a hefty price. At the same time, both neutrals allowed the belligerents to make good use of the fact that they were not at war with anyone. All belligerents benefited from trade with them (including weapon exports), had access to their currencies, could use their diplomatic services, and could gather intelligence in their capitals.[50] The message was simple; *"we are more valuable to you outside the conflict than under your occupation"*—the neutral carrot-and-stick approach. For this to work, the neutrals depended on credible military deterrents—which is anything but pacifists. That is what is usually called *armed neutrality*.

Inversely, well-intended attempts at neutral solutions have failed because of a lack of military preparedness. The most prominent and recent cases in South East Asia are those of Laos and Cambodia. Both tried to escape the slaughter of the Vietnam War through neutralist strategies but were ultimately drawn right into the conflict. Laos was even officially *neutralized* through the 1962 "Geneva accord on the Neutrality of Laos" with all sites of the conflict promising to respect Cambodian neutrality and its territorial integrity.[51] However, both countries lacked the military strength to guard their borders against the military operations of the belligerents. The Vietcong happily continued using supply-routes through both countries and recruited help from there. That, in turn, provoked the US into the bombing of Laotian and Cambodian territories, which then destabilized the national governments and drew them right into the conflict. Therefore, Taiwanese neutrality would not be a call to disarm the island or to cut it off from US weapon purchases. On the contrary, a well-prepared and adequately equipped army would be the backbone to a credible, permanently neutral island in the Pacific. Taiwan would need to be able to ensure that no nation could utilize either its airspace nor its territorial waters for military purposes and that it would not become an "unsinkable aircraft carrier" for the US nor a forward operating base for PRC Forces. Taiwan would be off-limits to all powers, thereby reducing the security dilemma toward both sides.

## THE CENTRALITY OF RECOGNITION

The crux of the issue, however, is that a "real" neutral solution to the Taiwanese question would need to be just that—a solution. Permanent neutrality is first and foremost a treaty agreement through which it becomes an official status under international law. Just as the State Treaty that neutralized Austria in 1955 was essentially an agreement between the USSR and the US to declare Austria off limits for military planning (it never joined NATO nor the Warsaw Pact), Taiwanese neutrality would have to be "imposed" from the outside as much as it would have to be "desired" from the inside. Taiwan, adopting the status of a permanent neutral nation, would require an international agreement to which all relevant global and regional powers would become signatories to include the PRC and the US, but also Japan, South Korea, the Philippines, Indonesia, and Vietnam. These states would have to agree to the terms of an international deal that would codify their future relationship with the island. Otherwise, regarding International Law—and for reasons of Realpolitik—a unilateral Taiwanese declaration of permanent neutrality would carry no weight, neither politically nor under international law.[52]

In short, if Taiwan was ever going to be a "real" permanent neutral, the neutralization of the island would need to happen through an international agreement, and it would need to be a process resulting in an improvement over the ambiguous status quo for all parties—otherwise, they would just not sign up for it. That would be the tricky part for Taiwan after a favorable neutrality referendum. Its diplomats would have to go out and "sell" Taiwan's neutrality, to make it truly permanent. Only a multilateral treaty would make a unilateral proclamation meaningful. However, that is not to say that a neutral solution cannot start locally. The Swiss are proud to this day that they were able to "defend" their neutrality during the Vienna Conference in 1815 when the High Powers neutralized their territory. One hundred forty years later, the Austrian Government convinced the US of the usefulness of its neutrality, despite Eisenhower's initial opposition. Another 40 years later, Turkmenistan became the latest example for a successful case of a self-proclaimed neutral, who managed to be recognized by the international community. Ashgabat had its permanent neutrality affirmed in 1995, by way of a

UN resolution—the first time that the UN was involved in the neutralization of a country.⁵³ The UN might become a significant international forum if Taiwan was ever to push for the recognition of its neutrality. In 2017, while declaring December 12 the *International Day of Neutrality*, the UN also acknowledged "that the national policies of neutrality of some States can contribute to the strengthening of international peace and security" and recognized "that such national policies of neutrality are aimed at promoting the use of preventive diplomacy."⁵⁴ The UN, thereby, threw its considerable weight behind permanent neutrality as something that was not only tolerable to the international community but worth fostering. It recognized that neutral actors, even when they are not members of the UN (like Switzerland until 2002), can contribute much to the peaceful development of international relations through active diplomatic contributions that only neutrals can deliver (mediation, good offices, fact-finding missions, negotiations, etc.).

## WHAT IS IN IT FOR THE BIG PLAYERS?

Most importantly, what Taiwan's neutralist approach would have to deliver would be a vision of benefits not only for itself but for all international actors—the value proposition is crucial. How could mainland China, the US, and East Asian Nations benefit from a permanently neutral Taiwan? First, despite its bellicose rhetoric, Beijing has an interest in maintaining its economically advantageous relationship with Taiwan. Trade between the two was worth 181.83 billion USD in 2017,⁵⁵ with over ninety thousand Taiwanese businesses investing into mainland China over the last thirty years and financial institutions of both sides operating on the soil of the other as part of an economic agreement. Furthermore, there are advantages if Taiwan remains an "offshore" market. For example, through its unique status Taipei would have the ability to intermediate the banking sectors. In 2012 Taiwan's Central Bank signed an agreement with the People's Bank of China, allowing for the direct settlement of Renminbi transactions. A year later it had already become the second largest trading place for China's foreign currency after Hong Kong.⁵⁶ The market has since moved but Taiwan remains and important trading place for the Renminbi and Beijing's aspirations to internationalize the currency to make it an alternative to the US Dollar or the Euro.⁵⁷ A neutral banking place will prove invaluable as it will increase trust in operations and the stability of its trading places.

Beijing could also benefit on a public diplomacy level form a neutral Taiwan. Despite its astounding and unique economic ascent, mainland China has failed to gather the kind of soft-power that was central to the success of other Powers. It has not produced a Blue-Jeans cult, or an Anime Pop-Culture diplomacy, or a K-pop style hype for the music of its younger generation. The over-arching perception in the western public is one of a China that patrols the internet, uses its tech companies for spying activities, and locks away dissidents in politics, arts, culture, and even incarcerates bookshop keepers. Taiwan, on the other hand, is a beacon of democratic freedom, human rights, and liberal thought. Instead of fending-off these values, the PRC could utilize a neutral Taiwan as an isolated but distinctly Chinese provider of liberal values to the rest of the world. Chinese humanitarianism, for example, delivered through neutral Taiwan, in the form of humanitarian assistance, diplomatic services, and peacekeeping missions around the world. A distinctly Chinese "Switzerland of the East" would be able to help in negotiations between the two Koreas and mediate during constitutional crises in places like Sri Lanka, or during ethnic tensions like in Myanmar. If the PRC encouraged instead of stifled a neutral Taiwanese diplomatic approach, it would immediately benefit from the positive image these efforts produced.

For the US, on the other hand, a permanently neutral Taiwan would be a way to ease tensions with Beijing, save money on military expenditures, and continue lucrative conventional arms sales, all while not changing the geostrategic balance. To talk about Taiwanese Neutrality would not suggest a step away from the US and undermine bilateral relations. Taiwan would still be part of the first island chain and not become a military base for the PRC's Pacific Fleet. Nor would the arrangement pose a danger to the US-Japan security alliance or influence the US relationship to the Philippines. Military relations in the Pacific would stay what they are—just with less tension toward Beijing. Strategically and financially, this would be the least expensive way to clean up a messy situation that has the potential to escalate into a scenario under which US troops and US money would be needed to defend a status quo that is bound to come to an end, one way or another. A sustainable deal with Beijing about the fate of a neutralized Taipei is in the interest of Washington.

Lastly, there is "the big" picture of regional security in East Asia.[58] A permanently neutral Taiwan would not only serve as a physical buffer zone between mainland China and the US, but it can become a blueprint for regional security agreements in the future—most prominently, for the Korean peninsula. Whatever the political course of the two Korean states, it is clear that Beijing will prevent at any cost the stationing of US troops or weaponry directly at its southern border. A unified Korea would need to be non-nuclear and neutral if it was ever to gain support from both superpowers for a common political future. The vision of politicians like Annette Lu go even further; her big picture also includes Japan and the Philippines as part of a "neutral belt" between China and the US. That would be an entire buffer region as a security guarantee to both nuclear powers that these countries and the exclusive economic zones of their maritime borders will not become threats. Whether or not such visions are ever to gain traction is another question, but it is clear that an armed permanently neutral Taiwan would be a potent testing ground for the viability of neutral zones between the big rivals of the twenty-first century.

## CONCLUSION

In conclusion, a unilateral declaration of neutrality, through a public referendum in Taiwan would be much less provocative than a declaration of independence. The *Territorial Neutrality* of Taiwan would even be compatible with a new consensus on a One China principle because it does not necessitate—nor invoke—sovereignty. On the other hand, such a proclamation would be only a first step toward a neutral solution for the island. "Real" permanent neutrality can only be achieved through a multilateral neutralization, which would need to involve the agreement of the PRC, the US, and other regional actors. Despite these challenges, a neutralist strategy would have a tremendous advantage over the current situation. It would give the foreign policy initiative back to Taipei and shift the toxic discourse about sovereignty to an innovative solution that offers more room for negotiation. The maintenance of peace and prosperity is undoubtedly preferable to a clear-cut definition of Taiwanese statehood. At the same time, Taiwanese neutrality would come with security and economic benefits to Beijing and Washington while de-escalating a significant source of military tension in East Asia. In short, territorial, armed neutrality might well be the key for Taiwan to transform the current uncertain status quo—peacefully—into a Chinese *modus vivendi*.

## NOTES

1. "Cairo Communiqué," *The National Diet Library of Japan*, accessed September 4, 2019, ndl.go.jp/constitution/e/shiryo/01/002 46/002_46_001r.html.
2. Chen Yi-shen, "The Shaping of Taiwan's Status after World War II," in *Taiwan's Struggle: Voices of the Taiwanese*, ed. Shyu-Tu Lee and Jack F. Williams (Lanham, MD: Rowman & Littlefield, 2014), 140.
3. Remembered as the "228 Incident." See Craig A. Smith, "Taiwan's 228 Incident and the Politics of Placing Blame," *Past Imperfect* 14 (2008). See also Stephen J. Hartnett, Patrick Shaou-Whea Dodge, and Lisa B. Keränen, "Postcolonial Remembering in Taiwan: 228 and Transitional Justice as 'The End of Fear,'" *Journal of International and Intercultural Communication* (2019).
4. Haruka Matsumoto, "The First Taiwan Strait Crisis and China's 'Border' Dispute Around Taiwan," *Eurasia Border Review* 3 (2012).
5. Only occasionally flair-ups of violent behavior occurred—the most serious one necessitating a third US military show of force in the Taiwan Straits in the mid-1990s.
6. Matsumoto, "The First Taiwan Strait Crisis and China's 'Border' Dispute Around Taiwan."
7. "Representation of China within the United Nations System," *International Legal Materials* 11, no. 3 (1972): 561–70.

8. US Congress, House, Taiwan Relations Act, HR 2479, 96th Cong., Introduction in House February 28, 1979, congress.gov/bill/96th-congress/house-bill/2479.

9. US Congress, House, Taiwan Relations Act, HR 2479, 96th Cong., Introduction in House February 28, 1979, congress.gov/bill/96th-congress/house-bill/2479.

10. Eun-Mee Kim, *The four Asian Tigers: Economic Development and the Global Political Economy* (San Diego: Academic Press, 1998).

11. "Diplomatic Allies" Ministry of Foreign Affairs Republic of China (Taiwan), accessed September 21, 2019, mofa.gov.tw/en/AlliesIndex.aspx?n=DF6F8F246049F8D6&sms=A76B7230ADF29736. See also Chris Horton, "El Salvador Recognizes China in Blow to Taiwan," *New York Times*, August 21, 2019, nytimes.com/2018/08/21/world/asia/taiwan-el-salvador-diplomatic-ties.html.

12. People's Republic of China, "China's Military Strategy," ed. State Council Information Office (Beijing: Foreign Languages Press, 2015).

13. Ibid., 5.

14. "Xi Jinping and My Ying-jeou summit," *South China Morning Post*, accessed September 5, 2019, scmp.com/topics/xi-jinping-and-ma-ying-jeou-summit.

15. "'All Necessary Means': Xi Jinping Reserves Right to Sue Force Against Taiwan," *The Guardian*, January 2, 2019, theguardian.com/world/2019/jan/02/all-necessary-means-xi-jinping-reserves-right-to-use-force-against-taiwan.

16. People's Republic of China, "China's National Defense in the New Era," ed. State Council Information Office (Beijing: Foreign Languages Press, 2019), 4.

17. Ibid., 7.

18. "US Approves $8bn Sale of 66 F-16 Fighters to Taiwan," *Aljazeera*, August 21, 2019, aljazeera.com/news/2019/08/approves-8bn-sale-66-16-fighters-taiwan-190821002905496.html.

19. US Congress, House, *Taiwan Travel Act*, HR 535, 115th Cong., Introduced in House January 13, 2017, congress.gov/bill/115th-congress/house-bill/535.

20. US Congress, House, *Taiwan Assurance Act of 2019*, HR 2002, 116th Cong., Introduction in House April 1, 2019, congress.gov/bill/116th-congress/house-bill/2002.

21. US Congress, House, *Taiwan Allies International Protection and Enhancement Initiative (TAIPEI) Act*, S 1678, 116th Cong., Introduction in House May 23, 2019, congress.gov/bill/116th-congress/senate-bill/1678.

22. US Congress, House, A resolution supporting measures taken by the Government of Taiwan to deter, or if so compelled, defeat, aggression by the Government of the People's Republic of China, S.Res. 228, 116th Cong., Introduction in Senate June 4, 2019, congress.gov/bill/116th-congress/senate-resolution/228.

23. Chris Horton, "Taiwan's President, Defying Xi Jinping, Calls Unification Offer 'Impossible,'" *New York Times*, January 5, 2019, nytimes.com/2019/01/05/world/asia/taiwan-xi-jinping-tsai-ing-wen.html.

24. Mary Hui, "Hong Kong's Protests Passed a Notable Milestone, and Sensitive Days Lie Ahead," *Quartz*, August 31, 2019, qz.com/1697901/hong-kongs-2019-protests-have-surpassed-2014-umbrella-movement/.

25. People's Republic of China, "China's National Defense in the New Era," 5 and 7.

26. Dean. P. Chen, "US-China Rivalry and the Weakening of the KMTs "1992 Consensus" Policy: Second Image Reversed, Revisited," *Asian Survey* 56, no. 4 (2016): 2–4.

27. Charlotte Gao, "Was It Wise for Tsai Ing-wen to Reject the '1992 Consensus' Publicly?" *The Diplomat*, January 4, 2019, thediplomat.com/2019/01/was-it-wise-for-tsai-ing-wen-to-reject-the-1992-consensus-publicly.

28. Speech of Lu Hsiu-lien at East Asia Peace Forum, "Peace in East Asia and the Neutrality of Taiwan," in *East Asia Peace Forum*, ed. Democratic Pacific Union (Taipei: Democratic Pacific Union, 2018).

29. Hsiu-lien Lu and Ashley Esarey, *My Fight for a New Taiwan: One Woman's Journey from Prison to Power* (Washington, DC: University of Washington Press, 2014).

30. East Asia Peace Forum, "Peace in East Asia and the Neutrality of Taiwan."

31. The question of the referendum reeds: "Do you agree that Taiwan should declare peace and neutrality to the international community?" See "呂秀蓮推和平公投 消除台灣與他國合作抗中的憂慮," *Newtalk*, March 4, 2019, newtalk.tw/news/view/2019-03-04/214756.

32. "Former vice president proposes Taiwan neutrality referendum," *Focus Taiwan*, March 5, 2019, focustaiwan.tw/news/aipl/201903050021.aspx.

33. Judy Lo, "No Referendums to Take Place in Taiwan until 2021," *Taiwan Times*, June 17, 2019, taiwannews.com.tw/en/news/3726253.

34. Publically initiated referendums have been possible since 2003 but the hurdles for them used to be discouragingly high. Under the new rules, however, the threshold of required signatures to initiate a national referendum was lowered from 5 percent of the electorate to 1.5 percent, and the requirement for a 50 percent voter turnout was reduced to 25 percent.

35. "Referendum on Changing Sports Team Name to 'Taiwan' Rejected" *Focus Taiwan*, November 24, 2018, focustaiwan.tw/news/aeas/201811250008.aspx.

36. On definitions of neutrality see also the introduction of this volume.

37. Cyril E. Black et al., *Neutralization and World Politics* (Princeton: Princeton University Press, 1968), xi.

38. Malbone W. Graham, "Neutralization as a Movement in International Law," *The American Journal of International Law* 21 (January 1927): 89.

39. See also Cyrus F. Wicker, "Some Effects of Neutralization," *The American Journal of International Law* 5, no. 3 (1911); Erving Winslow, "Neutralization," *American Journal of International Law* 2 (1908).

40. "Neutralization," 369–70.

41. Black et al., *Neutralization and World Politics*, 26.

42. Ibid., 33. See also Alexander Spring, *The International Law Concept of Neutrality in the Twenty-First Century* (Zurich: Dike Law Books, 20014), 42.

43. Lassa F. L. Oppenheim, *International Law: A Treatise—War and Neutrality*, vol. II (London: Longmans, Green, and Co., 1912), §301.

44. The term sometimes refers to just a neutral state but has also been used in context of non-sovereign territories in the early days of the twentieth century. See, for example, Erving Winslow, "Neutralization," *The North American Review* 186, no. 622 (1907): 83. See also chapter 8 of this volume.

45. Ken'ichi Goto, *Tensions of Empire: Japan and Southeast Asia in the Colonial and Postcolonial World*, Ohio University Research in International Studies—Southeast Asia series (Singapore: NUS Press, 2003), 33–38.

46. John Pownall Reeves et al., *The Lone Flag: Memoir of the British Consul in Macao during World War II* (Hong Kong: Hong Kong University Press, 2015).

47. For an account regarding Australian aggression see the Parliament of the Commonwealth of Australia, "Australian Policy: Indonesia's Incorporation of East Timor," in *East Timor: Final Report of the Senate Foreign Affairs, Defence and Trade References Committee* (Canberra: Senate Printing Unit, Parliament House, 2000), 111–15.

48. George Liska, *Nations in Alliance: The Limits of Interdependence* (Baltimore: Johns Hopkins Press, 1962).

49. It is uncertain if the relationship between the US and South Vietnam can be counted as a case of collective security, but there are authors who argue in that direction. See Edward Miller, *Misalliance: Ngo Dinh Diem, the United States, and the Fate of South Vietnam* (Cumberland: Harvard University Press, 2013).

50. See, for example, Herbert R. Reginbogin, *Faces of Neutrality: A Comparative Analysis of the Neutrality of Switzerland and other Neutral Nations during WWII*, trans. Ulrike Seeberger and Jane Britten (Berlin: Lit Verlag, 2009); Neville Wylie, *European Neutrals and Non-belligerents during the Second World War* (New York: Cambridge University Press, 2002).

51. Stephen C. Neff, *The Rights and Duties of Neutrals: A General History* (Manchester: Manchester University Press, 2000), 198.

52. Black et al., *Neutralization and World Politics*, 18.

53. General Assembly, "Maintenance of International Security: A—Permanent Neutrality of Turkmenistan," (A/RES/50/80, 1995). See also Spring, *The International Law Concept of Neutrality in the Twenty-First Century*, 81–82; David Noack, "Politics of Neutrality in the

Post-Soviet Space: A Comparison of Concepts, Practices, and Outcomes of Neutrality in Moldova, Turkmenistan, and Ukraine 1990–2015," in *Notions of Neutralities*, ed. Pascal Lottaz and Herbert R. Reginbogin (Lanham, MD: Lexington, 2019).

54. General Assembly, *International Day of Neutrality* (A/RES/71/275, 2017).

55. See trade date compiled by Eleanor Albert, "China-Taiwan Relations" Council on Foreign Relations, accessed September 5, 2019, cfr.org/backgrounder/china-taiwan-relations.

56. "Taiwan's Hunger for Renminbi Grows," *The Financial Times*, Febraruy 28, 2013, ft.com/content/033923f0-8163-11e2-904c-00144feabdc0.

57. By 2018, Taiwan was only the sixth largest RMB trading place. SWIFT, *RMB Tracker: Hong Kong, United Kingdom, Mainland China—Leading RMB Internationalization* (Belgium: SWIFT, 2018).

58. See chapter 8 of this volume.

## SELECTED REFERENCES

Black, Cyril E., Richard A. Falk, Klaus Knorr, and Oran R. Young. *Neutralization and World Politics*. Princeton: Princeton University Press, 1968.

Chen, Dean P. "US-China Rivalry and the Weakening of the KMTs '1992 Consensus Policy': Second Image Reversed, Revisited." *Asian Survey* 56, no. 4 (2016): 754–78.

East Asia Peace Forum. "Peace in East Asia and the Neutrality of Taiwan." In *East Asia Peace Forum*, edited by Democratic Pacific Union. Taipei: Democratic Pacific Union, 2018.

General Assembly. *International Day of Neutrality*. A/RES/71/275, 2017.

———. *Maintenance of International Security: A—Permanent Neutrality of Turkmenistan*. A/RES/50/80, 1995.

Goto, Ken'ichi. *Tensions of Empire: Japan and Southeast Asia in the Colonial and Postcolonial World*. Ohio University Research in International Studies—Southeast Asia series. Singapore: NUS Press, 2003.

Graham, Malbone W. "Neutralization as a Movement in International Law." *The American Journal of International Law* 21 (January, 1927): 79–94.

Hartnett, Stephen J., Patrick Shaou-Whea Dodge, and Lisa B. Keränen. "Postcolonial Remembering in Taiwan: 228 and Transitional Justice as 'The End of Fear.'" *Journal of International and Intercultural Communication* (2019): 1–19.

Kim, Eun-Mee. *The Four Asian Tigers: Economic Development and the Global Political Economy* [in English]. San Diego: Academic Press, 1998.

Liska, George. *Nations in Alliance: The Limits of Interdependence*. Baltimore: Johns Hopkins Press, 1962.

Lu, Hsiu-lien, and Ashley Esarey. *My Fight for a New Taiwan: One Woman's Journey from Prison to Power*. Washington, DC: University of Washington Press, 2014.

Matsumoto, Haruka. "The First Taiwan Strait Crisis and China's 'Border' Dispute Around Taiwan." *Eurasia Border Review* 3 (2012): 75–91.

Miller, Edward. *Misalliance: Ngo Dinh Diem, the United States, and the Fate of South Vietnam*. Cumberland: Harvard University Press, 2013.

Neff, Stephen C. *The Rights and Duties of Neutrals: A General History*. Manchester: Manchester University Press, 2000.

Noack, David. "Politics of Neutrality in the Post-Soviet Space: A Comparison of Concepts, Practices, and Outcomes of Neutrality in Moldova, Turkmenistan and Ukraine 1990–2015." In *Notions of Neutralities*, edited by Pascal Lottaz and Herbert R. Reginbogin, 267–88. Lanham, MD: Lexington, 2019.

Oppenheim, Lassa F. L. *International Law: A Treatise—War and Neutrality*. Vol. II. London: Longmans, Green, and Co., 1912.

People's Republic of China. *China's Military Strategy* (Beijing: Foreign Languages Press, 2015).

———. *China's National Defense in the New Era* (Beijing: Foreign Languages Press, 2019).

Reeves, John Pownall, Colin Day, Richard Garrett, and David Calthorpe. *The Lone Flag: Memoir of the British Consul in Macao during World War II*. Hong Kong: Hong Kong University Press, 2015.

Reginbogin, Herbert R. *Faces of Neutrality: A Comparative Analysis of the Neutrality of Switzerland and other Neutral Nations during WWII*. Translated by Ulrike Seeberger and Jane Britten. Berlin: Lit Verlag, 2009.

Smith, Craig A. "Taiwan's 228 Incident and the Politics of Placing Blame." *Past Imperfect* 14 (2008).

Spring, Alexander. *The International Law Concept of Neutrality in the Twenty-First Century*. Zurich: Dike Law Books, 2014.

SWIFT. *RMB Tracker: Hong Kong, United Kingdom, Mainland China—Leading RMB Internationalization*. Belgium: SWIFT, 2018.

The Parliament of the Commonwealth of Australia. "Australian Policy: Indonesia's Incorporation of East Timor." In *East Timor: Final Report of the Senate Foreign Affairs, Defence and Trade References Committee*. Canberra: Senate Printing Unit, Parliament House, 2000.

Wicker, Cyrus F. "Some Effects of Neutralization." *The American Journal of International Law* 5, no. 3 (1911): 639–52.

Winslow, Erving. "Neutralization." *The North American Review* 186, no. 622 (1907): 83–90.

———. "Neutralization." *American Journal of International Law* 2 (1908): 366–86.

Wylie, Neville. *European Neutrals and Non-belligerents during the Second World War*. New York: Cambridge University Press, 2002.

Yi-shen, Chen. "The Shaping of Taiwan's Status after World WarII." In *Taiwan's Struggle: Voices of the Taiwanese*, edited by Shyu-Tu Lee and Jack F. Williams. Lanham, MD: Rowman & Littlefield, 2014.

*Chapter Ten*

# Case Studies of Contemporary Neutrality Advocacy

Lu Hsiu-lien, Michael Tsai, and Michael O'Hanlon

EDITOR'S NOTE

Debates about the value of permanent neutrality are not confined to academic circles. There are policy advisors and politicians around the globe who think about the "neutral idea"[1] seriously and some have started their advocacy for it. This chapter presents three different thinkers; Lu Hsiu-lien (Annette Lu),[2] Vice president of the Republic of China (ROC–Taiwan) from 2000 to 2008, her colleague, Michael Tsai, former minister of defense of the ROC, and Michael O'Hanlon, director of research in foreign policy at the Brookings Institution and former member of the external advisory board the Central Intelligence Agency (2011–2012). The three practitioners participated in the conference "Permanent Neutrality: A Model for Peace Security and Justice" on March 25, 2019, in Washington, DC. They present their respective cases for the permanent neutrality of Taiwan (Lu and Tsai) and Ukraine (O'Hanlon). The former two are stated with a clear political purpose; to convince the audience of the moral and historical right for Taiwan to push for a neutral solution that would guarantee its security while allowing the Taiwanese population to steer the course of their political developments themselves. O'Hanlon's assessment of Ukraine, on the other hand, draws on a strategic assessment of the Eastern European region that he developed in earlier scholarship.[3] All three contributions were transcribed from their oral presentations and edited only for formality. They should be understood as primary sources that reflect contemporary neutrality advocacy.

## LU HSIU-LIEN (ANNETTE LU)

It's a great pleasure to have this opportunity to present the issue of Taiwan's pursuit for neutrality under the umbrella of global security architecture. Thank you for the auspices of the prestigious Catholic University of America. Thanks also for the kindness and hard work of Professor Herbert Reginbogin and his colleagues to conduct this workshop at the US Senate Hart Building.

This year 2019 marks the 40th anniversary of the termination of US diplomatic relations with ROC. It is also the 40th anniversary of the Kaohsiung Incident which caused 152 freedom fighters of Taiwan to be imprisoned, including myself. Eight leaders were court-martialed and sentenced to 12 years and more. The testimony by the co-defendants at the military court enlightened the general public who have been suppressed under 38 years of martial law regime. Years later, the flowers of democracy began to bloom. To commemorate 2019, a petition to pursue peace and neutrality, with 10,000 signatures were submitted to initiate the referendum on March 5. The second phase will need 281,745 signatures collected within six months after the approval. If everything goes well, the referendum will be voted along with the presidential election in January 2020. And it will become valid if 5 million people vote for it. The context of the referendum reads: "Do you agree that Taiwan shall declare peace and neutral to the world?"

### Historical Destiny Distorted

Historically, Taiwan did not suffer much from wars at home, but always became victimized by wars from outside. In 1894, Korea invited China and Japan to help crackdown a coup, which led to the Sino-Japanese War. China was defeated and Taiwan was ceded to Japan "in perpetuity." Thus, Taiwan became Japan's colony till 1945, when Japan surrendered to end World War II. The Allied Forces commanded Chiang Kai-shek to send troops to take over Taiwan. His troops never left Taiwan but treaded the native residents under foot. On February 28, 1947, a riot took place and Chiang sent more troops to suppress the riot and 10,000 people were slaughtered. Two years later, Chiang fled to Taiwan to resume his regime which was overthrown by Mao Tse-tung in China.

According to the UN Charter, the territory that is ceded from the rival at the end of World War II shall be entrusted by the UN to undertake a plebiscite for the residents to decide their future. Accordingly, the Allied Forces should have assisted Taiwan to have an opportunity to conduct a plebiscite. But it never happened. On the contrary, shortly after the outburst of the Korean War in June 1950, President Truman declared that the status of Taiwan was undetermined, and the Taiwan Strait became neutralized. Taiwan thus fell into the dilemma between the rivalry of PRC and ROC. Later in 1971, the UN General Assembly passed Resolution 2758 to recognize PRC as the sole representative of China, and Taiwan gradually became an international orphan. It is worthy of note that the UN Resolution 2758 only decided the representativeness of China. There was not a single word mentioned of ROC, nor Taiwan. Despite of it, the PRC has taken advantage of that resolution to mislead the world to believe that Taiwan is a part of China and the PRC represents Taiwan. The UN Resolution 2758 states that:

> THE GENERAL ASSEMBLY,
> Recalling the principles of the Charter of the United Nations.
> Considering the restoration of the lawful rights of the People's Republic of China is essential both for the protection of the Charter of the United Nations and for the cause that the United Nations must serve under the Charter.
> Recognizing that the representatives of the Government of the People's Republic of China are the only lawful representatives of China to the United Nations and that the People's Republic of China is one of the five permanent members of the Security Council.
> Decides to restore all its rights to the People's Republic of China and to recognize the representatives of its Government as the only legitimate representatives of China to the United Nations, and to expel forthwith the representatives of Chiang Kai-shek from the place which they unlawfully occupy at the United Nations and in all the organizations related to it.

As a matter of fact, during the 1971 UN debate on China issue, the Ambassador from Saudi Arabia reminded the General Assembly of the representativeness of the people on Taiwan and proposed that, the UN should conduct a plebiscite to allow the Taiwanese to choose among the following options:

1. To declare and maintain neutrality.
2. To become federal state with the PRC.
3. To join the PRC under confederation system.

This proposal was reluctantly accepted by the hardheaded Chiang Kai-shek, but abruptly rejected by US National Security Advisor Henry Kissinger as he had promised Beijing authority to accept One China Policy. Once more, the door to open the future of Taiwan was shut down. The miserable history of Taiwan made us believe that it is only when Taiwan becomes a neutral state that its people can be the master of their own.

After sacrifice and struggle for centuries, Taiwan stands up today as a modern democracy with a well-educated population of 23.6 million. It is also a beacon of soft power in Asia, with the most advanced high technology and earnest love for peace and human rights, as well as 28 harmonious religions. It is time for the people of Taiwan to solemnly declare to the world that

Taiwan refuses to become a pawn for negotiation, nor the battlefield of a war.

## The Strategic Interests of Taiwan's Neutrality

Taiwan is bordered between the largest ocean and continent and links the East China Sea, the Taiwan Strait, and the South China Sea. It is the pivot of the first island chain and is irreplaceable strategically. It is the leverage in the race for hegemony between China and the United States. That's why Taiwan is so attractive to China. The PRC has set up the agenda to annex Taiwan since the implementation of its Anti-Session Law in 2005. President Xi Jinping even officially made it clear to fulfill his historical duty for the reunification of the nation. In the latest statement delivered on January 2, "One China, Two Systems" is the formula to annex Taiwan. Regretfully, many Taiwanese businessmen and retired governmental officers and even elected politicians have either defected or cooperated with them. With the operation of their Fifth Column residing in Taiwan, the national security is seriously challenged by their infiltration. Moreover, the cyberattack tactics have tremendous impacts on the elections. It's no secret that some elected mayors and politicians are hand-picked by Beijing, especially the candidate for the next President, not to mention their drastically escalating military threat and globally diplomatic bullying over Taiwan.

The pursuit of neutrality through referendum, in strategic concern is a form of preventive diplomacy and preventive defense to counter China's invasion. The outcome of the neutrality referendum will be the best answer to China. This campaign deserves the world's attention and support, especially the US, which has been the major ally of Taiwan for over a century, even after recognition with China in 1979. The spirit and principles of the Taiwan Relations Act can become more effective when Taiwan becomes an armed neutrality country. Taiwan absolutely needs friendship and cooperation with the US and Japan as well, including arms sales.

## Would China Agree with Taiwan's Neutrality?

It is no surprise to say no. But China has always said no to Taiwanese democracy and referendums. Taiwan does not survive to please China. We did right things and did things right, before and in the future. We would try our best to convince China that Taiwan's neutrality would free China from the burden to liberate Taiwan, also from the fear that Taiwan might conspire with other countries against it. We believe that our neighboring countries including Japan, Korea, and the Philippines would also welcome Taiwan to become neutral. As a matter of fact, the Japanese Constitution serves the purpose for Japan's neutrality. Leaders from both North and South Korea also have indicated their intention to seek neutrality in the future. And the Philippines has been a member of the Nonaligned Movement within the ASEAN. Neutrality is not a naïve joke. It's a new philosophy and new strategy based on soft and smart power for international peace and justice. May God bless Taiwan to become neutral soon in the near future. Thank you.

## MICHAEL TSAI

*Michael Tsai*: As an American-trained attorney, I did study American law, I did study American Constitution. In its preamble it says that we, the people of the United States of America, we are born free and equal with dignity. I believe in that. But in Taiwan, the people of Taiwan, we are not born equal, free, with dignity. We had to fight for and pay the price. And this is what Madame Lu, she has been fighting for freedom and democracy, and had to serve seven years or six years in political prisoner herself. I'm also fighting for the freedom and democracy and human rights not only in Taiwan, but also I did fight the human rights and democracy in China, for Chinese friends, for the friends in Tibet, for Uighurs as well. Therefore, today we come here to seek the ways and means for Taiwan, among other small states, nations, seeking freedom and human rights.

Why Taiwan we are seeking armed neutrality across the Taiwan Strait between China and Taiwan? Why? My personal perspective, we are seeking the peace, security, and justice as our Taiwanese human rights for self-determination as stipulated under the UN Charter. The rights of self-determination of the people's own future should be a part of universal human rights. Is it? I believe so. Therefore, we are seeking the ways and means to realize if Taiwan can become free, equal, with dignity, and also have a security, peace, and justice in the Asia-Pacific as well as in the entire world. This is my personal conviction.

The second, why are we thinking that neutrality is so important for Taiwan and the surrounding area of Asian Pacific. The reason, we are going to advocate for the peace and neutrality in Taiwan Strait as a positive, preventive defense, Active Preventive Defense, APD. Because as Madame Lu mentioned that Taiwan, for the last 100 years, we are the victim, still the victim between the giant, powerful nations, used to be under the Japan after the Sino-Japanese War in 1894. And then up to the Korean War crisis, Taiwan became a victim of the PRC in China, tried to invade Taiwan, tried to take over Taiwan. And even now, Taiwan [is] still [a] conflict area and flashpoint of the global confrontation, particularly in this area, Taiwan Strait and South China Seas. Therefore, we are seeking for the freedom to seek for the peace, security, and justice, not only for Taiwan as human rights, but also for the peace and stability for the area in this Asia-Pacific.

Third, I would like to share with you, right after the Korean War Crisis in the 1950s, US President Harry Truman, he reported to the US Congress, saying that the US has dispatched its seven fleet Navy to patrol Taiwan Strait in order to prevent the crisis of the Korean War from extending from the Taiwan Strait, that is, to prevent China from intruding into the Taiwan, in order to maintain peace and stability in the Taiwan Strait and go beyond. And then in 1954, the US Pacific commander, four-star Admiral Davis, he asserted the so-called central line, middle line across the Taiwan Strait between China and Taiwan as a military buffer zone which prohibited both sides of Taiwan Strait, that is, China and Taiwan, sending the jet fighter and the navy apparatus into crossing, what we call the Davis Line, into the other area in order to maintain the peace and stability, and which Davis Line has been maintained for the last 65 years since 1955.

Therefore, we are asking what is possible, such kind of Davis Line or Demilitarized Zone can be still maintained for another 65 years? If it can be maintained and realized, hopefully, not only Taiwan Strait but also South China Seas, but also the East China Sea can be also effective and such kind of potential conflict or military confrontation can be avoided. And I believe the armed neutrality on Taiwan Strait not only benefits Taiwan's peace and security and justice, but also it would be beneficial to the United States, Japan, and some other nations in this area.

But what is the risk for our assertion of Taiwan's armed neutrality? The first one, China. I think our respectable Madame Lu mentioned that China has been claiming Taiwan as their part of territory. And they decreed they're going to take over Taiwan by all means, including the military or other coercive means to take over for annexation. That's not fair for Taiwan, because it's our basic human rights to determine our own futures, not dictated by China or some other nations.

Finally, in order to realize this kind of armed neutrality occurs in Taiwan for the past half century, I have honor to serve in the Taiwan national defense. We try very hard to train our armed forces, to increase our national defense budget. We try to cooperate closely with the United States to protect not only the security of Taiwan, but also protect the peace, security, and stability in this region of the Asia-Pacific. Therefore, I have proposed [the] establishment of military confidence building mechanism, MBCM. In short terms, under the framework of MBCM, in short term, we like to have change a discussion that occurs between Taiwan and the United States and Japan and other nations. And also we like to have dialog with our Chinese friends, how we can work together to view up this kind of confident beauty mechanism, how to preserve the Davis Line which has been maintained, as I mentioned, for the last 65 years.

The medium range, I hope, we can see this MCBM working together with the United States, Japan, and some other nations in the area, including China, how we can work out possible rules and regulations of codes and conduct of free navigations in that area of Asia-Pacific. And in long term, we are seeking for the international collective peace agreement, togetherness with China, United States, Japan, with some other Asian-Pacific nations, we're working together to have a European NATO in Asia-Pacific. Thank you.

*Moderator*: Thank you. Excellent. Michael, you say you're in favor of some kind of an Asian NATO if I heard you right. You wanna clarify that point briefly? And then we'll move on to a couple of audience questions.

*Michael Tsai*: There are two or three different kinds of ways or means when we're talking about the regional collective security cooperation. And NATO, of course, is very important and significant role during the last half century or so. Therefore, we are advocating for also some kind of regional security cooperation. And there are two ways or means. One, bilateral security cooperation like between the United States and Japan, the United States and South Korea, the United States with some other Asian countries. And another way is the multilateral regional security cooperation. For instance, there exists one, I think APEC, Asia-Pacific Economical Conference. They are twenty-three member nations now. Every year they have an APEC summit meeting. And Taiwan, China, United States, Japan, and also some other countries, Canada, Chile. Why not we use that APEC summit conference, that's talking about economy, economic cooperation, that's what has been done for the last 20 or 30 years. We can talk about the security cooperation as well, as I mentioned, how we can set up for the military confidence beauty mechanism, MCBM. For instance, we can establish the code of conduct of free navigation in the East China Sea, Taiwan Strait, and South China Sea. Because there are so many potential conference between the United States, China, Vietnam, and Philippines all together. So Taiwan use this existing mechanism, APEC, to talk about this.

Of course, my friend's talking about UN, United Nation. But China sits on the Security Council, they enjoy the veto power. Anything talking about the Taiwan Strait MCBM, China would veto. Therefore, kind of regional security cooperation among the superpower, including I would put in China, come together, talking about, as I mentioned, code of conduct of free navigation, and we can talk about the effort of how the anti-terrorism, anti-piracy, and some other crimes in open high seas. This has been working together with China, Japan, Taiwan, and the United States together for the last 10 to 15 years, because I was involved in that. How to work together for anti-terrorism, crimes on open high seas. In the spirit of good will, I remember the Chinese Communist leader, Hu Jintao, in 2011, he openly said that he would like to consider MCBM mechanism of confident beauty mechanism, between Taiwan and China. But unfortunately, the new leader, Xi Jinping, he's making the China dream of 2035 to become the world power. They're going to take over the Asia-Pacific political, military order to replace the United States' role for the past half century or so.

Therefore, Taiwan I say small-medium economic, political powers. We have 23 million population and territory with effective governments. Therefore we think we are entitled, as part of our human rights, for self-determination for our own future. We like to be involved in the spread of collective security. We shall succeed.

## MICHAEL O'HANLON

*Moderator*: You recently published on neutral solutions for Europe, arguing for the value of a neutral belt between NATO and Russia. Please tell us about your argument.

*Answer*: Over recent decades, while acknowledging the noble intentions behind NATO expansion since the Cold War ended, I have increasingly become persuaded that expansion has gone far enough. We should be resolute in defense of any and all existing NATO allies, because what's done is done in terms of previous rounds of expansion, and because any suggestion of a two-tier alliance (with some allies mattering more than others) invites deterrence failure. But we should particularly rethink aspirations of bringing any former Soviet republics into the North Atlantic Treaty Organization—by which we would be swearing to protect faraway lands with the blood of American troops. Such an idea, I am persuaded, is so counterproductive that it would not even be desirable for countries like Ukraine and Georgia themselves. Instead, I favor codification of permanent neutrality, in effect, for the former Soviet republics that are not currently in NATO provided that territorial disputes with Russia be satisfied, be resolved, to the satisfaction of Ukraine and Georgia and others, and provided that Russia acknowledge it has no right to thwart these countries' interest in joining the European Union if they're eligible some day for that, or any other organization. In making this argument, I begin, really with Thucydides, not with the last 12 months or the last 24 months, but with the last few thousand years. And Thucydides taught us that countries go to war for one of three reasons. They either go for interest and greed, or out of fear for their own security, or out of pride. And in my opinion, most Russian behavior in the post-Cold War era can be interpreted in terms of pride and wounded pride. I do not believe that NATO poses a serious security threat to Russia, but I believe that many Russians, including Vladimir Putin, find it offensive that the very organization that was set up to defeat the Soviet Union in the Cold War would then not only continue to exist after the cold war, but expand several hundred miles further east toward Moscow. Psychologically, that may be a threat. It certainly, I think to Russians, feels psychologically an insult. This is, to repeat, not an argument against NATO. I think NATO is a remarkably successful organization historically, and even though it expanded already, further than I would have recommended, I'm not in favor of dismantling it and I'm not in favor of apologizing to the Russians that we have expanded it.

All that said, Thucydides would have recognized current Russian thinking and Russian behavior. Because human beings are proud, when they feel that they've already suffered some kind of blow to their prestige, which is what happened at the end of the Cold War for the Soviet Union. And then on top of that their competitive counterpart has continued to amass more members with the same exact organization that was seen as the adversary through the Cold War. I believe that the Russian reaction, though not necessarily justifiable, was still predictable. And if it was predictable, then we should have been anticipating it. And if further NATO expansion would cause inevitable problems, I think we should anticipate that. I'm not trying to deny Ukraine or Georgia their rights as sovereign nations, but I would observe the United States and other existing NATO members, we have sovereign rights, too. We have the sovereign right to decide where we will send our sons and daughters to die in defense of someone else. That's about as profound as a sovereign right as can be imagined, and yet in many European dialogues, I wind up in debates with friends who feel that I'm somehow taking something away from Ukraine and Georgia and other eastern European countries. That they somehow rightfully deserve some inherent kind of right as a nation state in Europe to be in NATO. That is not correct and not consistent with the original framing of NATO or even its Article X provision that allows expansion *if* that expansion is in the interest of existing member states and *if* it will contribute to the stability of Europe. Such conditions do not apply in cases like those of Ukraine and Georgia in my view.

By the way, the right to join alliances is not in the UN charter, and I think alliances should always be justified in terms of serving specific purposes and specific circumstances. There's nothing inherently desirable or objectionable about an alliance. It is simply a potential vehicle that can be considered under certain circumstances. And if we think back to the origins of NATO after World War II, we know that George Kennan and other strategists identified the western European continental landmass, the British islands, Russia, Japan and the United States as the five key centers of global industrial and military power. And Kennan and others said we cannot afford to have most of those fall under the control of a single foreign hostile power because that would ultimately be a threat to the United States. That was the strategic logic by which NATO was formed. Kennan, himself, did not even support the formation of NATO at first, although he came over time to think that it had done some good things and perhaps that he had been mistaken in opposing it. But, the strategic focus was on the German industrial valleys, France to an extent, Britain and then Kennan also wanted to make sure that Japan did not fall under Soviet sway. And for these reasons, he supported the basic logic of the alliance system that was created during the Cold War. Now, today, the alignment of global power is a little different. Certainly, East Asia is, and China in particular, very important, very powerful. The broader Persian Gulf is still important for energy. So, maybe Kennan's five centers would now have to be seven or eight, but I still don't believe that his logic would require us to think that Ukraine or Georgia, or Moldova or Belarus, or even Finland or Sweden or the Balkans would have to fall within this core perimeter that Americans should be willing to send their sons and daughters to die in defense of as if it were American territory.

*Moderator*: Wouldn't more neutrals in Europe naturally weaken the NATO alliance and be to the detriment of the current security model? Wouldn't more allies for NATO make more sense than more neutrals?

*Answer*: As you can see, I'm making a specific argument. I'm not trying to say that the concept of neutrality is inherently good or inherently bad. I'm not trying to say the concept of alliances is inherently good or inherently bad. I think we have to apply these methods, think of these instruments, these potential options and develop them with the kind of expertise we have at this panel and this session overall today, and then ask with what we know about neutrality and what we know about alliances, what's the optimal security architecture for a given part of the world at a given period in time. So, I take that very pragmatic approach.

And the point I want to conclude on is to say those who would claim I'm depriving Ukraine and Georgia of their rightful sovereign prerogatives as nation states, in addition to the argument that I made before about how as an American, I feel like I should have some prerogatives too, I would also point out current policy is not doing Ukraine and Georgia any service whatsoever. Some 11 years ago, coming out of the Bucharest summit, NATO inadvertently painted a bullseye on the back of Ukraine and Georgia and did nothing to defend them. At the Bucharest summit NATO said someday we will bring Ukraine and Georgia into NATO, but there was no timeframe for when that will happen, no interim security guarantee for how we would protect those countries in the meantime, and by the way, there was a longstanding policy that you're not eligible for NATO membership if you have unresolved territorial disputes with your neighbors, even if those disputes are not your fault. Even if Russia invades your territory, we had and still have a NATO policy that says if there's an ongoing dispute, you're not eligible for membership. Because we don't want to bring somebody into NATO on one day and have to go fight to defend them the next day. We want to bring things in when they're calm, bring people in when they're calm, the situations are calm, and then extend the security blanket thereafter. But this concept will not work currently for Ukraine and Georgia. They both have unresolved conflicts with Russia. So, I think we have created, unintentionally, a perverse set of incentives which justifies in Vladimir Putin's mind his unacceptable and brutal behavior towards those countries. I make no defense of Russia's behavior, but I simply say Thucydides would not have been surprised. And ultimately, we not only have to do what we think is right in international politics, but what we think is smart and we have to anticipate the reactions of other countries. So, by elevating membership for new east European countries to a noble cause that must triumph above all else, I actually think we do these countries a disservice and hurt their security and hurt our own.

## NOTES

1. See chapter 3 of this volume.
2. Lu has a long political career to lock back on, including the struggle against the Kuomintang dictatorship in the 1970s and 1980s. Her memoires were published in English in Hsiu-lien Lu and Ashley Esarey, *My Fight for a New Taiwan: One Woman's Journey from Prison to Power* (Washington, DC: University of Washington Press, 2014).
3. Michael O'Hanlon, *Beyond NATO: A New Security Architecture for Eastern Europe* (Washington, DC: Brookings Institution Press, 2017).

## SELECTED REFERENCES

Lu, Hsiu-lien, and Ashley Esarey. *My Fight for a New Taiwan: One Woman's Journey from Prison to Power*. Washington, DC: University of Washington Press, 2014.
O'Hanlon, Michael. *Beyond NATO: A New Security Architecture for Eastern Europe*. Washington, DC: Brookings Institution Press, 2017.

# Conclusion

## Pascal Lottaz and Herbert R. Reginbogin

The ten chapters of this book explored various facets of neutrality in the international system, especially its underestimated security function. The main argument is that neutrality in general, and neutralization in particular, can function as useful tools of statecraft. Neutrality used to be an integral feature of international politics during the nineteenth-century balance of power.[1] However, neutralization as a way of creating stability in conflict areas started to fall out of fashion after the Second World War and declined even further after the Cold War. Austria and Finland, at the beginning of the Cold War, were two of the last successful cases, while Laos, during the Vietnam War, was the last unsuccessful attempt. Since then, only self-declared neutralities have emerged. Although the twenty-first century has inherited the work of the previous generations—there still is a "law of neutrality" that has not been revoked—neutrality has lost much of its previous esteem. Apart from a few "staunchly" neutral countries, the world community at large has not been using this potential route to organize state-to-state affairs. Occasional neutrality is not used anymore, while permanent neutrals are routinely portrayed as lethargic by design. So much so that there is an apologetic tone towards those who think that neutrality can be a legitimate foreign policy. The urge by politicians and researchers to combine the word "neutrality" with qualifications that balance the assumed apathy is symptomatic; "engaged neutrality,"[2] "active neutrality,"[3] "positive neutrality"[4] are neologisms mirroring the pathological complex that being neutral is incapacitating, passive, egoistic, isolationist, and needs an apology or correction of some form. In reality, neutrality has never been a passive or incapacitating policy. It never was about isolationism in the first place. It merely has been a means for states to protect their interests apart from joining alliances and fighting wars of others. Of course, in the eyes of those who fight, this naturally looks like cowardice because all sides in every war necessarily think that they fight on the right side. It is the nature of war that both sides believe with deadly passion that they have the right to fight; otherwise, they would not. But be it the US, the USSR, China, Japan, Great Britain, or other powers, big and small nations alike have been using neutral policies in one way or the other for centuries, whether they called them such or not.

The central thesis of this book is that by recognizing the potential of neutrality policies, international politics can gain an additional tool for the management of the great rivalry between states. The dynamics of multipolarity is already changing the discussion as the "American Century" is ending. The first two chapters illustrate that, on the one hand, neutrality is an alternative concept to collective security (and alliances), while, on the other hand, the difference between the two is opaque. Even at times when collective security approaches were relatively stable as, for example, in the early interwar period, traditionally neutral states did not easily give up their foreign policy. Furthermore, when conflict breaks out, even nonpermanent neutral countries can become neutral actors. To explain this, chapter 3 describes the logical position of different neutralities and that they are never outside the realm of a conflict; neutrals merely occupy a nonviolent space in a conflict constellation. Chapters 4 to 6 discuss cases of neutrality in contemporary Europe and how versatile neutralities today are—or, in the case of Ukraine, could be. Chapter 7 demonstrates how even the United States' long history of neutrality had varying interpretations, while chapters 8, 9, and 10 consider the possible applications of neutrality today.

This book acknowledges that states do not adopt permanent neutrality for its own sake. Neutrality is only a means to achieve an end. Some modern European neutrals might be on course to completely abandon the status, as discussed in chapter 5, and could join NATO at some point. However, the same is true in reverse. At the turn of the last century, some former communist republics discovered that their new security environment and the changed political positions are best served by communicating their general nonalliance with other powers. Serbia, Turkmenistan, and Moldova have adopted neutrality, and a sound argument can be made for Ukraine adopting the same approach. Mongolia, too, has become a permanent neutral while states in South East Asia have been using neutralist policies for decades but rather under the banner of nonalignment than traditional permanent neutrality. Even in unlikely places like Taiwan, there are policymakers who argue that neutrality would be the best solution for them.[5] It is not the urge to be passive or to remove themselves from world politics that drives politicians and their governments to seek neutral foreign policies but rational assessments of strategies within their possible scope of action. A scope that is, often, dictated by geography and historical trajectory. External pressure from different military powers and internal political dynamics are the reasons for voluntary self-neutralization. This is not to argue that permanent neutrality is a silver bullet to secure a territory against all threat or that it is always the best of all possible solutions. Much depends on the military strategies and the grand strategic aims of neighboring (great) powers. However, the argument stands that neutralization is a tool of statecraft with the potential to decrease the security dilemma and stabilize volatile or contested regions. There is nothing immoral nor unwarranted about permanent neutrality as a national grand strategy. Is it self-serving? Certainly, but so are all national security strategies. Their ultimate goal is to protect the interests of the state, not to create world peace.

Nonetheless, permanent neutrality is beneficial to the international system as a whole because of its positive side-effects; it can contain the spread of war or even forestall it, since (armed) neutrals can be buffer states between hostile parties. Furthermore, the unique capacity of neutral states to mediate, engage in preventive diplomacy, or do peacekeeping is another highly useful function to the international community. More research is needed, however, on the connection between neutral services and political systems. Is it right, for example, to consider the dictatorship of neutral Turkmenistan in the same category as the direct democracy of Switzerland and the representative democracy of Austria? Are these contemporary cases comparable to historical instances like the fascist neutralities of Portugal or Spain and the democratic neutralities of Sweden and Switzerland during the Second World War? In other words, can any regime, no matter its ideological orientation, use neutral policies in the same way or not?

It is important to point out that this book has not analyzed the connection between neutral impartiality and humanitarianism, although that is, of course, a most important topic for permanently neutral states in this century. It is astounding, for instance, that although neutrality and collective security are rival approaches to international security[6] the largest collective security organization in the world, the United Nations, is increasingly recognizing neutrality again as a pillar of international life. The UN was not only pivotal in the recognition of Turkmenistan's neutrality[7] but, in resolution 71/275 (2017), it also explicitly endorsed neutrality as a concept for peace. Today, the UN portrays the issue as follows:

> [T]he policy of neutrality contributes to the strengthening of peace and security in relevant regions and at the global level and plays an important role in developing peaceful, friendly and mutually beneficial relations between the countries of the world ... the policy of neutrality—a key factor for providing conditions and building a platform for peaceful negotiations—is also closely interconnected with and based on the tools of preventive diplomacy, such as early warning and prevention of conflict, mediation, good offices, fact-finding missions, negotiation, the use of special envoys, informal consultations, peace-building and targeted development activities. Consequently, ... countries with

the status of neutrality play an important role in providing and delivering humanitarian assistance in situations of complex emergencies and natural disasters.[8]

Unsurprisingly, the security function of permanent neutrality is not part of this renewed appreciation. The interest of the United Nations is confined to humanitarian aspects only. That, however, is inseparably connected to the strategic positions of neutrals. The capacity to reduce tensions and mediate among belligerents rests on their ability to remain outside conflicts while still being recognized by all belligerent parties as acting in their best interest. Only states that are engaged in world affairs and perceived as impartial by all sides can function as "honest brokers" between the trenches. Much remains to be explored. Only one thing is certain: neutrality is here to stay with the clear potential to function as a model for peace, security, and justice.

## NOTES

1. Maartje M. Abbenhuis, *An Age of Neutrals: Great Power Politics, 1815–1914* (Cambridge: Cambridge University Press, 2014).
2. Heinz Gaertner, ed., *Engaged Neutrality: An Evolved Approach to the Cold War* (Lanham, MD: Lexington, 2017).
3. Eidgenössisches Departement für Verteidigung, Bevölkerungsschutz und Sport (VBS), "Die Neutralität der Schweiz," (Berne: Schweizerische Eidgenossenschaft, 2014), 3.
4. Luca Anceschi, *Turkmenistan's Foreign Policy: Positive Neutrality and the Consolidation of the Turkmen Regime* (London: Routledge, 2008); Louis Clerc, "The Hottest Places in Hell? Finnish and Nordic Neutrality From the Perspective of French Foreign Policy, 1900–1940," in *Caught in the Middle*, ed. Johan den Hertog and Samuël Kruizinga, *Neutrals, Neutrality, and the First World War* (Amsterdam University Press, 2011); Karen Devine, "Values and Identities in Ireland's Peace Policy: Four Centuries of Norm Continuity and Change," *Swiss Political Science Review* 19, no. 3 (2013).
5. See chapters 9 and 10.
6. See chapter 1 by Stephen Neff of this volume.
7. Through UN resolutions 50/80 of 1996 and 69/285 of 2015.
8. "International Day of Neutrality 12 December," United Nations, accessed October 13, 2019, www.un.org/en/events/neutralityday/background.shtml.

## SELECTED REFERENCES

Abbenhuis, Maartje M. *An Age of Neutrals: Great Power Politics, 1815–1914.* Cambridge: Cambridge University Press, 2014.
Anceschi, Luca. *Turkmenistan's Foreign Policy: Positive Neutrality and the Consolidation of the Turkmen Regime* [in English]. London: Routledge, 2008.
Clerc, Louis. "The Hottest Places in Hell? Finnish and Nordic Neutrality from the Perspective of French Foreign Policy, 1900–1940." In *Caught in the Middle*, edited by Johan den Hertog and Samuël Kruizinga. *Neutrals, Neutrality, and the First World War*, 139–54: Amsterdam University Press, 2011.
Devine, Karen. "Values and Identities in Ireland's Peace Policy: Four Centuries of Norm Continuity and Change." *Swiss Political Science Review* 19, no. 3 (2013): 376–409.
Eidgenössisches Departement für Verteidigung, Bevölkerungsschutz und Sport (VBS). *Die Neutralität der Schweiz*. 4 ed. Berne: Schweizerische Eidgenossenschaft, 2014.

Gaertner, Heinz, ed. *Engaged Neutrality: An Evolved Approach to the Cold War*. Lanham, MD: Lexington, 2017.

# Index

Abela, Carmelo, 122
Abe, Shinzo, 178
absolutism, 42
Adams, John Quincy, 148
Afghanistan, 2, 97; combat mission in, 91; Soviet military occupation, 97
"Alabama Claims" arbitration case, 150
alliances: forming of, 44; membership in, 44–45, 49
Allison, Graham, 99
al-Qaeda, 133
Ameer, Ibrahim, 174
America/American: Civil War, 146, 150; contribution to international humanitarian law and neutrality, 150; epoch, 146; European colonial interference, 148; exceptionalism, 149; foreign policy, 156, 184; global supremacy, 167; impartiality and humanitarianism, 150; imperial power, 151; international law, 151; nation rises and expands with neutrality, 148; neutrality-Amnesia after 1945, 156; neutrality policies, 153; policymaking, 149; policy of neutrality, 148; total war, 151
Anglo-French warfare, 147
antagonistic security structure, 133
Arab Spring, 1
Argentina, 19

armed conflicts, 49, 104, 111, 146, 174; belligerents in, 49
armed neutrality, 40, 94, 103, 198, 199
arms control of conventional weapons, 180
arms-embargo policy, 24
ASEAN. *See* Association of Southeast Asian Nations (ASEAN)
Association Agreement, 136
Association of Southeast Asian Nations (ASEAN), 169, 176; China Declaration 2017, 174; impartiality and non-interference, 177; neutrality, 177; solidarity, 177
asymmetrical power distribution, 134
Austria/Austrian: analogy, 100; balancing act in Europe, 113; Central European Defense Cooperation (CEDC), 114; Common and Foreign Security Policy (CFSP), 113–114; coordination and collaboration within EU, 115; CSDP, 114; Federal Constitutional Law on, 113; foreign policies of, 196; for military planning, 200; model, 97; National Assembly, 94; national security policy, 112; neutrality, 90, 94, 96, 97, 101–102, 105, 112; neutralization, 58; 1955 Neutrality Act, 113; permanent neutrality, 89, 94, 113; State Treaty, 100; status of neutrality, 102
Austro-German initiative, 115

autonomy, 19, 100, 173, 176; policy of, 176

Baker, James, 133
balancing, 39
Balkans Regional Working Group, 114
bandwagoning, 39
Bauslaugh, Robert A., 60
Belarus: in Collective Security Treaty Organization (CSTO), 104; neutrality, 104
Belgium, 18, 23, 99
belligerency, recognition of, 26
belligerent neutrality, 70
bellum iustum, 145
Belt and Road Initiative, China, 138, 139, 171
benevolent neutrality, 67, 68
Bildt, Carl, 120
Bolivia, 24
Bosnian civil war of 1992–1995, 30
Bretton Woods principles, 145
Brezhnev, Leonid, 96
British-French conflict, 147
Brzezinski, Zbigniew, 98, 157
Bugajski, Janusz, 137
Burns, William, 133
Bush, George W., 129, 156

Cairo Declaration of 1943, 191
Cambodia/Cambodian: Conflict in 1991, 176; neutrality, 199; neutralization of, 30
Carter, Jimmy, 97, 98
centrality of recognition, 200
Central States Treaty Organization (CSTO), 48
CFSP. *See* Common Foreign and Security Policy (CFSP)
Chaco War, 24, 27, 30
Chamberlain, Neville, 22
Chile, 19
China/Chinese, 2, 3; authoritarian model, 167, 170; Belt and Road Initiative, 138, 139, 171; cross-strait relations, 194; *de facto* existence, 194; economic development and military modernization, 167; humanitarianism, 201; internal affairs, 173; invasion of, 212; military alliances, 172; military capabilities, 167; Military Strategy, 170, 193; minority populations, 3; national defense, 173; Renminbi transactions, 201
Chizhov, Vladimir, 135
Choi Kwang-soo, 180
"civilizational" values, 43
classical balance of power theories, 41
Cohn, Georg, 22, 27
Cohn's plan, 27, 28
Cold War, 2, 40, 43, 50, 64, 71, 90, 111, 112, 120, 130, 132, 133, 134, 176, 182, 221; alliances during, 129; block dynamics of, 59; collective defense, 91; containment analogy, 182; Finland neutrality during, 117; international distribution of power, 132; military blocs of, 95; political divisions of, 47; realignment of, 177
collective behavior, norms of, 45
collective defense, 42
collective security, 15, 26, 31–32, 40, 41, 46, 93, 156; approaches, 198; component of, 17; corps, 21; fall of, 22; first incarnation, 20; institutions, 45; League of Nations, 20; and neutrality, 20, 22, 30; provisions, 21, 25; resolution, 46; spirit of, 26; system of UN, 111
Common Foreign and Security Policy (CFSP), 118
Common Security and Defense Policy (CSDP), 93
Common Spaces agreement, 135
communism, 2, 43
communist ideology, 2
Conference on Security and Cooperation in Europe (CSCE), 48, 90; Helsinki Act, 122; role of, 48
confidence and security-building measures (CSBMs), 47
conflict prevention, 105
Conflict Prevention Centre, 48
conflict settlement, rules and mechanisms of, 169
contemporary neutrality advocacy, 209; editor's note, 209; historical destiny distorted, 210; O'Hanlon, 216; strategic

interests of Taiwan's neutrality, 212; Tsai, 213
cooperative security, 40, 91
Costa Rica, 49
Crimea, 137; annexation of, 119; Russia unification/annexation of, 137
crisis management, 105
Croatia, 114
CSBMs. *See* confidence and security-building measures (CSBMs)
CSDP. *See* Common Security and Defense Policy (CSDP)
CSTO. *See* Central States Treaty Organization (CSTO)
Customary International Law, 197

Damocles Sword of chain reaction, 75
Davidson, Philip S., 173
de-facto neutrality, 182
de Marco, Guido, 122
democracy, 153
democratic freedoms, 192
democratic governance, 43
Democratic Progressive Party (DPP), 193
Deng-Xiaoping, 170
deterrence, 183
differential neutrality, 63
Duterte, Rodrigo, 174

EAEU. *See* Eurasian Economic Union (EAEU)
EAPC. *See* Euro-Atlantic-Partnership Council (EAPC)
East Asia, neutrality in: ASEAN, 176; Cold War, 175; Japan, 177; millennium new security architecture, 175; neutral approaches of, 167; North Korea, 179; nuclear deterrence strategies, 167; Peace Forum in Taipei, 195; regional security in, 202; security architecture in, 167, 184; South Korea, 179; strategic options, 182; Taiwan, 181; US–Sino relations, 167; US view of "China challenge," 170
East Timor, 197
East-West European Peace initiatives, 177
EC. *See* European Communities (EC)
Egypt, 2
Eisenhower, Dwight D., 94, 200

enforceability, limits of, 3
engaged neutrality, Gärtner's concept of, 50
engaged neutrality, status of, 50
ENP. *See* European Neighborhood Policy (ENP)
Estonia, 114
Ethiopia, Italian invasion of, 22
EU. *See* European Union (EU)
Eurasian Economic Union, 171
Eurasian Economic Union (EAEU), 93, 139
Eurasian wars, 145
Euro-Atlantic-Partnership Council (EAPC), 114
Euro-Atlantic security process, 114
Europe: division of, 134; Russia role in, 133
European Communities (EC), 116
European conflicts, 18
European integration, 133
European Neighborhood Policy (ENP), 93
European neutrality, 132
"European Project," 3
European Recovery Program (Marshall Plan), 117
European security, 89
European Union (EU), 3, 89, 111; Austria, 112; capacity to conduct humanitarian, 116; Common Foreign and Security Policy (CFSP), 116; Finland, 117; humanitarian mission in Chad, 104; Ireland, 116; Malta, 122; militarization of, 132; neighborhood policy, 101; "open-door policy" of, 129; Permanent Structured Cooperation (PESCO), 115; Sweden, 120; Treaty of Lisbon of, 93; Treaty of Nice, 116
European war, 69
EU-Russian Common Spaces Agreement, 130

fatalism, 1
Fenghe, Wei, 173
Fenwick, Charles, 21
Finland, 96, 104, 111, 119; active neutrality, 118; active neutrality policy, 118; aggrandizement, 61; Diplomats, delegation of, 1; foreign policymakers,

118; Military Doctrine, 118; neutrality of, 117, 132; security concerns, 117; sovereign affairs, 119; trilateral statement of intent, 119
foreign policy, fundamental determinant of, 1
France, 23, 25, 31, 42, 61, 62, 75, 99, 101, 147; "suspicious quasi-neutrality," 154
Franco-Prussian War, 18

game-theoretical approaches, 57
Gärtner's concept of "engaged neutrality," 50
Gehler, Michael, 90
Geneva Convention in 1864, 150
geographical belonging, concepts of, 2
geography, 1
geopolitics, 2
Georgia, 130, 134; ethnic minorities, 103; model of neutrality, 102; permanent neutralities of, 134
German invasion of Poland, 154
Gonzi, Lawrence, 123
Göransson, Sverker, 120
Gorbachev, Michael, 89
Gorbachev, Mikhail, 179
Gorgé, Camille, 69
Graham, Malbone W., 197
grand summit conferences, 15
Greater Eurasia, neutrality in, 138
Grech, John Paul, 122
Greco-Turkish War, 152
Grotius, Hugo, 149

Hague Conferences, 154
Hague Convention of 1899, 150
Hague Conventions, 58, 111, 145
Hague Peace Conference of 1899, 146
Häikiö, Martti, 118
Haiti, military intervention in, 151
Harvard Draft Convention, 28
Helsinki Final Act of 1975, 90
Helsinki principles, 48
Helsinki summit of 1975, 122
Hitler, Adlof, 75
Honduras, neutralization of, 18
Hopmann, P. Terrence, 16
Hsiu-lien, Lu, 59, 195, 209, 210
Hultqvist, Peter, 121

humanitarian aid, 90
humanitarianism, 39
humanity, achievements of, 3
human rights abuses, 192
human security, 92
Humphrey, Hubert H., 95
Hungary, 114

IAEA. *See* International Atomic Energy Agency (IAEA)
ICA. *See* International Court of Arbitration (ICA)
IEDs. *See* Improvised Explosive Devices (IEDs)
Il-sung, Kim, 179
impartiality, 67
Improvised Explosive Devices (IEDs), 114
independent sovereignty, 122
India: alliance with China, 130; Russia and, 130
Indonesia, 50, 173, 200
Indo-Pacific, security architectures in, 169
INF Treaty. *See* Intermediate-Range Nuclear Forces (INF) Treaty
Ingwen, Tsai, 193; exponents of, 195
integral neutrality, 63
intercontinental ballistic missiles, 180
Intermediate-Range Nuclear Forces (INF) Treaty, 183
international agreements, 49
international alliances, 39, 43
International Atomic Energy Agency (IAEA), 96, 180
International Committee of the Red Cross, 150
international community, 15, 183
international conflicts, neutrality in, 156
International Court of Arbitration (ICA), 169
international disputes, settlement of, 70
international economic system, 138
international environment, development of, 63
international humanitarian law, 150
international law, 20, 57, 58, 200
international lawyers, 15
international peacekeeping mechanism, 24
international peacekeeping operations, 178

Index                                    231

international politics of twenty-first
  century, 2
International Relations, ix, 3, 4, 51
international sanctions, 180; gradual
  relaxation of, 180
international security policy, 50
international systems, 183
Iran, 3, 29, 61, 138; Japan's relations with,
  71; theocracy of, 2
Iraq, 31, 46; "coalition of the willing"
  invasion of, 156
Ireland: "against everybody neutrality,"
  154; independence and sovereignty,
  117; in military matters, 116; neutrality,
  111, 116
Israel, 2
Israel-Palestinian conflict, 122

Japan, 177, 191, 197; collective
  peacekeeping missions, 179;
  constitutional obligation, 179; foreign
  policy, 179; military role, 179; military
  strategy, 178; national seclusion, 60;
  neutralities of, 69; nondefensive armed
  forces, 177; pacifism, 178; postwar
  pacifism, 177; security, 178
Japanese–USSR relations, 69
Jefferson, Thomas, 147
Jinping, Xi, 170, 171, 174, 181, 193, 212
Johnson, President, 95
Jong-un, Kim, 180

Kai-shek, Chiang, 191, 192
Kekkonen, Urho K., 118
Kellogg-Briand Pact, 151–152
Kennan, George F., 95, 133, 182
Kennedy, John F., 96
Khrushchev, Nikita, 96
Kissinger, Henry, 1, 98, 157, 211
Kleen, Richard, 19
KMT. *See* Kuomintang Party (KMT)
Knowland, William F., 95
Korean Peninsula, 179, 180, 181
Korean War, 179, 210
Kozak Memorandum in 2003, 135
Kremlin, 98
Kuomintang Party (KMT), 193
Kuwait, 46

Laos, 199; neutralization of, 30
Laotian accord, 58
law-based international order, 3
Law of Neutrality, 59
League of Nations, 17, 21, 25, 29, 63
Lend-Lease Policy in 1941, 154
Libyan civil conflict of 2011, 31
Lieber Code, 150
Lisbon Treaty negotiations, 117
Luxembourg, independence and neutrality
  of, 18

MacArthur, Douglas, 177
Macau, 197
Makarov, Nikolai, 119
Malaysia, 173
man-made disasters, 93
Mao, communist forces, 181
Marshall, George C., 101
metarelational, 66
meta-relational neutral attitude, 67
meta-relational property, 57
Mexican-American War, 149
Mexican War, 148, 149
military alliances, 48
minimum winning coalition, 42
minority rights, 99
Minsk Agreement, 90, 99, 100, 137
Mitrany paradox, 131
Moldavian neutrality, 135
Moldova, 130, 134; permanent neutralities
  of, 134
Monroe Doctrine, 148, 172
Monroe, James, 148
Morgenthau, Hans J., 63–64, 132
"Moscow Memorandum" of April 15,
  1955, 113
multipolar security system, 176
Myanmar, ethnic tensions in, 201

NACC. *See* North Atlantic Consultative
  Council (NACC)
NAM. *See* Nonaligned Movement (NAM)
Napoleonic Wars, 156
national jurisdictions, fundamental
  distribution of, 3
national rejuvenation, 193
national security, 39
nation-states, violent aggrandizement of, 3

NATO. *See* North Atlantic Treaty Organization (NATO)
NATO Response Force (NRF), 92
natural disasters, 93
Neff, Stephen, 58, 59
neo-neutrality proposal, 28
the Netherlands, 18
network analysis, 57
neutral behavior, practice of, 64
neutrality, 8, 19, 66, 176, 197, 221; in Asia, 130; Austrian Model, 94; Chaco War, 24; codification of, 62; collective security *vs.*, 20, 45; concept of, 131, 134; connection to values, 57; decline of, 59; definition, 60; dichotomy of war, 146; in EU, 93; explicit policies of, 29; facets of, 221; Finland and Afghanistan, 96; as foreign policy, 60; future of, 104; geopolitical tools and humanitarian norms of, 157; Georgia, 102; great power balancing, 130; infringements of, 150; intellectual respectability of, 17; law of, 66; Moldova and Belarus, 103; NATO'S new role, 91; nature of, 26; neutral idea, 60; neutral solidarity and world peace, 23; nuclear-free zone in Central Europe, 95; permanent neutrality and security dilemma, 70; policy of, 153; politics of, 62, 64, 130; practice, 58; as problem-solving model, 97; recognition of, 200; road to respectability, 17; security function of, 64; soviet periphery in East and West, 96; Spanish Civil War, 25; strategy for peace, 18; Taiwanese declaration of, 197; through alliances, 41; triangular and bilateral, 64; for Ukraine, 99; UN Charter era, 29; US experience of, 157; validity of, 151; visions of future, 26
Neutrality Act, 153
Neutrality Act of 1937, 153
neutralization, 4, 9n8, 175; hallmark of, 58; instruments of, 58
neutral position, model of, 65
neutral solidarity, policy of, 24
neutral territory, ingrained respect for, 197
neutral trading partners, 176
new neutrality, 24

NGOs. *See* nongovernmental organizations (NGOs)
Nixon, Richard, 96
Nonaligned Movement (NAM), 59
nonbelligerency, 28
nongovernmental organizations (NGOs), 157
Nonintervention Committee, 26
North Atlantic Consultative Council (NACC), 132
North Atlantic Treaty Organization (NATO), 40, 73, 89, 132, 133, 134; Austrian collaboration with, 114; ballistic missile defense system, 119; Centre of Excellence (COE), 115; Crisis Management and Cooperative Security, 114; development of missile defense, 134; expansion, 137; expansionism, 134; Host Nation Support agreement, 121; International Security Assistance Force (ISAF), 102; membership, 99, 136; military alliances, 103; military integration with, 121; military links to, 89; military planes and ships, 137; mission in Georgia conflict, 104; 'open-door policy' of, 89, 129; Partnership for Peace (PfP), 90, 91, 120, 123, 129, 133; peacekeepers, 134; Planning and Review Process (PARP), 114; Political-Military Framework (PMF) for, 114; potential membership in, 95; revisionism of, 137; risk for, 43; from Russia, 74; status-quo in, 129; Treaty, 42; troops on Swedish territory, 121
NRF. *See* NATO Response Force (NRF)
nuclear-free zone in Central Europe, 95
Nuclear Non-Proliferation Treaty (NPT), 95
nuclear weapons, 29, 95; deployment of, 118; development of, 95; policy, 171
Nyon Agreement of September 1937, 26

occasional neutrality, 58, 67
Office of Democratic Institutions and Human Rights, 48
O'Hanlon, Michael, 98, 216
One Belt, One Road Initiative, China, 167, 174

One China Policy, 198
One China Principle, 194
"One Country, Two Systems" framework, 181
"One Country, Two Systems" principle, 181
Organization for Security and Cooperation in Europe (OSCE), 48; Istanbul Summit 1999, 134; peacekeepers, 134
OSCE. *See* Organization for Security and Cooperation in Europe (OSCE)

Pact of Paris of 1928, 29
Panama Canal, 151
pan-Europeanization, 3
Paraguay, 24
Paris Agreement of November 20, 1815, 111
partial neutrality, 197
Partnership for Peace (PfP), 90, 91, 99, 120, 123, 129, 133
peacekeeping: "direct approach" to, 15; military forces for, 46; mission, 105
People's Republic of China (PRC), 71, 169, 194; competitive strategy, 174; continental power, 176; decision-making process, 182; economic weight of, 193; electoral democracies, 170; energy companies, 172; fishing ships, 174; humanitarian intervention, 170; infrastructure projects, 174; Japan's security focus on, 178; liberal international order, 171; maritime expansionism, 172; mass internment of Uighurs, 173, "One China Principle," 181; operating system, 174; provocative actions, 170; relations with Vietnam, 172; reunification with, 181
permanent neutral, 75; countries, 180; disposition of, 71; potential adversaries and, 71
permanent neutrality, 15–16, 31, 32, 40, 70–71, 94, 111, 129, 175, 181, 196 9.17 9.19 9.22-9.23 B04n8: and collective security, 15; concept of, 59; development of, 17, 18; historical instances of, 197; hoc instances of, 20; implication of, 73; logical position of, 74; multilateral configuration of, 72; norms of, 184; potential value of, 17; reconceptualization of, 167; utility of, 131; value of, 209
permanent neutrals, 74; military requirements for, 63; states, 134
permanent territorial neutrality, 181, 198
perpetual neutrality, 32
PfP. *See* Partnership for Peace (PfP)
the Philippines, 151, 169, 184; drug victims, 3; nine-dash line, 174; US relationship to, 202
Phouma, Souvanna, 59
"pivot to Asia" strategy, 167
poisonous shrimp, 74
Poland, 3; German and Soviet invasions of, 152
political ideology, 2
political necessity, principles of, 63
politico-military power, 63
politico-moral tendencies, 63
politics of neutrality, 57, 62
Politis, Nicolas, 21
Polk, James K., 149
Portugal, 198; beneficial-to-everyone "strict" neutrality, 154
potential conflict, 70
Potsdam Declaration in 1945, 191
power, global distribution of, 176
power theories, balance of, 42
pragmatic neutrality, 112
pragmatic policymaking, 66
PRC. *See* People's Republic of China (PRC)
preventive diplomacy, 200
public diplomacy, form of, 183
Putin, Vladimir, 133, 171
Pyongyang, 180

Quasi-War, 147

Rainio-Niemi, Johanna, 98
Rapacki Plan, 95
Reagan, Ronald, 180
realism, 60, 64
Regan, Ronald, 179
regional autarky, 15
Republic of China (ROC), 192, 216; diplomatic ties with, 193; recognition of, 182

revanchism, 43
Rif War, 152
ROC. *See* Republic of China (ROC)
Roosevelt, Franklin D., 28, 152, 153, 154
Roosevelt, Theodore, 15
Russia/Russian, 130–131, 134, 171; agreement with, 129; annexation of Crimea, 118; Commonwealth of Independent States (CIS), 104; economy, 171; energy projects, 138; incentives for, 129; military technology of, 171; neutrality, 89, 130, 138; partnership against al-Qaeda, 133; permanent neutrality on, 129; promoting and imposing neutrality in Europe, 134; realism, 130; role in Europe, 133; source of conflicts between, 133; unification/annexation of Crimea, 137; West relations with, 133

Saudi Arabia, 2
Scenario Group Ukraine 2027, 93
Schweller, Randall, 132
security: alliances, 73; architecture, 4, 90; dilemma, 4; neutrality and (. *See* neutrality); systems, logic of, 57; through alliances, 41; through neutrality and nonalignment, 49
self-defense, capability of, 40
self-defense forces (SDF), 178, 179
Serbia, 74, 98, 114, 137, 222; "military neutrality," 59
Seville Declarations, 116
Shanghai Cooperation Organization (SCO), 138
Sherman Anti-Trust Act, 154
Sihanouk, Norodom, 59
Sino-American war, 175, 195
socioeconomic models, 2
Southern Rhodesia, comprehensive economic sanctions against, 30
sovereignty, 3, 46, 47; defense of, 134; issue of, 196; proclamations of, 195; undermined, 134; voluntary pooling of, 3
Soviet Union, 69, 132, 171; aggression against neighboring states, 2; collapse of, 3; Finnish bilateral security pact model, 104; military security, 1; neutralities of, 69, 96; security concerns of, 117
Spain: from nonintervention states, 25; "pro-Axis neutrality," 154
Spanish Civil War, 25, 26, 30
Sri Lanka, 201
state neutrality, 1
state-to-state interaction, 192
Stavridis, James, 123
strategic ambiguity, 191, 192
strategy diplomacy, 183
Suez and Panama Canals, 19
suspicious quasi-neutrality, 154
Sweden, 22, 111, 118; Armed Forces Command's (AFC) strategic assessment of, 120; Christian Democrats, 120; coalition government, 120; defense cooperation with, 119; foreign policies of, 196; militarily nonalignment, 120; neutrality, 120; Social Democrats, 120
Switzerland, 49, 69, 75, 111; foreign policies of, 196; permanent neutrality of, 18
Syria, 146

Taft, William Howard, 151
Taiwan, 181, 199, 210, 211; centrality of recognition, 200; danger in Pacific, 193; democracy, 211; diplomatic approach, 202; expulsion from the Olympic Games, 195; independence of, 172, 181, 193; neutralist approach, 201; neutrality, 195, 212; neutralization of, 181; peace and neutrality, 59; permanent neutrality, 198, 200; permanent, territorial, and armed, 199; permanent territorial neutrality, 196; public diplomacy level, 201; push for neutral, 195; reconciliatory approach toward, 193; relationship with, 201; reunification of, 170, 193; security architecture, 181; status of, 191; territorial neutrality of, 191; World War II, 191
Taiwan Allies International Protection and Enhancement Initiative (TAIPEI) Act, 193
Taiwan Relations Act, 182, 192

Taiwan Strait, 168, 192, 193–194; consensus on, 195
Taliban, 2
temporary neutrality, 111
Terminal High Altitude Area Defense system, 180
territorial conflicts, 2
territorial integrity, 197, 199
territorial neutrality, 197
terrorism, 90
Tiilikainen, Teija, 118
Timor, 198; counter-invasion of, 197
totalitarianism, 153
traditional neutrality policies, 27
traditional sovereign rights, 145
Transport Corridor Europe-Caucasus-Asia (TRACECA), 135
Treaty of Alliance 1778, 147
Treaty of Ghent 1814, 147
Trenin, Dimitri, 98
Trump, Donald, 170, 193
Tsai, Michael, 213

UAS. *See* Unmanned Aerial System (UAS)
UGS. *See* Unmanned Ground Systems (UGS)
UK: neutral commercial rights, 147; relations between US, 147
Ukraine, 98, 99, 130, 146; conflict with Russia, 136; crisis, 98; crisis in, 157; foreign policy, 136; minority rights in, 103; neutrality on, 137; O'Hanlon's assessment of, 209; presidential elections in, 134; territory of, 100; US military presence in, 134
Ukrainian conflict, 99
UN. *See* United Nations (UN)
UN Charter, 210
United Nations (UN), 2, 45, 111; Charter, 145; collective security, 46–47; Law of the Sea (UNCLOS), 3; military forces for peacekeeping, 46; peacekeeping troops, 100; resolution, 200; Security Council, 30, 31
United States, 2; advocacy for neutral rights, 147; alliance system, 183; armed conflicts, 146; armed forces, 151; benevolent neutrality, 147; and Britain relations, 147; Chinese direct investment in, 171; commercial and military areas in, 175; commitments to Britain, 147; constitutional democracy, 145; containment policy, 182; declaration of war against, 154; election of, 170; "engagement" with PRC, 170; European conflicts, 146; experience of neutrality, 147, 157; foreign policy, 145, 147; freedom of commerce, 147; humanitarianism, 146; military footprint, 156; military presence in Ukraine, 134; multilateral accord with Iran, 3; neutrality, 145, 146, 152; oil sanctions, 171; Pacific security architecture, 192; policy of "strategic ambiguity," 191; precedence, 146; products and raw materials, 152; public diplomacy, 183; society of nations, 147; strategic focus from Europe, 172; strategic options, 182; structural power of, 3; traditional neutrality, 154
Unmanned Aerial System (UAS), 115
Unmanned Ground Systems (UGS), 115
US-Japan alliance, 179
US-PRC military conflict, 175
U.S.-Russian proxy wars, 146
US-Sino relations, 173, 193; implications for, 168

Very High Readiness Joint Task Force (VJTF), 92
Vienna Conference in 1815, 200
Vietnam War, 176, 199
Vietnam, withdrawal of forces from Cambodia, 176
violent conflict, 40
VJTF. *See* Very High Readiness Joint Task Force (VJTF)
vulnerability, perceptions of, 43

Wales Summit in 2014, 92
Walt, Stephen, 39, 98
Warsaw Pact, 89; alliances, 40; states, 48
Warsaw Treaty Organization (WTO), 90
wars of aggression, 149
weapons of mass destruction, 90
Western Balkans, 114
Western expansionism, 130
Western "Open Door Policy," 169

Westphalian state system, 1
Widman, Allan, 120
Wilson, Woodrow, 21, 149, 151; military action in Latin America, 151
Winter War, 117
world peace, 20
World War I, 73, 146, 151, 176
World War II, 18, 61, 64, 67, 69, 73, 101, 131, 146, 181, 194, 198, 210; criminals and demons, 156; Jewish victims of, 156; "unfinished business" of, 167; unsettled issues of, 191
Wright, Quincy, 21, 60

WTO. *See* Warsaw Treaty Organization (WTO)

Yew, Lee Kuan, 74
Ying-jeou, Ma, 193
Yugoslavia, 50; violent dissolution of, 3

Zecha, Wolfgang, 113
Zedong, Mao, 192
zero-sum integration incentives, 135
Zone of Peace, Freedom, and Neutrality (ZOPFAN), 176
ZOPFAN. *See* Zone of Peace, Freedom, and Neutrality (ZOPFAN)

# About the Contributors

**Stephen C. Neff** has been based at the University of Edinburgh School of Law, in the United Kingdom, since 1983, where he is currently the Professor of War and Peace. He is a specialist in the history of international law in general, including the law of neutrality as a specialty. He is the author of *The Rights and Duties of Neutrals: A General History* (2000). He is also the author of *War and the Law of Nations: A General History* (2005) and *Justice Among Nations: A History of International Law* (2014).

**P. Terrence Hopmann** is professor of international relations at the Johns Hopkins School of Advanced International Studies. He is a former professor and chair of the Political Science Department at Brown University, where he was director of the Global Security Program of the Thomas J. Watson Jr. Institute for international Studies, the Center for Foreign Policy Development and the International Relations Program; was professor of political science at the University of Minnesota and director of its Centre for International Studies. Hopmann served as vice president of the International Studies Association and program chair of three ISA international meetings; was editor of the *International Studies Quarterly*, was a Fulbright Fellow in Belgium and Austria, and a senior fellow at the United States Institute of Peace and the Woodrow Wilson International Centre for Scholars. His main research focuses on the organization of security and co-operation in Europe; PhD, political science, Stanford University.

**Pascal Lottaz** is assistant professor for neutrality studies at the Waseda Institute for Advanced Study in Tokyo. His research focus is neutrality in world history and Japan's relations with neutral countries during the Second World War. He received his PhD from the National Graduate Institute for

Policy Studies (Tokyo) and lectures on international relations at Waseda University and Contemporary European Politics at Temple University, Japan Campus. He serves as secretary of the Diplomatic Studies Section (2019–2021) of the International Studies Association and he is the principal editor of *Notions of Neutralities* (2019).

**Heinz Gärtner** lectures at the department of political science at the University of Vienna and at the Diplomatic Academy of Vienna. He is former academic director of the Austrian Institute for International Affairs (oiip). He held a Fulbright Fellowship as well as the visiting Austrian chair at the Freeman Spogli Institute for International Studies at Stanford University, where he had further visiting fellowships. He was also visiting professor at the King's College, London; Johns Hopkins Institute for East-West Security Studies, New York; University of Erlangen, Germany; St. Hugh's College, Oxford; University of British Columbia; World Policy Institute, New York; and the University of New Haven. He lectures often at other American, European, and Asian universities and research institutes. Gärtner is senior external expert of the RAND-Corporation Europe. He chairs the advisory board ("Strategy and Security") of the Science Commission of the Austrian Armed Forces. His research areas are among others European, international security, arms control, and international relations theory. Gärtner received the Bruno Kreisky (legendary former Austrian chancellor) Award for most outstanding political books.

**Gunther Hauser** is honorary professor at the Danube University Krems and head of the Department International Security at the Austrian Defense Academy in Vienna. His research focus is European security and defense architecture, transatlantic relations and Chinese foreign, security and defense policies. He is member of the scientific board of the Department for Law and International Relations at the Danube University Krems and vice president of the Scientific Forum on International Security at the German Armed Forces Command and Staff College in Hamburg.

**Glenn Diesen** is professor at the faculty of World Economy and International Affairs of the National Research University Higher School of Economics in Moscow. Professor Diesen is also an editor at the journal *Russia in Global Affairs*. His research focus is the geoeconomics of Greater Eurasia and the emerging strategic partnership between Russia and China. Diesen's latest books are *Great Power Politics in the Fourth Industrial Rivalry: The Geoeconomics of Technological* Sovereignty (forthcoming); *Russia in a Changing World* (forthcoming); *The Decay of Western Civilisation and Resurgence of Russia: Between Gemeinschaft and Gesellschaft* (2018); *Russia's Geoeco-*

*nomic Strategy for a Greater Eurasia* (2017); and *EU and NATO Relations with Russia: After the Collapse of the Soviet Union* (2015).

**Herbert Reginbogin** is professor of international relations and international law and currently fellow at The Catholic University of America engaged in completing research on a New American Foreign Policy and International Security Architecture. Reginbogin has been a faculty member at several universities on both sides of the Atlantic. He has taught at Touro Law School (New York), the European University of Lefke (Cyprus), Bogazici University (Turkey), Cag University (Turkey), Potsdam University (Germany), in addition to guest lecturing at other institutions of higher learning around the world. Beyond his spending more than two decades teaching, he has specialized in US public policy; political, societal, economic, and security issues facing Europe; the Middle East; and East Asia. Throughout his career, Reginbogin has written and edited several books and publications on a broad range of topics related to energy and human security including neutrality from a historical and contemporary geopolitical security perspective. Over many years, Reginbogin has worked on several litigation cases; energy security issues in the Eastern Mediterranean, EU, and the US; international maritime law; international refugee issues; the nonproliferation and destabilization of the international world order; new international security architectures; and kleptocracy. PhD Certification from Touro College Jacob D. Fuchsberg Law Center, New York, Licentiatus Philosophiae from the University of Bern, and BA from Whittier College.

www.ingramcontent.com/pod-product-compliance
Lightning Source LLC
Chambersburg PA
CBHW050902300426
44111CB00010B/1347